Riddles,
Donkeys,
Wormy Cheese
and
Much More

Selected Writings on Jewish Themes

by

Rabbi Dr. Chaim Simons

Grosvenor House
Publishing Limited

This book is published by
Grosvenor House Publishing Ltd
Link House
140 The Broadway, Tolworth, Surrey, KT6 7HT.
www.grosvenorhousepublishing.co.uk

A CIP record for this book
is available from the British Library

ISBN 978-1-83975-904-8

CONTENTS

My Valedictory Speech delivered at King
David High School Liverpool, July 1978

Two articles I wrote for the King David
High School Liverpool Jewish Studies
magazine: "Well over the Fast" and
"Do-It-Yourself Shofar"

PREFACE

- Over 40 years, I have written a variety of papers in English and in Hebrew on Jewish themes, which of course include Israel.
- Many of these papers have been published either as books, papers in scholarly journals, or articles or letters to the Editor in various newspapers.
- Recently I published a selection of these papers in book form, and I am now publishing a further selection. Some of these papers are scholarly articles, the majority being interdisciplinary. Others consist of over 250 riddles in the field of Jewish Religious Knowledge, and yet others of 250 comments I have made on the series "Ten Minute Halacha" delivered by a well-known American Rabbi.
- I have included in the name of the title of the book the words "Riddles, Donkeys, Wormy Cheese" since these are a just a few of the subjects contained in this volume.
- In a few cases, I have included in the paper information stating why I wrote that particular article.
- Since the papers contained in this book were written at different periods, there is no consistency in the format of the references at the end of each paper. Likewise, transliterations of Hebrew words to English are not necessarily consistent for the same word throughout the book.
- I have made some small stylistic changes in the papers.

Section One

Catch Me if You Can!

Torah Riddles and Records

Rabbi Dr. Chaim Simons

(written January 2007)

PLEASE READ THIS FIRST!

In this book I have tried to do the near impossible! In other words, this book is intended for people of diverse ages, of diverse interests and of diverse background knowledge.

Layout of Book

The book contains over 250 Riddles or Records in the field of Jewish Religious knowledge.

Each Riddle/Record is divided into four parts:

1) The Question (designated by the letter Q). They are intentionally presented in a completely random order.
2) The Answer (designated by the letter A). It is possible that there are other equally acceptable answers to some of the questions.
3) An explanation and background knowledge to the Questions and Answers.
4) References in the Rabbinical literature for this information. In some cases, these References are very obvious (e.g. Siddur – Shacharit); nevertheless I included them to keep a uniform style throughout this book. As far as possible I tried to give reference works which are to be found in many Jewish homes (e.g. Mishnah Berurah). However, in some cases this was not possible and the user who is interested in looking them up, may have to go to a Torah library.

Let me now make some general comments:

- A serious problem is how to transliterate Hebrew words into English. Since this is not a research book, there is little point in using a scholarly transliteration scheme – this could make difficulties for some of the users. I have therefore not followed any recognised method, and this will thus lead to non-uniform transliterations throughout the book. However, I trust that this will not cause problems for the users.

- Another problem is when to use capital letters. Here I have been arbitrary.

- I am sure that the background knowledge of the different users will vary considerably. Since for some there will be difficulty in understanding the Hebrew words and expressions used throughout the book, I have included a Glossary at the beginning of the book.

- The explanations given in this book cannot cover every Rabbinic opinion and eventuality, and I am sure that some of the users will notice this fact.

- Since this book is in English, almost all the users will be Ashkenazim and, unless otherwise stated in a particular question, the answers are in accordance with Ashkenazi practice.

Suggestions on how to use this book

- *In Schools, Chederim, youth groups, and adult gatherings.* The instructor could use it as an activity such as a quiz between two teams. I should stress that it is not necessary to use consecutive questions as they appear in this book. The instructor can pick out questions he feels are suitable for the level of knowledge of his group. In addition to asking the participants for the answers to the questions, it might in some circumstances, be appropriate to ask the participants to answer questions from the explanations I have appended.

- *By an individual:* The user can cover up the answer, read the question and see if he can answer it, and possibly even explain his answer. If he is familiar with the use of (for example) the Mishnah Berurah, he can then go to the source material.

GLOSSARY

If the explanation of Hebrew word(s) used in this book includes another Hebrew word, it will be written in *italics* and it will be found elsewhere in this Glossary.

Adar — Month in the Jewish calendar when *Purim* occurs

Adar Rishon and *Adar Sheni* — The two months in a Jewish leap year in place of *Adar*

Afikoman — *Matzah* which is eaten as last item at Passover *Seder*

Akdomut — Liturgical poem recited on Pentecost before Reading the *Torah*

Akeidah — Chapter in the *Torah* dealing with the "Binding of Isaac"

Al achilat Maror — Blessing over the bitter herbs at the *Seder* service

Al achilat Matzah — Blessing over *Matzah* at the *Seder* service

Al biur Chametz — Blessing made before the search for *Chametz* on the night before Passover

Al Hanisim — Prayer recited on *Chanukah* and *Purim*

Aleinu — Prayer recited at the end of almost every service

Aliya — A term used to designate a person being called up to the Reading of the *Torah*

Ama (plural: *Amot*) — Linear measurement (about half a metre) used in Jewish law

Amidah (plural: *Amidot*) — Silent prayer recited at every service

Amud — Lectern at which the Reader in the Synagogue stands

Aneinu — Prayer added in the *Amidah* on most Fast days

Apocrypha — A number of books which were not included in the Jewish Bible

Aravot — Twigs of willows – one of the "Four Species" taken on the Festival of Tabernacles

Arba'at Haminim — The Four Species taken on the Festival of Tabernacles

Asara b'Tevet — Fast of 10th Tevet

Aseret hadibrot — The Ten Commandments

Aseret yemai teshuvah — Ten days of Penitence which occur from the Jewish New Year until the Day of Atonement

Ashkenazim — Jews coming from European countries

Ashrei — Psalm 145 together with a few other verses from Psalms, which is recited daily twice during the Morning service and once at the start of the Afternoon service.

Avinu Malkeinu — Prayer added on the Ten days of Penitence and on Fast days

Avodah — Term used for the service of the High Priest in the Temple on the Day of Atonement

Ba'al Koreh (plural: *Ba'alei Koreh*) — Man who reads from the *Torah* during the Synagogue service

Bamidbar — Biblical book of Numbers

Barmitzvah — Boy reaching the age of 13

Baruch Ata HaShem — First words of almost every Blessing

Berachah — (plural: *Berachot*) — Blessing which is recited at different occasions

Bereshit — Biblical book of Genesis

Birchat hailanot — Blessing recited when one sees fruit trees blooming during the month of *Nissan*

Birchat Hamazon — Grace after Meals after eating bread

Birchat Kohanim — Blessing the congregation by the *Kohanim* – Duchaning

Borachu — Very short prayer said mainly during the Evening and Morning services

Borei minei mezonot — Blessing said over flour products

Brit Milah — Ritual circumcision

Challot — Bread eaten (specially) on Shabbat

Chametz — Leaven food which may not be eaten on Passover

Chamishi — 5th person called up to the Reading of the *Torah*

Chanukah — Eight-day Festival - an increasing number of candles are lit on each successive night – hence the expression "Feast of Lights"

Chatan — Bridegroom

Chol Hamoed — Intermediate days of the Festivals of Passover and Tabernacles

Chumash — The *Torah*

Daven, Davening — Praying

Derashah — Religious discourse, given by (amongst others) the Rabbi or a *Barmitzvah* boy

Devarim — Biblical book of Deuteronomy

Duchan — Blessing of the congregation by *Kohanim* during the Synagogue service

Eichah — Biblical book of Lamentations recited on the Fast of Ninth of Av

Eiruv — Popularly used to designate area in which one may carry on the Sabbath

Eiruv Tavshillin — Ceremony made when a Festival occurs on a Friday to enable one to cook for the Sabbath

Elul — Month of the Jewish calendar occurring before the New Year

Eretz Yisrael — Land of Israel

Erev Pesach — Day before *Pesach*

Erev Shabbat — Day before *Shabbat* (i.e. Friday)

Erev Tisha b'Av — Day before *Tisha b'Av*

Erev Yom Kippur — Day before *Yom Kippur*

Etrog — Citron (similar to a lemon) which is taken as one of the "Four Species" on the Festival of Tabernacles

Gabbai — Synagogue official who is in charge of deciding who gets called up to the *Torah* or who leads the services

Gemara — The major part of the *Talmud*

Hadassim — Twigs of myrtle which is taken as one of the "Four Species" on the Festival of Tabernacles

Haftarah (plural: *Haftarot*) — Reading from the Prophets following the Reading of the *Torah* on the mornings of Sabbaths and Festivals

Hagadah — Book from which the Passover *Seder* is read

Hakafot — Circuits made with the *Sifrei Torah* on *Simchat Torah*

Halachah — Jewish law

Halachah leMoshe miSinai — Laws handed to Moses on Mount Sinai but do not appear directly in the *Torah*

Hallel — Psalms 113-118 which are recited on certain Festivals during the Morning service

Hamavdil — Main blessing of the *Havdalah* ceremony

Hamotzi — Blessing before eating bread

Havdalah — Ceremony made using wine, spices and a light at the termination of Sabbaths, and only wine at the termination of Festivals

Hoshana Rabba — 7th day of the Festival of Tabernacles

Isru Chag — The day after the Festivals of Passover, Pentecost and Tabernacles

Kabbalat Shabbat — Synagogue Service for the Inauguration of the Sabbath

Kaddish — Prayer taking various formats recited during the course of all Synagogue Services

Kaddish d'Rabbanon — One of the various formats of the *Kaddish* which is recited after learning in public

Kapparot — Symbolic ceremony performed on the day before the Day of Atonement

Karet — A severe Heavenly punishment

Karpas — Vegetable which is dipped in salt water towards the beginning of the Passover *Seder*

Kashering — Making non-kosher crockery, cutlery etc. kosher, or fit to be used on Passover

Kedushah — Addition during the Reader's repetition of the 3rd blessing of every *Amidah*

Kelim — Eating utensils

Kezayit — The size of an olive – taken as about the volume of a matchbox today

Kiddush — Prayer made over wine before most meals on Sabbaths and Festivals

Kiddush Levanah — Prayer blessing the Creator of the Moon recited each month

Kislev — Month in Jewish calendar in which *Chanukah* occurs

Kohelet — Biblical book Ecclesiastes

Kohen (plural: *Kohanim*) — Jew who is descended in the direct male line from the Biblical Aaron

Kohen Gadol — High Priest chosen from amongst the other *Kohanim*

Korban Pesach — Paschal lamb sacrifice

Korbanot — Sacrifices which were offered up in the Temple in Jerusalem

Kriyat haTorah — Reading from the *Torah* during the Synagogue service

Lag b'Omer — 33rd day of the *Omer*

Lecha Dodi — Liturgical poem recited during the Inauguration of the Sabbath service

Lechu Neranana — First words of *Kabbalat Shabbat*

Lein, Leining — Reading of the *Torah* in the synagogue

Levi — Jew descended in the male line from the tribe of Levi (and who is not a *Kohen*)

Ma'ariv — Evening service

Maftir — Last Reading from the *Torah* on Sabbath and Festival mornings. It is always followed by a *Haftarah*

Mah Nishtanah — The 4 questions asked by the child at the Passover *Seder*

Malachi — Last of the "Minor Prophets" in the Bible

Marcheshvan — Month in the Jewish calendar

Masechet — A Tractate of the *Talmud*

Mashiv Haruach, Barech Aleinu, and *V'tain Tal Umatar* — Changes made in the *Amidah* during the winter in order to pray for rain

Matzah (plural: *Matzot*) — Unleavened bread eaten during Passover

Me'ain Shalosh — Blessing recited after eating flour products, wine and certain fruits

Me'ain Sheva — Abbreviated repetition of the *Amidah* recited on the Evening service of Sabbaths

Megillah — Usually refers to the Book of Esther which is read on *Purim*

Melave Malka — Meal eaten after termination of Sabbath

Mezonot – see *Borei minei mezonot*

9

Mezuzah (plural: *Mezuzot*) — Scrolls attached to every door post which contain two portions from the *Torah*

Mikva — Ritual bath

Minchah — Afternoon service

Minyan — Ten adult males who have to be present in a Synagogue in order to say certain prayers

Mishloach Manot — Two food items that must be sent to a friend on *Purim*

*Mitzvah (*plural: *Mitzvot)* — A commandment

Mizmor Letodah — Psalm 100 which is recited during the *pesukei dezimrah* on almost every weekday

Mohel — Person performing ritual circumcisions

Moshe or *Moshe Rabbeinu* — Biblical Moses

Motzaei Shabbat — Termination of the Sabbath

Muktzah — Objects which may not be moved on Sabbaths and Festivals

Mussaf — Additional service recited mainly on Sabbaths and Festivals

Ne'ilah — Concluding service on the Day of Atonement

Nevi'im — Prophetical books of the Bible

Nishmat — Addition towards the end of the *pesukei dezimrah* on Sabbaths and Festivals

Nissan — Month in the Jewish year when Passover occurs

Omer – see *Sefirat haOmer*

Pagum — Blemished

Parashah (plural: *Parashiot*) — Portion of the *Torah* read during the Synagogue service on Sabbath morning

Parashat — Every *Parashah* has a name taken from one of its first words (e.g. Parashat Yitro)

Parev — Food which is neither milky nor meaty

Pesach — Festival of Passover

Pesach Sheni — The "Second Passover" which was observed in Temple times a month after Passover

Pesukei dezimrah — Psalms and verses of Praise to the Almighty recited towards the beginning of the Morning service

Pidyan Haben — Ceremony of Redeeming of the First born if a boy

Pikuach Nefesh — Saving of life. This overrides almost every law in the *Torah*

Pirsumei nisa — Proclaiming a miracle – an example is lighting the *Chanukah* candles in front of the window in order to proclaim the miracle which occurred with the oil in the Temple

Piyut (plural: *Piyutim*) — Liturgical Poem

Pizmon — Liturgical poem with a refrain

Possul — Expression used when an object is disqualified for a ritual use

Purim — Feast of Lots which commemorates the Jews' victory over Haman as recounted in the Book of Esther. Haman drew lots to decide on which day to kill the Jews and hence the name "Feast of Lots"

Rambam — Moses Maimonides – a great Rabbi who lived in the 12th century

Rav — Rabbi

Retzai — Addition to Grace after Meals made on Sabbaths

Revi'i — 4th person called up to the Reading of the *Torah*

Revi'it — Minimum quantity of a liquid (at least 86mls) required for certain *Mitzvot*

Rosh Chodesh — Beginning of New Month in Jewish calendar

Rosh Hashanah — Jewish New Year

Sandak — Person holding the baby during a circumcision

Schach — Roof of the *Sukkah* which is made of flora

Seder — Service in the home on the first night(s) of Passover

Sefer Torah (plural: *Sifrei Torah*) — Handwritten *Torah*

Sefirat haOmer — Daily counting of the 49 days between Passover and Pentecost

Selichot — Penitential Prayers recited mainly during the days before the Jewish New Year and thereafter until the Day of Atonement

Sepharadi — Jews generally from Oriental countries

Seudah — A meal – usually used for a festive meal

Seudat Mitzvah — Meal given on a religious occasion, such as a wedding, *Barmitzvah* or *Brit Milah*

Seudat Purim — Special festive meal eaten during the day of *Purim*

11

Shaatnez — Garment containing both wool and linen

Shabbat — Jewish Sabbath

Shabbat Hagadol — Sabbath before Passover

Shabbat Mevorachin — The last Shabbat of a month at which the following month is blessed

Shabbat Shuva — Sabbath between the New Year and the Day of Atonement

Shacharit — Morning service

Shamash — Sexton in a Synagogue. Another meaning: the candle used to light all the *Chanukah* candles

Shavuot — Festival of Pentecost

Shehecheyanu — Blessing of praise recited at start of Festival or on eating a new fruit or wearing a new garment

Shema — Prayer containing three passages from the *Torah* recited during the Evening and Morning services

Shemini Atzeret — Festival occurring immediately after the Festival of Tabernacles. [It is popularly called the 8th day of Tabernacles, but strictly this is incorrect.]

Shemot — Biblical book of Exodus

Shemura Matzah — Specially baked *Matzot* which are eaten at Passover *Seder*

Shevat — Month in Jewish calendar

Shevi'i — 7th person called up to the Reading of the *Torah*

Shir Hama'a lot Mimaamakim — Psalm 130. It is added to the morning service during the Ten days of Penitence

Shir Hashirim — Biblical book "Song of Solomon"

Shir shel Yom — Psalm recited at the end of the Morning service which is specific for a particular day of the week

Shishi — 6th person called up to the Reading of the *Torah*

Shiur — A *Torah* lesson

Shiva — First week of mourning for a close relative

Shliach Tzibur — Reader at a Synagogue service

Shloshim — 30 days of mourning following the death of a close relative

Shofar — Ram's horn blown mainly on the Jewish New Year

Shul — Synagogue

Siddur (plural: *Siddurim*) — Prayer book

Simchat Torah — Rejoicing of the Law - Last day of the Festival of Tabernacles

Sivan — Month in the Jewish calendar in which Pentecost occurs

Siyum — Celebration made when one finishes usually a Tractate of the *Talmud*

Sukkah — Temporary hut lived in during the Festival of Tabernacles

Sukkot — Festival of Tabernacles

Ta'anit Esther — Fast of Esther which is observed on the day before *Purim*

Ta'anit Shaini Batra — Last of three fasts which some are accustomed to fast after the Festivals of Passover and Tabernacles

Tachanun — Supplicatory prayer said immediately after the *Amidah* of the Morning and Afternoon services on most days of the year

Tallit — Garment with *Tzitzit* worn by men during the Morning service

Talmud — A multi-volume book containing Rabbinic discussions on all aspects of Jewish law

Techum — Boundary as to how far one may walk outside the city limits on Sabbaths and Festivals

Tefillah (plural: *Tefillot*) — Daily prayers

Tehilim — Biblical book of Psalms

Tenach — Entire Jewish Bible

Tephillin — Phylacteries – Black boxes containing 4 portions from the *Torah* worn by men during the weekday Morning service.

Tevet — Month in the Jewish calendar

Tisha b'Av — Fast of 9th of Av commemorating the destruction of both Temples in Jerusalem

Tishri — Month in the Jewish calendar when the New Year, Day of Atonement and Tabernacles occur

Toiveling — Immersing certain items of eating and cooking utensils in a ritual bath

Torah — Pentateuch or Five Books of Moses. A *Torah* scroll used in the Synagogue service is a handwritten copy of the entire Pentateuch

Trumot and *Ma'asarot* — Tithes taken from produce grown in *Eretz Yisrael*

Tu biShevat — New Year for Trees which occurs on 15th *Shevat*

Tzitzit — Special fringes attached to each corner of a 4 cornered garment

Tzom Gedaliah — Fast of Gedaliah which is observed on 3 Tishri

Tzur Mishelo — One of the *Zemirot* sung at the Sabbath meals

Va'ani Tefilati — Short prayer recited at the Sabbath Afternoon service

Vayechal — Portion of the *Torah* read in the Synagogue on most Fast days

Vayikra — Biblical book of Leviticus

Vidui — Confession of sins which is recited at the end of every *Amidah* on the Day of Atonement

Vilna Gaon — a great Rabbi and scholar living in Vilna in Lithuania during the 18th century

Ya'aleh v'yavo — Addition to *Amidah* and Grace after Meals made on *Rosh Chodesh* and Festivals

Yahrzeit — Anniversary of the death of a relative

Yechezkel — Biblical book of Ezekiel

Yehoshua bin Nun — Biblical Joshua

Yeshayahu — Biblical book of Isaiah

Yishtabach — Final blessing of the *Pesukei dezimrah*

Yitzchak — Biblical Isaac

Yom Kippur — Day of Atonement

Yom Tov — Generic name for a Jewish Festival

Zemirot — Songs sung during the meals on Sabbaths and Festivals

RIDDLES AND RECORDS

Q. Where and when does one say "Ashrei" at midnight?

A. In many Shuls on the first night of Selichot.

Selichot are recited by the Ashkenazim from a number of days before Rosh Hashanah and on weekdays during the "aseret yemai teshuvah." They are invariably said immediately before the Shacharit service. However, on the first day of Selichot, which is always on Motzaei Shabbat, many congregations hold them at midnight. Maybe the reason is that contained in the Pizmon, are the phrases "who cry to you while it is still night" and "accept their entreaties when they tarry at night." These Selichot begin with Ashrei.

(Shulchan Aruch Orach Chaim 581:1 Rema; Selichot books)

🔶 🔶 🔶 🔶 🔶 🔶 🔶 🔶 🔶 🔶

Q. Why when Dan increased the size, (its height as well as its area), of his Sukkah, he made it possul?

A. He increased its height to above 20 amot.

There is no limit to the maximum area of a Sukkah. In theory one could build one enormous Sukkah in which all the Jews in the world could sit in! However, there is a maximum height, which is 20 amot (An ama is about half a metre.) A Sukkah above this height is possul.

(Shulchan Aruch Orach Chaim 634:1, 633:1)

🔶 🔶 🔶 🔶 🔶 🔶 🔶 🔶 🔶 🔶

Q. Why when Naftali put on his Tephillin at night he observed the Mitzvah?

A. Because he had to get up early for work and it was still dark.

When wearing Tephillin one must always be aware of their holiness. The Rabbis therefore made a decree that it is forbidden to sleep in Tephillin. One might then well ask what happens if one has to get up early to go to work before it is light in the morning. The answer is that in such a case, since there is no chance of a person falling asleep with his Tephillin on, he is permitted to put them on then. However, according to most opinions, he should not make a berachah over them. This question also arose in the Nazi concentration camps, where Tephillin had been smuggled in. The inmates began work when it was still dark and the Rabbis in the camp permitted them to lay Tephillin before it got light. There, there was certainly no chance of one falling asleep wearing them, since one would then certainly have been shot by the Nazis guards.

(Shulchan Aruch Orach Chaim 30:2; Igrot Moshe Orach Chaim 10)

❀ ❀ ❀ ❀ ❀ ❀ ❀ ❀ ❀ ❀ ❀

Q. Which of the "Tehilim for the Day" is most appropriate for Rosh Hashanah?

A. The one recited on Thursdays.

It contains the verse "Tik'u bachodesh shofar..." (Blow the Shofar on the new moon.... for our day of Festival.) Rosh Hashanah occurs on the 1st and 2nd of the month, namely when there is a new moon, and the Shofar is blown on Rosh Hashanah. Indeed, according to some opinions, one always recites this Tehilim on Rosh Hashanah irrespective of the day of the week on which it actually occurs.

(Tehilim 81:4; Luach l'Eretz Yisrael [Rav Tukachinski] any year, "Shacharit Rosh Hashanah")

❀ ❀ ❀ ❀ ❀ ❀ ❀ ❀ ❀ ❀ ❀

Q. Why, when choosing his etrog for the Mitzvah, did Aaron pierce it with a needle and thread?

A. To check that it has not dried up inside.

An etrog which has dried up is possul. One can know whether it is dry inside by piercing it with a needle and thread. If there is moisture inside, the thread will become wet. [Unless one is an expert and knows how to pierce it, one should not do so, since one can easily make it possul, if one doesn't pierce it in the right place!]

(Shulchan Aruch Orach Chaim 648:1)

🕍 🕍 🕍 🕍 🕍 🕍 🕍 🕍 🕍 🕍 🕍

Q. What seems strange about the content of "al hanisim" said on Chanukah?

A. It does not mention the miracle of the oil.

The Gemara explains that the reason for the celebration of Chanukah is because of the miracle of the oil. One would therefore expect this to be the main theme of the "al hanisim" addition to the Amidah and Birchat Hamazon. However, it is not even briefly mentioned there!

(Shabbat 21b; Siddur - "Al Hanisim")

🕍 🕍 🕍 🕍 🕍 🕍 🕍 🕍 🕍 🕍 🕍

Q. Why did Yehoshua read Eichah on Tisha b'Av, sitting on the floor but wearing his Shabbat clothes?

A. Tisha b'Av occurred on Motzaei Shabbat and he had no time before Ma'ariv to change out of his Shabbat clothes.

Many Shuls will daven Ma'ariv when Tisha b'Av occurs on Motzaei Shabbat, immediately after Shabbat. The Halachah is that one removes one's leather shoes after Borachu (the beginning of Ma'ariv). Obviously, one cannot change into weekday clothes on Shabbat and so one has to sit on the floor with one's Shabbat clothes!

(Shulchan Aruch Orach Chaim 559:3; 553:2 Rema)

🙠 🙠 🙠 🙠 🙠 🙠 🙠 🙠 🙠 🙠 🙠

Q. Where are there more berachot in the Ma'ariv service - in Israel or in the Diaspora?

A. In the Diaspora.

After the berachah "Hashkivainu" recited soon after the Shema at Ma'ariv, there is an extra berachah "Baruch haShem leolam." Some Siddurim might state that this berachah is said only in the Diaspora. However, it was the custom of the Vilna Gaon not to say this berachah, even in the Diaspora. Many of the customs of the Vilna Gaon are followed in Israel by the Ashkenazim, since the followers of the Vilna Gaon were the first of the settlers to go to Israel in the early 19th century. Therefore, this berachah is not recited in Israel.

(Siddur – weekday Ma'ariv service; Luach l'Eretz Yisrael [Rav Tukachinski] all years," Motzaei Rosh Hashanah")

🙠 🙠 🙠 🙠 🙠 🙠 🙠 🙠 🙠 🙠 🙠

Q. For which Parashah does one lein on Shabbat Minchah, Monday and Thursday up to Chamishi?

A. Parashat Vayelech.

The smallest number of verses from the Torah that may be read for a person called up to the Torah is three. On Shabbat Minchah, and Monday and Thursday mornings, three people are called up. However, a total of 9 verses is not sufficient – one has to read a minimum of 10. In Parashat Vayelech, the division of the Parashah is such that for the first three people called up on Shabbat morning, only three verses are read for each of them. Therefore, on Shabbat Minchah, Monday and Thursday, one must continue reading up to Chamishi when the third person is called up to the Torah.

(Chumash – Parashat Vayelech, Devarim chap 31; Shulchan Aruch Orach Chaim 135:1; 137:1)

🔔 🔔 🔔 🔔 🔔 🔔 🔔 🔔 🔔 🔔 🔔

Q. Why did Rivkah, who one Shabbat had gone for a walk outside the town, suddenly stop and then not move more than a few steps in any direction?

A. She suddenly realised that she had gone outside the Techum.

On Shabbat and Yom Tov, one may not walk more than about one kilometre beyond the last houses of the settlement. [The laws on this are very complicated.] Should however one find that one has done so, one would then be "trapped" there and could only walk no more than about two metres in any direction! [Therefore take care where you walk on Shabbat and Yom Tov!]

(Shulchan Aruch Orach Chaim 396:1 & Rema)

🔔 🔔 🔔 🔔 🔔 🔔 🔔 🔔 🔔 🔔 🔔

Q. Why and when did Shaul bow 8 times during the Amidah?

A. He was the Shliach Tzibur during Mussaf on Yom Kippur.

During every Amidah, the congregation and also the Shliach Tzibur during his repetition bow 4 times - at the beginning at end of both the first berachot and the berachah "Modim" which occurs towards the end of the Amidah. The repetition of the Mussaf amidah on Yom Kippur includes "Aleinu" and the Avodah (describing the service of the Kohen Gadol in the Temple on Yom Kippur). During these two sections, the Shliach Tzibur and the congregation bow a total of 4 times right on to the floor. Thus the Shliach Tzibur bows a total of 8 times.

19

RABBI DR. CHAIM SIMONS

(Shulchan Aruch Orach Chaim 113:1; 621:4 Rema; Machzor for Yom Kippur - Mussaf)

🐒 🐒 🐒 🐒 🐒 🐒 🐒 🐒 🐒 🐒 🐒

Q. Where is the fast longer on Tisha b'Av - in Israel or in England?

A. In England.

The fast begins at sunset and ends at "tzait hakochavim" (when it gets dark and one can see the stars) on the following day. The period between sunset and "tzait hakochavim" is known as twilight. The further north or south one travels from the equator, the longer is this period of twilight. Hence the length of the fast!

(tables in "Or Meir" by Rabbi Meir Posen, London 5733)

🐒 🐒 🐒 🐒 🐒 🐒 🐒 🐒 🐒 🐒 🐒

Q. When on Rosh Hashanah occurring on a weekday may no-one blow the Shofar?

A. During the nighttime.

On Rosh Hashanah there is the Mitzvah of blowing the Shofar. This Mitzvah can only be observed during the daytime. Since one is only allowed to blow the Shofar on Rosh Hashanah when actually performing the Mitzvah and not just to practice or for the fun of it, one may not blow it during the nighttime of Rosh Hashanah.

(Shulchan Aruch Orach Chaim 588:1, 596:1 Rema)

🐒 🐒 🐒 🐒 🐒 🐒 🐒 🐒 🐒 🐒 🐒

Q. What did Leah have to say when she saw a monkey for the first time?

A. The berachah "M'shaneh haBriyot"

20

Amongst the various berachot which one recites are berachot of praise to G-d. One of them is "M'shaneh haBriyot" (who varies the forms of His creatures). The recital of this berachah includes seeing for the first time an elephant or a monkey.

(Shulchan Aruch Orach Chaim 225:8; Mishnah Berurah 225:29)

❀ ❀ ❀ ❀ ❀ ❀ ❀ ❀ ❀ ❀

Q. When is Havdalah divided into two parts, with a separation of about 24 hours between the parts?

A. When Tisha b'Av occurs on a Sunday (or is postponed from Shabbat).

At the termination of every Shabbat one makes Havdalah over wine. However, if Tisha b'Av occurs after Shabbat, one will not be able to drink the wine. Since Havdalah after Shabbat can be made until Tuesday night, one makes the part of Havdalah - the berachah over the wine and "Hamavdil" on Sunday night after the end of Tisha b'Av. The part of Havdalah consisting of the berachah over the light can only be said on Motzaei Shabbat. This is therefore said on the night of Tisha b'Av.

Thus Havdalah is divided into two parts with a separation of about 24 hours between the parts.

(Shulchan Aruch Orach Chaim 299:6, 556 :1)

❀ ❀ ❀ ❀ ❀ ❀ ❀ ❀ ❀ ❀

Q. Why did Malachi say the Tehilim of Hallel on the 24th day of *each* month?

A. He would read the entire book of Tehilim over the course of *each* month.

It is always praiseworthy to recite Tehilim. Some read the entire book once each month. According to the accepted division, on day 24 of the month, Tehilim 113 - 118 (i.e. the Tehilim comprising the Hallel) are recited.

(Some books of Tehilim show this division.)

🕊️ 🕊️ 🕊️ 🕊️ 🕊️ 🕊️ 🕊️ 🕊️ 🕊️ 🕊️ 🕊️

Q. What is the longest Kaddish possible?

A. The Kaddish said at a siyum of a Masechet during the "aseret yemai teshuvah."

When finishing learning a Masechet, one makes a Siyum (a finishing ceremony which includes a special prayer, a Kaddish and drinks and the serving of refreshments). This Kaddish includes a longish addition towards its beginning, the additional paragraph of Kaddish d'Rabbanon, and if it is during the "aseret yemai teshuvah" there is the addition of the word (u)l'eila.

(Hadran at end of any Masechet from the Talmud)

🕊️ 🕊️ 🕊️ 🕊️ 🕊️ 🕊️ 🕊️ 🕊️ 🕊️ 🕊️ 🕊️

Q. Why did Yonah send "Mishloach Manot" three days running?

A. He lived in a city in which there was a doubt whether it was walled at the time of Yehoshua bin Nun, and that year, Purim occurred on a Friday.

The date of Purim in an unwalled city is 14 Adar. Cities walled from the time of Yehoshua bin Nun celebrate Purim on 15 Adar. Cities where there is a doubt whether or not they were walled have 2 days Purim - 14 and 15 Adar. One of the Mitzvot of Purim is "Mishloach Manot." This is performed in non-walled cities on the 14th, walled cities on 15th and "doubtful cities" on both 14th and 15th. When 15 Adar occurs on Shabbat, walled cities spread the celebration of Purim over 3 days - Friday 14th, Shabbat 15th and Sunday 16th Adar. To keep all the various opinions, residents of such walled cities send "Mishloach Manot" both on Shabbat

15th and Sunday 16th. Thus one can see from all this, that residents of doubtful cities will, to keep all the opinions, send them on all 3 days.

(Shulchan Aruch Orach Chaim 688:4, Mishnah Berurah 688:10; Shulchan Aruch Orach Chaim 688:6; Mishnah Berurah 688:18)

🕎 🕎 🕎 🕎 🕎 🕎 🕎 🕎 🕎 🕎

Q. Why nearly 2 weeks after the burial of a relative, family Levy who were present at the burial, were still sitting Shiva?

A. The burial took place at the beginning of Chol Hamoed.

From the time of the burial of a close relative, one sits Shiva for (almost) a week. However, if the burial takes place during Chol Hamoed Pesach or Sukkot, the Shiva only starts at the end of that Festival. If therefore a burial were to take place on the first day of Chol Hamoed, the Shiva would only start about a week later, and would hence end about two weeks after the burial.

(Shulchan Aruch Orach Chaim 548:1)

🕎 🕎 🕎 🕎 🕎 🕎 🕎 🕎 🕎 🕎

Q. When (according to some opinions) does one say "Migdol" in Birchat Hamazon, but does not say either "retzai" or "ya'aleh v'yavo"?

A. At the Melave Malka on Motzaei Shabbat.

Towards the end of Birchat Hamazon one says on weekdays "Magdil yeshuot ..." and on Shabbat, Festivals, and Rosh Chodesh, "Migdol yeshuot..." On Shabbat there is an additional paragraph in Birchat Hamazon beginning with "retzai" and on Yom Tov and Rosh Chodesh, the addition of "ya'aleh v'yavo." According to some opinions, at the Melave Malka, the meal held on Motzaei Shabbat, (when one is of course not adding either "retzai" or "ya'aleh v'yavo") one says Migdol.

23

(Siddur – Birchat Hamazon; Shulchan Aruch Orach Chaim 188:5; Ben Ish Chai, Year 2 Parashat Vayetzei, para. 27)

🙏 🙏 🙏 🙏 🙏 🙏 🙏 🙏 🙏 🙏 🙏

Q. From where in the *Tefillot* can one learn the laws of Pesach?

A. From a Piyut which is recited during the repetition of the Shacharit Amidah on Shabbat Hagadol.

A number of piyutim have been written and are incorporated in the repetition of the Amidah on many special Sabbaths, including Shabbat Hagadol, the Shabbat before Pesach. Amongst those recited on that Shabbat, is one which has the laws of Pesach in a rhymed manner. In practice, very few Shuls say these piyutim.

(some Siddurim - The Piyut for Shacharit of Shabbat Hagadol, "Elokei haruchot lechol basar...")

🙏 🙏 🙏 🙏 🙏 🙏 🙏 🙏 🙏 🙏 🙏

Q. When during Kriyat haTorah does the entire congregation call out part of the leining?

A. When reading "Vayechal" on Fast Days.

During Kriyat haTorah on Fast Days, there are three occasions when the Ba'al Koreh stops, the congregation call out together in a special tune the subsequent words and the Ba'al Koreh then repeats them when continuing with the Torah reading. The first is during the Aliyah for the Kohen; the second and third are during the third Aliyah.

(Shemot 32:12, 34:6-7, 9; Shulchan Aruch Orach Chaim 565:1; Mishnah Berurah 565:3)

🙏 🙏 🙏 🙏 🙏 🙏 🙏 🙏 🙏 🙏 🙏

Q. Why did Yoel say Ashrei (for the first time during that service) *after* saying the Amidah of Minchah?

A. He had arrived in Shul for Minchah and the congregation were already saying the Amidah.

The important thing about congregational prayer is for everybody to say the silent Amidah together. If one arrives a few minutes late for Minchah and the congregation is already saying the silent Amidah, by starting with Ashrei, one is likely to miss out on saying the Amidah with the congregation. One therefore first says the Amidah and afterwards Ashrei.

(Shulchan Aruch Orach Chaim Be'er Heteiv 234:2)

❀ ❀ ❀ ❀ ❀ ❀ ❀ ❀ ❀ ❀ ❀

Q. On the board in a Shul appeared "Mashiv Haruach" and under it "Barech Aleinu." Why did not "V'tain Tal Umatar" appear instead of "Barech Aleinu" on this board?

A. It was a Sepharadi Shul and "Barech Aleinu" is said during the winter instead of "Barachenu."

In the blessing "barech aleinu" in the Amidah, a request for rain is added during the winter months. Ashkenazim say "v'tain tal umatar livrachah" instead of just "v'tain berachah." Sephardim however, in the summer say a shortish berachah beginning "barachenu" whilst in the winter say a much longer berachah beginning "barech aleinu."

(Siddurim "Nusach Ashkenaz (or Sephard)" and "Nusach "Eidot Hamizrach (Sepharadi)" – weekday Amidah)

❀ ❀ ❀ ❀ ❀ ❀ ❀ ❀ ❀ ❀ ❀

Q. Why on some occasions was Yechezkel permitted to bite his nails on Shabbat?

A. That part of his nail was mostly hanging off.

One of the 39 of forbidden work on Shabbat is "gozez" (shearing). Included under this heading is detaching anything from a creature, whether living or dead. For example, cutting or even biting one's nails is forbidden. However, if the majority of a certain portion of the nail is already detached, one may in an unusual way (such as with one's hand or teeth) detach the remaining part.

(Mishnah Berurah 328:96)

✢ ✢ ✢ ✢ ✢ ✢ ✢ ✢ ✢ ✢ ✢

Q. On which Rosh Chodesh does one recite whole Hallel?

A. Tevet.

Whole Hallel is recited on Chanukah, but only half Hallel on Rosh Chodesh. Rosh Chodesh Tevet always occurs during Chanukah. It hence follows that on this Rosh Chodesh, whole Hallel is recited.

(Shulchan Aruch Orach Chaim 683:1)

✢ ✢ ✢ ✢ ✢ ✢ ✢ ✢ ✢ ✢ ✢

Q. When did Yankel Cohen have to especially search for the beginning of his leining when he was called up first to the Torah?

A. When it was Parashat Vayechi.

In a Sefer Torah there is a form of "paragraphing." Sometimes, the writing stops in the middle of a line and the rest of the line is blank - this is known as a Parashah Petuchah (an open portion). In other cases, after a space in the middle of a line, there are more words. This is known as a Parashah Setuma (a closed portion). With one exception, every new weekly Parashah begins after a Parashah Petuchah or a Parashah Setuma. A Kohen who is always called up for this first portion, will therefore not have to search in the middle of a paragraph for the beginning of his reading. The exception is Parashat Vayechi (the last reading in the book of Bereshit) which follows the previous Parashah without a space.

[A Kohen will also have to search on a Fast Day where reading begins with Vayechal, which is in the middle of a paragraph.]

(Bereshit 47:28; Chumash which indicates paragraphing with the letters "pe" and "samech")

🕮 🕮 🕮 🕮 🕮 🕮 🕮 🕮 🕮 🕮 🕮

Q. When did Binyamin read half a verse from the Torah backwards?

A. Whilst he was saying Kiddush Levanah.

Towards the beginning of each month, one has the ceremony of Kiddush Levanah, blessing the Creator of the moon. During this ceremony one reads 3 times half the verse from the song of Moshe, "Tipol aleihem..." and then follows it by reading it 3 times backwards.

(Shemot 15:16; Siddur – Kiddush Levanah; Shulchan Aruch Orach Chaim 426: 2 Rema)

🕮 🕮 🕮 🕮 🕮 🕮 🕮 🕮 🕮 🕮 🕮

Q. When on Shabbat Minchah does one not say "Va'ani Tefilati" before taking out the Sefer Torah?

A. When Yom Kippur falls on Shabbat.

Every Shabbat Minchah immediately before the leining one says the verse from Tehilim "Va'ani Tefilati." However, when Yom Kippur occurs on Shabbat it is not said. The reason for saying it is that it is praise to the Jewish people, who even though they eat and drink on Shabbat they don't neglect the Shabbat prayers. Since one fasts on Yom Kippur this reason is not relevant.

(Tehilim 69:14; Shulchan Aruch Orach Chaim 622:1; Mishnah Berurah 622:2)

🕮 🕮 🕮 🕮 🕮 🕮 🕮 🕮 🕮 🕮 🕮

Q. When during a particular period of the year was Tsephania careful not to write the date in a particular form?

A. It was nighttime during Sefirat haOmer and he had not yet counted that particular day?

There are some opinions which say that the performance of a Mitzvah does not require intent. To observe the Mitzvah of counting the Omer, all one has to do is say, for example, on the fifth night, "Today is the fifth day." Therefore, if before one has counted, someone was to ask, "How many does one count tonight?" and one were to answer "today is the fifth day," it is likely that by saying this, one has observed the counting for that night, and it is then questionable whether one could then count that night with a berachah. There is an opinion, that by writing the date, one fulfils the Mitzvah of counting. Therefore one should not write the date in the form "Today is the fifth day of the Omer" until one has counted that night.

(Shulchan Aruch Orach Chaim 489:4; Responsa by R' Wolf Eiger (printed in Responsa of R' Akiva Eiger, responsa no. 29))

Q. What is not used on Shabbat and must always be black on the outside?

A. The straps of the Tephillin.

There are a number of things in the construction of a pair of Tephillin which are "Halachah leMoshe miSinai." One of these is that the straps of the Tephillin must be black on the outside.

(Shulchan Aruch Orach Chaim 33:3)

Q. Why did Yocheved prefer to drink from a plastic cup rather than a glass one?

A. She was in a place where she did not know whether the kelim had been toiveled.

Kelim made from certain materials which have been manufactured or purchased from a non-Jew requires immersion ("toiveling") in a Mikva before they may be used. These materials include metal, glass, glazed china, but NOT plastic. Thus by using a plastic vessel, there is no problem regarding toiveling.

(Shulchan Aruch Yoreh Deah 120:1)

✥ ✥ ✥ ✥ ✥ ✥ ✥ ✥ ✥ ✥ ✥

Q. When do some ba'alei koreh use the "upper notes" whilst others the "lower notes"?

A. When reading the "aseret hadibrot" in Parashat Yitro and Parashat Vaetchanan.

All the books in the Tenach have musical notes on each of the words (not the same symbols as used in musical scores for an orchestra!). In many Chumashim, one sees two different sets of notes (known as the "upper notes" and the "lower notes") on the same words for the "aseret hadibrot" ("Ten Commandments") in both Parashat Yitro and Parashat Vaetchanan. The difference is that the "upper notes" divide each of the Commandments into a separate verse and the "lower notes" keep the natural division of the verses. Some congregations use the "upper notes" on Shavuot, the anniversary of the giving of the Torah, and the "lower notes" on Shabbat Parashat Yitro and Shabbat Parashat Vaetchanan. Other congregations always use the "upper notes."

(Mishnah Berurah 494:3 and Biur Halachah "Mibachodesh Hashlishi")

✥ ✥ ✥ ✥ ✥ ✥ ✥ ✥ ✥ ✥ ✥

Q. What might happen if one pours the wine left in the Kiddush cup back into the wine bottle after Kiddush?

A. The wine could become "pagum."

When one drinks from a cup of wine, what remains in the cup becomes "pagum" ("blemished"). If one pours this wine back into the bottle, the whole bottle becomes "blemished" and it is then better not to use it for Kiddush etc. One can remove this blemish by, before pouring it back in the bottle, pouring some wine from the bottle into the "blemished" cup. Following this, the wine can be poured from the cup back into the bottle with no problem.

(Shulchan Aruch Orach Chaim 182:6; Mishnah Berurah 182:27)

🔸 🔸 🔸 🔸 🔸 🔸 🔸 🔸 🔸 🔸 🔸

Q. In the mnemonic "at-bash" to remember the days of the various Festivals throughout the year, the letter "koof" stands for Kriyah – Simchat Torah, *as observed in the Diaspora.* However, in Israel, Simchat Torah is on the previous day. Suggest an alternative occasion for "koof" which can also be used in Israel.

A. Purim KATAN. This occurs on the same day of the week as the 4th day of Pesach occurs that year.

What is the mnemonic "at-bash"? From the various days of the week when Pesach occurs, one can determine on what day of the week most of the other notable days in the year will occur. The first letter of the Hebrew alphabet is "aleph" and the last letter is "taff" - hence the phrase "at" in at-bash; "taff" stands for Tisha b'Av and this will occur on the same day of the week as the first day of Pesach. The second letter is "bet" and the second from last letter is "shin" (hence the phrase "bash') "Shin" stands for Shavuot and this will occur on the same day as the week as the second day of Pesach, and so on... However, to apply this

30

mnemonic in Israel, there is a problem with the fourth day, since in Israel, Simchat Torah occurs one day earlier than in the Diaspora. This can be solved, in leap years by utilising Purim Katan. "Katan" begins with a "koof," the fourth from last letter of the alphabet. [Purim Katan only occurs in a leap year and is on 14 Adar I.]

(Shulchan Aruch Orach Chaim 428:3; Mishnah Berurah 428:5)

🝰 🝰 🝰 🝰 🝰 🝰 🝰 🝰 🝰 🝰 🝰 🝰

🝰. Where in the Yom Kippur service can one learn to count up to at least seven?

🅰. In the Avodah - achat, achat veachat, achat ushtayim …

During the Mussaf service for Yom Kippur, one reads the order of the service for the Kohen Gadol on Yom Kippur. In it he counts "one, one and one, one and two…."

(Machzor for Yom Kippur - Mussaf)

🝰 🝰 🝰 🝰 🝰 🝰 🝰 🝰 🝰 🝰 🝰

🝰. When and why did Miryam use a brush made from pig's hair?

🅰. On Shabbat, because (according to some opinions) one can then brush one's hair with it.

One of the forbidden labours of Shabbat is "gozez" (shearing) and this includes detaching anything from a living creature. Pulling out one's hair comes under this category. If one uses a comb or a hard brush, one is sure to detach hairs. However, a brush made from pig's hair is very soft and thus won't pull out any hairs.

(Shulchan Aruch Orach Chaim 303:27, Be'er Heteiv 303: 13)

🝰 🝰 🝰 🝰 🝰 🝰 🝰 🝰 🝰 🝰 🝰

Q. Why did the waiter at the wedding dinner remove *only* the knives from the table, yet leave all the other dirty cutlery and plates?

A. It was time for Birchat Hamazon

It is customary to cover or remove the knives from the table before Birchat Hamazon. One of the reasons is that the table is like an altar and the stones on the altar may not be cut with metal since weapons for war are made of metal.

(Shulchan Aruch Orach Chaim 180:5; Mishnah Berurah 180:11)

✿ ✿ ✿ ✿ ✿ ✿ ✿ ✿ ✿ ✿ ✿

Q. Since it was not Tisha b'Av, why did Yosef put on Tephillin in the afternoon?

A. The Tephillin only became available in the afternoon.

Although it is normal to put on Tephillin first thing in the morning for Shacharit, if for some reason one is prevented from doing so, they can and should be put on when one is able to do so. (It is only on Tisha b'Av that one specifically waits until Minchah to put on Tephillin.)

(Mishnah Berurah 30:1; Shulchan Aruch Orach Chaim 555:1

✿ ✿ ✿ ✿ ✿ ✿ ✿ ✿ ✿ ✿ ✿

Q. When on Rosh Chodesh does one omit reading the korbanot for Rosh Chodesh?

A. When it is Rosh Chodesh Tishri

On Rosh Chodesh, the korbanot are recited at the beginning of the service following the daily sacrifices; at Kriyat haTorah; and in the Mussaf Amidah. Rosh Chodesh Tishri is also Rosh Hashanah and the korbanot for Rosh Chodesh are not directly mentioned in the davening. However, contained in the Rosh Hashanah korbanot is the phrase, "Milvad olat hachodesh" (apart from the Rosh Chodesh sacrifice).

(Shulchan Aruch Orach Chaim 591:2 Rema; Mishnah Berurah 591:3)

❀ ❀ ❀ ❀ ❀ ❀ ❀ ❀ ❀ ❀ ❀

Q. When does one say "Clear the table," without having yet eaten the meal?

A. On the Seder night before Mah Nishtanah.

The Torah phrases the commandment for the Seder night "And you shall relate it to your son." Unusual things are thus done, such as dipping a vegetable in salt water, and giving the children nuts, in order to encourage them to ask questions about the Seder. Another one of these unusual things is before the "Mah Nishtanah" to call out "Clear the table." The natural reaction of a child is to say "but we haven't eaten yet!" One hopes by this that the children will then continue asking questions about the Seder.

(Shulchan Aruch Orach Chaim 473:6, 472:16)

❀ ❀ ❀ ❀ ❀ ❀ ❀ ❀ ❀ ❀ ❀

Q. Why was Chaimke's birthday cake not iced with words such as "Happy Birthday"?

A. It was going to be cut on Shabbat.

One of the forbidden labours of Shabbat is "mochaik" (erasing). Included in this labour is cutting through letters. When a cake is iced with words, one must be particularly careful on Shabbat when cutting the cake not to cut through any letters.

(Shulchan Aruch Orach Chaim 340:3 Rema)

❀ ❀ ❀ ❀ ❀ ❀ ❀ ❀ ❀ ❀ ❀

Q. How many times is Moshe Rabbeinu's name mentioned in the Pesach Hagadah?

A. Only once

One would have thought that since Moshe is the central character in the Exodus from Egypt, the Hagadah would be full of his name. But this is not so! It occurs only once and even that is only incidentally in a quote.

(Hagadah - the paragraph beginning "Rabbe Yossi Haglili ..." (immediately after the ten plagues))

🔯 🔯 🔯 🔯 🔯 🔯 🔯 🔯 🔯 🔯 🔯

Q. Which weekly meal is good for a certain limb in one's body?

A. The Melave Malka.

By tradition, there is a limb in one's body known as the "niscoi" or "luz" and it gets its sustenance from the food eaten at a Melave Malka, the meal eaten after the termination of Shabbat. This is the limb which will not rot in the grave after one's death and will remain until "techiyat hameitim."

(Mishnah Berurah 300:2)

🔯 🔯 🔯 🔯 🔯 🔯 🔯 🔯 🔯 🔯 🔯

Q. What is the maximum number of Chanukah candles (not counting the Shamash) that are lit throughout Chanukah in the Shul in the MORNING?

A. 34

It is customary to light Chanukah candles in the Shul just before Shacharit throughout Chanukah, the number being the same number that was lit on the previous evening. Needless to say, they are not lit on Shabbat morning and the smallest number not to be lit on Shabbat morning is when the 2nd day of Chanukah falls on

Shabbat. Since 36 candles are lit throughout the nights of Chanukah, the maximum number lit in the mornings will be 34.

(Luach l'Eretz Yisrael [Rav Tukachinski], all years, "1st day Chanukah")

✤ ✤ ✤ ✤ ✤ ✤ ✤ ✤ ✤ ✤ ✤

Q. When (in Israel) do some people recite "Shir Hashirim" three times on the same day?

A. When the 1st day of Pesach occurs on Shabbat.

It is customary to read Shir Hashirim at the commencement of Shabbat. Some read this book at the end of the Pesach Seder. On Shabbat Chol Hamoed Pesach, this book is read in the morning service before Kriyat haTorah. When there is no Shabbat Chol Hamoed and the 1st day occurs on Shabbat, it is read on that Shabbat in Israel. (In such a case, in the Diaspora, it is read on the 8th day.) It is thus read 3 times on that Shabbat.

(Luach D'var B'ito 5758 ["Achiezer" Bnei Brak] p.696)

✤ ✤ ✤ ✤ ✤ ✤ ✤ ✤ ✤ ✤ ✤

Q. What is the shortest leining read during the year?

A. The leining for Purim.

The smallest number of people called up when one reads from the Torah is 3. Although for each person one must read at least 3 verses, the smallest total number of verses that may be read are 10. There is one exception to this rule which is Purim when just 9 verses are read. The reason is that the subject being read is the war with Amalek (Haman's ancestor) and this is contained in just 9 verses.

(Shulchan Aruch Orach Chaim 693:4 & Rema; Mishnah Berurah 693:10; Shemot 17:8-16)

✤ ✤ ✤ ✤ ✤ ✤ ✤ ✤ ✤ ✤ ✤

Q. For what food does one say the berachah "Borei minei mezonot," but the after berachah is "Borei nefashot"?

A. Cooked rice

Although rice is not one of the "five species of grain" (wheat, barley, spelt, oats and rye), the Rabbis attached a special importance to it, since it satisfies one's hunger. They therefore ruled that before eating cooked rice, one would say the same berachah over it as for dishes prepared from the five species of grain, namely "Borei minei mezonot." However, since it is not one of these five species, the after berachah is just "Borei nefashot."

(Shulchan Aruch Orach Chaim 208:7; Mishnah Berurah 208:28, 29)

❀ ❀ ❀ ❀ ❀ ❀ ❀ ❀ ❀ ❀ ❀

Q. In which Shul (which has daily services) is Tachanun rarely said?

A. In a Shul where a Mohel attends every day and performs a Brit Milah almost every day.

One of the occasions when Tachanun is omitted is when a Ba'al Brit is present. A Ba'al Brit is the father, the Mohel or the Sandak. Thus a Mohel who is well occupied will enable his Shul to omit Tachanun almost every day!

(Shulchan Aruch Orach Chaim 131:4; Mishnah Berurah 131:22)

❀ ❀ ❀ ❀ ❀ ❀ ❀ ❀ ❀ ❀ ❀

Q. Why of all the worshippers in the Shul did just Elimelech grow a beard?

A. He was appointed as the permanent Shliach Tzibur.

The Gemara tells us that out of respect for the congregation, a permanent Shliach Tzibur should have a beard. In particular, the

Shliach Tzibur on Fast days, Rosh Hashanah and Yom Kippur should have a beard.

(Chullin 24b; Shulchan Aruch Orach Chaim 53:6; Mishnah Berurah 53:24)

🕎 🕎 🕎 🕎 🕎 🕎 🕎 🕎 🕎 🕎 🕎

Q. Why did Tomar who was caught selling hadassim with the sign "Hadassim grown in the North of England" end up in Court?

A. Hadassim don't grow there. The climate is not suitable.

Different plants grow in different parts of the world, depending on the climatic conditions, etc. Hadassim need a warm climate and there is not such a climate in the North of England.

(an appropriate book on botany!)

🕎 🕎 🕎 🕎 🕎 🕎 🕎 🕎 🕎 🕎 🕎

Q. What is the minimum number of leaves one can have on one's aravot (used for the Mitzvah of the "aravah") on Hoshana Rabba?

A. One twig with one leaf.

On Hoshana Rabba, in addition to taking the Arba'at Haminim, one also takes the aravot, shakes them and then beats them. The ideal number of twigs to take is 3, 5 or 7 (depending on one's custom). However, one could take just one twig with one leaf, although this is frowned upon.

(Shulchan Aruch Orach Chaim 664:4 & Rema; Mishnah Berurah 664:16)

🕎 🕎 🕎 🕎 🕎 🕎 🕎 🕎 🕎 🕎 🕎

Q. Which Shabbat do the birds look forward to?

A. Shabbat Parashat Beshalach.

On Shabbat Parashat Beshalach, the portion concerning the manna is read. There was a command not to go out to gather the manna on Shabbat since it would not fall that day. The trouble makers, Datan and Aviram, who wanted to "prove" that this was not so, would get up early on Shabbat morning and sprinkle on the ground manna they had collected on Friday. But their plot did not work. The birds came and ate it up. As a reward, it is customary to feed them on Shabbat Parashat Beshalach each year.

[Because there are some problems in the laws of Shabbat on the feeding of these birds, there are various permissible ways to do it.]

(Aruch Hashulchan Orach Chaim 324:3)

🔸 🔸 🔸 🔸 🔸 🔸 🔸 🔸 🔸 🔸

Q. When and on which day of the year does one read (the letter) "pe" before (the letter) "ayin"?

A. In three of the chapters of Eichah on Tisha b'Av.

The first four chapters of the Book of Eichah consist of 22 (or 66) verses written in alphabetical order. However, in chapters 2, 3 and 4 the verses beginning with the letter "pe" comes before the verses beginning with the letter "ayin." The Gemara explains this reversal of the letters as follows. The spies who returned from spying out Eretz Yisrael spoke evil about it - they said what they had not seen. Their mouth [pe] came before their eyes [ayin].

(Eichah 2:16-17, 3:46-51, 4:16-17; Sanhedrin 104b)

🔸 🔸 🔸 🔸 🔸 🔸 🔸 🔸 🔸 🔸

Q. Why did Tirzah light a Yahrzeit candle specifically in the dining room?

A. She lit it on Yom Tov

On Yom Tov, one may light a candle from an existing light, provided one intends making use of the light, e.g. for reading, to light up the room, etc. A Yahrzeit candle is not usually lit for making use of, and so if one wants to light it on Yom Tov, one must do so in a place where one will use it, for example in the dining room.

(Shulchan Aruch Orach Chaim 502:1; Mishnah Berurah 502:1; Shemirat Shabbat K'hilchata 13:6)

🕯 🕯 🕯 🕯 🕯 🕯 🕯 🕯 🕯 🕯

Q. In Israel there are 5 berachot which are said only once a year and in the same month. Which is the month and what are the berachot?

A. The month is Nissan and the berachot are:

1. al biur Chametz
2. birchat hageulah (before 2nd cup of wine at the Seder)
3. al achilat Matzah
4. al achilat Maror
5. birchat hailanot

The first of these berachot is made before one searches for chametz on the night before Pesach.

The next 3 berachot are recited at the Seder: namely the berachah recited before the berachah over the second cup of wine, before eating the matzah, and before eating the maror. (In the Diaspora where one has two Seders, these 3 berachot are recited twice in the year.)

The last of these berachot is one said specifically in the month of Nissan when one sees fruit trees beginning to blossom.

(Shulchan Aruch Orach Chaim 432:1, 473:7, 475:1, 226:1)

🙠 🙠 🙠 🙠 🙠 🙠 🙠 🙠 🙠 🙠 🙠

Q. An entire congregation was seen reciting Tachanun resting their foreheads on their arms but there was no Sefer Torah in the room. In which city was the congregation?

A. Jerusalem.

When one recites Tachanun and there is a Sefer Torah in the room, one says this prayer reclining one's forehead on one's arm. However, in Jerusalem, even if there is no Sefer Torah present, one does this reclining.

(Shulchan Aruch Orach Chaim 131:1; Luach l'Eretz Yisrael [Rav Tukachinski], all years, "Tzom Gedaliah")

🙠 🙠 🙠 🙠 🙠 🙠 🙠 🙠 🙠 🙠 🙠

Q. On which two Festivals does one get the punishment of "karet" for eating chametz?

A. Pesach and Yom Kippur.

The punishment for eating chametz on Pesach is karet - a severe Heavenly punishment. The punishment for eating *anything* on Yom Kippur is karet - and this of course includes chametz!

(Rambam Hilchot Chametz uMatzah 1:1; Rambam Hilchot Shvitat Asor 1:4)

🙠 🙠 🙠 🙠 🙠 🙠 🙠 🙠 🙠 🙠 🙠

Q. Where in the davening did Binyamin mention Shabbat every day of the week?

A. In the introduction to the Shir shel Yom (e.g. hayom yom sheini b'SHABBAT ...)

Every morning towards the end of Shacharit, one says one of the Tehilim. These were the Tehilim which was said by the Levi'im in the Temple service. It is introduced by the words, (for example), "Today is the second day of the week b'SHABBAT. This is in fact the proper title for the days of the week. According to the Ramban, one has to remember the Shabbat every day of the week.

(Siddur - end of weekday Shacharit service; Ramban, commentary on Shemot 20:8)

Q. Which double Parashah is shorter than almost all the single Parashiot?

A. Nitzavim-Vayelech.

The last 4 Parashiot in the Torah are the shortest ones in the Torah. When Rosh Hashanah occurs on a Thursday or Shabbat, Nitzavim and Vayelech are joined together. Nitzavim is of length 40 verses and Vayelech is 30 verses. *Together* they are just 70 verses which is much shorter than the length of most of the Parashiot, whose lengths are generally over 100 verses.

(Shulchan Aruch Orach Chaim 428:4; Devarim 29:9 – 30:20 (Nitzavim); Devarim 31:1 – 31:30 (Vayelech))

Q. "Mayim Shelanu" translates as "our water" – or does it have another meaning?

A. It means water which has been allowed to stand all night for the purpose of baking Matzot for Pesach.

Great precautions have to be taken when baking the Matzot for Pesach to ensure they don't become chametz. Any rise in temperature will cause the dough to become chametz quicker. Therefore one requires the water used to be as cool as possible. To do this the water is drawn just before night and allowed to stand all night. The cool spring night air, compared with the hotter daytime air, will cool down the water. Only such water may be used for baking Matzot for Pesach. In Hebrew the expression "mayim shelanu" also means water which has been allowed to stand all night.

(Shulchan Aruch Orach Chaim 455:1)

🕎 🕎 🕎 🕎 🕎 🕎 🕎 🕎 🕎 🕎 🕎

Q. Apart from living creatures (e.g. chicken, fish) or money, what can one use for Kapparot on erev Yom Kippur?

A. A plant

On the morning of erev Yom Kippur, it is customary to do the Kapparot ceremony. It is symbolic of transferring one's sins on to some living creature or an object. [It should be stressed that this is only symbolic. The only way to be free of sin is by repentance.] Some people use a chicken, some a fish and others money. One authority quotes the possibility of using a plant.

(Shulchan Aruch Orach Chaim 605:1; Matei Ephraim 604-605:4)

🕎 🕎 🕎 🕎 🕎 🕎 🕎 🕎 🕎 🕎 🕎

Q. When did Malachi make a point of not sleeping during the Rav's derashah or shiur in the Shul?

A. During Sukkot.

On Sukkot, one is obligated to sleep in the Sukkah. One is even forbidden to take a short nap outside the Sukkah. Therefore one must keep awake whilst the Rabbi is giving his derashah or shiur outside the Sukkah. (It is impolite at any time to fall asleep when the Rabbi is talking!)

(Shulchan Aruch Orach Chaim 639:2)

🙏 🙏 🙏 🙏 🙏 🙏 🙏 🙏 🙏 🙏 🙏

Q. When is the longest interval of time between 2 successive readings of whole Hallel?

A. In a non-leap year: from Shavuot to Sukkot.
In a leap year: from Chanukah to Pesach.

Whole Hallel is recited on the first day(s) Yom Tov of Pesach – 15 (and 16 in Diaspora) Nissan; Shavuot – 6 (and 7 in Diaspora) Sivan; Sukkot – 15–22 (and 23 in Diaspora) Tishri; Chanukah – 25 Kislev and following 7 days. In a leap year there is an additional Adar consisting of 30 days. From this one can see that the interval from Shavuot to Sukkot is 4 months and 9 days, and in a leap year the interval from the end of Chanukah to Pesach is 4 months and 12 or 13 days.

(Arachin10a-b; any Luach of the Jewish year)

🙏 🙏 🙏 🙏 🙏 🙏 🙏 🙏 🙏 🙏 🙏

Q. In which prayer does one give the answer to a question and only afterwards ask the question?

A. Ein kElokenu

Ein kElokenu is said or sung towards the end of the morning service on Shabbat and Yom Tov (and by some also on weekdays). The first verse begins "Ein kElokenu" (there is none like our G-d). The second verse begins "Mi kElokenu" (who is like our G-d?). Logically these two verses should be reversed. The reason is that one must accept absolutely unconditionally the

43

uniqueness of G-d. Only after such an acceptance can one ask who is like our G-d.

(Siddur – end of Shabbat Mussaf)

🔹 🔹 🔹 🔹 🔹 🔹 🔹 🔹 🔹 🔹 🔹

Q. On which 3 occasions does the leining at Shabbat Minchah not come from the following Shabbat's Parashah?

A. 1. The following Shabbat is Yom Tov or Chol Hamoed
2. Yom Kippur occurs on Shabbat
3. The following Shabbat is Parashat Bereshit

On Shabbat Minchah, one normally reads from the Torah the beginning of the following week's Parashah. However there a few exceptions:

1) When Yom Tov or Chol Hamoed occurs on Shabbat, one does not read the regular Parashah, but a special appropriate reading. On the previous Shabbat Minchah, one doesn't read the beginning of this special reading but the beginning of the Parashah of the Shabbat after the Festival.

2) There is a special reading for the afternoon of Yom Kippur, irrespective of whether it occurs on Shabbat or on a weekday.

3) The last Parashah in the Torah (Vezot Haberachah) is read on Simchat Torah - in Israel usually on a weekday and in the Diaspora always. If for example Simchat Torah occurs on a Tuesday, then on the following Shabbat, Bereshit is read. However on the previous Shabbat, one reads at Minchah the next Parashah, namely Vezot Haberachah and not Bereshit.

(Luach l'Eretz Yisrael [Rav Tukachinski])

🔹 🔹 🔹 🔹 🔹 🔹 🔹 🔹 🔹 🔹 🔹

Q. When did Akiva recite the entire Aleinu prayer not at the end of the service?

A. During the Mussaf Amidah on Rosh Hashanah.

The entire Aleinu prayer is said in the middle of the 4th Berachah of the Mussaf Amidah on Rosh Hashanah.

(Shulchan Aruch Orach Chaim 591:7 Rema; Rosh Hashanah Machzor - Mussaf Amidah)

⚜ ⚜ ⚜ ⚜ ⚜ ⚜ ⚜ ⚜ ⚜ ⚜

Q. What is the minimum time that can elapse between 2 different Festivals?

A. Zero.

Immediately following Sukkot is Shemini Atzeret which is a new Festival. For example, the berachah "Shehecheyanu" which is said on a new Festival is recited on Shemini Atzeret. Therefore, there is zero time from the end of the 7th day of Sukkot to the beginning of Shemini Atzeret.

(NOTE: Unlike Shemini Atzeret, the 7th day of Pesach is a continuation of the Festival of Pesach.)

(any Jewish calendar!)

⚜ ⚜ ⚜ ⚜ ⚜ ⚜ ⚜ ⚜ ⚜ ⚜

Q. Is it better to eat exclusively meat foods OR exclusively milk foods on Shavuot?

A. Exclusively meat foods.

It is a custom to eat milk foods on Shavuot. However, in common with the other Festivals, there is a Torah command to rejoice on the Festival and "there is no rejoicing other than by eating meat and wine." To observe all the foregoing, it is the norm to have one meaty and one milky meal on Shavuot. If one has to choose between the two, surely a Torah commandment would come before a custom!

(Shulchan Aruch Orach Chaim 494:3 Rema; Mishnah Berurah 529:11)

🪶 🪶 🪶 🪶 🪶 🪶 🪶 🪶 🪶 🪶 🪶

Q. When does everybody have to daven early on Shabbat morning?

A. When erev Pesach occurs on Shabbat.

On Shabbat one is obliged to eat three meals. According to all opinions, at the second meal one must eat bread. On erev Pesach one may only eat chametz until the end of the first third of the day (about nine o'clock in the morning). Matzah may not be eaten that day. Therefore, one has to daven early in order to finish the service, go home, make kiddush and finish at least a small meal by nine o'clock.

(Shulchan Aruch Orach Chaim 274:4, 444:1; Mishnah Berurah 444:4, 5)

🪶 🪶 🪶 🪶 🪶 🪶 🪶 🪶 🪶 🪶 🪶

Q. Why is it a good idea to check one's Mezuzot every Adar Rishon?

A. A Mezuzah should be checked twice in 7 years and this is about the frequency of Adar Rishon.

Mezuzot of a private house should be checked twice in 7 years. The month of Adar Rishon occurs in every Jewish leap year and there are at least 2 Adar Rishons during every 7 years. There are no Festivals in this month, which leaves one ample time to deal with the checking of Mezuzot and thus fulfilling the requirement of their checking,

(Shulchan Aruch Yoreh Deah 291:1; end of section 4 of Mishnah Berurah, very short account of calendar principles)

🪶 🪶 🪶 🪶 🪶 🪶 🪶 🪶 🪶 🪶 🪶

Q. When might some say "Vayanuchu VOM" in an Amidah on Shabbat, other than at Minchah?

A. At Ne'ila when Yom Kippur occurs on Shabbat.

Many congregations in the Shabbat prayers say Vayanuchu VAH in the Ma'ariv Amidah, Vayanuchu VO in the Shacharit and Mussaf Amidot, and Vayanuchu VOM in the Minchah Amidah. Logically when Yom Kippur falls on Shabbat, at Ne'ilah one should say Vayanuchu VOM, and some suggest this distinction.

(Mishnah Berurah 268:1; Siddur – Shabbat services; Shulchan Aruch Harav 3-4 additions 141(1447))

🔸 🔸 🔸 🔸 🔸 🔸 🔸 🔸 🔸 🔸 🔸

Q. Why did Ruchama not say "al hanisim" in Birchat Hamazon after the Seudat Purim?

A. It was in Jerusalem when (Shushan) Purim occurred on Shabbat.

In such a case, the celebration of Purim is spread over 3 days with the Purim Seudah being held on the Sunday which is *after* Purim. Therefore "al hanisim" is not said in Birchat Hamazon after the Seudah.

(Shulchan Aruch Orach Chaim 688:6; Luach l'Eretz Yisrael [Rav Tukachinski] 5765, "Purim Meshulash")

🔸 🔸 🔸 🔸 🔸 🔸 🔸 🔸 🔸 🔸 🔸

Q. What is sometimes classed as a plant and sometimes not?

A. Mushrooms.

When one eats mushrooms, one says the berachah "shehakol" and not "adamah" because they don't feed from the ground but from the air. However on Shabbat, if one were to detach them, one would be guilty of "ketzirah" (reaping) like for any other plant or tree which grows from the ground.

(Shulchan Aruch Orach Chaim 204:1; Chaye Adam Hilchot Shabbat 12:1)

✿ ✿ ✿ ✿ ✿ ✿ ✿ ✿ ✿ ✿ ✿

Q. Why had Aaron who had been born on the 7th day of Chanukah not yet reached the age of Barmitzvah 13 years later on the 7th day of Chanukah?

A. He was born on 2 Tevet in a year when there were 29 days in Kislev, and 13 years later, there were 30 days in Kislev.

The month of Kislev can have either 29 or 30 days. When it has 29 days, the 7th day of Chanukah will be 2 Tevet. When it has 30 days it will be 1 Tevet. It is the date of birth and not the day in Chanukah which determines when a boy is to be Barmitzvah. In this case, the boy must wait until 2 Tevet for his Barmitzvah which will be the 8th day of Chanukah.

(c.f. Mishnah Berurah 55:42)

✿ ✿ ✿ ✿ ✿ ✿ ✿ ✿ ✿ ✿ ✿

Q. When is "Baruch Ata HaShem," not part of a berachah?

A. When one is saying the verse in Tehilim, "Baruch ata HaShem lamdaini chukecha."

One may always recite Tehilim including saying the Divine Name which often occurs in their verses. "Baruch ata HaShem lamdaini chukecha" is a complete verse in Tehilim 119.

(If one says "Baruch ata HaShem" with the intention of saying a berachah and one suddenly realises that one should not be saying that berachah, one should finish off by saying "lamdaini chukecha.")

(Tehilim 119:12; Shulchan Aruch Orach Chaim 206:6)

✿ ✿ ✿ ✿ ✿ ✿ ✿ ✿ ✿ ✿ ✿

Q. When leining which Parashah (excluding Sefer Bereshit and Parashat T'zaveh) did Shmuel not mention Moshe Rabbeinu's name?

A. Parashat Nitzavim.

The reason people usually quote *just* T'zaveh, (but not Nitzavim), as a Parashah when Moshe's name is not mentioned, is that Moshe is talking to the Jewish people in Nitzavim and he is thus not "out the picture" as in T'zaveh.

(Devarim chap. 29:9 – 30:20)

🕊 🕊 🕊 🕊 🕊 🕊 🕊 🕊 🕊 🕊 🕊

Q. Why was it permitted to strain the water on Shabbat in a certain city, yet in the adjoining city it was forbidden?

A. In the first city, the water was drinkable without straining. In the second city it wasn't.

One of the forbidden labours of Shabbat is "meraked" (straining). Liquids which are fit to be drunk without straining may be strained on Shabbat. Those which are not, may not.

(Shulchan Aruch Orach Chaim 319:10)

🕊 🕊 🕊 🕊 🕊 🕊 🕊 🕊 🕊 🕊 🕊

Q. When one says Tachanun at Minchah one reclines one's forehead on one's left arm. At Shacharit because one is wearing Tephillin on the left arm, one reclines on the right arm. On Tisha b'Av one puts on Tephillin at Minchah but not Shacharit. Therefore on which arm does one recline one's forehead when one says Tachanun at Shacharit and Minchah on Tisha b'Av?

A. On Tisha b'Av one does not say Tachanun!

On the surface it may seem strange that Tachanun is omitted on Tisha b'Av. On all other fast days it is said. The reason is that Tisha b'Av is referred to (in the book of Eichah) as a Festival in the hope that in the near future it will indeed become one.

(Shulchan Aruch Orach Chaim 131:1 Rema, 559:4; Eichah 1:15)

🕮🕮🕮🕮🕮🕮🕮🕮🕮🕮🕮

Q. What is the connection between "shaatnez" and "15 tagin"?

A. On each of the 5 letters of the word "shaatnez" (shin, ayin, tet, nun, zayin) are 3 "tagin" i.e. a total of 15 "tagin.

On a number of letters in the Torah are "decorations" called "tagin." These consist of either one or three little "zayins" on top of the letters. Five of the seven letters with three tagin are shin, ayin, tet, nun, zayin and these spell out the word "shaatnez."

(Shulchan Aruch Orach Chaim 36:3; Mishnah Berurah 36:12; Vayikra 19:19; Devarim 22:11)

🕮🕮🕮🕮🕮🕮🕮🕮🕮🕮🕮

Q. When is it most possible that one's Tephillin will get mixed up with someone else's?

A. During Mussaf on Rosh Chodesh.

On Rosh Chodesh one removes one's Tephillin before Mussaf. It is rare that the service will be held up until everyone has wound up and put away his Tephillin. Therefore, in a Shul they are invariably left on the table during Mussaf and mix ups could occur!

(Shulchan Aruch Orach Chaim 423:4)

🕮🕮🕮🕮🕮🕮🕮🕮🕮🕮🕮

Q. How (according to some opinions) can some members of a congregation be saying "v'tain berachah" whilst others are saying "v'tain tal umatar" at the same service? No-one is making a mistake!

A. It is in the Diaspora, but some of the worshippers have arrived from Israel after 7 Marcheshvan and it is before about 5 December.

During the rainy season, a request for rain is made during the saying of the Amidah. In Israel one starts this prayer on 7 Marcheshvan. In the Diaspora however, the date is about 5 December, which is usually more than a month later than in Israel. The practical question which arises is when one travels from Israel to the Diaspora between 7 Marcheshvan and the beginning of December. One would then have already started praying for rain in Israel. Should one then stop when one reaches the Diaspora? The generally accepted opinion is that if one has started, one continues saying "v'tain tal umatar" in the Diaspora. One can therefore have a situation in a particular congregation when some people are praying for rain whilst others are not!

(Shulchan Aruch Orach Chaim 117:1; Sha'arei Teshuvah Orach Chaim 117:4)

✿ ✿ ✿ ✿ ✿ ✿ ✿ ✿ ✿ ✿

Q. What did Tzvika the magician say to his audience before beginning his act?

A. It is not magic, but a sleight of hand.

Any form of sorcery is strictly forbidden by the Torah. If therefore one wants to put on a conjuring show, at, for example, a children's party, then the "magician" must announce at the start that what he is about to perform is not magic but a sleight of hand.

(Meorot Hadaf Hayomi vol. 2 p.246)

✿ ✿ ✿ ✿ ✿ ✿ ✿ ✿ ✿ ✿

Q. What does baldness not change during davening on every weekday morning?

A. The position of the head Tephillin.

The position of the head Tephillin is behind the hair line. However, with increasing age there is increasing baldness and the hair line recedes. However, the Tephillin remains in the same position as before the baldness began.

(Shulchan Aruch Orach Chaim 27:9; Ben Ish Chai, First year, Parashat Chaye Sarah, para. 1)

🔯 🔯 🔯 🔯 🔯 🔯 🔯 🔯 🔯 🔯 🔯

Q. What are the greatest number and the smallest number of the 4 special Parashiot that can be read *during* the month of Adar?

A. greatest number – 4; smallest number – 2.

Around the period of the month of Adar (or Adar Sheni in a leap year), 4 special additional Parashiot are read:

1. Shekalim - on the Shabbat before Rosh Chodesh Adar or if it occurs on Shabbat, on Rosh Chodesh itself.
2. Zachor - on the Shabbat before Purim.
3. Parah - on the Shabbat following Purim. If however Purim occurs on Thursday or Friday, Parah is read one week later.
4. Hachodesh - on the Shabbat before Rosh Chodesh Nissan, or if it occurs on Shabbat on Rosh Chodesh itself.

There are 29 days in Adar (or Adar Sheni).

From the above one can easily work out that when Rosh Chodesh Adar occurs on Shabbat, all 4 Parashiot are read in Adar. When Rosh Chodesh Nissan occurs on Shabbat, only 2 are read during Adar. In the majority of years, 3 are read during Adar.

(Shulchan Aruch Orach Chaim 685:1-6)

🔯 🔯 🔯 🔯 🔯 🔯 🔯 🔯 🔯 🔯 🔯

Q. Which prayer by tradition "fell from Heaven" and was found by the "Anshei Knesset Hagdolah"?

A. Baruch Sheamar

The prayer "Baruch Sheamar" is at (or near) the beginning of the "pesukei dezimrah" which are recited towards the beginning of Shacharit. By tradition, this prayer fell from Heaven and was found by the "Anshei Knesset Hagdolah" (the Rabbis who organised the Prayer Book).

(Siddur – towards the beginning of Shacharit; Mishnah Berurah 51:1)

🕊 🕊 🕊 🕊 🕊 🕊 🕊 🕊 🕊 🕊

Q. When do Jerusalemites read the Megillah (Esther) whilst fasting?

A. When Purim occurs on Shabbat in Jerusalem.

In unwalled cities the Megillah (Esther) is read on 14 Adar, which immediately follows Ta'anit Esther and so the congregation hear the Megillah whilst still fasting. Walled cities (in practice only Jerusalem) read the Megillah a day later and so are not fasting when they hear it. However, when 15 Adar occurs on Shabbat, even in Jerusalem they read the Megillah on 14 Adar which means that even they are fasting at the time.

(Shulchan Aruch Orach Chaim 686:2, 688:6)

🕊 🕊 🕊 🕊 🕊 🕊 🕊 🕊 🕊 🕊

Q. Why on Shabbat did Tamar scatter over the table the mixed cutlery (which had already been dried)?

A. She wanted to return it to its respective compartments in the cutlery tray in a manner which was permitted on Shabbat.

One of the forbidden labours of Shabbat is "borer" (selecting). After washing cutlery, the knives, forks and spoons are usually all mixed up together. One often wants to return each item to its correct compartment in the cutlery tray, but as such one cannot, since they are all mixed together. To solve the problem, one can scatter them over the table in a way that each item will separate from the others. They will then no longer be mixed together and can be returned to their respective compartments in the cutlery tray.

(Igrot Moshe Orach Chaim 4:74 "Borer" 11)

🙞 🙞 🙞 🙞 🙞 🙞 🙞 🙞 🙞 🙞 🙞

Q. Who and when do those reciting a berachah turn through a half circle in the middle of the berachah?

A. The Kohanim during the berachah for Birchat Kohanim.

In most of Israel, the Kohanim duchan every morning, although in the Diaspora, this only takes place on Festivals. Before they begin the duchaning they make a berachah. When they begin this berachah they are facing the Ark and about three quarters way through the berachah they turn through a half circle to face the congregation.

(Mishnah Berurah 128:40)

🙞 🙞 🙞 🙞 🙞 🙞 🙞 🙞 🙞 🙞 🙞

Q. Why was Amos the Shliach Tzibur instantly dismissed?

A. Because he omitted the berachah "vlamalshinim" in the repetition of the Amidah

The weekday Amidah originally consisted of 18 berachot. Later, an additional berachah "vlamalshinim" was instituted against the Jewish heretics, Should the Shliach Tzibur leave it out during his repetition of the Amidah, we suspect he may be a heretic and we therefore immediately dismiss him!

(Shulchan Aruch Orach Chaim 126:1)

🙞 🙞 🙞 🙞 🙞 🙞 🙞 🙞 🙞 🙞 🙞

Q. What is the shortest span of time that something is leined from *all* 5 Books of the Torah?

A. If in that year there is a Shabbat Chol Hamoed Sukkot - 8 days. However, if this is not the case - 9 days, namely from the 2nd day of Rosh Hashanah to Yom Kippur.

The readings from the Torah during this period include the following: the 2 days of Rosh Hashanah - Bereshit and Bamidbar; the Fast of Gedaliah - Shemot; Shabbat Shuva - Devarim; Yom Kippur - Vayikra and Bamidbar; the first day of Sukkot in Israel [and first 2 days in the Diaspora] - Vayikra and Bamidbar; if there is Shabbat Chol Hamoed Sukkot - Shemot, Bamidbar and Devarim; Shemini Atzeret - Devarim, Bereshit and Bamidbar in Israel [and Devarim and Bamidbar in the Diaspora], [Simchat Torah (Diaspora) - Devarim, Bereshit and Bamidbar.]

From this one can see that when there is a Shabbat Chol Hamoed Sukkot, from the first day of Sukkot to Shemini Atzeret in Israel, [and 2nd day Sukkot to Simchat Torah in the Diaspora] – namely in a span of 8 days, one reads from all the 5 Books in the Torah. When there is no Shabbat Chol Hamoed Sukkot – it is a span of 9 days, from 2nd day Rosh Hashanah to Yom Kippur.

(Megillah 30b-31a)

Q. Why on Shabbat could the knot be untied but not tied?

A. It was a bow that accidentally became a knot on Shabbat.

Two of the forbidden labours of Shabbat are "koshair" (knotting) and "matir" (unknotting). The tying and untying of a tight knot on Shabbat is forbidden. The tying of a bow, (which will be untied within a day) is permitted. If however, such a bow accidentally becomes a knot, the knot may be untied on Shabbat.

(Shulchan Aruch Orach Chaim 317:5; Mishnah Berurah 317:23)

Q. Why did Haggai, the Shliach Tzibur, say the Kedushah (which is recited during the repetition of the Amidah) even though there was no minyan present?

A. When he began the repetition of the Amidah there was a minyan present. However, before the Kedushah, several people left the Shul, and since at least 6 people still remained he could continue the repetition including the Kedushah.

Although most of the prayers can be recited even when davening alone at home, there are some prayers which require a minyan in order to be recited. These include the repetition of the Amidah, which in turn includes the Kedushah. The Kedushah is an addition in the third berachah of the Shliach Tzibur's repetition. However, if one begins the repetition with a minyan in the Shul and then some people leave the room, provided that there remain at least 6 people, one can continue the repetition of the Amidah, (which of course includes the Kedushah), until its conclusion.

(Shulchan Aruch Orach Chaim 55:2; Mishnah Berurah 55:8)

⚜ ⚜ ⚜ ⚜ ⚜ ⚜ ⚜ ⚜ ⚜ ⚜ ⚜

Q. When should one avoid having one's fingerprints taken?

A. On Shabbat and Yom Tov.

"Koteiv" (writing) is one of the forbidden labours on Shabbat and Yom Tov. Writing includes meaningful symbols. Fingerprints are a meaningful symbol for police and fingerprint experts and are therefore classed as writing.

(Shemirat Shabbat K'hilchata 41:29)

⚜ ⚜ ⚜ ⚜ ⚜ ⚜ ⚜ ⚜ ⚜ ⚜ ⚜

Q. Why month after month did only *some* members of the congregation say the berachah?

A. It was the berachah over "Half Hallel."

On the days when the whole Hallel is said, all communities of Jews in the world precede it by a berachah. When however only "Half Hallel" is recited (on the last 6 days of Pesach and on Rosh Chodesh) there are differences of opinions regarding the berachah. Ashkenazim say it, whilst Sephardim omit it. Thus if there is a mixed congregation, some will say it, whilst the remainder will omit it.

(Shulchan Aruch Orach Chaim 422:2 and Rema)

Q. How many times should one wash one's hands during the Pesach Seder?

A. Three

(i) "urchatz" - washing before eating the karpas dipped in salt water.
(ii) "rachtza" - washing before eating the Matzah.
(iii) The third time, which is obligatory, but generally people are very lax about, is "mayim acharonim" - washing one's hands before Birchat Hamazon.

(Shulchan Aruch Orach Chaim 473:6, 475:1, 181:1)

Q. Why did Reuven not have to repeat the evening Amidah, but during the following day he had to do so?

A. It was Rosh Chodesh and at the respective Amidah he had forgotten to say "ya'aleh v'yavo"

On Chol Hamoed and Rosh Chodesh, one adds "ya'aleh v'yavo" in the weekday Amidah. Should one forget, one is obligated to go back and say it. The only exception is Ma'ariv of Rosh Chodesh. The reason is that when witnesses came to Jerusalem to report that had seen the new moon, and their evidence was accepted, the Court did not sanctify the new month at night.

(Shulchan Aruch Orach Chaim 422:1)

🐜 🐜 🐜 🐜 🐜 🐜 🐜 🐜 🐜 🐜 🐜

Q. When did Shifrah intentionally boil up water, and allow it to overspill to put out the gas?

A. On Yom Tov.

If for some reason, one no longer requires a lighted gas on Yom Tov, one is not allowed to directly turn off the gas. In the case of a financial loss, one may however do it indirectly by the following method. Fill a saucepan to the top with water, boil the water and when it boils it will automatically spill over and put out the flame, and one can then turn off the gas. One has to then use some of this water, such as for making a cup of tea.

(Shemirat Shabbat K'hilchata 13:13)

🐜 🐜 🐜 🐜 🐜 🐜 🐜 🐜 🐜 🐜 🐜

Q. What is the only occasion in the year that one has an *obligatory* leining from the book of Bereshit? (not including when one is reading the Parashiot from Bereshit)

A. Rosh Hashanah

On the 2 days of Rosh Hashanah one leins from Parashat Vayera - on the first day from the birth of Yitzchak until the Akeidah, and on the second day the Akeidah.

[The leining from Bereshit on Simchat Torah is strictly speaking not an obligatory reading, but an extra! Having finished reading the Torah, one immediately begins again from Bereshit, so as not to give the opportunity for the Satan to say that the Jews have finished reading the Torah and do not want to read it again!]

(Shulchan Aruch Orach Chaim 584:2, 601:1, 668:2; Mishnah Berurah 668:10)

❀ ❀ ❀ ❀ ❀ ❀ ❀ ❀ ❀ ❀ ❀

Q. Why did Yitzchak omit "Tzur Mishelo" from the Zemirot he sang?

A. Because he might fulfill the Mitzvah of Birchat Hamazon when singing it!

"Tzur Mishelo" is a paraphrase of Birchat Hamazon and according to some opinions, one might fulfill the Mitzvah of Birchat Hamazon by singing it. Therefore when one sings it, it is preferable to have the active intention of not fulfilling the Mitzvah of Birchat Hamazon. [Of course, in all instances, one should not say that having sung it, one does not then have to say Birchat Hamazon!]

(Orchot Chaim of Rav Chaim Volozhin on customs of the Vilna Gaon, para. 94 and footnote no.52 of "Ohalei Chaim" – found in Siddur "Ishei Yisrael" of the Vilna Gaon.)

❀ ❀ ❀ ❀ ❀ ❀ ❀ ❀ ❀ ❀ ❀

Q. How many "Avinu Malkeinu's" are there?

A. One

Judaism is a monotheistic religion. There may be 44 verses in "Avinu Malkeinu" - but there is only *one* Avinu Malkeinu!

(Siddur – weekday Shacharit and Minchah, Machzor for Rosh Hashanah and Yom Kippur.)

❀ ❀ ❀ ❀ ❀ ❀ ❀ ❀ ❀ ❀ ❀

Q. When does the Shul omit "vihi noam" on Motzaei Shabbat even though *none* of following 6 days are Yom Tov?

A. There are 3 possibilities:

1. Pesach begins on the following Shabbat.
2. In Israel, if Yom Tov of Sukkot is on Shabbat.
3. Tisha B'Av is on Motzaei Shabbat.

After the Amidah on Motzaei Shabbat, "vihi noam" is said. It speaks of "ma'asei yadeinu" (the work of our hands) and so when there is not a complete week of workdays, (i.e. a Yom Tov will occur before the following Shabbat), it is omitted. There are however a few exceptions:

1. If Pesach begins on the following Shabbat - the reason being that the afternoon of erev Pesach, namely Friday afternoon, is the time for offering the "Korban Pesach." This time is regarded like a Yom Tov and certain labours (approximately those forbidden on Chol Hamoed) are forbidden. Hence, there is less than a complete week for "ma'asei yadeinu."
2. *In Israel,* if Yom Tov of Sukkot is on Shabbat. The entire following week is then Chol Hamoed, when many labours are forbidden. [This cannot arise in the Diaspora since the Sunday will be Yom Tov as well.]
3. If Tisha b'Av occurs on Motzaei Shabbat, one begins after reading the book of Eichah from "v'ata kadosh." The reason is that the words "vihi noam" are not appropriate for a day such as Tisha b'Av.

(Shulchan Aruch Orach Chaim 295: Rema; Mishnah Berurah 295: 3; Luach l'Eretz Yisrael [Rav Tukachinski]: 5758 "Shabbat Hagadol," 5764 "1st day Chol Hamoed Sukkot"; Shulchan Aruch Orach Chaim 559:; Mishnah Berurah 559:7)

🔸 🔸 🔸 🔸 🔸 🔸 🔸 🔸 🔸 🔸

Q. At which Minchah does one not say Ashrei?

A. Yom Kippur

On Yom Kippur, Minchah begins with Kriyat haTorah. Ashrei is left over to the Ne'ilah service.

(Shulchan Aruch Orach Chaim 622:1 Rema)

✿ ✿ ✿ ✿ ✿ ✿ ✿ ✿ ✿ ✿ ✿ ✿

Q. When does one read the same Haftarah two weeks running?

A. In Jerusalem, when Purim occurs on Shabbat.

In Jerusalem (a city which was walled at the time of Yehoshua bin Nun), Purim is celebrated one day later than the rest of the world. Only in Jerusalem, Purim can occur on Shabbat, and in such a case its observance is spread over 3 days - Friday, Shabbat and Sunday. On the Shabbat, "al hanisim" is said and the Torah reading for Purim is read as the Maftir. The question then arises which Haftarah is read on that Shabbat. One reads the same Haftarah as on the previous Shabbat, which was Shabbat Zachor. The Haftarah deals with King Shaul fighting the Amalekites, something which is most appropriate for both Shabbat Zachor and Purim.

(Shulchan Aruch Orach Chaim 688:6; Mishnah Berurah 688:16; Shmuel I 15:2-34)

✿ ✿ ✿ ✿ ✿ ✿ ✿ ✿ ✿ ✿ ✿ ✿

Q. What is the connection between duchaning and worrisome dreams?

A. Whilst the Kohanim are stretching out the tune during duchaning, there is a prayer to be recited by a person who has had such a dream.

Sometimes a person wakes up having dreamed something which troubles him. The Gemara gives various remedies to put one's mind at rest after such a dream. One of them is saying a special prayer whilst the Kohanim are duchaning. The reason for stretching out the tune at the last words of each of the verses of the duchaning is to give the congregation time to say this supplication.

(Berachot 55b; Shulchan Aruch Orach Chaim 130:1; Mishnah Berurah 130:3; some Siddurim and Machzorim - duchaning)

🪷 🪷 🪷 🪷 🪷 🪷 🪷 🪷 🪷 🪷 🪷

Q. Where does one omit the same 2 paragraphs in the davening month after month?

A. In the Hallel on Rosh Chodesh and last 6 days of Pesach.

The Gemara gives a list of days when one is obligated to say the Hallel. In addition, by established custom, Hallel is also recited on Rosh Chodesh and the last 6 days of Pesach. However on these occasions, two paragraphs are omitted - those beginning with "lo lanu" and "ohavti" - and it is then popularly known as "Half Hallel."

(Arachin 10a-b; Ta'anit 28b; Shulchan Aruch Orach Chaim 422:2; Mishnah Berurah 422:12)

🪷 🪷 🪷 🪷 🪷 🪷 🪷 🪷 🪷 🪷 🪷

Q. When does one read from *three* Sifrei Torah on the same morning?

A. There are 4 possibilities:

    (i)   Shabbat Chanukah which falls on Rosh Chodesh
    (ii) Shabbat Shekalim which falls on Rosh Chodesh
    (iii) Shabbat Hachodesh which falls on Rosh Chodesh
    (iv) Simchat Torah

Every Shabbat (unless it is a Yom Tov or Chol Hamoed) one reads the week's Parashah from the Sefer Torah. If it is Rosh Chodesh, one takes out an additional Sefer Torah to read the portion for Rosh Chodesh. If it is also Parashat Shekalim or Parashat Hachodesh (which are two of the special readings which take place around the month of Adar) or Chanukah, then a third Sefer Torah is taken out that Shabbat for the appropriate reading. On Simchat Torah one also takes out three Sifrei Torah – one to read from the end of the Torah, one for the beginning and one for the Maftir for that day.

(Shulchan Aruch Orach Chaim 684:3; 685:1; Mishnah Berurah 685:13; Shulchan Aruch Orach Chaim 668:2, 669:1)

🔅 🔅 🔅 🔅 🔅 🔅 🔅 🔅 🔅 🔅 🔅

🔎. What and when is the maximum number of days in a row that one can read the Torah?

🅰. *In Israel*: 10 – When Chanukah begins on a Friday or a Sunday. [*In the Diaspora*: 11 – When Sukkot begins on a Tuesday.]

In addition to every Shabbat, Monday and Thursday, the Torah is read every day during the 8 days of Chanukah. Therefore, in a year when Chanukah begins on a Friday, one reads the Torah on: the day before Chanukah which is Thursday; the 8 days of Chanukah; and the day after Chanukah which is Shabbat. A similar calculation can be made when Chanukah begins on a Sunday. One thus has a Torah reading on 10 consecutive days.

[One likewise has Torah readings every day throughout Sukkot (including Shemini Atzeret/Simchat Torah) which in the Diaspora continues for 9 days. In a year when the day before Sukkot occurs on a Monday, one reads the Torah on that day, on each of the 9 days of Sukkot, and also on the following day (Isru Chag) which will be a Thursday. Thus in the Diaspora there is a Torah reading on 11 consecutive days.]

(Shulchan Aruch Orach Chaim 684:1)

🔅 🔅 🔅 🔅 🔅 🔅 🔅 🔅 🔅 🔅 🔅

Q. In Israel, for which Festivals does one never make Eiruv Tavshillin?

A. Sukkot and Shemini Atzeret.

On Shabbat, cooking is strictly forbidden. On Yom Tov it is permitted for that day alone. What then can one do when Yom Tov occurs on Friday? How can one have fresh cooked food for Shabbat? This is done by performing Eiruv Tavshillin - taking a cooked dish and bread on the day before Yom Tov and making a certain declaration.

In Israel, where there is only one day Yom Tov (except for Rosh Hashanah), Sukkot and Shemini Atzeret cannot occur on Friday - (in the Diaspora they can be the 2nd day of these Festivals) - Eiruv Tavshillin is thus not applicable to Sukkot and Shemini Atzeret. The reason for these limitations is that due to calendar principles, there are three days during the week, when the various Festivals cannot occur.

(Shulchan Aruch Orach Chaim 527:1. 2. 12; 428:1)

🕯️ 🕯️ 🕯️ 🕯️ 🕯️ 🕯️ 🕯️ 🕯️ 🕯️ 🕯️ 🕯️

Q. Apart from "aseret yemai teshuvah," when do some say "Shir Hama'alot Mimaamakim" after Yishtabach?

A. On Hoshana Rabba.

During the Festival of Sukkot, the world is judged for how much rain will fall that coming winter. The last day of Sukkot is Hoshana Rabba and being the last day, it is very crucial for this judgment. The day thus takes on the appearance in the Shul's morning service as a "Mini Yom Kippur." Just as in the "aseret yemai teshuvah" when one says "Shir Hama'alot Mimaamakim" after Yishtabach, some places likewise do so on Hoshana Rabba.

(Shulchan Aruch Orach Chaim 664:1; Mishnah Berurah 664: 2, 7; Luach D'var B'ito ["Achiezer" Bnei Brak] all years "Hoshana Rabba")

🕯️ 🕯️ 🕯️ 🕯️ 🕯️ 🕯️ 🕯️ 🕯️ 🕯️ 🕯️ 🕯️

Q. What is the longest weekday Amidah?

A. Minchah of erev Yom Kippur.

Every Amidah recited on Yom Kippur ends with a long Vidui. In addition, this Vidui is also recited at the end of the Amidah of Minchah of erev Yom Kippur; the reason being in case there should be a mishap whilst one is eating one's meal before the fast one might not be able to recite Vidui during Yom Kippur itself. This Vidui easily makes this Amidah the longest weekday Amidah.

(Shulchan Aruch Orach Chaim 607:1; Mishnah Berurah 607:1; Machzor for Yom Kippur- Minchah for erev Yom Kippur)

🦯 🦯 🦯 🦯 🦯 🦯 🦯 🦯 🦯 🦯

Q. What is the connection between elephants and Chanukah?

A. During the war with the Greeks at the time of the Chanukah miracle, the Greeks used elephants.

This is found in the Book of Maccabees, which is one of the books of the Apocrypha. "...and for every *elephant* they appointed a thousand men, armed with coats of mail, and with helmets of brass on their heads; and beside this, for every beast were ordained five hundred horsemen of the best."

(Maccabees I 6:33-35)

🦯 🦯 🦯 🦯 🦯 🦯 🦯 🦯 🦯 🦯

Q. Why (according to some opinions) when Moshe heard the Megillah not in the original Hebrew, nor in a language which he understood, he fulfilled the Mitzvah of reading the Megillah?

A. He heard it in Greek.

To fulfill the Mitzvah of Reading the Megillah on Purim, one must hear it either in the original Hebrew, even if one does not understand Hebrew, or (at least in theory) in a language that one understands. An exception to this rule, according to the Rambam, is if that one hears the Megillah in Greek, even if one does not understand Greek, one fulfills the Mitzvah.

(Shulchan Aruch Orach Chaim 690:8, 9; Rambam, Hilchot Megillah 2:3)

✤ ✤ ✤ ✤ ✤ ✤ ✤ ✤ ✤ ✤ ✤

Q. When is the longest Rosh Chodesh weekday Mussaf Amidah recited?

A. On Rosh Chodesh Tevet during a leap year.

Every Rosh Chodesh there is an additional service after Shacharit known as Mussaf. During every service during Chanukah, an additional passage "al hanisim" is added in every Amidah. Since Rosh Chodesh Tevet occurs during Chanukah, "al hanisim" is added into the Rosh Chodesh Tevet Mussaf Amidah. In addition, in (at least the first half of) a Jewish leap year, the two additional words "ulachaparat posha" are added into this Amidah.

(Shulchan Aruch Orach Chaim 423:3, 682:2; Mishnah Berurah 423:6)

✤ ✤ ✤ ✤ ✤ ✤ ✤ ✤ ✤ ✤ ✤

Q. How many times (in the vast majority of years) is there Kriyat haTorah during the "aseret yemai teshuvah"?

A. 10.

On Shabbat, Yom Kippur and the Fast of Gedaliah, the Torah is read at both Shacharit and Minchah; on Rosh Hashanah (unless it is Shabbat) and on any remaining Mondays and Thursdays, just at Shacharit. One can now easily work out that when Rosh Hashanah occurs on Monday, Thursday or Shabbat, the total number of

Torah readings during the "aseret yemai teshuvah" is 10. However, when Rosh Hashanah occurs on Tuesday, it is only 9.

(Siddur; Machzorim for Rosh Hashanah and Yom Kippur)

🕮 🕮 🕮 🕮 🕮 🕮 🕮 🕮 🕮 🕮 🕮

Q. Why on a winter's night did Katriel not close the shutters on the windows?

A. It was Chanukah and the Chanukah lights were burning in front of the window.

The Chanukah lights should be placed where those passing by the outside of the house will see the lights and thus there will be "pirsumei nisa." They should therefore be placed outside the front door or next to the window. If they are next to the window, one should obviously not close the shutters, since then passersby will not then see the Chanukah lights!

(Shulchan Aruch Orach Chaim 671:5; Mishnah Berurah 671:21)

🕮 🕮 🕮 🕮 🕮 🕮 🕮 🕮 🕮 🕮 🕮

Q. During which two months does one say Tachanun during every Shacharit (except for Shabbat and Rosh Chodesh)?

A. Marcheshvan and Tammuz.

Tachanun, a supplicatory prayer, follows the Shacharit Amidah on weekdays. It is however omitted on Festivals and many other notable days, although it is said on many fast days such as 17 Tammuz. Marcheshvan and Tammuz have no days which come into the category of omitting Tachanun.

(Shulchan Aruch Orach Chaim 131:6, 7)

🕮 🕮 🕮 🕮 🕮 🕮 🕮 🕮 🕮 🕮 🕮

Q. What is the only day in the week on which all 6 fasts in the year can occur?

A. Thursday

The six fasts of the year are: Yom Kippur, 9 Av, Fast of Gedaliah, 10 Tevet, 17 Tammuz and Fast of Esther. The principles of the calendar prevent the fasts from occurring on certain days of the week and also, with the exception of Yom Kippur, if they fall on Shabbat they have to be moved to a different day.

(Shulchan Aruch Orach Chaim 428:1)

🔱 🔱 🔱 🔱 🔱 🔱 🔱 🔱 🔱 🔱 🔱

Q. What is the longest period of time between two successive recitals of Hallel (either whole or half Hallel)?

A. Just over six weeks – from second day Rosh Chodesh Elul until first day of Sukkot.

Hallel is recited on Pesach, Shavuot, Sukkot, Shemini Atzeret, Chanukah and Rosh Chodesh. It is not recited on Rosh Hashanah and Yom Kippur, since it is inappropriate to say it on the Days of Judgment. [Rosh Hashanah occurs on Rosh Chodesh Tishri.] Therefore the longest period between two successive recitals of Hallel is just over six weeks - from the second day of Rosh Chodesh Elul until the first day of Sukkot.

(Arachin 10a-b; Ta'anit 28b; Shulchan Aruch Orach Chaim 584:1)

🔱 🔱 🔱 🔱 🔱 🔱 🔱 🔱 🔱 🔱 🔱

Q. When on Shabbat Rosh Chodesh does one read the Maftir for Rosh Chodesh but not the Haftarah for Rosh Chodesh?

A. When Rosh Chodesh Av falls on Shabbat.

When Rosh Chodesh falls on Shabbat, and one reads as the Maftir the portion for Rosh Chodesh, then the Haftarah is that read for

Rosh Chodesh. During the "Three Weeks" between 17 Tammuz and 9 Av, special Haftarot are read – Haftarot whose message is rebuking the Jewish people and warning them of the imminent destruction. In some years Rosh Chodesh Av occurs on Shabbat and then there is a "conflict" of which Haftarah to read. The one read is the one for the "Three Weeks" even though the Maftir read on that Shabbat is the one for Rosh Chodesh.

(Shulchan Aruch Orach Chaim 428:8; 425:1 Rema; Mishnah Berurah 425:8)

🐾 🐾 🐾 🐾 🐾 🐾 🐾 🐾 🐾 🐾 🐾

Q. According to the Ashkenazi order of service, on which day is the Shacharit service the shortest in the year?

A. Erev Pesach - when it occurs on a Friday.

During Shacharit on the day before Pesach, a number of things are *omitted*:

i) Mizmor Letodah, which is one of the Tehilim recited in the "pesukei dezimrah."

ii) Tachanun, which is omitted during the entire month of Nissan.

iii) Lamnatzeach, which is said between Ashrei and Uvo leZion, towards the end of the service.

At the end of the service, each day of the week a different one of the Tehilim is read. The one for Friday is the shortest of these Tehilim.

(Shulchan Aruch Orach Chaim 429:2 & Rema; Tehilim 93)

🐾 🐾 🐾 🐾 🐾 🐾 🐾 🐾 🐾 🐾 🐾

69

Q. Apart from Yom Kippur, when can one have a Ne'ilah service (at least theoretically)?

A. On the last 7 fast days proclaimed when there is no rain in Eretz Israel.

On Yom Kippur, after Minchah one has an additional service called Ne'ilah. Ne'ilah means "closing," as this is the time when the gates of Heaven are closing and it is thus the last opportunity to pray for forgiveness before the day ends. On a practical level, this is the only occasion in the year when Ne'ilah is said, since on our other fast days observed every year there is no Ne'ilah service. However in addition to these fast days, should there be no rain in Eretz Israel, a series of fasts are proclaimed, with increasing severity. During the last 7 of these fast days, there is, at least theoretically, a Ne'ilah service.

(Shulchan Aruch Orach Chaim 623; Tur Orach Chaim 579)

✿ ✿ ✿ ✿ ✿ ✿ ✿ ✿ ✿ ✿

Q. What do the longest Parashah in the Torah, the longest of the Tehilim, and the longest Masechet (in pages) in the Talmud have in common?

A. The number 176.

The longest Parashah - Naso (the second Parashah in Bamidbar) has 176 verses, the longest of the Tehilim - no. 119 has 176 verses and Bava Batra - the longest Masechet in the Talmud has 176 pages. [NOTE: Although it only has 64 pages, the longest Masechet *in words* is Berachot.]

(Tenach; Masechet Bava Batra)

✿ ✿ ✿ ✿ ✿ ✿ ✿ ✿ ✿ ✿

Q. Why was Moishe's Sukkah which *looked* perfectly kosher and could withstand a normal wind, possul?

A. The schach was put on before building the walls.

To be a kosher Sukkah, it has to be built in a specific order – namely the walls must be built before putting on the schach. (Should one happen to put the schach on first, after building the walls, it would be sufficient to lift up the schach and then return it in order to make the Sukkah kosher.)

(Shulchan Aruch Orach Chaim 635:1 Rema; Sefer Sukkah Hashalem by Eliahu Weissfish p.337)

🕯️ 🕯️ 🕯️ 🕯️ 🕯️ 🕯️ 🕯️ 🕯️ 🕯️ 🕯️ 🕯️

Q. On which three consecutive days in the year has the time of *midday* a special significance?

A. Erev Tisha b'Av, Tisha b'Av and the day after Tisha b'Av.

On erev Tisha b'Av, according to some authorities, one may not learn Torah after midday. The study of Torah gives one joy and therefore it is forbidden on Tisha b'Av and this has been extended to the afternoon of erev Tisha b'Av. From midday of Tisha b'Av, some of the mourning restrictions are relaxed and sitting on a chair is permitted. On the day after Tisha b'Av, the mourning restrictions end at midday. During the 3 weeks from 17 Tammuz until Tisha b'Av and especially from Rosh Chodesh Av there are various laws of mourning to be observed. The reason they continue until midday on the 10 Av, is that the Temple continued burning during 10 Av.

(Shulchan Aruch Orach Chaim 553:2 Rema, 559:3, 558:1 Rema)

🕯️ 🕯️ 🕯️ 🕯️ 🕯️ 🕯️ 🕯️ 🕯️ 🕯️ 🕯️ 🕯️

Q. Why did Daniel make Kiddush at the conclusion of a public fast?

A. It was Asara b'Tevet which that year occurred on a Friday.

The only fast that can occur on a Friday is Asara b'Tevet. The fast will end after Shabbat comes in. One is not allowed to eat or drink anything after the commencement of Shabbat until one makes Kiddush. One therefore ends this fast with Kiddush.

(Mishnah Berurah 550:10; Shulchan Aruch Orach Chaim 271:4)

🏮 🏮 🏮 🏮 🏮 🏮 🏮 🏮 🏮 🏮 🏮

Q. When and by how much are the "pesukai dezimrah" (from Baruch Sheamar to Yishtabach) longer – on Shabbat or on Yom Kippur?

A. On Shabbat, *by one letter*

Towards the beginning of Shacharit are the "pesukei dezimrah." On Shabbat, Yom-Tov and Hoshana Rabba a number of Tehilim are added to them. On Rosh Hashanah and Yom Kippur, towards the end of the "pesukei dezimrah," one replaces the words "Hamelech Hayoshev" (the King who sits) with "Hamelech Yoshev" (the King is *now* sitting). The reason being that on these days, which are the days of judgment, the Almighty - the King - is *at that moment* sitting and judging the world. Thus there is one letter fewer in the "pesukei dezimrah" - namely the letter "he" in "hayoshev."

(Siddur – Shacharit for Shabbat; Yom Kippur Machzor - Shacharit)

🏮 🏮 🏮 🏮 🏮 🏮 🏮 🏮 🏮 🏮 🏮

Q. Why did Reuven wait until the *second* night of Rosh Hashanah to eat an apple?

A. His new fruit was an apple.

At the beginning of every Festival, one says the berachah "Shehecheyanu," at the joy of having lived to see the Festival. The question therefore arises whether one should say it again on the second night of Rosh Hashanah. To help solve this problem, one takes a new fruit on the second night and has the intention when saying Shehecheyanu during Kiddush, that the berachah is also over this new fruit. In addition, it is customary to eat an apple dipped in honey on the first night of Rosh Hashanah. But what if one has not eaten an apple that year (and they are not found in the shops for the remainder of the year) and one has no other new fruit? It would in such a case seem best to keep this apple for the second night.

(Shulchan Aruch Orach Chaim 600:2, 583:1 Rema)

🐟 🐟 🐟 🐟 🐟 🐟 🐟 🐟 🐟 🐟 🐟

Q. Which Mitzvah is one unlikely to perform more than 4 times during one's lifetime?

A. Birchat Hachamah

Birchat Hachamah (blessing the Creator of the sun) is said only once in 28 years. Even a person saying it the first time at the age of 6, might subsequently say it at the ages of 34, 62, 90. Although we wish a person to live to 120, it is unlikely he will live to say Birchat Hachamah at 118.

(Shulchan Aruch Orach Chaim 229:2)

🐟 🐟 🐟 🐟 🐟 🐟 🐟 🐟 🐟 🐟 🐟

Q. When is the only occasion when one begins leining less than three verses from an open or closed paragraph?

A. For the Levi on Rosh Chodesh.

In a Sefer Torah there is a form of "paragraphing." Sometimes the writing stops in the middle of a line and the rest of the line is blank - this is known as a "Parashah Petuchah" (an open portion). In other cases, after a space in the middle of a line, there are more words. This is known as a "Parashah Setuma" (a closed portion). The end of such paragraphs can be considered as "natural breaks." The minimum number of verses that one can read for a person called up to the Torah is 3. Also one is not allowed to stop less than three verses from such a "natural break." The reason for this is that a person coming in or leaving the Shul between people being called up to the Torah might come to think that one may read less than three verses. However there is a problem in the splitting up the leining on Rosh Chodesh and one is left with no option but to begin reading for the Levi less than three verses from an open paragraph.

(Shulchan Aruch Orach Chaim 137:2, 138:1, 423:2, Mishnah Berurah 423:2)

🔯 🔯 🔯 🔯 🔯 🔯 🔯 🔯 🔯 🔯

Q. When (not including Friday or Shabbat) does one not say "Avinu Malkeinu" at Minchah on Rosh Hashanah?

A. When one davens Minchah immediately after Mussaf.

After saying the Amidah at Minchah on Rosh Hashanah, one says "Avinu Malkeinu." In many Shuls, Mussaf on Rosh Hashanah finishes well after noon, when one is able to daven Minchah. In such a case, "Avinu Malkeinu" is omitted.

(Machzor for Rosh Hashanah - Minchah; Luach l'Eretz Yisrael [Rav Tukachinski], any year, towards end of Mussaf for Rosh Hashanah.)

🔯 🔯 🔯 🔯 🔯 🔯 🔯 🔯 🔯 🔯

Q. When is the longest Maftir read?

A. When the 8th day of Chanukah falls on Shabbat.

Following the reading of the Parashah each Shabbat, the Maftir is read. This is usually a repeat of the last few verses (about 3 - 5 verses) of the Parashah. On some occasions, there is a special Maftir, which is often much longer; for example, on Rosh Chodesh, on Chanukah, and on the 4 special Parashiot read about the month of Adar. When the last day of Chanukah is on Shabbat, the Maftir is particularly long and is of length 40 verses.

(Shulchan Aruch Orach Chaim 282:4, 684:1, 2; Bamidbar 7:54-89, 8:1-4)

✿ ✿ ✿ ✿ ✿ ✿ ✿ ✿ ✿ ✿ ✿

Q. Why did Meir drink lemonade (not during a meal), but not say a berachah before drinking it?

A. He had already drunk wine and the lemonade was (preferably) on the table when he said the berachah over the wine.

Normally on has to say the appropriate berachah before eating any food. Sometimes one berachah will also cover various subsequent foods. When one says the berachah "Hamotzi" before eating bread at the beginning of a meal, almost all the foods eaten and drunk during that meal are included by that "Hamotzi." Another example is when one says "Borei Pri Hagafen" over wine. This will include any other drink subsequently drunk. It is however preferable that the drink be on the table when the person says the berachah over the wine.

(Shulchan Aruch Orach Chaim 177:1, 174:2; Mishnah Berurah 174:3)

✿ ✿ ✿ ✿ ✿ ✿ ✿ ✿ ✿ ✿ ✿

Q. Since he did not give a Derashah, why was the Festive meal at Yehudah's Barmitzvah considered a "Seudat Mitzvah"?

A. It was precisely the day he became 13 years old.

Certain meals on special occasions, such as the meal after a wedding or a Brit Milah are known as a "Seudat Mitzvah." One such meal is to mark a Barmitzvah. If it is given on the day a boy becomes 13 years old, it is a "Seudat Mitzvah" even if the Barmitzvah boy does not give a derashah. If however it is held on a different day, it is only called a "Seudat Mitzvah" if the Barmitzvah boy gives such a derashah.

(Mishnah Berurah 225:6)

✿ ✿ ✿ ✿ ✿ ✿ ✿ ✿ ✿ ✿

Q. On which two nights in the year does the congregation wear a Tallit for Ma'ariv?

A. Yom Kippur and the night after Yom Kippur.

A Tallit is only worn at Shacharit and Mussaf. However on Yom Kippur it is worn at all the services. Ma'ariv after Yom Kippur follows immediately after Ne'ilah. It is unusual to remove one's Tallit between Ne'ilah and Ma'ariv!

(Mishnah Berurah 619:4; Shulchan Aruch Harav 4: additions 137 (1443))

✿ ✿ ✿ ✿ ✿ ✿ ✿ ✿ ✿ ✿

Q. When does one say "Mizmor Letodah" and *also* the extra Tehilim (not recited on an ordinary weekday) which follow it?

A. On Hoshana Rabba.

In the "pesukei dezimrah" on Shabbat, Yom Tov and Hoshana Rabba a number of extra Tehilim are added before "yehi chavod." On Shabbat, Yom Tov, erev Pesach, Chol Hamoed Pesach and erev Yom Kippur, one of the Tehilim, "Mizmor Letodah" is omitted. Thus on Chol Hamoed Sukkot it is said - Hoshana Rabba is the last day of Chol Hamoed Sukkot.

(Siddur – Shacharit for weekdays, Shabbat and Yom Tov; Shulchan Aruch Orach Chaim 664:1 and Rema)

✿ ✿ ✿ ✿ ✿ ✿ ✿ ✿ ✿ ✿

Q. How did Yoezer make Kiddush since he did not have a cup holding a "revi'it"?

A. He held the wine bottle (in which there was a revi'it of wine) whilst making Kiddush.

When one makes Kiddush, one requires a certain minimum quantity of wine. This quantity is a "revi'it" (at least 86 mls). If one does not have a cup which holds that minimum size, one can hold the wine bottle during Kiddush, provided the wine in this bottle is at least this quantity. After finishing Kiddush, one pours wine from the bottle into one's cup and drinks it.

(Shemirat Shabbat K'hilchata 47:10 and footnote 48)

🙟 🙟 🙟 🙟 🙟 🙟 🙟 🙟 🙟 🙟 🙟

Q. Why when Yehudah counted the correct number for the Omer (without having omitted any previous days' counting), did he not fulfill the Mitzvah?

A. He read from the Siddur the correct number, but not understanding the Hebrew words, he did not know which number it referred to.

Each night from the 2nd night of Pesach until Shavuot, one counts the Omer. The actual counting is not a prayer but a counting and thus one has to know which number one is counting. Even if one reads it in the original Hebrew but does not know which number is referred to, one does not fulfill the Mitzvah.

(Mishnah Berurah 489:5)

🌱 🌱 🌱 🌱 🌱 🌱 🌱 🌱 🌱 🌱 🌱

Q. Apart from Yom Kippur, for which fast is the date never changed?

A. 10 Tevet.

With the exception of Yom Kippur, fasts occurring on Shabbat are moved to the next day – Sunday, (except for the Fast of Esther which is advanced to Thursday). However, the fast of 10 Tevet can never fall on Shabbat, and so it is always observed on 10 Tevet.

(Shulchan Aruch Orach Chaim 550:3; Mishnah Berurah 550:8)

🕎 🕎 🕎 🕎 🕎 🕎 🕎 🕎 🕎 🕎 🕎

Q. Why does one eat gefilte fish on Shabbat rather than on Yom Tov?

A. One eats it on Shabbat to avoid the problems of borer. On Yom Tov, such borer is permitted.

One of the forbidden labours of Shabbat is "borer" (selecting). This means that one may not remove unwanted material from wanted material. An example is not removing fish bones (which are unwanted) from the fish (which is wanted). A person can easily transgress this either inadvertently or by lack of knowledge. Therefore, sometime in the past, someone "invented" gefilte fish (minced fish balls) for Shabbat. However, on Yom Tov one may remove the fish bones, and because of this, there is no reason to eat gefilte fish on Yom Tov.

(Shemirat Shabbat K'hilchata 3:15)

🕎 🕎 🕎 🕎 🕎 🕎 🕎 🕎 🕎 🕎 🕎

Q. How did Yoel keep the Mitzvah of "Kiddush Levanah" on a month when it was so cloudy every night that he could not see the moon during the entire period when one could perform this Mitzvah?

A. He went up in airplane above the clouds!

There is a monthly Mitzvah to bless the Creator of the Moon. This Mitzvah is known as "kiddush levanah" and it is performed during most of the first half of the month on a night when the moon is visible. Cases have been reported when it was cloudy every night and when the last night was reached and the Mitzvah would thus be lost for that month, some Rabbis went up in an airplane above the clouds!

(Shulchan Aruch Orach Chaim 426:1 Rema; Meorot Hadaf Hayomi 2:219)

🖰🖰🖰🖰🖰🖰🖰🖰🖰🖰

🖰. When did Chaim say Hallel *sitting down?*

🅐. On Seder night(s).

In addition to the various daytime readings of Hallel, it is also said during the Seder service. It is begun before the meal and continued after the meal. When the Hallel is recited during the daytime, one stands when reading it. At the Seder however it is read whilst seated as a symbol of freedom.

(Hagadah of Pesach; Mishnah Berurah 480:1)

🖰🖰🖰🖰🖰🖰🖰🖰🖰🖰

🖰. How did Eliahu fulfill the Mitzvah of Kiddush, which requires speaking, yet he did not even open his mouth and say anything?

🅐. Using the principle "shomea k'o-ne.

Literally the words "shomea k'o-ne" mean "listening is like answering." To fulfill certain Mitzvot, one has to say something. Common examples are Kiddush and Havdalah. In practice however, (indeed it is preferable), that just the master of the house says these things in the presence of the family and the guests. They just listen silently with the intention of fulfilling the Mitzvah, and thereby, it is, as if they have said these things with their own mouths. [Although it is proper to answer "Amen," nevertheless by not answering Amen, one still fulfills the Mitzvah.]

(Mishnah Berurah 271:5; Shemirat Shabbat K'hilchata 47:32; Encyclopedia Talmudit 4:197)

🖰🖰🖰🖰🖰🖰🖰🖰🖰🖰

Q. Which prayer is said on a particular day, just at Minchah by some communities, in Shacharit and Minchah by others, and at Ma'ariv, Shacharit and Minchah by yet others?

A. "Aneinu" on fast days.

On fast days one adds in the Amidah, the prayer beginning "Aneinu." However different communities say it at different times. Ashkenazim (Jews of European origin) say it just at Minchah, Sephardim (Jews of Oriental origin) at Shacharit and Minchah, and Taymanim (Jews of Yemenite origin) at all three services. It is of interest to note that the fasts (except Tisha b'Av) have not yet begun when Taymanim say it at Ma'ariv!

(Shulchan Aruch Orach Chaim 565:3 & Rema; Mishnah Berurah 565:9; Kaf Hachaim 565:14; Shtilei Zeitim 565:1 & Zayit Ra'anan 565:1)

Q. The congregants were not talking or making any other disturbances. So why month after month did the Shamash bang on the table during the service?

A. To tell the congregation to begin saying the Mussaf Amidah on Rosh Chodesh.

After the Kaddish before the Mussaf Amidah on Rosh Chodesh, there is a short pause to enable the congregants to take off their Tephillin. Since the entire congregation should start the silent Amidah together, the shamash or the gabbai bangs on the table to signal to the congregation to start saying the Mussaf Amidah.

(Shulchan Aruch Orach Chaim 423:4, 90:10; Mishnah Berurah 90:35)

Q. What in connection with the afflictions on Yom Kippur can a Kohen do up to three times during that day which is forbidden to a non-Kohen?

A. Wash his hands (or preferably have his hands washed by a Levi) *up to the wrists* before Duchaning.

One of the prohibitions on Yom Kippur is washing any part of the body. Before Kohanim go up to Duchan, their hands are washed *up to the wrists*, preferably by a Levi. In Israel there is Duchaning three times during Yom Kippur – at Shacharit, Mussaf and Ne'ilah - and so the Kohanim have their hands washed *up to their wrists*, three times during Yom Kippur.

(Shulchan Aruch Orach Chaim 613:1, 613:3 Rema, 128:6; Mishnah Berurah 613:7)

🕎 🕎 🕎 🕎 🕎 🕎 🕎 🕎 🕎 🕎

Q. Which berachah is sometimes said only once in a lifetime, sometimes never and rarely more than once?

A. The berachah for a "Pidyan Haben."

The ceremony of "Pidyan Haben" by a Kohen is performed when the firstborn is over 30 days old. It is only performed if the firstborn child of the mother is a boy. In addition, it must not be a Caesarian birth, nor may the father be a Kohen or Levi nor the mother the daughter of a Kohen or Levi. At this ceremony the father says the appropriate berachah. Should a man marry more than once and each wife give birth to a first-born son, only then will the father will have the opportunity to say this berachah more than once in his lifetime!

(Shulchan Aruch Yoreh Deah 305:1, 18, 24)

🕎 🕎 🕎 🕎 🕎 🕎 🕎 🕎 🕎 🕎

Q. When was Shimon particular to eat "Seudah Shlishit" twice on a certain Shabbat?

A. When erev Pesach occurred on that Shabbat.

On Shabbat one is obligated to eat three meals. For the first two meals one must eat bread and for the third meal (Seudah Shlishit) it is preferable. According to many opinions one can only eat the third meal on the *afternoon* on Shabbat. From the foregoing, a problem will arise when erev Pesach occurs on Shabbat. One may only eat bread until one third of the day has passed - about 9 o'clock in the morning. Matzah may not be eaten the entire day. What then is the best way to observe the Mitzvah of eating the third meal? Some people have two meals with bread – the second one being for the "Seudah Shlishit" – on Shabbat morning whilst one can still eat Chametz, and, in the afternoon an additional "Seudah Shlishit" (without bread or Matzah, of course!) is eaten with, for example, fish, fruit, etc.

(Shulchan Aruch Orach Chaim 274:4; 291:5 & Rema; 444:1 & Rema; Mishnah Berurah 444:8)

🌱🌱🌱🌱🌱🌱🌱🌱🌱🌱

Q. When Asher the Ba'al Koreh first learned Parashat Masei, what unusual thing did he notice with the singing notes?

A. He saw two notes which occurred nowhere else in the Torah.

The Torah is read to various musical notes which are indicated in the printed Chumash on the words themselves. Most of these notes are very common. However, there are a few rare ones, the rarest being "Yerach ben Yomo" and "Karnei Foro" which only occur once in the Torah and that is in Parashat Masei.

[These notes also occur once in Megillat Esther. In both the case of the Torah and Megillat Esther they occur on words connected with measurements.]

(Bamidbar 35:5; Esther 7:9)

🌱🌱🌱🌱🌱🌱🌱🌱🌱🌱

Q. Why did Gad search for specially spun 4 or 8 ply wool?

A. He wanted the wool for the making of Tzitzit.

Wool used in most clothing is two ply, namely two threads twisted together. In the wool for Tzitzit, however, it is customary to use 4 ply or better still 8 ply, which has been spun for the express purpose of wool to make Tzitzit.

(Shulchan Aruch Orach Chaim 11:2, Biur Halachah "v'tzrichin")

* * * * * * * * * *

Q. When can a person be called up to the Torah for "shishi" and "chazak" simultaneously?

A. When Parashat Pekudai is read on Shabbat Rosh Chodesh.

Four special Parashiot are read around the month of Adar (Adar Sheni in a leap year). The first is Shekalim which is read on the Shabbat before Rosh Chodesh Adar, or if Rosh Chodesh Adar is on Shabbat, on the Shabbat itself. When such a Rosh Chodesh occurs on Shabbat, 3 Sifrei Torah are taken out. In the first one reads the Parashah to *six* people; in the second Sefer Torah one reads for Rosh Chodesh for the 7th person and in the third Sefer Torah the Maftir for Parashat Shekalim. When one finishes reading any of the 5 books of the Torah, the congregation followed by the Reader says "Chazak..." In a year when Parashat Pekudai is read on Rosh Chodesh Adar Sheni (this can only occur in a leap year), it is also Parashat Shekalim. Thus only *six* people are called up for Parashat Pekudai, and "Chazak" (which is said at the end of the Parashah) will thus be said at the end of Shishi (namely, the 6th person called up).

(Shulchan Aruch Orach Chaim 685:1; Mishnah Berurah 685:4, 5; Shulchan Aruch Orach Chaim 139:1 Rema)

* * * * * * * * * *

Q. Why could Yonatan move the object on Shabbat but not on Yom Tov?

A. Certain things are Muktzah on Yom Tov but not on Shabbat.

The term "Muktzah" is used for objects which may not be moved on Shabbat or Yom Tov. In fact, Muktzah is stricter for Yom Tov than for Shabbat. For example, peels and bones which are fit for consumption by animals are Muktzah on Yom Tov but not on Shabbat.

(Shulchan Aruch Orach Chaim 495:4, Mishnah Berurah 495:15, 17)

Q. When on *every* Yom Tov is it forbidden for Leah to do cooking?

A. After sunset (towards the end of Yom Tov).

Cooking is only permitted on Yom Tov *for that day*. We do not know *exactly* when between sunset and "tzeit hakochavim" the day begins or ends. [This is the reason that Shabbat and Yom Tov are more than 24 hours long; we start some minutes before sunset and finish at tzeit hakochavim.] Thus by cooking after sunset, we could well be cooking on Yom Tov and eating the food after Yom Tov is out.

(Shulchan Aruch Orach Chaim 503:1; Luach D'var B'ito ["Achiezer" Bnei Brak] 5758 page 835)

Q. When do all Shuls leave out "Me'ain Sheva" on a Friday night?

A. When the first night of Pesach is on Shabbat?

Normally there is no repetition of the Amidah at Ma'ariv. However on Ma'ariv of Shabbat, there is an abridged repetition in which the 7 berachot of the Shabbat Amidah are incorporated into 1 berachah - hence the term "Me'ain Sheva" (an abridged 7 berachot). It was instituted to give an opportunity to latecomers to catch up with their prayers. The importance of this was that they should not finish after everybody else and thus have to go home alone in the dark. However, the Seder night is known as "Leil Shimurim" - the night when the Jewish people are specially guarded and so there is no worry for latecomers to go home alone in the dark. Thus "Me'ain Sheva" is omitted.

(Shulchan Aruch Orach Chaim 268:8; Mishnah Berurah 268:20; Shulchan Aruch Orach Chaim 487:1; Mishnah Berurah 487:9)

🏛️🏛️🏛️🏛️🏛️🏛️🏛️🏛️🏛️🏛️

Q. When and why did Shimon *intentionally* make his kosher Sukkah possul?

A. It was at the end of Hoshana Rabba, in Israel, since he needed to use the Sukkah on Shemini Atzeret/Simchat Torah.

It is a Torah commandment to dwell in the Sukkah all 7 days of Sukkot (8 days in the Diaspora). In Israel one returns to the house on the evening of Shemini Atzeret. Now supposing someone needs to use the Sukkah on Shemini Atzeret. (For example, one has a lot of guests and there is insufficient room in the house to feed and sleep them on Shemini Atzeret.) In order to be able to use the Sukkah on Shemini Atzeret, one must intentionally make it possul just before Shemini Atzeret. The reason is that one should not give the appearance that one is adding to the Mitzvah of Sukkah by using it after the end of Sukkot.

(Shulchan Aruch Orach Chaim 666:1)

🏛️🏛️🏛️🏛️🏛️🏛️🏛️🏛️🏛️🏛️

Q. When did Ovadiah not make Havdalah at the end of Yom Tov?

A. When Yom Tov ended on a Friday.

At the end of every Shabbat and Yom Tov, one makes Havdalah, a ceremony which separates the holy from the profane. When a Yom Tov ends on Friday, Shabbat then begins at the termination of Yom Tov and because Shabbat has a greater holiness than Yom Tov, one does not make Havdalah.

(Rambam, Hilchot Shabbat 5:21)

✝✝✝✝✝✝✝✝✝✝

Q. Which two words seem out of place in "vatodiainu" said when the second day of Rosh Hashanah begins on Motzaei Shabbat?

A. Vachagigat Haregel.

At Ma'ariv at the termination of Shabbat, ones adds in the Amidah, the prayer "ata chanantanu" whose content is the separation between the Shabbat and the weekdays. When Yom-Tov occurs immediately after the Shabbat, the addition begins "vatodiainu" and it is differently phrased. Since most of the occasions when one says this addition is one of the "Foot Festivals" (Pesach, Shavuot, Sukkot), it includes the phrase "Vechagigat Haregel" - celebration of the "Foot Festival." Even though Rosh Hashanah is not one of the "Foot Festivals," this phrase is not omitted when it occurs on Sunday.

(Shulchan Aruch Orach Chaim 294:1, 599:1; Mishnah Berurah 599:2)

✝✝✝✝✝✝✝✝✝✝

Q. What is wrong with the following instruction appearing in a Siddur: "On erev Yom Kippur, omit Lamnatzeach and Kel Erech Apayim."?

A. Kel Erech Apayim is only said on Mondays and Thursdays. Erev Yom Kippur cannot fall on these days!

On most Mondays and Thursdays throughout the year one says Kel Erech Apayim immediately before Kriyat haTorah. From the principles of the calendar, Yom Kippur cannot fall on Sunday, Tuesday or Friday. Thus erev Yom Kippur cannot fall on Monday or Thursday.

(Kitzur Shulchan Aruch 25:2; Shulchan Aruch Orach Chaim 428:1)

Q. In which well-known prayer recited three times each day has the "nun fallen out"?

A. Ashrei

"Ashrei" begins with two verses from different Tehilim which both begin with the word "Ashrei"; it is then followed by Tehilim 145 in its entirety; finally there is a verse from another one of the Tehilim. Tehilim 145 is an alphabetic acrostic. However, there is no verse in it beginning with the letter "nun." The Gemara explains the reason for such an omission. "Nofel" (whose first letter is nun) means falling and since this is a hint at the Jewish people falling, there is no verse in Ashrei beginning with the letter nun.

(Tehilim 84:5, 144:15, 145, 115:18; Berachot 4b)

Q. In which berachah did Leah make a distinction between fruits grown in Eretz Yisrael and fruits grown in the Diaspora?

A. Me'ain Shalosh.

After eating bread one recites the full "Birchat Hamazon," which consists of 3 berachot (of Torah origin) plus an additional one (of Rabbinical origin). After eating flour products, wine and certain fruits one recites "Me'ain Shalosh" - an abridged 3 berachot. In it the 3 berachot of "Birchat Hamazon" plus the additional berachah are incorporated into one berachah. For fruits grown in Eretz Yisrael, this berachah finishes with the words "ve'al pairoteha" (and for its [i.e.Eretz Yisrael's] fruits); for Diaspora fruits it finishes with "ve'al hapairot" (and for the fruits).

(Shulchan Aruch Orach Chaim 208:1, 10)

🏵️🏵️🏵️🏵️🏵️🏵️🏵️🏵️🏵️🏵️🏵️

🔍. What is the longest period of time that one omits Tachanun?

🅰. The entire month of Nissan. To be exact from Minchah on 29 Adar (Adar Sheni in a leap year) to Shacharit of 2 Iyar.

Tachanun is the supplicatory prayer recited after the Amidot of Shacharit and Minchah. It is omitted on Festivals and various other notable days in the year and (almost invariably as well) on the Minchah preceeding these days. Included in these days is the whole month of Nissan. The longest period for its omission will therefore be from Minchah on 29 Adar to (but not including) Shacharit of 2 Iyar.

(Shulchan Aruch Orach Chaim 131:7)

🏵️🏵️🏵️🏵️🏵️🏵️🏵️🏵️🏵️🏵️🏵️

🔍. When did Naftali read the Haftarah for Parashat Miketz?

🅰. When Chanukah began on a Friday.

Every Shabbat morning, following the Kriyat haTorah, one reads a Haftarah. The Haftarah is almost always related to the week's Parashah. When Shabbat occurs, for example, on Chanukah or Rosh Chodesh, the Haftarah is special for these days. In almost every year, Parashat Miketz is read during Chanukah. However, when Chanukah begins on Friday, Parashat Miketz is read *after* Chanukah and so the Haftarah for Miketz will be read.

(Shulchan Aruch Orach Chaim 684:2; Luach l'Eretz Yisrael [Rav Tukachinski] 5761, "Miketz")

🕎🕎🕎🕎🕎🕎🕎🕎🕎🕎

Q. Why in Israel may one sweep the floor of the house on Shabbat, but this was not allowed in pre-Second World War Europe?

A. Almost all the house floors in Israel are tiled, which was not the case in Europe.

One of the forbidden labours of Shabbat is "boneh" (building). This includes leveling any holes in the ground. Houses such as in pre-Second World War Europe had earthen floors and since by sweeping one would level holes, it was forbidden to sweep such floors. Today, in Israel, as in much of the developed world, floors are not earthen. If the majority of the floors in a city are tiled or wooden, one is allowed to sweep the floor on Shabbat.

(Shulchan Aruch Orach Chaim 337:2, Biur Halachah 337 "v'yesh machmirim.")

🕎🕎🕎🕎🕎🕎🕎🕎🕎🕎

Q. Apart from Lag b'Omer, what are bonfires and haircuts connected with?

A. The Nazir

Due to certain mourning practices during part of the period of the Omer, haircutting is not allowed. On the 33rd day of the Omer - known as Lag b'Omer, mourning is suspended and haircutting is permitted. Also, Lag b'Omer is a celebration in memory of Rabbi Shimon bar Yochai, a Rabbi who lived nearly two thousand years ago. At this celebration, bonfires are lit. The Nazir is a person who has taken a vow to abstain from wine and grape products and cutting his hair. At the end of his period of being a Nazir he cuts his hair and then burns it.

(Shulchan Aruch Orach Chaim 493:2, Rema and Ateret Zekainim; Bamidbar 6:18)

🪔🪔🪔🪔🪔🪔🪔🪔🪔🪔🪔

Q. What in a house sometimes points inwards, sometime outwards and sometimes upwards?

A. A Mezuzah

A Mezuzah contains the first two paragraphs of the Shema and is attached to the doorpost of almost every door in a house on the upper third of the doorpost. There are different customs regarding the direction of affixing a Mezuzah on the doorpost. Some have it pointing inwards, others outwards whilst yet others upwards.

(Shulchan Aruch Yoreh Deah 289:6 & Rema, Terumat Hadeshen part 1 chapter 52)

🪔🪔🪔🪔🪔🪔🪔🪔🪔🪔🪔

Q. Why is the Halachah which says that a Kohen who pronounces his "ayins" as "alephs" not permitted to Duchan, not relevant for *any* Jews in the world?

A. There is no letter "ayin" in Birchat Kohanim!

Most Western Jews cannot pronounce the letter "ayin" correctly and thus we are lenient on this question. But even if we were not lenient, this problem cannot arise with Birchat Kohanim since there is no letter "ayin" in Birchat Kohanim!

[It also applies for a Shliach Tzibur and here it can be relevant.]

(Shulchan Aruch Orach Chaim 128:33, Mishnah Berurah 128:120, Be'er Heitev 128: 55; Bamidbar 6:24-26)

🪔🪔🪔🪔🪔🪔🪔🪔🪔🪔🪔

Q. Why on one Friday night when Yosef made Kiddush in accordance with the Halachah, did he not fulfil this Mitzvah?

A. He did not eat anything after making Kiddush.

In order to fulfil the Mitzvah of Kiddush, one must eat a meal immediately after it. This meal need not be a full meal but can just be a piece of bread or cake. Without this, one has not fulfilled the Mitzvah of Kiddush, even if one has made it meticulously in accordance with all its other laws.

(Shulchan Aruch Orach Chaim 273:3 & Rema, 273:5)

Q. Why when Mordechai nullified his Chametz in Chinese, did he fulfil the Mitzvah of nullifying Chametz?

A. He understood the Chinese language!

After searching for Chametz on the night before Pesach and also after burning or disposing of it the next morning, one makes a declaration of nullification. This is not a prayer but a declaration and one must understand what one is saying. Even if one says it in the original Aramaic and doesn't understand what one is saying, one has not fulfilled the obligation of nullification. Therefore if one understands Chinese, one can say it in Chinese. Moreover, if one only understands Chinese, one *has to* say it in Chinese!

(Shulchan Aruch Orach Chaim 434:2 Rema; Mishnah Berurah 434:9)

Q. When whilst dressing does one act daily "Right and then left and then left and then right"?

A. When one puts on one's shoes and ties up the laces.

One first puts on the right shoe and then the left one. Afterwards one ties up the left lace and then the right one. The reason that one puts on the right one first is that the Torah gives importance to the right hand and foot over the left ones. With regards to the laces however it is the left which is given the greater importance as can be seen from the binding of the Tephillin which is done on the left arm.

(Shulchan Aruch Orach Chaim 2:4; Mishnah Berurah 2:5, 6)

♧ ♧ ♧ ♧ ♧ ♧ ♧ ♧ ♧ ♧

Q. For which Parashah may one *not* call up additional people, all the way up to Shevi'i?

A. Ha'azinu.

Towards the end of the Torah is the song "Ha'azinu" which is the content of almost the entire Parashat Ha'azinu. It was also the song of the Levi'im in the Temple during the Shabbat Mussaf sacrifice. It was then divided into six portions and every week one portion was sung. Today when we read it from the Torah, we may only make stops where the Levi'im stopped in the Temple. Thus only shevi'i (the portion for the 7th person being called to the Torah) may be split up.

(Devarim 32:1-43; Shulchan Aruch Orach Chaim 428:5, Mishnah Berurah 428:11, 12, 14)

♧ ♧ ♧ ♧ ♧ ♧ ♧ ♧ ♧ ♧

Q. Which fast (according to some opinions) is postponed every year?

A. Tzom Gedaliah.

Tzom Gedaliah commemorates the murder of Gedaliah after the destruction of the First Temple. It is observed on the day after Rosh Hashanah. Some however, say that Gedaliah was killed on

Rosh Hashanah. Since one cannot fast on Rosh Hashanah, the fast is every year postponed until after Rosh Hashanah.

(Shulchan Aruch Orach Chaim Be'er Heteiv 549:1)

❡ ❡ ❡ ❡ ❡ ❡ ❡ ❡ ❡ ❡ ❡

Q. Why when Shmuelik, who lived in a village in England had a daily national newspaper delivered to his house on Yom Tov, was he forbidden to carry it in the street?

A. Because it had come from outside the Techum on Yom Tov.

On Yom Tov it is permitted to carry outside the Eiruv (e.g. in the street, in a place where there is no Eiruv). However, the laws regarding the Techum - going about a kilometre outside the "city boundaries" applies in the same way as on Shabbat.

If a daily newspaper has been printed in a different city, it has come from outside the Techum on Yom Tov. In such a case one may not carry it outside the Eiruv.

(Shulchan Aruch Orach Chaim 495:1, 397:3; 515:5, 9; Mishnah Berurah 515:49)

❡ ❡ ❡ ❡ ❡ ❡ ❡ ❡ ❡ ❡ ❡

Q. What is the longest Amidah that can be recited during the year?

A. Mussaf on Rosh Hashanah when it occurs on Shabbat.

All the Amidot recited on Shabbat and Yom Tov consist of 7 berachot – with one exception. This is the Mussaf Amidah for Rosh Hashanah which consists of 9 berachot, with the middle three of them being very long. When Rosh Hashanah occurs on Shabbat, there are also a number of additions appertaining to Shabbat.

(Shulchan Aruch Orach Chaim 591:1; Machzor for Rosh Hashanah – Mussaf)

❡ ❡ ❡ ❡ ❡ ❡ ❡ ❡ ❡ ❡ ❡

Q. Where and when (according to some opinions), (after the fixed calendar was already in operation), did one lay Tephillin on 2 Tishri?

A. In Eretz Yisrael, until about the 13th century.

When the fixed calendar was instituted, at about the middle of the 4th century, the observance of two days Yom Tov in the Diaspora was retained. In Eretz Yisrael only one day was observed and according to some opinions, this included Rosh Hashanah. Thus Tephillin were laid on 2 Tishri. According to these opinions, when Jews arrived from France in about 13th century, after the expulsion of the Crusaders from Eretz Yisrael, they instituted 2nd day Rosh Hashanah. As a result, the Jews of Eretz Yisrael no longer lay Tephillin on that day.

(Beitzah, Ba'al Hamaor 3a)

Q. Apart from pikuach nefesh, when may one, *today*, intentionally cause bleeding on Shabbat?

A. When performing a Brit Milah.

There are only a few things *today* which override Shabbat. They are pikuach nefesh and a Brit Milah. If a baby boy is 8 days old on Shabbat, the Brit Milah takes place on that day. During a Brit Milah, there is, of course, bleeding.

(Shulchan Aruch Orach Chaim 331:1)

Q. In which three consecutive Parashiot in the Torah did David the Ba'al Koreh encounter a rare note?

A. Vayeira, Chayei Sarah and Toldot.

The Torah is read to specific musical notes which are printed above or below the words in a Chumash. Most of these notes are common but there are a few rare ones.

In three consecutive Parashiot in Bereshit there are rare notes. These are:

Vayeira - "shalshelet"; Chayei Sarah – "shalshelet"; Toldot – "merchah k'fulah."

(Bereshit 19:16, 24:12, 27:25)

🐝 🐝 🐝 🐝 🐝 🐝 🐝 🐝 🐝 🐝 🐝

Q. When are there more words in the Kaddish – during the year or during the "aseret yemai teshuvah"?

A. The same.

Kaddish is a prayer largely in Aramaic which has various formats and is said in a number of places in every service. During the "aseret yemai teshuvah" there is a slight change in the wording as follows: Whilst during the year one says "leaylah min kol" – 3 words, during the "aseret yemai teshuvah" one says: "leaylah (u) leaylah mikol" – 3 words. The number of words remains constant!

(Kitzur Shulchan Aruch 129:1)

🐝 🐝 🐝 🐝 🐝 🐝 🐝 🐝 🐝 🐝 🐝

Q. When did Yechezkel lein in Aramaic?

A. When he leined Parashat Vayetzei.

The entire Torah is in Hebrew with the exception of 2 words spoken by Lavan which appear towards the end of Parashat Vayetzei. These words are "Y'gar sahaduta"

(Bereshit 31:47)

🐝 🐝 🐝 🐝 🐝 🐝 🐝 🐝 🐝 🐝 🐝

Q. On which Shabbat may one not eat gefilte fish?

A. When Yom Kippur falls on Shabbat.

The origin of eating gefilte fish on Shabbat (minced fish balls) stems from the prohibition of "borer" (selecting) on Shabbat. Because of this prohibition, one may not remove the bones from fish. Since this may create difficulties when eating fish on Shabbat, it became customary to eat gefilte fish on Shabbat. On Yom Kippur one must fast and thus gefilte fish is forbidden!

(Shemirat Shabbat K'hilchata 3:15)

🕎 🕎 🕎 🕎 🕎 🕎 🕎 🕎 🕎 🕎

Q. Why when Shmuel drank on Purim until he reached the state of "ad dlo yada" did he not fulfill the Mitzvah of drinking on Purim?

A. He drank alcoholic beverages other than wine.

On Purim one is commanded to drink until one does not know the difference ("ad dlo yada") between "Blessed be Mordecai" and "Cursed be Haman." According to most opinions, the drinking must be done with wine only. Therefore by getting drunk on liqueurs, one will not fulfill the Mitzvah!

(Shulchan Aruch Orach Chaim 695:2; Mevakshei Torah 3:14 "Purim and the Month of Adar" 146:2 (pp.162-63))

🕎 🕎 🕎 🕎 🕎 🕎 🕎 🕎 🕎 🕎

Q. Which scissors are never Muktzah on Shabbat?

A. A grape scissors.

The term "Muktzah" is used for objects which may not be moved on Shabbat. It is divided into different categories. One of these categories is implements which are normally used for doing work forbidden on Shabbat: for example, a hammer. However, objects in this group may be used to do permitted works. For example, one may use a hammer to crack open nuts. One can likewise use an ordinary scissors to cut grapes from a bunch

(which has of course been detached from the tree before Shabbat!)
When not using the scissors for this purpose the scissors are
Muktzah and (if one does not require the space they are occupying)
they may not be moved on Shabbat. The sole function of grape
scissors is cutting grapes from a bunch, (in the same way as a table
knife is used for cutting food), and they are thus not Muktzah
on Shabbat.

(Shulchan Aruch Orach Chaim 308:3, 4)

🌱 🌱 🌱 🌱 🌱 🌱 🌱 🌱 🌱 🌱 🌱

Q. What is the minimum quantity of food over which one has to
say a berachah before eating?

A. There is no minimum - even one grain of sugar!

Before eating or drinking any food, one blesses the Creator for
benefit one gets from the food. However small the quantity, there
is a benefit and one thus makes a berachah.

(For a berachah said after eating food, one requires a definite
quantity of food.)

(Shulchan Aruch Orach Chaim 210:1; Mishnah Berurah 210:3)

🌱 🌱 🌱 🌱 🌱 🌱 🌱 🌱 🌱 🌱 🌱

Q. Where is Rosh Chodesh Tishri "hidden" in the Amidah of
Rosh Hashanah?

A. In the expressions: i) Yom Hazikaron, ii) Milvat olat
hachodesh, iii) Musfei.

  i) Yom Hazikaron – this is an expression used for both
      Rosh Hashanah and Rosh Chodesh
  ii) Milvad olat hachodesh – apart from the Rosh Hashanah
      Mussaf sacrifice, there is a Rosh Chodesh Mussaf
      sacrifice.

iii) Musfei – the Mussaf sacrifices *(plural)* offered on Rosh Hashanah – one for Rosh Hashanah and one for Rosh Chodesh.

(Shulchan Aruch Orach Chaim 582:6, Mishnah Berurah 582:18; Shulchan Aruch Orach Chaim 591:2 Rema; 591:3)

Q. Why did Ezra talk about Pesach during his Purim seudah?

A. Pesach occurs 30 days after Purim and one begins studying the laws of Pesach 30 days before this Festival.

Because of the numerous laws on the various aspects of Pesach, one should start to learn them 30 days before Pesach. Thirty days before Pesach is exactly Purim.

(In addition, on the Shabbat before Pesach, the Rav of the Shul gives a derashah on the laws of Pesach.)

(Shulchan Aruch Orach Chaim 429:1; Mishnah Berurah 429:1, 2)

Q. What was the profession of Dov who potentially had to work *every* day of the year and only had holidays and rest periods during the night?

A. A Mohel.

A Brit Milah can take place every day of the year without exception - including Shabbat, Yom Kippur and Yom Tov - but only during the daytime. It may never take place during the night. Thus a Mohel who performs Brit Milah has his "holidays" only at night-time! [In practice he is not free even at night. Parents often contact the Mohel, at all times including nighttime, to ask questions.]

(Shulchan Aruch Yoreh Deah 262:1 & Rema, 266:2)

Q. When did Nachum put on Tephillin on Shabbat?

A. When he found them in the street on Shabbat and there was no Eiruv.

One of the prohibitions of Shabbat is "hotza'ah" (carrying in a place where there is no Eiruv - an enclosed area). A classic example is a street situated in a town which has no Eiruv. What then happens if one finds a pair of Tephillin in such a street on Shabbat? On Shabbat one is forbidden to put on Tephillin for the purpose of the Mitzvah of Tephillin. However in this situation, by wearing the Tephillin they become an adornment on the wearer and he may thus walk in the street with them.

(Shulchan Aruch Orach Chaim 301:7, 42; Mishnah Berurah 301:158)

ⓧ ⓧ ⓧ ⓧ ⓧ ⓧ ⓧ ⓧ ⓧ ⓧ ⓧ

Q. Apart from Kabbalat Shabbat, when does one say "Lechu Nerananah" every week?

A. On Wednesday morning, at the end of the Tehilim for that day.

Before Ma'ariv on Shabbat, there is a service called "Kabbalat Shabbat." It consists of a number of Tehilim, beginning with "Lechu Nerananah," and also the poem "Lecha Dodi." At the end of every Shacharit one says a different one of the Tehilim for each day of the week. Wednesday's is Tehilim 94. The following one – Tehilim 95 - begins with "Lechu Nerananah" and the first three verses of it are read. It is appropriate that these 3 verses are read on Wednesday, since Sunday, Monday and Tuesday "belong" to the previous Shabbat, and Wednesday, Thursday and Friday to the following Shabbat. So saying these verses on Wednesday is a reminder that Shabbat is "on the way."

(Siddur – Kabbalat Shabbat; Tehilim 94, 95; Mishnah Berurah 299:16)

ⓧ ⓧ ⓧ ⓧ ⓧ ⓧ ⓧ ⓧ ⓧ ⓧ ⓧ

Q. Shimon heard Reuven repeat the same thing 90 times in rapid succession. What might Reuven have been saying?

A. (e.g.) V'et kol minai tevuata l'tova, v'tain tal umatar livrachah

During the winter, prayers for rain are added into the weekday Amidah. One of these additions is in the berachah "Barech Aleinu" (the blessing for sustenance) and the added wording is "v'tain tal umatar livrachah" - and give us dew and rain for blessing.

However, during the course of the previous over half a year, one has not made this addition and by habit one could err and not say it, or be doubtful whether one had said it. If one has not said it, one has to go back. However, what is the rule if one is not sure whether one has made this addition? The answer is that if one has already said it 90 times, then one can assume that one has not made a mistake. However, rather than wait for about a month until one has davened 90 times, one can say the words "v'et kol minai tevuata l'tova, v'tain tal umatar livrachah" 90 times in rapid succession. Having said this 90 times, should one be in doubt whether one had said this addition when subsequently saying the Amidah, one would not have to go back or repeat the Amidah.

(Shulchan Aruch Orach Chaim 117:1, 114:8, 9)

Q. For what on Friday night does one use the bottom one and on Shabbat morning the top one?

A. On Friday night one cuts the bottom of the two Challot and on Shabbat morning the top one.

On each meal on Shabbat and Yom Tov, one makes "Hamotzi" over two loaves of bread (the "Challot"). The reason for two loaves is that a double portion of manna fell on Fridays. It is customary to cut the top loaf on all occasions, except Friday night when one cuts the bottom one.

(Shulchan Aruch Orach Chaim 274:1 & Rema. Mishnah Berurah 274:1)

✿ ✿ ✿ ✿ ✿ ✿ ✿ ✿ ✿ ✿ ✿ ✿

Q. When did Zevulun read a Haftarah in Shul on a Friday afternoon?

A. When the fast of 10 Tevet occurred on Friday.

On Minchah on fast days one reads from the Torah and there is also a Haftarah. The only fast that can fall on Friday is 10 Tevet.

(Shulchan Aruch Orach Chaim 550:3 Rema; Mishnah Berurah 550:10)

✿ ✿ ✿ ✿ ✿ ✿ ✿ ✿ ✿ ✿ ✿ ✿

Q. The Shulchan Aruch says that one should hurry up Shacharit on Yom Kippur in order not to delay the davening of Mussaf. In fact, there is another day in the year when the problem is even more acute. When is it?

A. Simchat Torah.

The reason for hurrying up Shacharit is that one should begin Mussaf before the time for Minchah, otherwise there will be the problem of what to daven first – Mussaf or Minchah. This stems from the principle that when there is something which is frequent and something which is less frequent, the frequent takes priority. Since Minchah is said every day of the week but Mussaf only on Sabbaths and Festivals and Rosh Chodesh, Minchah would take priority over Mussaf. In practice however, on Yom Kippur almost every Shul has already started Mussaf before the time for Minchah. However on Simchat Torah, by the time one finishes the Hakafot with their accompanying dancing and all the numerous Aliyot in calling up the entire congregation (and possibly a Kiddush in the middle of it all!), it is already probably the time for Minchah!

RABBI DR. CHAIM SIMONS

(Shulchan Aruch Orach Chaim 620:1; Mishnah Berurah 620:2; Shulchan Aruch Orach Chaim 669:1 Rema)

🌸🌸🌸🌸🌸🌸🌸🌸🌸🌸🌸

Q. What is the maximum number of times a Kohen can Duchan at different services on a particular day?

A. 4 times

This could occur *in theory* on Yom Kippur. In Israel there is Duchaning at Shacharit, Mussaf and Ne'ilah on Yom Kippur. However, if a Kohen goes up to Duchan at Minchah on Yom Kippur, one does not tell him not to Duchan.

(Shulchan Aruch Orach Chaim 129:1, 2, 622:4)

🌸🌸🌸🌸🌸🌸🌸🌸🌸🌸🌸

Q. Which 5 successive paragraphs in the davening begin and end with the same words?

A. The 5 Tehilim of the "pesukei dezimrah" which follow Ashrei.

Following Ashrei, which is in the main Tehilim 145, the "pesukei dezimrah" continue with Tehilim 146 - 150, each of them beginning and ending with the word "Hallelukah"

(Siddur – Shacharit service.)

🌸🌸🌸🌸🌸🌸🌸🌸🌸🌸🌸

Q. What is permitted on Shabbat and Yom Tov, yet forbidden on Chol Hamoed?

A. Having a non-Jewish contractor build a house for a Jew outside the Techum.

On Shabbat and Yom Tov (but *not* Chol Hamoed) it is forbidden to go more than about a kilometre outside the city boundaries.

102

The boundary until where one may go is known as the Techum. For a number of reasons including "ma'arit ayin" (doing things which could appear to be forbidden), one may not employ non-Jewish workers to do work for a Jew on Shabbat, Yom Tov and Chol Hamoed. Since on Shabbat and Yom Tov one may not go outside the Techum, a question of "ma'arit ayin" cannot arise when a non-Jewish contractor builds a house for a Jew outside the Techum. However, since on Chol Hamoed one can leave the Techum, a Jew may not employ a non-Jewish contractor on these days.

(Shulchan Aruch Orach Chaim 397:1, 543:2, Mishnah Berurah 543:4)

🌱🌱🌱🌱🌱🌱🌱🌱🌱🌱🌱

Q. Why was Reuven at first reluctant when he was asked to be the Shliach Tzibur?

A. The Halachah says that only when pressed should one accept.

A person should not "push himself" to be the Shliach Tzibur in a Shul. The first time he is asked he should refuse, the second time he should prepare himself to get up from his seat and only on the third occasion go up to the Amud.

(Shulchan Aruch Orach Chaim 53:16)

🌱🌱🌱🌱🌱🌱🌱🌱🌱🌱🌱

Q. When is salt regarded as a product which grows from the ground?

A. In the laws of Imur on Shabbat.

One of the headings of forbidden work on Shabbat is "imur" (gathering together of produce). The prohibitions regarding imur only apply to things that grow from the ground. However, for the

103

purpose of imur, salt is regarded by the Rabbis as something which grows from the ground (i.e. in salt mines).

(Shulchan Aruch Orach Chaim 340:9; Mishnah Berurah 340:36)

🏵 🏵 🏵 🏵 🏵 🏵 🏵 🏵 🏵 🏵 🏵

🏵. Where in the davening on a Yom Tov which occurs on Shabbat, does one conclude a berachah *solely* with "Mekadesh haShabbat"?

🏵. In the berachah "Me'ain Sheva."

On Shabbat one concludes the middle berachah of the Amidah with the words "Mekadesh haShabbat" and on Yom-Tov "Mekadesh Yisrael vehazmanim." On Friday night, including when Friday night is also Yom Tov, one says immediately after the Amidah, "Me'ain Sheva" – an abbreviated repetition of the Amidah. However one *always* concludes it with just the words "Mekadesh haShabbat." The reason is that this is a prayer written specially for Shabbat.

(Siddur – Ma'ariv for Shabbat and Yom Tov; Shulchan Aruch Orach Chaim 268:8, 9)

🏵 🏵 🏵 🏵 🏵 🏵 🏵 🏵 🏵 🏵 🏵

🏵. Why did Dinah never take Trumot and Ma'asarot from rice?

🏵. Because rice is not grown in Israel.

Produce grown *in Israel* in Jewish fields has to have Trumot and Ma'asarot taken from it. It happens that rice is not at present grown in Israel. Were it to be grown it would of course have to be tithed.

Shulchan Aruch Yoreh Deah 331:1)

🏵 🏵 🏵 🏵 🏵 🏵 🏵 🏵 🏵 🏵 🏵

Q. On Chanukah it is customary to eat cheese dishes. How is it possible to go through Chanukah and *not be able* to eat any cheese dish?

A. One continually eats meat at intervals of less than 6 hours.

It is a custom to eat cheese dishes on Chanukah. This commemorates Yehudit who cut off the head of a wicked king by feeding him cheese dishes and wine until he fell asleep. After eating meat, one has to wait 6 hours before partaking of any milk dishes. Therefore if one were continually to eat meat throughout Chanukah in intervals of less than 6 hours, one would be precluded from keeping the custom of eating cheese dishes!

(Shulchan Aruch Orach Chaim 670:2 Rema; Mishnah Berurah 670:10; Shulchan Aruch Yoreh Deah 89:1)

Q. On what days does one say Ashrei 4 times?

A. On the days when one says Selichot before Shacharit.

Every day of the year during the course of the davening, one says Ashrei three times. The Selichot (recited before Shacharit in the days before Rosh Hashanah and during the "aseret yemai teshuvah"), begins with Ashrei. Thus on these days Ashrei is said 4 times.

(Berachot 4b; Siddur - Shacharit and Minchah; Book of Selichot)

Q. When cannot a Kohen or Levi receive Maftir?

A. At Minchah on fast days and at Shacharit on Tisha b'Av.

The first person called up to the Torah is a Kohen and immediately after him is a Levi. From then on, only a Yisrael is called up. On Shabbat and Yom Tov, the Maftir is additional to the obligatory number and so a Kohen or Levi can be called up for it. However, on the afternoon of Fast days and at the morning of Tisha b'Av, the Maftir is the third person called up and being part of the obligatory number, only a Yisrael can be called up for it.

(Shulchan Aruch Orach Chaim 135:3; 282:4 & Rema, 566:1 Rema)

🌸🌸🌸🌸🌸🌸🌸🌸🌸🌸🌸

🔍. Why on an erev Shabbat was Reuven given the book (and it was not a mistake!) designated for the Barmitzvah boy Shimon, whose Barmitzvah was on that Shabbat?

🅰. Generally speaking, one may not give a present on Shabbat.

The Rabbis have forbidden giving a present on Shabbat since it resembles a business transaction and could lead to writing on Shabbat. However there are ways of giving a Barmitzvah boy his present on Shabbat. One way is by someone else receiving the present before Shabbat on the Barmitzvah boy's behalf, even if the Barmitzvah boy does not know about it. It can then be given to the Barmitzvah boy on Shabbat, since technically he has received it before Shabbat.

(Shemirat Shabbat K'hilchata 29:29)

🌸🌸🌸🌸🌸🌸🌸🌸🌸🌸🌸

🔍. Apart from Rosh Hashanah and Yom Kippur, when does one say "Avinu Malkeinu" but omit Tachanun?

🅰. The morning of erev Yom Kippur when it occurs on a Friday.

Avinu Malkeinu is said during the "aseret yemai teshuvah," and on most fast days throughout the year. It is omitted when these days occur on Shabbat, Friday afternoon and erev Yom Kippur. When however the latter occurs on Friday, it is said at Shacharit - the reason being that Yom Kippur of that year will be on Shabbat and Avinu Malkeinu will only be said on that day at Ne'ilah. During the "aseret yemai teshuvah," Tachanun is omitted on Rosh Hashanah, Yom Kippur, Shabbat, Friday afternoon and erev Yom Kippur. It thus follows, that apart from Rosh Hashanah and Yom Kippur, the only time one says Avinu Malkeinu but omits Tachanun is the morning of erev Yom Kippur when it occurs on a Friday.

(Shulchan Aruch Orach Chaim 602:1 Rema, 604:2 Rema)

Q. Why did Reuven's father not worry when his son demanded an excessive ransom for the Afikoman?

A. If the Afikoman gets lost, one can take *any other* Shemurah Matzah and use it for the Afikoman.

Towards the beginning of the Seder, the middle Matzah is broken and the bigger portion (the Afikoman) is put away to be eaten as the last course of the meal. It is customary for the children to "steal" the Afikoman and demand a "ransom" for its return. There is however a halachah that should the Afikoman get lost, one can take another Shemurah Matzah in its place.

[But be careful – one's son might get clever and hide all the Shemurah Matzot which are in the house!!]

(Shulchan Aruch Orach Chaim 473:6, 477:2 Rema)

Q. How did Zechariah reach the age of Barmitzvah 23 hours before he completed his 13 years?

A. He was born at the end of a day. 13 years later he reached the age of Barmitzvah at the beginning of that day.

A boy reaches the age of Barmitzvah when he is 13 years old. There is a principle that part of day is regarded as a whole day.

RABBI DR. CHAIM SIMONS

Therefore if a boy is born just before sunset on, for example 3 Kislev, then 13 years later when 3 Kislev begins at the previous nightfall, he will be 13 years old, even though on an hourly count, he is missing about 23 hours.

(Mishnah Berurah 55:42)

✿ ✿ ✿ ✿ ✿ ✿ ✿ ✿ ✿ ✿ ✿

Q. When, for a religious reason, did Dan return home and wake somebody up at 2 o'clock in the morning (i.e. 2 a.m.)?

A. When he returned home at 2 o'clock in the morning during Chanukah, no-one in the house was awake and he needed to light Chanukah candles.

At the beginning of each night during the 8 days of Chanukah, candles are lit. (On Shabbat of course, they are lit before the commencement of Shabbat.) They are lit in a place where people outside in the street or members of the household can see the lights. The reason is to proclaim the miracle of Chanukah ("pirsumei nisa"). If the hour is so late (such as 2 o'clock in the morning) that there is no-one in the street and the entire household is asleep, one cannot say a berachah over the lights. Therefore one should wake up a member of the family to watch the lighting of the candles.

(Shulchan Aruch Orach Chaim 672:2 & Rema; Mishnah Berurah 672:11).

✿ ✿ ✿ ✿ ✿ ✿ ✿ ✿ ✿ ✿ ✿

Q. Why was Micha trapped up a tree for almost the entire Shabbat?

A. He, knowing that the Halachah forbade it, climbed up a tree towards the beginning of Shabbat.

One of the work prohibitions of Shabbat is "kotzer" (detaching something which grows from the ground). Since by climbing a

108

tree, one can easily break off branches and twigs, the Rabbis forbade climbing a tree on Shabbat. Included in this prohibition is the "punishment" that if one knowing the law regarding climbing trees on Shabbat, still does so, one must remain in the tree till the termination of Shabbat.

(Shulchan Aruch Orach Chaim 336:1; Mishnah Berurah 336:7)

🐞🐞🐞🐞🐞🐞🐞🐞🐞🐞🐞

🐞. When does one say "Sephardim, go back; Ashkenazim, continue"?

🅰. If in the Amidah during the "aseret yemai teshuvah," one says in error "Melech oheiv tzedaka umishpat." Ashkenazim continue with the Amidah, whilst Sephardim must go back to this berachah.

Several changes are made in the Amidah during the "aseret yemai teshuvah." If one erred, in some cases one must go back; in others one does not return. One of the changes made during these days is, instead of concluding one of the berachot. "Melech oheiv tzedaka umishpat," one says "Hamelech hamishpat." If one errs here there is a difference of opinion what to do. Ashkenazim continue with the Amidah, whilst Sephardim go back.

(Shulchan Aruch Orach Chaim 582:1, 118:1 Rema.)

🐞🐞🐞🐞🐞🐞🐞🐞🐞🐞🐞

🐞. Why did Rabbi Zielin *not* give a Derashah on a certain Shabbat Hagadol?

🅰. That year Shabbat Hagadol occurred on erev Pesach.

It is an established custom for the Rabbi of a Shul to give a Derashah on Shabbat Hagadol, the Shabbat before Pesach. In it, the Rabbi talks about the laws of Pesach. However, when Pesach begins on a Sunday, some of the laws, such as the search for

109

chametz, selling the chametz, kashering vessels, must be performed before Shabbat and it will thus be too late for the Rabbi to talk about them on that Shabbat. The Derashah is therefore advanced to the previous Shabbat.

(Mishnah Berurah 429:2)

⚜ ⚜ ⚜ ⚜ ⚜ ⚜ ⚜ ⚜ ⚜ ⚜

Q. What new clothes may be bought during "the 9 days"?

A. Non-leather shoes for Tisha b'Av.

During the 9 days (the first nine days of the month of Av), no new clothes may be bought, even such mundane clothes such as socks. On Tisha b'Av one may not wear leather shoes. If one does not possess non-leather shoes, one may buy such shoes for use on Tisha b'Av.

(Shulchan Aruch Orach Chaim 551:7 Rema, Mishnah Berurah 551:49; Kaf Hachaim, Orach Chaim 551: 97, Igrot Moshe 3:80)

⚜ ⚜ ⚜ ⚜ ⚜ ⚜ ⚜ ⚜ ⚜ ⚜

Q. When does one say the extra Tehilim for Shabbat and Yom Tov but omit Nishmat?

A. On Hoshana Rabba

Towards the beginning of Shacharit are the "pesukei dezimrah." On Shabbat and Yom Tov they are longer than on weekdays with a number of Tehilim being added before the paragraph "yehi chavod." In addition, on Shabbat and Yom Tov, "Nishmat" is added before yishtabach. On Hoshana Rabba, these Tehilim are added before "yehi chavod" but "Nishmat" is not said.

(Shulchan Aruch Orach Chaim 664:1 & Rema)

⚜ ⚜ ⚜ ⚜ ⚜ ⚜ ⚜ ⚜ ⚜ ⚜

SECTION ONE: CATCH ME IF YOU CAN!

Q. When were the Arba'at Haminim taken on Chanukah?

A. At the time of the Hasmoneans.

Because of the war with the Greeks, the Jews were not able to celebrate Sukkot at the proper time. Therefore, after they cleansed the Temple on 25 Kislev (which then became Chanukah), they celebrated Sukkot and took the Arba'at Haminim.

(Maccabees II 10: 5-7)

🕎 🕎 🕎 🕎 🕎 🕎 🕎 🕎 🕎 🕎

Q. How, for three and a half months in a year, can there be a difference in the Parashiot read in Israel and in the Diaspora?

A. When the 8th day of Pesach in the Diaspora occurs on Shabbat, in a Jewish leap year.

Throughout the year successive Parashiot of the Torah are read on Shabbat mornings. When however, a Festival or Chol Hamoed occurs on Shabbat, an alternative portion of the Torah is read. In Israel, Pesach is 7 days and in the Diaspora 8 days. If this 8th day occurs on Shabbat, in Israel the normal Parashah will be read, whereas in the Diaspora there will be the special leining for Pesach. As a result, Israel will be one Parashah ahead of the Diaspora. The only way for the Diaspora to catch up will be that when one comes to a double Parashah, in Israel it will be split up into two single Parashiot. In a leap year, the first double Parashah after Pesach will be Matot-Masei, but it is only read about three and a half months after Pesach.

(Luach D'var B'ito ["Achiezer" Bnei Brak] 5755)

🕎 🕎 🕎 🕎 🕎 🕎 🕎 🕎 🕎 🕎

Q. When does 7 become 1, and when does 3 become 1?

A. 7 becomes 1 in the prayer "Me'ain Sheva"
3 becomes 1 in the berachah "Me'ain Shalosh"

Normally the Amidah is not repeated at Ma'ariv. However on Friday night there is a form of repetition of the Amidah called "Me'ain Sheva" when the 7 berachot of the Amidah are "telescoped" into 1 berachah.

After eating bread, one must, according the Torah, say a full "Birchat Hamazon" comprised of 3 berachot from the Torah (plus one added by the Rabbis). After eating from the "seven species" (flour products, wine and certain fruits) one says a berachah called "Me'ain Shalosh" in which the 3 (plus one) berachot of "Birchat Hamazon" are made into 1 berachah; (for flour products it begins "al hamichya," for wine, "al hagefen" and for certain fruits, "al haetz.")

(Shulchan Aruch Orach Chaim 268:8, 208:1)

Q. When is wool preferred for a garment?

A. In the Mitzvah of Tzitzit.

According to the Torah, a garment having 4 corners requires Tzitzit to be attached to each of the corners. Garments can be made of various materials - wool, cotton, linen, etc. Do they all require Tzitzit? Opinions are divided on this question, but all agree that according to the Torah, a garment made of *wool* requires Tzitzit.

(Shulchan Aruch Orach Chaim 9:6)

Q. Why on a certain Ta'anit Sheni Batra, did Binyamin who usually said the Selichot for that day, omit them?

A. Because it occurred on Pesach Sheni.

A few weeks after Pesach and Sukkot, there are three days - Monday, Thursday and the following Monday - designated as fasts, or in practice as days for saying Selichot. The reason for these days, is that due to levity during the *week-long* Festivals, one might have come to sin. A day known as Pesach Sheni - a minor festival today - occurs on 14 Iyar, and should this clash with the second Monday, some omit the Selichot.

(Shulchan Aruch Orach Chaim 492:1; Luach Eretz Yisrael, [Rav Tukachinski] 5765,"Iyar – Ta'anit Sheni Tanina")

🕎 🕎 🕎 🕎 🕎 🕎 🕎 🕎 🕎 🕎 🕎

🕎. Which three numbers follow 13, 12, 11, 10, 9 in the Amidot for Mussaf recited on Sukkot (including Shemini Atzeret)?

🅰. 8, 7, 1.

During every Mussaf Amidah during the year, details of the Mussaf sacrifices are included. Generally they are not the same for the various Festivals. On the first day of Sukkot this sacrifice includes 13 cows. On successive days during Sukkot, the number of cows decreases by one each day. Thus on the sixth day, 8 cows are offered up and on the seventh day 7 cows. However on the eighth day which is known as Shemini Atzeret, and which is in fact a new Festival, not 6 cows are offered up but only 1.

(Machzor for Sukkot- Mussaf; Bamidbar 29:12-38)

🕎 🕎 🕎 🕎 🕎 🕎 🕎 🕎 🕎 🕎 🕎

🕎. How did Yissachar fry an egg on Shabbat in a permitted way?

🅰. In the direct heat of the sun.

One of the categories of work forbidden on Shabbat is "ofeh" (baking/cooking). However, this prohibition is limited to cooking by a man-made source of heat, e.g. oil, gas, electricity. Cooking by the direct heat of the sun is not included. Therefore, in theory at least, one can fry an egg by the heat of the sun on Shabbat.

(Shulchan Aruch Orach Chaim 318:3)

♔ ♔ ♔ ♔ ♔ ♔ ♔ ♔ ♔ ♔ ♔

Q. Why did Yossi prefer a wooden seat to a padded one in a train or bus?

A. In case there was Shaatnez in the material of the padded seat.

The Torah forbids the wearing of a garment containing both wool and linen. Such a mixture is known as Shaatnez. In addition, some people are particular not to sit on a seat containing Shaatnez.

(Shulchan Aruch Yoreh Deah Be'er Heteiv 301:2; "The Chazon Ish" by Shimon Finkelman [Art Scroll History Series, Mesorah Publications] pp.164, 234)

♔ ♔ ♔ ♔ ♔ ♔ ♔ ♔ ♔ ♔ ♔

Q. What berachah did Akiva say when he saw "ROYGBIV"?

A. "Zocher Habrit …" - the berachah recited when seeing a rainbow.

After the flood, G-d promised Noach that he would not destroy the world in the future by flood and as a sign he gave the rainbow. When one sees a rainbow, one must say the berachah "Zocher habrit, v'neeman bivrito v'kayom b'maamaro."

The colours of the rainbow are Red, Orange, Yellow, Green, Blue, Indigo and Violet. Their initial letters spell out ROYGBIV.

(Bereshit 9:8-17; Shulchan Aruch Orach Chaim 229:1)

♔ ♔ ♔ ♔ ♔ ♔ ♔ ♔ ♔ ♔ ♔

🪲. Where is Yom Kippur called Rosh Hashanah?

🅰. In the book of Yechezkel - "On Rosh Hashanah, on the tenth of the month [of Tishri]."

This is the only occasion in the whole of the Tenach where the expression "Rosh Hashanah" is used but it refers to Yom Kippur!

(Yechezkel 40:1.)

🌷🌷🌷🌷🌷🌷🌷🌷🌷🌷🌷

🪲. When does one not reply when spoken to by a king and when does one reply?

🅰. During the Amidah. To a Jewish king, one does not reply but to a non-Jewish king, if necessary, one does.

The central prayer in every service is the Amidah. On weekdays it consists of 19 berachot and on Sabbaths and Festivals almost invariably 7 berachot. There are very strict laws regarding not speaking during the saying of the Amidah. If a Jewish king were to address someone, he would understand why he could not reply. With a non-Jewish king however, it could prove uncomfortable if not outright dangerous!

(Shulchan Aruch Orach Chaim 104:1)

🌷🌷🌷🌷🌷🌷🌷🌷🌷🌷🌷

🪲. What is the difference between a miniscule insect and a caterpillar on a lettuce on Shabbat?

🅰. The miniscule insect cannot be removed, the caterpillar may.

The forbidden labour of "borer" (selecting) on Shabbat does not apply to big objects. An insect on a vegetable is miniscule; a caterpillar is relatively large and may therefore be removed.

(Shemirat Shabbat K'hilchata 3:36)

🌷🌷🌷🌷🌷🌷🌷🌷🌷🌷🌷

Q. When in some years does one say Tachanun on every day of a particular month (except Shabbat and Rosh Chodesh) whereas in other years one does not?

A. In Shevat, when Tu biShevat occurs on Shabbat.

Tachanun is a supplicatory prayer said after the Amidah on most week days during the year. On almost all days which have some special significance, Tachanun is omitted. One of these days is Tu biShevat - the 15th Shevat, the New Year for Trees. This is the only occasion during the month of Shevat when Tachanun is omitted. Should Tu biShevat occur on Shabbat in any particular year, then Tachanun in any case is not said, and Tachanun will thus be said every day of that month except Shabbat and Rosh Chodesh.

(Shulchan Aruch Orach Chaim 131:6)

※ ※ ※ ※ ※ ※ ※ ※ ※ ※ ※

Q. Which Haftarah has the most verses?

A. The Haftarah for Parashat Beshalach.

Every Shabbat and Yom Tov morning and on a few other occasions during the year, a Haftarah, which is a reading from the Nevi'im, directly follows the leining. These Haftarot vary considerably in length from each other. The longest is for Parashat Beshalach and it is 52 verses long.

(Shulchan Aruch Orach Chaim 284:1; Shoftim 4:4 – 5:31)

※ ※ ※ ※ ※ ※ ※ ※ ※ ※ ※

Q. When did Sa'adia, who was a Sepharadi say a berachah over Hallel on Rosh Chodesh?

A. On Rosh Chodesh Tevet

Whole Hallel is recited on the first day(s) of Yom Tov of Pesach, Shavuot, every day during Sukkot and every day during Chanukah.

Half Hallel is recited on the last six days of Pesach and Rosh Chodesh. Everyone says a berachah over whole Hallel. In the case of half Hallel, Ashkenazim say a berachah whereas Sephardim do not. Rosh Chodesh Tevet occurs during Chanukah and even Sephardim will thus say a berachah before reciting Hallel on that Rosh Chodesh.

(Arachin10a-b; Ta'anit 28b; Shulchan Aruch Orach Chaim 422:2 Rema)

🌱🌱🌱🌱🌱🌱🌱🌱🌱🌱🌱

Q. Which prayers, which are special for Shabbat, are recited every Shabbat throughout the year without exception?

A. 1. Mizmor Shir Leyom haShabbat during Kabbalat Shabbat
2. Vayechulu after the Ma'ariv Amidah
3. Kel Adon
4. Yekum Purkun

1. Following Lecha Dodi on Friday night, "Mizmor Shir Leyom haShabbat" is recited. Although many Shuls omit Lecha Dodi and the Tehilim preceding it when Shabbat occurs on Yom Tov, Chol Hamoed or immediately after Yom Tov, one always says "Mizmor Shir Leyom haShabbat."
2. Even when Shabbat occurs on Yom Tov, "Vayechulu" is recited after the Ma'ariv Amidah
3. On every weekday throughout the year, even if it is a Festival, one says the berachah "Hamayir Laaretz" after Borachu in Shacharit. On Shabbat however, this is always replaced by "Hakol Yoducha" and then "Kel Adon."
4. Following the Haftarah on every Shabbat during the year, "Yekum Purkun" is recited.

(Siddur – Shabbat services; Machzorim for the different Festivals)

🌱🌱🌱🌱🌱🌱🌱🌱🌱🌱🌱

Q. Why could Yocheved eat Parev foods but not milky or meaty foods?

A. It was at the beginning of the "nine days" (at beginning of the month of Av) and she had just eaten a meaty meal. (Likewise, after Shabbat during the "nine days.")

The two Temples were both destroyed on the 9 Av. Because of this, a number of rules of mourning were instituted during the 9 days from the beginning of Av until after 9 Av. One of them is not eating meat during this period, except for Shabbat. There is also a rule that after eating meat, one must wait a period of time, (according to most authorities - 6 hours), before partaking of milk foods. Therefore, if just before the beginning of the 9 days, or towards the end of Shabbat during these 9 days, one has partaken of meat, one will not be able to eat even milk foods at the beginning of the 9 days or after the termination of Shabbat.

(Shulchan Aruch Orach Chaim 551:9; Yoreh Deah 89:1)

Q. What use can one make of the Shofar on Rosh Hashanah occurring on Shabbat which one cannot do when it occurs on a weekday?

A. Use it as a cup for drinking.

When Rosh Hashanah occurs on a weekday, the Shofar is blown. The Shofar is therefore set aside for the Mitzvah of blowing it and it cannot be used for any other purpose. When Rosh Hashanah is however on Shabbat, there is no blowing and it can therefore be used for other purposes, such as a cup for drinking! (One would of course have to close up the narrow open end with one's finger!)

(Mishnah Berurah 588:15)

Q. Which four books in the Tenach, all of which are read during the Shul service, does one "go back" after reaching the end of the book?

A. Yeshayahu, Malachi, Eichah, Kohelet.

These 4 books of the Tenach end on a bad note. Since we do not like to finish off anything on a bad note, after reading the last verse we again read the verse preceding it. During the course of the year, all four of them are read as part of the Shul service - two of them as Haftarot and the other two as Megillot.

(Tanach)

✿✿✿✿✿✿✿✿✿✿✿✿

Q. When on a Wednesday or Thursday should one not "rely" on one's Rabbi?

A. For the making of Eiruv Tavshillin.

On Shabbat, cooking is strictly forbidden. On Yom Tov it is permitted for that day alone. What then can one do when Yom Tov occurs on Friday? How can one have fresh cooked food for Shabbat? This is done by performing a ceremony known as Eiruv Tavshillin - in which one takes a cooked dish and bread on the day before Yom Tov (which for this Mitzvah will always be a Wednesday or Thursday) and making a certain declaration. Although the Rabbi of the town includes in his Eiruv Tavshillin, all the inhabitants of his town, this is only for people who genuinely have themselves forgotten to make it. A person may not deliberately rely on his Rabbi in this matter.

(Shulchan Aruch Orach Chaim 527:1, 2, 7)

✿✿✿✿✿✿✿✿✿✿✿✿

Q. When on Yom Tov is it obligatory to have a Seudah Shlishit?

A. When Yom Tov occurs on Shabbat.

119

On Shabbat it is obligatory to eat 3 meals. On Yom Tov, 2 meals are sufficient. Obviously when Yom Tov occurs on Shabbat, three meals are required.

(Shulchan Aruch Orach Chaim 291:1, 529:1)

🌱 🌱 🌱 🌱 🌱 🌱 🌱 🌱 🌱 🌱 🌱

Q. On which Shabbat Mevorachin does one *always* take out 2 Sifrei Torah?

A. Nissan.

On the last Shabbat of each month (except Elul), before returning the Torah to the Ark, the blessing for the coming month is recited. Such a Shabbat is thus known as "Shabbat Mevorachin." When Rosh Chodesh Nissan occurs on a weekday, Shabbat Mevorachin is Shabbat Parashat Hachodesh. When however, Rosh Chodesh occurs on Shabbat, Shabbat Mevorachin will be Parashat Parah. On both these Shabbatot, 2 Sifrei Torah are taken out.

(Siddur - Shabbat Shacharit; Luach l'Eretz Yisrael [Rav Tukachinski] 5766 "Parashat Hachodesh," 5758 "Parashat Parah")

🌱 🌱 🌱 🌱 🌱 🌱 🌱 🌱 🌱 🌱 🌱

Q. What is the minimum period of time to finish the "shloshim" after the death of a relative?

A. Six days.

After a close relative dies, there is first of all a period of mourning lasting seven days, known as the "shiva." This is followed by a period of 23 days, making a total of 30 days - "shloshim." However, should a Festival begin during these two periods, then such a period will be immediately terminated. When a burial takes place on erev Yom Kippur, the shiva will end with Yom Kippur and 5 days later the shloshim will end at the commencement of Sukkot.

(Shulchan Aruch Yoreh Deah 399:10)

🌱 🌱 🌱 🌱 🌱 🌱 🌱 🌱 🌱 🌱 🌱

Q. Why did Reuven say a berachah over food which he knew not to be kosher?

A. He was eating it for "Pikuach Nefesh."

Before eating any item of food or drink, one has to make a berachah. Should however one eat a food which is not kosher, such as pork, shell fish, non-kosher cakes or non-kosher confectionery, one does not make a berachah. However, if one is seriously ill and one requires to eat such foods to become healthy, then it is permitted, even obligatory, to eat such forbidden foods in order to recover. This is known as "pikuach nefesh." In such a case, one says a berachah over these forbidden foods.

(Shulchan Aruch Orach Chaim 196:1, 2, 204:9; Mishnah Berurah 204:47)

✣ ✣ ✣ ✣ ✣ ✣ ✣ ✣ ✣ ✣ ✣

Q. Why was Tachanun said in a Shul at Minchah, even though they had not said it at Shacharit that very same day?

A. At Shacharit that day, there had been present in the Shul a Chatan and he was not present at Minchah.

The Tachanun prayer is said at Shacharit and Minchah each weekday unless it is a special day in the Jewish year: For example: Tu biShevat, Purim, Lag b'Omer. It is also omitted when there is present in the Shul a Chatan - a man who has got married during the previous seven days. Thus if the Chatan was present at Shacharit but not Minchah, Tachanun would only be recited at the Minchah service that day.

(Shulchan Aruch Orach Chaim 131:4)

✣ ✣ ✣ ✣ ✣ ✣ ✣ ✣ ✣ ✣ ✣

Q. What is the maximum and minimum number of days during Chanukah that one can say Mussaf?

A. Maximum – 4; Minimum – 2

During Chanukah, Mussaf is said on Shabbat Chanukah and on Rosh Chodesh Tevet which always occurs during Chanukah. Since Chanukah is 8 days long, there can be two Shabbatot during Chanukah. The month of Kislev has either 29 or 30 days. When there are 30 days in a month, Rosh Chodesh is on the 30th day and on the 1st day of the new month; when there are 29 days, it is only on the 1st day of the next month. For Chanukah itself, there is no Mussaf, since there was no Mussaf sacrifice specifically for Chanukah.

The maximum number of days during Chanukah that one can say Mussaf is 4. This occurs when the first and last days occur on Shabbat and there are 2 days Rosh Chodesh Tevet.

The minimum number of days is 2. There are two possibilities for this: i) when Rosh Chodesh Tevet occurs on Shabbat and Sunday, ii) when Shabbat is not Rosh Chodesh, nor the first and last days, and there is just one day Rosh Chodesh Tevet. [*Note:* If there is just one day Rosh Chodesh Tevet, due to the principles of the calendar, it cannot occur on Shabbat. Thus the minimum number of days for saying Mussaf during Chanukah *cannot* be 1.]

(Shulchan Aruch Orach Chaim 286:2, 423:3, 428:2)

❧ ❧ ❧ ❧ ❧ ❧ ❧ ❧ ❧ ❧

Q. What is the maximum number of consecutive days on which one does not lay Tephillin (under normal circumstances)?

A. For those who lay Tephillin on Chol Hamoed: 3
For those who do not lay Tephillin on Chol Hamoed: 8 in Israel 10 in the Diaspora

Tephillin must be put on every day with the exception of Shabbat and Festivals. Regarding Chol Hamoed, there are different opinions. In Israel, no-one lays Tephillin on Chol Hamoed

For those who lay Tephillin on Chol Hamoed:

When a Festival occurs on Thursday and Friday or on Sunday and Monday, the maximum number of days will be 3.

For those who do not lay Tephillin on Chol Hamoed :

In Israel: For Sukkot in every year, and for Pesach beginning on Shabbat or Sunday, the maximum number of days will be 8. (Sukkot cannot begin on a Friday or Sunday and so the number cannot increase to 9).

In the Diaspora: When Sukkot begins on a Thursday, Simchat Torah will be on day 9 which is a Friday. Thus the maximum number of days will be 10.

(Shulchan Aruch Orach Chaim 31:1, 2 & Rema)

🪷 🪷 🪷 🪷 🪷 🪷 🪷 🪷 🪷 🪷 🪷

Q. Why did Tzuriel say the berachah "Hamotzi" over cake?

A. He intended eating a very large quantity of it.

The berachah over bread is "Hamotzi" and over cake "Mezonot." However should, for example, one intend to eat a *large* quantity of cake, which others would make a whole meal of, one would then have to wash one's hands beforehand, say the berachah "Hamotzi" over the cake and the entire "Birchat Hamazon" after eating this large quantity of cake.

(Shulchan Aruch Orach Chaim 168:6)

🪷 🪷 🪷 🪷 🪷 🪷 🪷 🪷 🪷 🪷 🪷

Q. When was Sarah permitted on Yom Kippur to smell a fruit which was attached to the tree?

A. When Yom Kippur occurred on a weekday.

Picking something which is attached to the ground is forbidden on Shabbat. Because of this, on Shabbat the Rabbis forbade one to smell a fruit on a tree in case one came to pick it in order to eat it. This prohibition does not apply when Yom Kippur occurs on a weekday, since one cannot eat the fruit. It does however apply when Yom Kippur falls on Shabbat, in case one would come to do likewise on another Shabbat.

(Shulchan Aruch Orach Chaim 336:10; Shemirat Shabbat K'hilchata 26: footnote 72)

🌱 🌱 🌱 🌱 🌱 🌱 🌱 🌱 🌱 🌱 🌱

Q. When are the berachot recited after a Haftarah the longest?

A. On the morning of Yom Kippur occurring on Shabbat.

Following any Haftarah, at least 3 berachot are recited. On Shabbat and Yom Tov there is an additional berachah, the wording depending on whether it is Shabbat or a Yom Tov. When a Yom Tov occurs on Shabbat, a number of words relating to Shabbat are contained in this berachah. This berachah is the longest on Yom Kippur morning and when it occurs on Shabbat it includes these additional words, making it even longer.

(Machzor for Yom Kippur – end of Shacharit)

🌱 🌱 🌱 🌱 🌱 🌱 🌱 🌱 🌱 🌱 🌱

Q. On which day of the year does one, in some years say Hallel, and in other years Tachanun?

A. 3 Tevet.

Chanukah begins on 25 Kislev and always lasts 8 days. Every day during Chanukah, one says the whole Hallel and omits Tachanun. The latter is resumed on the day after Chanukah. Since in some years, the month of Kislev has 30 days and in others 29 days, the last day of Chanukah will occur on either 2 or 3 Tevet. In the former case Tachanun and not Hallel will be said on 3 Kislev, and in the latter case the opposite.

(Shulchan Aruch Orach Chaim 683:1, 131:6; Luach l'Eretz Yisrael [Rav Tukachinski] – at end of Chanukah)

🕎 🕎 🕎 🕎 🕎 🕎 🕎 🕎 🕎 🕎

Q. When are there 20 berachot in the weekday Amidah?

A. In the Shliach Tzibur's repetition of the Amidah at both Shacharit and Minchah on a Fast Day.

The normal weekday Amidah has 19 berachot. However, when the Shliach Tzibur repeats the Amidah on a Fast Day, he adds a berachah "Aneinu" before the berachah "Refoeinu" thus increasing the Amidah to 20 berachot.

(Shulchan Aruch Orach Chaim 566:1; Siddur – Shacharit and Minchah for weekdays)

🕎 🕎 🕎 🕎 🕎 🕎 🕎 🕎 🕎 🕎

Q. When did Zevulun shorten the length of "Birchat Hamazon" day by day for 4 successive days?

A. When Shabbat Chanukah occurred on Rosh Chodesh Tevet.

On Shabbat ones adds "retzai" in "Birchat Hamazon"; on Rosh Chodesh "ya'aleh v'yavo"; on Chanukah "al hanisim." When Shabbat Chanukah occurs on Rosh Chodesh Tevet – (it has to be the first day of Rosh Chodesh since 1 Tevet cannot fall on Shabbat) – then on that Shabbat one has all these three additions. On the following day, namely the 2nd day of Rosh Chodesh – 1 Tevet – one adds just two of them – "ya'aleh v'yavo" and "al hanisim." The following day is the 8th day of Chanukah and the only addition is "al hanisim." The day after is an ordinary weekday with no additions.

(Shulchan Aruch Orach Chaim 188:5; 187:4 Rema)

🕎 🕎 🕎 🕎 🕎 🕎 🕎 🕎 🕎 🕎

Q. On which Shabbat Amidah does one *omit* "retzai bimnuchatenu, kadsheinu b'mitzvotecha...."?

A. The Mussaf Amidah for Shabbat Rosh Chodesh.

The final paragraph of the fourth berachah of any Amidah said on Shabbat, even if it is also a Yom Tov, is "retzai bimnuchatenu, kadsheinu b'mitzvotecha...." The only exception is the Mussaf Amidah for Shabbat Rosh Chodesh, when these words (which all in all are several lines of print!) are absent. It has been suggested that at some time in the past they were *accidentally* missed out and they were never replaced. Indeed, there have been suggestions to replace them!

(Siddur - Amidot for Shabbat and Yom-Tov; Aruch Hashulchan Orach Chaim 425:2)

🌿🌿🌿🌿🌿🌿🌿🌿🌿🌿

Q. How did Amos (according to some opinions) avoid observing Purim and not transgress the Halachah?

A. He traveled from Jerusalem to Tel Aviv during the daytime of 14 Adar and remained there till the following day.

Purim is celebrated in non-walled cities (such as Tel-Aviv) on 14 Adar. However, in cities, such as Jerusalem, which were walled at the time of Yehoshua bin Nun, it is celebrated on the 15 Adar. Numerous questions and discussions arise regarding people traveling between these two types of cities on 14 and 15 Adar as to when they should celebrate Purim. According to some opinions if one were to travel during the *daytime* of 14 Adar from Jerusalem to Tel-Aviv and remain there till the following day, one would be exempt from Purim.

(Needless to say, this is not the proper way to act!!)

(Har Tzvi, (Responsa of Rav Tzvi Pesach Frank), Orach Chaim, volume 2, chapter 628, summary, paragraph 11)

🌿🌿🌿🌿🌿🌿🌿🌿🌿🌿

Q. When did Nechemiah (who davened "Nusach Ashkenaz") say "Amen" after his own Berachah?

A. After saying "bonei brachamov Yerushalayim" in Birchat Hamazon.

The first 3 berachot of Birchat Hamazon are from the Torah. The 4th berachah is a Rabbinical enactment. One thus says "Amen" after the end of the 3rd berachah to indicate the separation between the Torah and the Rabbinical berachot.

(Shulchan Aruch Orach Chaim 188:1; Mishnah Berurah 215:4)

Q. When and what is the largest number of verses leined for a *single* Aliyah?

A. Revi'i of the joined Parashiot Matot-Masei – 72 verses.

There are some weeks in the year, especially in a non-leap year when two Parashiot are read and in such a case, they are always joined together at revi'i. Since 2 Parashiot are read, the total number of verses being read that Shabbat are almost always greater than with the reading of a single Parashah. Matot-Masei are the last two Parashiot in the book of Bamidbar.

(Mishnah Berurah 282:5; Bamidbar 32:20 - 33:49)

Q. When might Channah say the berachah "borei minei mezonot" over bread?

A. (For example) When she breaks the bread into pieces each smaller than a "kezayit" and then cooks the bread

The berachah over bread is "Hamotzi" and over cake "Mezonot." However, bread can lose its "status" in various manners. One of them is to first break the bread into pieces each of which is less than a "kezayit" (the size of an olive - about the volume of a

RABBI DR. CHAIM SIMONS

matchbox today). The bread is then cooked (but not baked) in a saucepan over the stove. It will then be regarded like "cake" whose berachah is "mezonot."

(Shulchan Aruch Orach Chaim 168:10)

🌼🌼🌼🌼🌼🌼🌼🌼🌼🌼

Q. On which occasion during the year do some Shuls interrupt the Kriyat haTorah to read a Piyut?

A. On (the first day of) Shavuot to read "Akdomut."

Akdomut is a Piyut written by R' Meir ben R' Yitzchak nearly one thousand years ago in the city of Worms and its language is Aramaic. It used to be recited in most places after the first verse of the leining on (the first day of) Shavuot. However today most Shuls read it before the Kohen recites the berachot over the Torah.

(Machzor for Shavuot – beginning of leining (for first day); Shulchan Aruch Orach Chaim Be'er Heteiv 494:2)

🌼🌼🌼🌼🌼🌼🌼🌼🌼🌼

Q. When did Yankel shave 2 days before Lag b'Omer?

A. When Lag b'Omer occurred on a Sunday.

The Gemara states that 24,000 pupils of Rabbi Akiva died between Pesach and Shavuot. Because of that, it has become customary not to marry or cut one's hair during a part of that period. There are differing customs as to which part of the Omer these restrictions apply. However, all the various customs include the weeks before Lag b'Omer – the 33rd day of the Omer. When however, Lag b'Omer (a day during the Omer when these restrictions don't apply) falls on a Sunday, one may cut one's hair on the previous Friday, in honour of Shabbat.

(Yevamot 62b; Shulchan Aruch Orach Chaim 493:1, 2 & Rema)

🌼🌼🌼🌼🌼🌼🌼🌼🌼🌼

Q. Which is the only Haftarah *always* read on a Shabbat, which comes from the book of Yehoshua?

A. The Haftarah for Parashat Shelach Lecha.

Every Shabbat and Yom Tov, following the leining, a portion is read from the Nevi'im, which is known as the Haftarah. Although during the course of the year the Haftarot are read from all of the books of the Nevi'im, the vast majority come from the latter Nevi'im, in particular from the prophet Yeshayahu. In contrast there are only 3 which come from the book of Yehoshua, two of which are read on Yom Tov (Simchat Torah and the 1st day of Pesach) and only one which is *always* read on a Shabbat (Parashat Shelach Lecha).

(Haftarot which are read during the entire year)

🌾🌾🌾🌾🌾🌾🌾🌾🌾🌾

Q. For which month during some years was Motty Klein, a caterer for *Barmitzvahs*, without any work?

A. Adar Rishon – if 13 years earlier was a non-leap year.

A boy reaches Barmitzvah age on the date he becomes 13 years old. But what happens when a boy is born in the month of Adar in a Jewish non leap year and 13 years later it is a leap year – namely there is both Adar Rishon and Adar Sheni? In such a case, his Barmitzvah is in Adar Sheni, since only then is he considered to have *completed* 13 years of his life. Thus in such a year there will be no Barmitzvahs in Adar Rishon.

(Shulchan Aruch Orach Chaim 55:10 Rema)

🌾🌾🌾🌾🌾🌾🌾🌾🌾🌾

Q. When does one have 7 successive Readings of the Torah, without missing a day, without reciting Hallel?

A. When Rosh Hashanah occurs on Thursday and Friday.

129

Included in the occasions when one has Kriyat haTorah are Rosh Hashanah morning, Shabbat morning and afternoon, Fast of Gedaliah morning and afternoon, and Monday morning. On none of these occasions does one say Hallel. When Rosh Hashanah occurs on Thursday and Friday there is a total of 2 Readings of the Torah; the next day is Shabbat with a further 2 Readings; the following day is the Fast of Gedaliah (postponed from Shabbat) with 2 Torah readings; the next day is Monday with its Reading. Thus we have a total of 7 Readings of the Torah without having said Hallel.

(Shulchan Aruch Orach Chaim 584:2, 601:1, 282:1, 292:1, 566:1, 135:1)

🌺 🌺 🌺 🌺 🌺 🌺 🌺 🌺 🌺 🌺 🌺

Q. When during the period of the Omer did Menashe answer his friend's question in an indirect manner?

A. When (prior to his own counting) he was asked one night "how many do we count tonight in the Omer?"

Every night from the 2nd night of Pesach until Shavuot one counts the Omer. To keep this Mitzvah, it is sufficient to just say (for example) "Today is the third day." There is a dispute whether when counting the Omer, one must have the intention of fulfilling the Mitzvah. If the answer is in the negative, then (prior to one's own counting) by answering one's friend "Today is the third day," one fulfills the Mitzvah and so cannot subsequently count that night *with a berachah.* To avoid this problem one answers one's friend "Last night was the second day."

(Shulchan Aruch Orach Chaim 489:1, 4)

🌺 🌺 🌺 🌺 🌺 🌺 🌺 🌺 🌺 🌺 🌺

One can go on and on composing questions such as these – but as with all things, one has to stop somewhere!!

Section Two

You too may Comment!

COMMENTS WHICH I MADE ON THE TEN MINUTE HALACHA SHIURIM GIVEN BY RABBI ARYEH LEBOWITZ OF YESHIVAH UNIVERSITY, NEW YORK

(As can been seen from the dates of each of my comments, they were all written in 2011.)

(Yeshiva University in New York had (as of 2011) put 50,000 of its shiurim on the Internet, and they should be praised for making all these shiurim freely available to the public. Amongst these shiurim are several hundred "ten minute halachah" shiurim delivered by Rabbi Aryeh Lebowitz. In this limited time, the Rabbi goes through the different subjects magnificently. I myself have learned much new material from these shiurim and they have also enabled me to revise subjects which I have learned in the past. For each shiur, there is a space for the users to add their own comments. I myself have used this opportunity to add interesting or unusual comments. In a few of the cases I have described my personal reminiscences or have made a humerous point or given a riddle for the users to solve. Since these comments of mine can also be used independently of the actual shiur, I am reproducing them here. The heavy print in capital letters is the name of Rabbi Lebowitz' shiur and the small letters in heavy print is my title to the comments which follow. I have kept the comments in the order that I made them. I have also added the date that I wrote them.)

CHANUKAH GELT

Further reason for Chanukah gelt

There is another source for Chanukah gelt, which is brought by Rabbi Yosef Kapach in his book Halichot Taiman, (Jerusalem: Machon Ben-Zvi, 5762), p.64. He writes that in Yemen every day during Chanukah, Jewish mothers would give their children a small coin. The child would then hurry to the market and with half of this money would purchase some small and tender carrots and with the remainder some fine sugar which the shopkeeper would put in small paper containers and add some red colouring matter. The child would then happily return home, put this red-coloured sugar in a bottle, fill it with water and it would then resemble the wine which the grownups drank.

20 July 2011

KASHRUS OF MEDICINE AND VITAMINS

Gelatin and glycerin in medicaments

This question was also discussed in a lecture entitled "Kashrus, Food and Chemicals" delivered by Dayan Gavriel Kraus of the Manchester Beth Din (England) in April 1972, and this lecture was reproduced in a booklet. In it, Dayan Kraus states on page 7, "… gelatin and glycerin are used extensively in medicines. … However, one can be 'mekil' – lenient, with regard to many medicaments, especially if they are tasteless or better still if they have an unpleasant taste."

21 July 2011

LECHEM MISHNAH FOR SEUDA SHELISHIS

Rav Chidka's 4 meals on Shabbos

Rav Avraham Yitzchak Sperling in his book "Ta'amei Haminhagim Umekorei Hadinim" writes on page 140, that it is commonly said that by eating of the various foods served at a kiddush on Shabbos morning one fulfils the opinion of Rav Chidka that one must eat 4 meals on Shabbos. Since this book gives no source for this statement, can any reader supply it? However, since the halachah is not in accordance with Rav Chidka, is it not problematic to intend that the eating of this food at the kiddush is to fulfil this opinion?

24 July 2011

SHABBOS ZEMIROS

Tzur Mishelo

Rav Chaim Volozhin in his work "Orchot Chaim" which speaks about the practices of the Vilna Gaon, writes that the Vilna Gaon did not sing "Tzur Mishelo" (end of paragraph 94). I have heard that the reason was that the content of "Tzur Mishelo" includes a summary of the three Torah berachos of birchas hamazon, and by singing it one might fulfil the mitzvah of birchas hamazon. Furthermore, I have heard that to avoid this problem, when singing it one should say "Hashem" instead of the actual Divine Name.

24 July 2011

CORRECTING THE BAL KOREI

Who should correct the Ba'al Koreh?

A question which can well be asked is whether there should there be a specific person present to correct the mistakes of the Ba'al Koreh, or may anyone in the congregation call out the correction? Rabbi Chaim David Halevi writes on this subject in his Mekor Chaim (part 3 125:9) that it is bad when the whole congregation call out such corrections, but instead a knowledgeable person should stand by the side of the reader and only he should correct any mistakes made by the reader. Incidentally, this was the procedure followed by the Chinese Jews of Kaifeng.

24 July 2011

PESACH SHEINI

Date of Pesach Sheini

Although calendars invariably give the date of Pesach Sheini as 14 Iyar, it would seem to be more correct to give its date as the afternoon of 14 Iyar and the night of 15 Iyar. One can possibly bring a proof from the services in which one does not say tachanun. The practice is that on a day that one does not say tachanun, one also omits it on the previous minchah. This is not the case with Pesach Sheini. Although tachanun is omitted on the 14 Iyar, it is recited at minchah of 13 Iyar (see "Luach l'Eretz Yisrael" by Rav Tuchachinsky). In the case of Pesach Sheni, the service prior to the afternoon of 14 Iyar is shacharis, and in accordance with the practice to also omit tachanun on the service prior to a specific occasion, it is omitted at shacharis of 14 Iyar.

26 July 2011

SIYUM

Ta'anis Bechorim and Women

According to the Shulchan Aruch, first-born women must also fast on Erev Pesach, and this is possibly the custom amongst some sefaradi women. Also, if the father is a first-born and so is his infant son, then the mother should fast for her son. There are discussions regarding whether such women participate in such a siyum. In Pressburg (Bratislava) the women would participate. (Piskei Teshuvos vol.5 chap.570 fn.21). Rav Ovadiah Yosef says it is good for such women to hear the siyum from the ezras nashim, but it is also sufficient to bring some cake home from the siyum for them. (Yalkut Yosef - Kitzur Shulchan Aruch 570:2).

26 July 2011

SIMANA MILSA

Apple only on 2nd night of Rosh Hashanah

I recollect that my grandmother had the custom to eat apple dipped in honey on the 2nd night of Rosh Hashanah and not on the 1st night, and I assume she had this custom from Poland where she was born. A possible reason for this is that unlike today when apples are on the market throughout the year, in those days in Poland, they were seasonal, and it was at Rosh Hashanah time that they became available. To avoid the shehecheyanu problem on the 2nd night of Rosh Hashanah, one takes a new fruit. Quite possibly the apple was the new fruit and for this reason eating an apple dipped in honey was delayed until the 2nd night.

27 July 2011

MISHLOACH MANOS

Lomdisher Mishloach Manos

One cannot give seforim for mishloach manos, but one can give "lomdisher mishloach manos" where the recipient needs to do halachic research. It should be stressed that this should only be done with, for example, fellow kollelniks who will not take offence, and will take it in the spirit of Purim. One sends them "unusual" mishloach manot and the recipients must answer in writing giving sources, explaining whether they think the sender has fulfilled the mitzvah. Examples are: an uncooked potato and some tea bags; a packet of salt and a bottle of tap water; orange peel and apple peel – they are both edible!; two different sorts of vitamin pills. A further suggestion is that one could send just one very nice item of food and the recipient has to answer whether or not the sender has performed part of the mitzvah of mishloach manos. Another possibility is to make the recipient sign that he has received the mishloach manos and the recipient must also explain why his signature has been asked for. A final word – send at least one mishloach manos which one fulfills the mitzvah without any doubt!

28 July 2011

MAYIM ACHARONIM

Finger Bowls

At dinners, especially in past generations, a "finger bowl" containing water with a flower petal floating in it would be passed around towards the end of the meal and the diners would dip their fingers in it. The question is: Does one fulfill the mitzvah of mayim acharonim by this method? The Kaf Hachaim discusses this question (Kaf Hachaim 181:9) and states that if there was a lot of water in the "finger-bowl" it would then be permitted, although this is not the preferred method for mayim acharonim.

28 July 2011

KISSING THE MEZUZAH

The Sharp Pointed Shin

Over forty years ago, I went to visit a friend and when I reached his front door, I kissed the mezuzah, The mezuzah case had a metal letter "shin" on it and the points at the top of this letter were sharp. As a result, when I kissed the mezuzah I cut my hand! I mentioned this to the master of the house (who incidentally today is the Rabbi of an Israeli town and a Rosh Yeshivah). He answered me that the protection afforded by a mezuzah is only when you are already inside the house but you were still outside when this happened! [see Bavli Avodah Zarah 11a and Yerushalmi Peah chapter 1 halachah1]

28 July 2011

KITNIYOS (AND QINOA)

Are Potatoes Kitniyos?

Although the vast majority of Jews in the world do not regard potatoes as kitniyos and therefore eat them on Pesach, there are opinions which rule otherwise. The community of Padua forbade the eating of potatoes during Pesach since they regarded them as kitniyos. The author of the Chayei Odom in his additions/commentary Nishmas Odom [hilchos Pesach responsa 20] states that in the years 5531-2 (1771-2) there was a famine in Germany and the Beth Din permitted the eating of potatoes, because in Germany they did not eat them on Pesach since flour was made from potatoes. The Pri Megadim, [Mishbetzos Zahav Orach Chaim 453:1] who lived in Berlin, also mentions the opinion that potatoes are kitniyos, but in a more indirect manner.

29 July 2011

BERACHOS ON DESSERT

Is Ice Cream a Solid or a Liquid?

When one puts ice cream into one's mouth it is a solid but it turns into a liquid in one's mouth before one swallows it. This could have ramifications on whether one says a berachah on it when it is eaten as a dessert during a meal which has begun with hamotzi. It is the general practice not to say a berachah on liquids drunk even towards the end of a meal. Therefore what is the halachah regarding ice cream eaten as a dessert? Today's poskim are divided on whether one says a berachah on it. [see Rav Alexander Mandlebaum, Vezos Haberachah p.74 fn.12]

29 July 2011

✡ ✡ ✡ ✡ ✡ ✡ ✡ ✡ ✡ ✡ ✡

USING AUTOMATIC BATHROOMS ON SHABBOS

Public Toilets versus Private Toilets

Rabbi Lev-Bochbot, a Rosh Kollel in Bnei Brak, researched this question and came to a conclusion which could possibly distinguish between a hotel's public toilet and the toilet in one's own hotel room. In the former case one can utilise the principles "p'sik reisha d'lo niche lei" and "kel'achar yad." However, in one's own hotel room, one obviously does not want a toilet to be unflushed and thus this makes the automatic flushing more questionable.

31 July 2011

✡ ✡ ✡ ✡ ✡ ✡ ✡ ✡ ✡ ✡ ✡

LAUNDRY DURING THE NINE DAYS

T-shirts and Jeans

The heter to change one's clothes several times throughout a Shabbos which occurs during the 9 days, will only be valid for those clothes suitable for Shabbos wear – such as white shirts. However, if on weekdays one wears T-shirts, coloured shirts and jeans, one would not be permitted to put them on for short periods of time during Shabbos. [see Rav Shimon Eider, A Summary of Halachos of the Three Weeks].

1 August 2011

GREETINGS BEFORE DAVENING

"Shabbat Shalom"

It is the accepted practice that when one meets someone that one knows one greets them. In Israel, on a weekday one says "boker tov," on Shabbos "Shabbat shalom" and on Yom Tov "Chag sameach." The Shabbos greeting includes the word "shalom." If therefore one meets someone on Shabbos morning before davening, is it preferable to give a greeting which does not include the word "shalom" such as "Gut Shabbes," or can one say that "Shabbat shalom" just parallels the words "boker tov" which one says on a weekday, and that it is not one's intention to give shalom?

2 August 2011

MINHAGIM

Sukkah or House on Shemini Atzeres?

According to the Gemara and Shulchan Aruch, a person in the Diaspora is required to live in his sukkah also on Shemini Atzeres. In practice, many people do not act this way. Both "**Sha'arim Metzuyanim** Behalachah" (138:3) and "Piskei Teshuvos" (668:1) write on the question and bring many sources which justify this.

5 August 2010

AL NAHAROS BAVEL AND SHIR HAMA'ALOS
Seudah Hamafsekes before Tisha b'Av

On the afternoon of erev Tisha b'Av one does not say tachanun. Therefore, what does a person (who is always particular to say shir hama'alos when tachanun is not said and al naharos bovel when it is) recite after sitting on the floor, eating his seudah hamafsekes before Tisha b'Av?

7 August 2011

HAVE WE FOUND THE CHILAZON?
University Degree D.Litt

The degree which was awarded to Rabbi Herzog by London University for his work on techeles was a D.Litt. degree and not a Ph.D. The D.Litt. degree is a higher doctorate, namely it is a degree which is higher than a Ph.D. He was awarded this degree in 1913 for his thesis entitled "Hebrew Porphyrology," which means the study of purple dye. About 50 years ago I read this extremely interesting thesis at the University of London Senate House Library. Unlike theses today which have to be bound to rigid specifications, this thesis consisted of piles of pages which were just clipped together!

8 August 2011

SHNAYIM MIKRA
The Verse "Shema Yisrael"

According to the halachah, one is not permitted to say the verse in the Torah "Shema Yisrael" twice in rapid succession. What then does one do when reading "shnayim mikra" on Parashas Voeschanan where this verse occurs? The Kaf Hachaim discusses

142

this question (chapter 61 paragraph 35), and brings an opinion that on the second occasion one should say this verse silently.

15 August 2011

⚜ ⚜ ⚜ ⚜ ⚜ ⚜ ⚜ ⚜ ⚜ ⚜ ⚜

MELAVE MALKA

Migdol vs Magdil

It is the general custom to say "migdol" on days when one says mussaf and "magdil" on all other days. However, there are some Sefaradi poskim, including the Ben Ish Chai (first year Chukas paragraph 19) and the Kaf Hachaim (chapter 189 paragraph 11 and chapter 300 paragraph 14) who extend the saying of "migdol" to the melave malka.

15 August 2011

⚜ ⚜ ⚜ ⚜ ⚜ ⚜ ⚜ ⚜ ⚜ ⚜ ⚜

KIDDUSH LEVANAH

3 Days after the Molad

According to many opinions, the earliest time for kiddush levanah is 3 days after the molad. It is an error to think that a person can take the time which is given for the molad, add 72 hours to it, and consider this to be the earliest time for him to recite kiddush levanah. One needs to know in which part of the world the time given for the molad refers to. In fact, there are numerous opinions on the location. These include: "sof hamizrach" – 130 degrees east of Jerusalem; "ketzai hamizrach" – 90 or 114 degrees east of Jerusalem; "tabor haaretz" – 24 degrees east of Jerusalem; near to Netzivin in Babylon; Eretz Yisrael – probably Jerusalem, but Yavneh and Jericho have also been suggested. It would seem that there is no authoritative ruling on which opinion is correct. In practice however, since the vast majority of the Jews in the world live to the west (or virtually to the west) of all these locations,

143

there would be no problem for them to recite kiddush levanah 72 hours after the time given for the molad. The problem will only arise regarding the latest time for this mitzvah.

16 August 2011

🏵 🏵 🏵 🏵 🏵 🏵 🏵 🏵 🏵 🏵 🏵

WEARING A HAT FOR DAVENING

Hat plus Yarmulka

Ideally, a hat is not in place of a yarmulke but in addition to it (Mishnah Berurah 91:12; Piskei Teshuvos 2:10). There are thus two layers of covers on one's head during davening. At shacharis, the tallis covering one's head will be the second layer. This reminds me of the time when I attended a Chabad bris. Since those who were to receive kibudim were only wearing a yarmulka, one of the Ba'alei Bris went around putting an additional yarmulka on the heads of these people.

16 August 2011

🏵 🏵 🏵 🏵 🏵 🏵 🏵 🏵 🏵 🏵 🏵

WEARING A JACKET FOR DAVENING

Jacket or Tallis

In a shul I davened in, which is situated in the Har Nof area of Jerusalem, there are on the wall regulations for a shaliach tzibur. One of them is that he has to wear a jacket and hat. However, it continues that if he does not have these garments, then he has to put on a tallis.

16 August 2011

🏵 🏵 🏵 🏵 🏵 🏵 🏵 🏵 🏵 🏵 🏵

GEBRUKTS

Only after a Leap Year

I have heard (but have not seen it in writing) that a person using his Pesach kelim for gebrukts on the 8th day of Pesach, would only use them on the next Pesach if that following year was a leap year, and in this way more than 12 months would have passed. If however the following year was not a leap year, then less than 12 months would have passed, and they would wait until yet the following Pesach to use the kelim.

16 August 2011

WHO CAN COUNT TOWARD A MINYAN?

Karaites

Although is it customary today to allow a non-observant Jew to be counted in a minyan, on the grounds that he comes under the category of "tinok shenishbah," does this permission also include Karaites? Karaites are definitely Jews but they do not accept the Oral Law. The Rambam wrote a teshuvah on this question (edition "Mekitzei Nirdamim" responsum14), where he clearly rules in the negative, the reason being that Karaites do not accept the idea of a minyan.

17 August 2011

NETILAS YADAYIM IN THE BATHROOM

With a Keli or Without a Keli?

In many washrooms in or adjacent to a toilet, one will find a keli for netilas yadayim. According to the halachah, is one required to use such a keli? The answer is no. It was a personal custom of the Chazon Ish to use a keli. However, Rabbi Abba Shaul would intentionally not use a keli, even if one was to be found in the washroom.

18 August 2011

⚜⚜⚜⚜⚜⚜⚜⚜⚜⚜⚜

SHOVELING SNOW ON SHABBOS

Salt – yes, Sand – possibly no!

Although the spreading of salt onto snow on Shabbos is permitted, the spreading of sand is more problematic. Some authorities forbid it saying that one is adding a new permanent layer to the ground and it would thus be forbidden under the prohibition of boneh. Others however hold that it is permitted since this layer cannot be considered as permanent. [see Rabbi Dovid Ribiat, "The 39 Melochos," volume 2, pages 368-69].

18 August 2011

⚜⚜⚜⚜⚜⚜⚜⚜⚜⚜⚜

PEYOS

Twirling of Peyos on Shabbos

A question connected with peyos is whether one is permitted to twirl one's peyos on Shabbos or Yom Tov with the intention of forming them into curls. Rav Dovid Ribiat mentions this question and recommends that it is preferable not to do so. ("The 39 Melachos" volume 4, page 1061).

22 August 2011

⚜⚜⚜⚜⚜⚜⚜⚜⚜⚜⚜

WALKING IN FRONT OF SOMEBODY DAVENING

Reaction of a Gadol

I read of an incident where a boy davened the amidah very slowly directly behind one of our Gedolim. As a result, this Gadol had to wait until the boy finished his amidah before he could step backwards. The boy's father, who was present in the Shul, went afterwards and apologised to the Gadol. The latter however replied that it was wonderful to see a boy davening like that.

22 August 2011

SEUDAS PURIM

What if one omits "Al Hanisim"?

Since one is obligated to eat one meal during the daytime of Purim, what happens if one omits "Al hanisim" when bensching after the first meal eaten during the day of Purim. On this there are discussions by the poskim with the suggestion that one would have to bensch again. (see: Taz Orach Chaim 693:2)

23 August 2011

WASHING FOR DAVENING

Washing between Services

What would those who are particular to wash between minchah and ma'ariv do in the following cases? If on Rosh Hashanah one davens minchah immediately after mussaf; between minchah and ne'ilah (fingers only!); between ne'ilah and ma'ariv.

23 August 2011

CONSIDEARTIONS IN ADOPTION

Not a Levi

Nearly 40 years ago, I had a problem with regards to one of my teenage pupils who had been adopted, but his adopted parents did not want him to know this fact. His adopted father was a Levi, but from the information I had obtained from the Beth Din who had a file on his adoption, I learned that this boy was a Yisrael. The problem was in connection with an Aliyah to the Torah at the school's weekday morning services. All the pupils in his class regularly had Aliyos, and thus a way had to be found to give him an Aliyah. Sometimes I gave him hagba or gelila and when there was no Kohen present, I gave him the first Aliyah. On one occasion there were two Kohanim present but no Levi. I got around the problem by asking the two Kohanim to "forgo" their right to the first Aliyah, (of course without telling them the reason), which they agreed to, and I then called up this adopted boy to the first Aliyah.

23 August 2011

DRINKING ON PURIM

Leil Shikurim

In "Machzor Vitri," a work written by Rabbeinu Simchah a student of Rashi, appears "ma'arovis" (piyutim for the ma'ariv service for Purim) which begin with the words "leil shikurim" and repeatedly mention wine. (Ish Horovitz edition, volume 2, pages 583-84). They are interposed in the birchos kriyas shema of the ma'ariv service of Purim, and this could give support to the fact that the drinking of wine and becoming shikur is an integral part of Purim.

24 August 2011

MEDICINE ON SHABBOS II

Cannot Decide

What happens when a person cannot decide whether or not he has reached the state of choleh kol gufo? In such a case we allow him to take medication on Shabbos, the reason being that today we are not proficient in the grinding up of herbs, which was the reason for the Rabbinic ordinance of not taking medication on Shabbos. (see: Rabbi Dovid Ribiat, "The 39 Melochos" volume 2, pages 492-93, and footnote 175a).

24 August 2011

EATING MATZAH ON EREV PESACH

Hamotzi on Afternoon of Erev Pesach

A riddle type question that one can ask is how can one make the berachah hamotzi on the afternoon of erev Pesach (before the tenth hour)? At this period, one may not eat bread or matzah or even cakes containing matzah meal. (The answer is based on the writings of Rav Ovadiah Yosef regarding erev Pesach which occurs on Shabbos and one wants to make hamotzi at the seudah shlishis.) One takes a whole matzah and puts it in a hot meat or chicken soup (in a keli rishon), so that it absorbs the taste of the soup. One then takes out the matzos from the soup in one piece. They will then be cooked matzos (which may be eaten on erev Pesach), the pieces of which are larger than a kezayis, and so the berachah will be hamotzi.

24 August 2011

EINO YEHUDI AT THE SEDER

Date not convenient

When I was at university, a fellow non-Jewish student told me that he was interested to attend a Seder. I said that I would see if it could be arranged. However, when I told him the date of the Seder, he told me that it was not convenient for him and asked if it could therefore be held on a different date!!

25 August 2011

TZITZIS: IN OR OUT?

Tzitzis Inside on Tisha b'Av

Some people who throughout the year have their tzitzis outside their clothes, will on Tisha b'Av until noon, have them inside. (see: Piskei Teshuvos, volume 6, 555:2).

25 August 2011

HAVDALAH FOR WOMEN

Havdalah in Shul

In some shuls, havdalah is made at the end of the ma'ariv service on motzaei Shabbos. Although this can be advantageous for a single person, it can be problematic for a married man who has his wife and daughters at home. Should he fulfil the mitzvah of havdalah in shul, he will not be able to make it when he gets home. It would thus seem that he should have the intention not to fulfil this mitzvah when havdalah is being made in shul.

25 August 2011

KAPAROS

Flora for Kaparos

Rashi writes about taking flora for kaparos on erev Rosh Hashanah. The use of flora for kaparos is also mentioned by both Rav Yaakov Emden in his siddur (Shaarei Shamayim, page 112b) and the Mate Efraim (604-05: 4), but unlike Rashi, they state that the flora is used on erev Yom Kippur.

25 August 2011

HAFTARAH

"Ben Rosho"

On Shabbos and Yom Tov, four berachos are recited after the haftarah. From Maseches Sofrim (13:10) we can see that the first of these four berachos is "semi-divided" into two, with the second part beginning with the words "ne'eman ata hu." Machzor Vitri (section 166) goes as far as to state that "ne'eman ata hu" is the beginning of a separate berachah. It was once pointed out to me that if we take the acrostic of these berachos (including "ne'eman"), we have beis, nun, reish, shin, ayin which spells out "ben rosho." Can we learn from this that the father of the composer of these berachos was a rosho?

26 August 2011

BIRCHAS HAMAPIL

Aninus

An omen (a person who is obligated to mourn for certain relatives is known as an "onen" between the time of death and the burial of that relative) is forbidden (or at least has an exemption) to recite berachos. However, (according to Rav

151

Shlomo Zalman Auerbach z'tl), an exception to this rule is that an onen is obligated to say the berachah hamapil before going to sleep. (see: Rav Chaim Binyamin Goldberg, "Penei Baruch," page 21 and footnote 19).

28 August 2011

KASHRUS OF CHEWING GUM
Chewing Gum on Furniture

Although many aspects concerning "chewing gum" which are solely "bein odom laMakom" are often discussed, there is an aspect which is also "bein adom l'chaveiro." How often have people gone into a shul (or other public building) and found chewing gum stuck to the furniture or floor? Sadly, often! A child must be taught that before going into a shul (or other public building), he must throw away any chewing gum he has in his mouth into the nearest dust bin.

28 August 2011

SHEMURA MATZAH
Satmar Matzos

There is almost no limit to the number of chumros that one can do when baking matzos for Pesach. The late Satmar Rebbe, Rav Yoel Teitelbaum z'tl declared, "Every single chumrah that can possibly exist in industrial matzoh production, I have instituted in my bakery." These included: discarding wheat if the slightest scent of onion or garlic could be detected in it; the wheat could only be reaped between noon and five o'clock in the afternoon; the farmers were forbidden to drink water (despite the intense heat) whilst harvesting; there was absolutely no trace of salt or other chemicals in the water drawn from the Satmar's own well for the "mayim shelanu." (see: Mishpacha (English edition), 13 April 2011, pages 56 – 67).

28 August 2011

❧❧❧❧❧❧❧❧❧❧

WEARING A GARTEL FOR DAVENING

Forgetting one's Gartel!

What happens if one arrives in shul and finds that one has forgotten one's gartel? Does one return home for it and in this way lose out on tefillah betzibur, or does one daven without a gartel? This question is brought in "Piskei Teshuvos" (volume 1 page 692) and the ruling given there is to daven without a gartel.

29 August 2011

❧❧❧❧❧❧❧❧❧❧

WHEN A SEFER TORAH FALLS

Sending a Sefer Torah by Post

Suppose one needs to transfer a Sefer Torah from a shul which has closed down in the Diaspora to a shul in Eretz Yisroel. The ideal way is for a traveller to take it personally with him all the way. However, a number of innocent travellers who have been asked to transport a package to another country and unknown to them hidden in the package are drugs, and as a result these innocent couriers have found themselves thrown into jail. For this reason, people usually refuse to carry any packages. The question thus arises can one send such a Sefer Torah by post? It is well known that in transit, postal packages sometimes fall (or are put) onto the floor. Some poskim have dealt with this question and when there is no alternative, the post may be used. However, before sending the Sefer Torah, the gidim between two yerios should be removed, thus making the Sefer Torah posul, and it should then be placed in a container which in turn is in a further container, and one should also ensure that the package is waterproof. (see: Piskei Teshuvos, volume 2, page 134).

29 August 2011

⚜ ⚜ ⚜ ⚜ ⚜ ⚜ ⚜ ⚜ ⚜ ⚜ ⚜

STANDING FOR THE READING OF ASERES HADIBROS

Upper or Lower Notes

For shuls who always lein the aseres hadibros with the "ta'am hoelyon," one could argue that one stands during the reading, since the sound of the leining is different from other parts of the Torah, especially at the end of each dibrah. This is admittedly not a strong argument, but maybe one can make a comparison with "oz yoshir" which is leined to a special tune and one stands. On Shavuos, there is an additional reason to stand when reading the aseres hadibros, namely, that this Festival marks the anniversary of receiving the Torah. However, according to "Luach l'Eretz Yisroel" of Rav Tukachinski, one only uses the "ta'am hoelyon" on Shavuos, but for the parshios Yisro and Voeschanan, he writes that one reads the aseres hadibros, as for other parts of the Torah, namely with the "ta'am hatachton." Since the above two reasons for standing do not apply on these two Shabbosos, it could therefore be argued that one should remain seated.

30 August 2011

⚜ ⚜ ⚜ ⚜ ⚜ ⚜ ⚜ ⚜ ⚜ ⚜ ⚜

HALF KEDUSHA

Heicha Kedusha in Kollel

One day I attended a minchah minyan of a kollel (in Eretz Yisroel), and was quite shocked to see that they did a heicha kedusha. Since it was minchah gedolah, there was no chance of them overstepping shekiyah. Being a kollel minyan I sincerely hope that at least nine of those present would have answered amen to the berachos. The minyan was followed by the afternoon break and so one could not give the answer "bitul Torah." The answer that Chazal did not institute the repetition of the amidah for people like kollelniks, which even if acceptable, is based on the assumption that no people living in the area or those passing by at the time attend the minyan, which is often not the case.

30 August 2011

✤ ✤ ✤ ✤ ✤ ✤ ✤ ✤ ✤ ✤ ✤

WRITING BS"D AND B"H

B.H. = B'ezras Hashem or Birchas Hamazon

I recollect an amusing incident which occurred nearly 40 years ago. At that time, in England, one would head correspondence with the letters Beis Hei in Hebrew, whereas in the United States, they would often use the transliterated equivalent of B.H. One day I received a letter from the U.S. which was headed B.H. and dealt with some Birchas Hamazon booklets I had ordered. I showed the letter to somebody, mentioning that the B.H. stood for B'ezras Hashem. This person, who had never heard of writing B.H. instead of Beis Hei, argued that the B.H. was in fact the sender's reference, which often appeared towards the top of business letters, to the fact that the letter dealt with booklets for Birchas Hamazon!

30 August 2011

✤ ✤ ✤ ✤ ✤ ✤ ✤ ✤ ✤ ✤ ✤

CHALAV AKUM

Saudi Arabian Milk

I heard that during the Gulf War (1990-91) when Jewish soldiers were stationed in Saudi Arabia, the question was asked whether

155

they could rely on Rav Moshe Feinstein's heter for cholov akum. The answer given was they could not, since unlike in the United States where all the milk is cow's milk, in Saudi Arabia there was also camel's milk.

31 August 2011

NEWSPAPER ON SHABBOS

Keep it in your house!

The following point should be noted for Yom Tov regarding newspapers. Should a newspaper (and according to some opinions, even that day's newspaper) arrive at one's house on Yom Tov (in a permitted manner!) and it was in a location outside the techum at the start of Yom Tov, one would be forbidden to carry it outside the Eiruv. (see: Shulchan Aruch, Orach Chaim 515:9; Piskei Teshivos, volume 5, pages 404-05).

31 August 2011

KASHRUS OF GLASS

3 times 24

There is a method of kashering glass for Pesach, known as "milui veirui." In this method the glassware is soaked in water for 3 days, changing the water every 24 hours. (see: Mishnah Berurah. 451:154). Although I saw this method bring used when I was young, I can say that I have not seen it used during the last 50 years. It is very possible that due to the cheap price of glassware today, this method is rarely used today.

1 September 2011

EARLY SHABBOS

Retract!

After a person had accepted Shabbos early, he realised that he had not put on tefillin that day. He asked one of today's Gedolim what to do and he told him to do hataras nedarim to cancel his early acceptance of Shabbos. (see Piskei Teshuvos, volume 3, chapter 261, paragraph 9, for a discussion on this question).

1 September 2011

SHABBOS HAGADOL

Rhymed Laws of Pesach

Toward the end of the "yotzros" for Shabbos Hagadol is a piyut composed by R' Yosef Tov Elem (who lived 1,000 years ago) and which begins "Elokei haruchos l'chol bosor." This piyut gives the whole spectrum of the laws of Pesach in a rhymed form, and it begins with an alphabetical acrostic. A slow reading of this piyut can serve as an excellent introduction to one's learning the detailed laws of Pesach.

1 September 2011

NER HAVDALAH

A New Fire on Motzaei Shabbos?

The reason for saying a berachah over fire on motzaei Shabbos is as a remembrance that Hakadosh Baruch Hu instructed Adam harishon on the first motzaei Shabbos how to rub two stones together and create a fire. (Pesachim 54a). One could think from this that the fire to be used at havdalah on motzaei Shabbos must be a new fire made on motzaei Shabbos, and that one cannot use a ner sheshovas as is required on motzaei Yom Kippur. However, no one seems to suggest this, even as a hiddur.

2 September 2011

✿ ✿ ✿ ✿ ✿ ✿ ✿ ✿ ✿ ✿ ✿

SHINUY MAKOM AND BERACHOS

Corridors of an Apartment Building

Consider the case of a person living in an apartment building who whilst eating goes outside his front door into the corridor. Is this regarded as shinui makom? In Israel, every apartment dweller pays local taxes (arnona) on a certain proportion of the area of these corridors at the same rate as if it was an integral part of his apartment. Thus it might be considered that the apartment dweller has a part-ownership of this corridor, and thus going into the corridor will not be considered as shinui makom. Today's poskim are divided on this question. (see: Rav Alexander Mandelbaum, Vezos Haberachah, page 57).

4 September 2011

✿ ✿ ✿ ✿ ✿ ✿ ✿ ✿ ✿ ✿ ✿

ELEVATORS ON SHABBOS

Height of Apartment Buildings in Bnei Brak

"Since Bnei Brak rabbanim do not endorse the use of Shabbos elevators, seven stories is the maximum height for Bnei Brak housing projects." (from an article in Mishpacha (English edition) 31 August 2011, page 50).

4 September 2011

✿ ✿ ✿ ✿ ✿ ✿ ✿ ✿ ✿ ✿ ✿

ASSORTED SHEIMOS ISSUES

Genizah or Recycle?

In Israel, an "exponentially" increasing number of Torah pamphlets are to be found in the shuls on Shabbos. (It has become "big business" and in some of these pamphlets one has to search out the words of Torah from amongst the advertisements!!) After each Shabbos they would reach the genizah and it was becoming impossible to deal with such quantities of material. As a result, there are some poskim who have ruled that these pamphlets can be recycled, and there are special containers provided in which to put them.

4 September 2011

BEDIKAS CHAMETZ PART 1

Take a New Fruit

Although the custom is not to say bircas shehecheyanu over the mitzvah of bedikas chametz, there are in fact some authorities who rule that one does recite it. Thus some are accustomed to take a new fruit and when saying the berachah shehecheyanu over it, have in mind that it is also for bedikas chametz. (see: Piskei Teshuvos, volume 5, 432:2).

5 September 2011

ELECTRIC SHAVERS

No Problem for a Shliach Tzibur!

A person who is a regular shaliach tzibur or is one on Rosh Hashanah, Yom Kippur or Fast Days does not have to worry whether or not an electric shaver is permitted – according to the halachah he has to have a beard! (Shulchan Aruch, Orach Chaim 53:6 and Mishnah Berurah 53:23-24).

5 September 2011

⚜ ⚜ ⚜ ⚜ ⚜ ⚜ ⚜ ⚜ ⚜ ⚜

NER SHABBOS

Electric Shabbos "candles"

Instead of the conventional candles or oil for ner Shabbos, may one instead use an electric light? Today's poskim are divided on the question and of those who allow an electric light, some prefer a light powdered by a battery. There are reported cases of poskei hador in the United States, who in exceptional cases used an electric light for neros Shabbos. One of them was Rav Moshe Feinstein who when he was once in a hotel and unable to light candles, lit a flashlight and made a berachah over it. Another possible case was with Rav Aharon Kotler, who being in a hotel room where it was forbidden to kindle a flame, and he therefore utilised the electric light; (one should add that it is not clear from the context whether this was an actual occurrence with him or he just held this opinion). (see:http://ohr.edu/ask_db/ask_main.php/93/Q2/ AND http://www.dailyhalacha.com/m/halacha.aspx?id=1655).

5 September 2011

⚜ ⚜ ⚜ ⚜ ⚜ ⚜ ⚜ ⚜ ⚜ ⚜

FISH AND MEAT

Beware at Buffets!

In a wedding in Israel, a buffet is often held before the chuppah, and depending on the grandiose of the buffet, all sorts of foods appear on the various tables. Some of them are fried pâtés which could be filled with either vegetables or fish or meat. Without tasting them, one has no idea of the filling. When going around the tables, one can thus easily put onto one's plate both fish and meat pâtés and start eating both of them almost simultaneously. So when in doubt, ask the waiters what the filling is!

6 September 2011

☙ ☙ ☙ ☙ ☙ ☙ ☙ ☙ ☙ ☙

VISITORS KEEPING TWO DAYS OF YOM TOV IN ISRAEL

Money Collectors leave Disappointed!

There was an occasion when I went into a shul in Jerusalem to daven minchah on the Second Day of Yom Tov of the Diaspora. When after ashrei they began uvo letzion, I realised it was a minyan for tourists. During the service, some locals came into the shul, and as often happens in many shuls in Israel, went around the shul shaking their cupped hands hoping to receive money. Needless to say, they left the shul disappointed and empty handed!

6 September 2011

☙ ☙ ☙ ☙ ☙ ☙ ☙ ☙ ☙ ☙

HAVDALAH B'TEFILAH

First or Second Amidah?

A person who forgets to daven ma'ariv on motzaei Shabbos is required to recite the amidah twice at shacharis on Sunday morning. In the event of him not having made havdalah, he would have to say "ato chonantonu" in one of the amidahs. In which one does he say it? On the one hand, the first amidah he recites, namely the amidah for shacharis, is the first amidah for him after Shabbos. On the other hand, the second amidah is the tashlumin for the previous ma'ariv, the service at which chazal ruled one must say ato chonantonu. The poskim are divided on this question. (see: Talmudic Encyclopedia, volume 8, columns 95-96).

7 September 2011

☙ ☙ ☙ ☙ ☙ ☙ ☙ ☙ ☙ ☙

161

BENTCHING AFTER AL YICHASREINU (ON SHABBOS)

Leave the Knives on Shabbos?

Is there any difference between Shabbos and weekdays with regards to removing or covering the knives before bentching? Some authorities hold that this only applies on weekdays (Shulchan Aruch, Orach Chaim 180:5), whilst others hold that it includes Shabbos and Yom Tov (Be'er Heteiv, Orach Chaim 180:4; Kaf Hachaim, Orach Chaim 180:15).

7 September 2011

⚜ ⚜ ⚜ ⚜ ⚜ ⚜ ⚜ ⚜ ⚜ ⚜

BERACHOS ON SMELLS

Smelling instead of Arbes

What does one do when the Shabbos for a shalom zachor is Yom Kippur? One obviously cannot serve the arbes and the other foods. An answer to this appeared in "Ohr Somayach, Ask the Rabbi," issue 267, and it stated that one makes a "besamim shalom zachor." Instead of the foods, the parents of the new born boy set out various items for smelling and the participants say the appropriate berachos over these items. Incidentally, this is a good opportunity to help arrive at one's 100 berachos on that Yom Kippur. (see: Mishnah Berurah 46:14).

7 September 2011

⚜ ⚜ ⚜ ⚜ ⚜ ⚜ ⚜ ⚜ ⚜ ⚜

BORROWING A SEFER, TALLIS OR TEFILLIN WITHOUT PERMISSION

30 or 100

It is permitted to borrow someone's shofar on Rosh Hashanah without asking the owner and say over it the berachos for blowing the shofar. It may well be asked whether under such circumstances, one is limited to the 30 obligatory notes, or may one also blow a further 70 notes which are customarily blown in order to reach the number 100. The answer is 100 – but no more than that! (Mate Efraim 586:5).

7 September 2011

✾ ✾ ✾ ✾ ✾ ✾ ✾ ✾ ✾ ✾ ✾

TRYING ON CLOTHING BEFORE CHECKING FOR SHATNES

Sample Check for Shaatnez

In a large batch of identical garments, is a sample check for shaatnez sufficient to permit the remaining garments to be worn without checking? "The Shaatnez Newsletter" (volume 1, Issue 2) bought out in 5765/2005 answered this question in the negative and brought an actual case from Cleveland to prove it. It happens that sometimes oddments of material are used for functions such as padding in a jacket, and in just some of the clothing within the same batch these oddments may be made of linen. A few years ago, I asked the same question in Jerusalem on a jacket which stated it had been sample tested for shaatnez and was told that it needed to be sent for testing.

8 September 2011

✾ ✾ ✾ ✾ ✾ ✾ ✾ ✾ ✾ ✾ ✾

SAYING L'DOVID DURING ELUL

The Judge who recited Psalm 27

In a certain shul in an Anglo-Saxon country there was an argument between the chazan and the gabbai as to what date one finishes saying "L'Dovid Hashem Ori" (Psalm 27) and because of this the chazan was dismissed from his post. The chazan took the matter to court and when the non-Jewish judge heard that the dispute

163

was about the recital of Psalm 27, the judge began to recite this Psalm by heart (in English) and commented that it is such a beautiful Psalm and thus it ought to be recited every day of the year!

8 September 2011

🏵 🏵 🏵 🏵 🏵 🏵 🏵 🏵 🏵 🏵

RETZUOS OF TEFILLIN

No to two sides

A tefillin batim maker offered to paint black the backside of the retzuos of Rav Eliashiv's tefillin. The Rav, whilst agreeing it was a hiddur mitzvah to do so, declined the offer. He explained that if he had both sides of the retzuos of his tefillin painted black, many others would rush to do so, and there is no hiddur mitzvah when this results in others having to spend money. (see: Mishpacha (English edition) 16 February 2011, page 24).

9 September 2011

🏵 🏵 🏵 🏵 🏵 🏵 🏵 🏵 🏵 🏵

SHOALIN V'DORSHIN B'HILCHOS HACHAG

What about Rosh Hashanah?

The poskim write about learning the halachos of Pesach, Shavuos and Sukkos before these Festivals, with the Shulchan Aruch Harav ruling that 30 days applies to all these three Festivals. (Orach Chaim 429:1-3). But what about Rosh Hashanah? In fact for Rosh Hashanah one does more than theoretically learn the dinim. For (almost) the entire month of Elul, the baal tokea blows the shofar every morning with the tekiah, shevarim and terua. This should be an inducement for him to learn (or revise) the various dinim concerning the mitzvah of shofar, in particular the many dinim concerning the blowing of the different notes for the shofar, including such details such as the length of each note and at which stages to take a new breath.

11 September 2011

⚜ ⚜ ⚜ ⚜ ⚜ ⚜ ⚜ ⚜ ⚜ ⚜

BEHAVIOR DURING CHAZARAS HASHATZ

Standing during the Piyutim?

What should a person whose custom is to stand during the chazoras hashatz do during the time when the piyutim which are found within the amidah on Rosh Hashanah and Yom Kippur, and in some places also on other occasions during the year, are being recited? Are these piyutim to be regarded as part of the amidah and thus require standing? The poskim write that even when one is able to rely on the chazoras hashatz as one's own amidah, one cannot do so when there are piyutim. (Mate Efraim 591:1). Thus these piyutim are not regarded as part of the amidah, and maybe one could sit down when they are being recited.

12 September 2011

⚜ ⚜ ⚜ ⚜ ⚜ ⚜ ⚜ ⚜ ⚜ ⚜

WEARING TEFILLIN FOR MINCHA (AND ALL DAY)

Tefillin on Shabbos?

Nearly 40 years ago, the Rabbi of a shul in England told me that the mother of a boy who had had his Barmitzvah on the previous Shabbos, had proudly told the Rabbi that her son had put on his tefillin before going to shul that Shabbos! I later spoke to this boy and said to him that surely he knows that one does not put on tefillin on Shabbos. He answered that he knows that, but considered that the Shabbos of his Barmitzvah was an important occasion and therefore he put on tefillin. There is an "upside" to this incident and that is that the boy saw the importance of the mitzvah of tefillin. This reminds me of the incident when Rav Levi Yitzchak of Berdichev saw a man oiling the wheel of his cart whilst wearing tefillin. Rav Levi Yitzchak said "Look how the man loves the mitzvah of tefillin, that even when he oils wheels he does not remove his tefillin." I hope that after all these years this Barmitzvah boy is still laying tefillin – every weekday.

13 September 2011

GEZEL SHEINA: "STEALING" SLEEP

Wake up for my Chanukah Lighting!

A person arrives home at two o'clock in the night during Chanukah whilst everybody is asleep, but he has not yet lit Chanukah lights. Under such circumstances he would not be able to recite the berachos over the lighting. The Mishnah Berurah writes (672:11) that he should wake up people in order that he may say the berachos over the lighting. Thus we can see from this that one may wake up third parties in order that the person himself might perform this mitzvah.

14 September 2011

BOWING AND BOUNCING DURING DAVENING

3 or 6

The universal custom before reciting "oseh shalom" at the end of the amidah is to go back 3 steps – left, right, left. However, there are poskim who write there should be 6 steps backwards, namely three steps with each foot, and this is done as follows: left, then right to make it level with the left, and the same thing is then repeated twice more, thus making a total of 6 steps backwards. (see: Divrei Chamudos on Rosh, Berachos, perek "ain omdim" paragraphs 67 and 68; Machatzis Hashekel Orach Chaim 123:10).

15 September 2011

TEFILAS HADERECH

How to carry around a Tefilas Haderech card

It is advisable to carry around in one's pocket the text of tefilas haderech. However, in the course of travelling one is sure to need to use a toilet. One may well ask whether or not one is allowed to enter a toilet with this prayer in one's pocket, and furthermore in some cases it may even contain the name of Hashem written in full. The answer is that it is preferable to have a small durable container for this prayer and this container is put in one's pocket. This arrangement is known as a keli within another keli, and one can then enter a toilet with it in one's pocket without any problem. (Mishnah Berurah 43:25).

15 September 2011

COMING LATE FOR DAVENING

Latecomers not admitted for Kol Nidrei

About half a century ago I heard about the following incident which occurred in a Shul in England, which obviously did not like its worshippers arriving late for davening. What occurred was that when the time the Shul had announced for Kol Nidrei had arrived, they locked the doors of the Shul and did not let in anyone who arrived late. I wonder if that Shul then omitted the pronouncement "Al daas Hamakom …. onu matirim lehispalel im ha'avaryanim"!!

15 September 2011

WAITING BETWEEN MEAT AND DAIRY

Space Between Meat and Dairy sinks

Some kitchens are built with just one sink and this will necessitate the use of separate washing up bowls for meat and dairy. Others have two sinks. However, in some cases they are placed right next to each other and this can be a liability, since if one is not very careful there may be some splashing from sink to sink. The ideal is to have the two sinks in separate parts of the kitchen.

15 September 2011

🏵 🏵 🏵 🏵 🏵 🏵 🏵 🏵 🏵 🏵

BAL TISHAKTSU

No torn toilet paper on Shabbos

What if one is in a place on Shabbos where one needs to use the toilet and discovers that there are only rolls of toilet paper? By then not using the toilet could result in transgressing bal tishaktsu. Not using toilet paper would be contrary to kavod labriyos. What then should one do? Under such circumstances the poskim rule that one may tear the toilet paper using a shinui, such as unrolling a length of paper, pressing it on the wall with one's two fists and then pulling the fists apart in order to tear the paper. (see: Rav Dovid Ribiat, The 39 Melochos, volume 3, page 843). To avoid this situation, if one is living in area where there is an Eiruv, it is a good idea to carry a supply of toilet paper in one's pocket.

18 September 2011

🏵 🏵 🏵 🏵 🏵 🏵 🏵 🏵 🏵 🏵

MATANOS L'EVYONIM

Matanos L'evyonim from Schnorrers

On Purim, the proper way is to give each of two evyonim an honourable amount of money or food so that they can celebrate Purim with great enjoyment. But unfortunately there are schnorrers in this world who want to get away with the minimum! According to the Ritva, one fulfils the mitzvah by giving just one pruta to each evyon. (Mishnah Berurah 694:1) A super schnorrer might want to go further and give his pruta "al m'nat l'hachzir," namely, on condition that the evyon returns this pruta! Is such a condition valid? The poskim hold that one cannot make such a condition with mishloach manos, but they are not sure about it with matanos l'evyonim. (first Biur Halachah to Orach Chaim chapter 694). Let us hope that this discussion is theoretical and every evyon will have a Happy Purim.

18 September 2011

THE BERACHOS ON THUNDER AND LIGHTNING

Thunder and Lightning on Purim

The Noda Beyehudah rules that one is allowed to interrupt the reading of the megillah on Purim in order to recite kiddush levanah. It would seem that the same should apply if there is thunder and lightning whilst reading the megillah. However here there could be some additional points. Since one must recite the berachah for these things "toch kedai dibur," which is about three seconds, one might well have to say these berachot even in the middle of a verse of the megillah. In such a case would one return to the next word or the beginning of that verse? Another point is that because light travels much faster than sound, there could well be a space of over half a minute between seeing the lightning and hearing the thunder. Would one wait in silence after saying the berachah over the lighting until one hears the thunder, or alternatively would one meanwhile read another verse or so of the megillah? A related issue is if during the reading the megillah, someone calls out that there is a rainbow outside, would one then interrupt the reading and go outside to recite the berachah, as in the case of kiddush levanah?

18 September 2011

NETILAS YADAYIM IN THE BATHROOM

Asher Yotzer Card

In order to remind people to say "asher yotzer" and /or to give them the text of this berachah, during the last years, some very decorative "asher yotzer" cards have been been produced to attach to the wall near the washbasin for netillas yadayim, with some of them having the name of Hashem written in full. According to the Tzitz Eliezer one may recite this berachah in a room where there is a toilet, washbasin and various other facilities. On the basis of this, is it permitted to hang up such a card in such a room? One should also remember that there are times when the toilet in such a room is in actual use.

18 September 2011

HAFTARAH

Kohanim and Leviim Excluded

Here is a riddle that one can ask people? Which haftorahs cannot be recited by a kohen or levi? The answer is haftorahs which are recited at minchah on Yom Kippur and other fast days and on the morning of Tisha b'Av. The reason is that they are read by the person called up for shlishi and this can only be a yisrael.

18 September 2011

SHABBOS ZEMIROS

Suspected Maskil Authorship

Should one find in a zemiros book brought out by an organisation whose orthodoxy has much to be desired, a zemer not appearing elsewhere, one might justifiably assume that it was written by a maskil. But this might not always be the case. One such example was the zemer "Al Ahavoscha Eshte G'vi'i" which I found in such an organisation's zemer book. As a result, for several decades I would not sing it. It was by hashgacha pratis that I found this zemer in Machzor Vitri (Hurwitz edition, pages 147-48), a work written by Rabbeinu Simchah a student of Rashi, and that the authorship was Rav Yehudah Halevi. Since then it forms part of my repertoire of zemiros, and I would like to see zemiros books incorporating this zemer.

18 September 2011

TZITZIS: IN OR OUT

Everyone's Tzitzis Out at Night

Ask your friends the following question. On which two ma'ariv services during the year does one wear a tallis? They are sure to give one occasion – namely Yom Kippur, but they may find it difficult to think of the second occasion. It is ma'ariv of motzaei Yom Kippur – a person does not take off their tallis between ne'ilah and ma'ariv.

19 September 2011

PRACTICAL TEVILAS KELIM ISSUES

Snow for Toiveling

There has been a snowstorm and a substantial amount of snow has settled. The kelim mikvah is a long way away and difficult to get to, and one has kelim to toivel. Can one use the snow? Under such conditions the book "Tevilas Kelim" (by Rav Tzvi Cohen, page 150) allows one to toivel glass kelim in the snow.

19 September 2011

GEZEL SHEINAH: "STEALING" SLEEP
Waking up People with the Shofar

Sefardim start reciting selichos daily from the beginning of Elul, and they are often recited each night at midnight or in the early morning. The shofar is blown on a number of occasions during the recital of these selichos. However, the Rav of the Porat Yosef Yeshivah in Jerusalem has ruled that one should omit blowing the shofar since one has no right to deprive the neighbours of their sleep, and to do so would be gezel sheinah. (Mishpacha, English edition, 14 September 2011, p.28).

20 September 2011

❦ ❦ ❦ ❦ ❦ ❦ ❦ ❦ ❦ ❦ ❦

BIRCHAS HAMAPIL
Even on Tisha b'Av

Kriyas shema al hamita consists of the beracha "hamapil," the first paragraph of the shema, and many other pesukim and prayers. One might reasonably expect that on the night of Tisha b'Av it would be limited to just hamapil and shema. One might especially expect to have to omit the part beginning "vihi noam," which is indeed omitted at the ma'ariv service when Tisha b'Av occurs on motzaei Shabbos. However, the poskim rule that on Tisha b'Av one recites kriyas shema al hamita with all the pesukim and prayers as on any other night of the year. (see: Rav Moshe Harari, "Mikroei Kodesh, Hilchos Ta'aniyos," page 285)

21 September 2011

❦ ❦ ❦ ❦ ❦ ❦ ❦ ❦ ❦ ❦ ❦

LAWS AND CUSTOMS OF CHODESH NISSAN

Shelumiel on Shabbos

It is customary during the first 12 (or 13) days of Nisan to read each day the korban which a nasi brought for the the chanukas hamizbeiach. This is also the leining for Chanukah. The only day Chanukah cannot begin on is Tuesday, which means that the 5th day of Chanukah can never fall on Shabbos, and as a result the korban for Shelumiel ben Tsurishadai is never read on Shabbos. (Because of this, some say that Shelumiel is the origin of the word schlemiel!!) However, Shelumiel does get his opportunity to be read on Shabbos - during Nisan, since the 5th day can fall on Shabbos!

21 September 2011

TORN TZITZIS STRINGS

More than just torn!

Tzitzis can often get torn if one does not use sufficient care when laundering them. There are various patents in how to launder them without damage. However, sending them to a non-Jewish laundry can indeed create problems. One person reports that the laundry charged him a large sum and when queried they answered that "it was hard work undoing all those knots." At least the tzitzis were not ruined – they could be reknotted. However, in another story I heard, (I cannot vouch for its accuracy), the tzitzis beged was returned minus the tzitzis together with a note that the laundry had cut off the threads hanging from the corners – in this case the tzitzis threads were more than just torn!!

22 September 2011

DAVENING ON A PLANE

Tal Umotor or Berachah?

About 40 years ago, I had occasion to fly from Israel to Europe, (it was an occasion when it was halachically permitted for me to leave Israel). The date was when one was already saying "vesein tal umotor" in Israel but not yet in the Diaspora. During the flight, whilst already over Europe, a minyan was arranged to daven minchah on the airplane (in an area of the plane which did not disturb other passengers). I recollect someone questioning whether to say "vesein tal umotor" or "vesein berachah." However, the general custom is that since one has already begun to say "vesein tal umotor" whilst in Israel, one should continue to say it when outside Israel. (Sha'arei Teshuvah, Orach Chaim 117:4).

22 September 2011

SHLISSEL CHALLAH

Berachah over the Shlissel

What berachah does one say over the shlissel?! Baruch ato bevoecha, ubaruch ato betseisecha. (Devarim 28:6).

22 September 2011

WHO CAN COUNT TOWARD A MINYAN?

He could not make up the Minyan!

He was born on the 7th day of Chanukah. Thirteen years later on the 7th day of Chanukah there were 9 Jewish men above the age of Barmitzvah plus him in the Shul. Yet there was not a minyan! How could this be? In the year he was born, there were 29 days in Kislev; thus he was born on 2 Teves. Thirteen years later there were 30 days in Kislev and the 7th day of Chanukah was thus on

1 Teves. Therefore he only became a man on the following day, the 8th day of Chanukah. Incidentally, over 40 years ago I was in a Shul where this actually occurred, but they incorrectly decided that there was a minyan.

22 September 2011

MINYAN: CAKE OR ICING?

"Minyan and Cake with Icing"

Ten men, a minyan, met together, and amongst the food in front of them was a cake with icing. This iced cake looked so appetising that at least seven of these men decided they would "koveya seudah" on it; the others ate a more limited quantity. This means that at least seven have to do netillas yadayim, make hamotzi over this cake and after eating it have to recite birchas hamazon. Since at least seven have to say birchas hamazon and because a minyan has eaten, they have to add the name of Hashem into the zimun.

22 September 2011

EREV ROSH HASHANA

Everyone "Dayanim Mumchim"

The minhag in many shuls is that immediately after shacharis on erev Rosh Hashanah, the congregation disperses into various groups for hataras nedarim. Three of the worshippers, usually chosen randomly, sit on a row of chairs, and another worshipper or sometimes a group of worshippers stand before them and recite the long nusach for hataras nedarim which begins "shimu noh rabosei dayanim mumchim ...." These "dayanim mumchim" can somtimes be the biggest amei haaretz, who do not even have a clue of the halachos of hataras nedarim. At least once a year, some people have the "honour" to be called "dayanim mumchim"!

This is unless one follows the opinion of Rav Eliyahu Dovid Rabinowitz-Teomim, (the "Aderet") who wrote that one should omit these two words!

23 September 2011

✿✿✿✿✿✿✿✿✿✿

EREV ROSH HASHANA

Shofar on Friday Erev Rosh Hashanah?

It is customary to blow the shofar at the end of every weekday shacharis service during Elul with the exception of erev Rosh Hashanah, even if it occurs on a Friday. However, the instruction in the "Singer's Prayer Book" which has been the standard siddur used in England since the early 1890s, and was originally authorised by the then British Chief Rabbi Nathan Adler, states that when erev Rosh Hashanah occurs on Friday the shofar is blown. The same instruction is to be found in the edition of this siddur with the commentary of the then British Chief Rabbi Joseph Hertz. However, despite searching, I have never found a source for shofar blowing on erev Rosh Hashanah occurring on a Friday.

23 September 2011

✿✿✿✿✿✿✿✿✿✿

EREV ROSH HASHANA

Fasts with an increasing intensity

Based on a Midrash Tanchuma about a king who remitted taxes in three stages, one learns about fasting in three stages: erev Rosh Hashanah; during the aseras yemai teshuvah; Yom Kippur. When comparing these fasts with this Midrash, in going from stage to stage, these fasts could well be with an increasing intensity. However, Rav Yosef Karo in his Shulchan Aruch writes about fasting on erev Rosh Hashanah but omits fasting during the aseres yemai teshurah. Maybe a Talmudic support can be found for giving a specific mention to fasting on erev Rosh Hashanah, (as distinct from the aseres yemai teshuvah), from a Yerushalmi in maseches Ta'anis (perek 2, halachah 12) where it states that Rav Yonoson fasted every erev Rosh Hashanah.

23 September 2011

🏺🏺🏺🏺🏺🏺🏺🏺🏺🏺🏺

EREV ROSH HASHANA

A Mikvah in the House

In 1930, Rav David Miller of New York, published a book entitled "The Secret of the Jew: His Life – His Family" which includes how one can easily build a mikvah in one's house at a very low cost. Although he claimed that this mikvah was also kosher for women, this came under criticism due to the fact that some opinions held that the water was "sh'uvim." However, as far as a men's mikvah is concerned this criticism is irrelevant, since one can use ordinary tap water. Men who want to use the mikvah but prefer the privacy of a mikvah in their own house, can study the relevant chapters of Rav Miller's book which appear online: http://www.homemikveh.org/sotj/sotj.html

25 September 2011

🏺🏺🏺🏺🏺🏺🏺🏺🏺🏺🏺

EATING ON EREV SHABBOS

Very late Friday meal

If one eats a meal on Friday and before one has finished it, it is sunset, namely Shabbos begins, one must stop eating, put out a covered lechem mishnah, make kiddush and eat at least a kezayis from this lechem mishnah – (no netillas yadayim or hamotzi is required). It is best to avoid being in such a situation, but there could be occasions when one does need to eat such a meal.

177

Consider the case in the summer in a very northern location where Shabbos begins very late indeed. For children or elderly people eating at a very late hour could well be very difficult. They could start a meal with a "Shabbos type" menu and when at least "plag minchah" arrives, they could accept Shabbos, stop eating, make kiddush and eat at least a kezayis from the lechem mishnah. (see: Piskei Teshuvos, volume 3, 271:14).

25 September 2011

BIRTHDAYS

Beware if born after nightfall!

The date of one's birthday in the secular calendar will have two equivalents in the Jewish calendar, the first if one is born before nightfall, the second if after nightfall. If one is fortunate to be born in Israel, both the correct Jewish and secular dates will appear on one's "teudat zehut" (identity card). However, if one was born in the Diaspora, the Hebrew date appearing will automatically be as if one was born before nightfall. If one were born after nightfall, unless one can produce an official documentation to prove it, something which is almost impossible to obtain, they will register one's Jewish birth date as if one was born before nightfall, despite what one might tell the registrations clerk. I was in this situation and when I complained about this, was told that I could now celebrate two birthdays!

25 September 2011

COMING LATE FOR DAVENING

The Chazzan who arrives late!

If one recites "baruch sheamar" and "yishtabach," one is required to say a minimum of pesukei dezimrah between them. It is also possible to say just either "baruch sheamar" or "yishtabach," plus a minimum of pesukei dezimrah. What happens if the chazzan for shacharis on Shabbos arrives in shul immediately before "shochen ad"? Would the saying of the very short passage between "shochen ad" and "yishtabach" be sufficient to justify him saying "yishtabach"?

26 September 2011

BEDIKAS CHAMETZ PART I

Lights on or off?

Rav Moshe Sternbuch in his Hagadah "Moadim Uzmanim" discusses whether one should leave the electric lights on or turn them off during bedikas chametz. On the first year after I was married, I could not decide what to do in this matter. It was the electric corporation who finally decided the matter for me! When I began bedikas chametz there was power outage, but during the bedikah the power returned. I was thus able to follow both opinions! Since then I have followed this procedure each year, I begin with the electric lights off and then during the course of the bedikah, I turn on the lights.

26 September 2011

BENTCHING AFTER AL YICHASREINU (ON SHABBOS)

Also on Weekdays

In an article on Rav Menachem Manes Moore who studied in the Mir Yeshiva before the Second World War, Rav Moore says in describing his experiences. "In Bircas Hamozone we would only bentsch until 'al yechasreinu,' and from there on not another word." (Yated Ne'eman, English edition, 2 May 2003, page 20).

It would seem from the context, that he his speaking of any time and not just Shabbos.

26 September 2011

✤✤✤✤✤✤✤✤✤✤✤

EIRUV TAVSHILIN (THEORY)

1 or 2 or 3

In the Diaspora, one can have a situation when one needs Eiruv Tavshilin three times within a short period of just three weeks, namely when Rosh Hashanah, Succos and Shemini Atzeres occur on Thursday and Friday. The general custom is to make it on the day before each of these Festivals. One might well ask whether one can make Eiruv Tavshilin just once before Rosh Hashanah, then preserve the tavshilin, for example in the freezer? The poskim are divided on this question. There is also a third intermediate opinion, which allows one to make Eiruv Tavshilin before Succos to also include Shemini Atzeres, the reason being that they are regarded as the same Festival. (Shulchan Aruch Orach Chaim 527:14 and Mishnah Berurah (including Biur Halachah) on it).

27 September 2011

✤✤✤✤✤✤✤✤✤✤✤

EIRUV TAVSHILIN (PRACTICAL)

Washing the dishes

It was over 40 years ago at a period where there was communal kitchen at the kollel where I was studying at. On an occasion when Yom Tov was on Friday, the women in the kitchen, who were kollel wives, themselves decided that they they had to wait till Shabbos began to wash up the dishes from the Friday Yom-Tov meal. Their reasoning was that since one was allowed to wash up dishes on Shabbos, this was not covered by Eiruv Tavshilin. The women in fact had support for their actions – the Mishnah

Berurah! There it states that Eiruv Tavshilin only permits things which are "tzorchei seudah." (Mishnah Berurah 528:3). It should be mentioned however that the custom is to allow things such as hachanah, which would include washing up the dishes on Yom Tov for Shabbos.

27 September 2011

✢ ✢ ✢ ✢ ✢ ✢ ✢ ✢ ✢ ✢

THE PROCEDURE FOR GETTING AN ALIYAH

No work for the Gabbai

When one is called up for an aliyah, the Torah should already be rolled to the correct place. This is one of the many functions of a shul gabbai to ensure that this has been done, the reason being to avoid inconveniencing the congregation. We learn this from the Kohen Gadol on Yom Kippur who would first read from parashas Acharei Mos, (which today is the leining for Yom Kippur) and he would then roll the Torah to parashas Emor, which is very close and again read, (which today is part of the leining for the first day of Succos). He would not however roll the Torah to parashas Pinchas which is a relatively long way away. (Yoma 68b, 69b-70a). Thus in a shul which uses a specific Sefer Torah just for Shabbos and Yom Tov, the gabbai does not need to roll the Torah between Yom Kippur and Succos (in years when there is no Shabbos between them).

5 October 2011

✢ ✢ ✢ ✢ ✢ ✢ ✢ ✢ ✢ ✢

ONE WHO CAN'T FAST BOTH TSOM GEDALYA AND YOM KIPPUR

Seems more theoretical

There has been a lot of discussion by the Poskim on the question of when one can only fast either on Tsom Gedaliah or on Yom

Kippur. However, I have always thought that this discussion is theoretical. Surely a person who for medical reasons would not be able to fast on Yom Kippur if he fasted a week earlier (or in some years six days), would be forbidden to fast on any fast day.

5 October 2011

TOILETRIES AND CHAMETZ

Schnitzel on Serviettes

I have been informed by a mashgiach that serviettes (table napkins) could contain amylene, which could have been derived from wheat. Often when frying schnitzel or potato chips, one places the boiling hot food after removing it from the frying pan onto such serviettes in order that the serviette absorb any excess oil, but in the process the food might well absorb some of this amylene. There would seem to be room to investigate whether or not this is a problem on Pesach.

5 October 2011

KITTEL ON YOM KIPPUR

Kittel and Burial

In the Diaspora, men are often buried wearing their kittel, the garment they wore each Yom Kippur. In Israel however, the custom is not to add to detract from the tachrichim. Therefore, in answer to a question on this subject, Rav Tukachinski (Gesher Hachaim, part 2, 28:3) writes that if there is time to convert the kittel into the ktones garment of the tachrichim, it is proper to do so.

5 October 2011

HELLO, BLESS ME AND GOODBYE (SHALOM ALEICHEM ON FRIDAY NIGHT)

When Yom Tov occurs on Shabbos

Is there any difference regarding the singing of Shalom Aleichem when a Yom Tov occurs on Shabbos? According to "Luach l'Eretz Yisrael" of Rav Tukachinshi, one says it, including when Seder night or Rosh Hashanah occurs on Shabbos. "Luach Dvar B'ito" writes that according to minhag Vishnitz when Yom Kippur occurs on Shabbos, Shalom Alecheim and some Shabbos zemiros are sung in the Shul.

6 October 2011

✤ ✤ ✤ ✤ ✤ ✤ ✤ ✤ ✤ ✤

MECHITZAH PART 2 – HEIGHT, MATERIAL AND CIRCUMSTANCES

Lovud and Mechitzos

Consider the following scenario: The mechitzah in a shul consists of metal poles which are of the correct height for a mechitzah but there is more space between the metal poles than the width of the metal itself. The space between the poles is however less than 3 tefachim. There is no curtain covering these poles. The women's section is at the same level as the men's and is situated both the right and the left of the men's section. Needless to say, one can see the women. The question: Can one apply the principle of "lovud" to call this a mechitzah, and hence it would be permitted to daven at such a shul?

11 October 2011

✤ ✤ ✤ ✤ ✤ ✤ ✤ ✤ ✤ ✤

INVITING PEOPLE TO A BRIS

Mixed Seating at a Bris Milah?

According to Rav Moshe Feinstein (Igros Moshe, Orach Chaim, volume1, responsum 41), one can have mixed seating at a wedding since people are there by invitation. However, for a bris milah, one specifically does not "invite" people, but one just "informs" them. Will this affect the seating arrangements?!

11 October 2011

🌿🌿🌿🌿🌿🌿🌿🌿🌿🌿

CLAPPING AND DANCING ON SHABBOS

Dancing at an Aufruf

Rav Shlomo Aviner in answer to a question on this subject relates the following incident: "There is a story about Rav Moshe Feinstein that a student in his Yeshiva finally got married after many, many years. At the Aufruf they were so excited that they, including Rav Feinstein, began to dance around the bima. A student asked him. 'Isn't it forbidden to dance on Shabbos?' Rav Feinstein responded, 'You call this dancing?!'"
(see: www.ravaviner.com/2011_04_01_archive.html).

11 October 2011

🌿🌿🌿🌿🌿🌿🌿🌿🌿🌿

MAKING A ZECHER L'CHURBAN IN OUR HOMES

Additions to House

Consider the following scenario (which is in fact relevant to my apartment). A person makes the "zecher l'churban" in his house opposite the front door as required by halachah. At a later date he builds additions to his house and as a result this "zecher l'churban" is no longer opposite his front door. Is he required to make another "zecher l'churban" opposite his new front door?

24 October 2011

🜚 🜚 🜚 🜚 🜚 🜚 🜚 🜚 🜚 🜚

REMOVING RINGS FOR NETILAS YADAYIM

Use the side of one's Spectacles

If one is concerned that one may forget one's rings after doing netilas yadayim and one is wearing spectacles, one can put them on the side frame of the spectacles.

24 October 2011

🜚 🜚 🜚 🜚 🜚 🜚 🜚 🜚 🜚 🜚

MECHIRAS CHAMETZ

Detail your Sale!

The author of the Kitzur Shulchan Aruch gives a sample deed of sale which he used for mechiras chametz. (end of chapter 114). In this deed he gives a detailed list of the chametz items to be sold, the sale value of each item and its precise location in the house of the seller. In contrast, I have seen such deeds in which there is barely room for the members of the community to write just their name and address!

25 October 2011

🜚 🜚 🜚 🜚 🜚 🜚 🜚 🜚 🜚 🜚

MACHNISEI RACHAMIM AND PRAYING TO ANGELS

Mentioning Angels by Name every Night

Every night in Krias Shema al Hamita, we invoke that specific angels should be in various positions surrounding us – "Mimini

185

Michael, umismoli Gavriel ..." The source is from the Zohar parashas Bamidbar.

25 October 2011

✿ ✿ ✿ ✿ ✿ ✿ ✿ ✿ ✿ ✿

NEFILAS APAYIM WHEN THERE IS NO SEFER TORAH

Tachanun in Hebron

Rav Eliyahu Mani, who was the Chief Rabbi of Hebron in the mid-19th century wrote in his book "Zichronos Eliyahu" (part 1, Orach Chaim, page 14) concerning the reciting of tachanun in Hebron, that one does not rest one's head on one's arm (paragraph 16). However, a few paragraphs later (paragraph 19) one could understand him to have written that in Hebron one rests one's head on one's arm even when there is no Sefer Torah in the room and even if one is davening alone. How does one resolve this apparent contradiction? Perhaps the meaning is that wherever one is located in Hebron, and even if davening alone, one always recites tachanun. However even if there is a Sefer Torah in the room in Hebron, and even if there is a minyan, one does not rest one's head on one's arm.

26 October 2011

✿ ✿ ✿ ✿ ✿ ✿ ✿ ✿ ✿ ✿

NEFILAS APAYIM WHEN THERE IS NO SEFER TORAH

Tachanun on Tisha b'Av!!

Here is a riddle. When one recites tachanun at minchah, one rests one's head on one's left arm. At shacharis, because one is wearing tefillin on the left arm, one rests one's head on one's right arm. On Tisha b'Av, one puts on tefillin at minchah and not at shacharis. Therefore on which arm does one rest one's head on when one says tachanun at shacharis and minchah on Tisha b'Av? The answer: One does not say tachanun on Tisha b'Av!!

26 October 2011

✿ ✿ ✿ ✿ ✿ ✿ ✿ ✿ ✿ ✿ ✿

INTRODUCTION TO HILCHOS CHOL HAMOED

No Succah – no Tiyul?

Although people often utilise Chol Hamoed to go on tiyulim, this could be a potential problem on Succos if there will be no succah on the route. Does the exemption that travellers have from dwelling in the succah also apply to those going on a mere tiyul. Rav Moshe Feinstein writes that such people are not exempt from the mitzvah of succah. (Igros Moshe, Orach Chaim, volume 3, responsum 93). Although there are other poskim who disagree, they add that it is not proper to go on a tiyul when there will not be a succah on the route. (Sefer Hasuccah by Rav Eliahu Weissfish, page 433).

27 October 2011

✿ ✿ ✿ ✿ ✿ ✿ ✿ ✿ ✿ ✿ ✿

SUMMARY OF HILCHOS CHOL HAMOED

Driving a Car on Chol Hamoed – Maaseh Hedyot???

To be able to drive a car, one takes numerous lessons, does countless hours of supervised practice and then has to pass a rigorous test. Driving a public vehicle, such as a bus, coach or taxi is tzorchei rabim and is thus permitted even though it is maaseh uman. If there would be a real financial loss if one did not drive, it would be permitted even though it is maaseh uman. However, driving for pleasure, which could be classed as tzorech hamoed, is only permitted if it is maaseh hedyot and surely driving a vehicle cannot be so classed!

27 October 2011

✿ ✿ ✿ ✿ ✿ ✿ ✿ ✿ ✿ ✿ ✿

SUMMARY OF HILCHOS CHOL HAMOED

Photography on Chol Hamoed

In the era when one photographed onto a photographic film, such photography was halachically writing. (The 39 Melachos by Rav Dovid Ribiat, volume 4, pages 952-53). One sees numerous photographs of gedolei hador carrying their arbaas haminim and the fact that they did not prevent the photographers strongly indicates that it is permitted to take such photographs on Chol Hamoed. Since the only time in the year that one can take such photographs is during Chol Hamoed Succos, it might be classed as davar haovud. Furthermore, since almost every child can use a home camera, it could be classed as maaseh hedyot. Possibly today's digital cameras are even more permissible.

27 October 2011

❈ ❈ ❈ ❈ ❈ ❈ ❈ ❈ ❈ ❈

PAS PALTAR (DURING ASERES YEMEI TESHUVA)

Parisian Bread in London

Nearly 50 years ago, I heard the following incident related in the course of a shiur. A person bought a loaf of bread in Paris where no pas yisrael was available. He ate half of the loaf in Paris. He then flew with what was left of it to London. In London pas yisrael was readily available. The question was could he finish eating this loaf of bread in London. He submitted the question to a posek. I don't recollect the answer, but in this case it was theoretical, since by that time the bread was no longer fit to be eaten!

27 October 2011

❈ ❈ ❈ ❈ ❈ ❈ ❈ ❈ ❈ ❈

CHECKING TEFILLIN AND MEZUZOS

Every Adar Rishon

I have seen it suggested that one have one's mezuzos checked every Adar Rishon. In this way one will have had them checked twice within a period of 6 years (or sometimes even 5 years) and thus will have fulfilled the requirement of checking them twice in 7 years. Also since there are no days in Adar Rishon which require special preparations, one has the time to arrange for this checking.

28 October 2011

HAIRCUTS AND SHAVING DURING SEFIRA

When 3 Sivan is on Sunday

When Lag b'Omer occurs on Sunday, the Rema writes that one may cut one's hair on the previous Friday in honour of Shabbos. Those who follow Minhag Vilna observe the mourning laws of sefirah until the morning of 3 Sivan. From the case of Lag b'Omer, we can possibly derive that should 3 Sivan occur on a Sunday, one may cut one's hair on the previous Friday.

30 October 2011

HAIRCUTS AND SHAVING DURING SEFIRA

Shaving – Haircutting

In the case of sefirah, the Shulchan Aruch (Orach Chaim 493:2) uses the word "lehistaper" (haircutting). However, in the case of Chol Hamoed the word "megalchin" (shaving) is used (Orach Chaim 531:2). Why the difference in wording for the same actions? It is possible that the reason is that the third perek of

189

Moed Koton which includes the subject of cutting any human hair on Chol Hamoed begins with the words "v'ailu megalchin".

30 October 2011

⚜ ⚜ ⚜ ⚜ ⚜ ⚜ ⚜ ⚜ ⚜ ⚜ ⚜

ISSUES OF AIRPLANE TRAVEL

Tal u'Matar or Berachah?

In Eretz Yisroel one begins "v'sein tal u'matar" on 7 Marcheshvan, and this includes areas close to Eretz Yisroel (Rav Yehosef Schwartz, "Divrei Yosef", responsum 4); elsewhere in the world, one begins 60 days after tekufa of Tishri. Consider the following scenario: a person is on an airplane going towards Israel (and especially in a case where he intends remaining in Israel) on a date between 7 Marcheshvan and 60 days after tekufa of Tishri. He davens on the airplane over the Mediterranean, when he is close to Israel. Does he say "v'sein tal u'matar" or "v'sein berachah"?

30 October 2011

⚜ ⚜ ⚜ ⚜ ⚜ ⚜ ⚜ ⚜ ⚜ ⚜ ⚜

CELEBRATING ROSH CHODESH

Rosh Chodesh Fasts

The Mishnah Berurah writes (418:1) that the community of Worms in Germany fast on Rosh Chodesh Sivan and recite selichos, to commemorate the evil degrees enacted against the Jews on that date in the year 4856 (1096). What is the leining on this fast? In the morning one does the leining for Rosh Chodesh and in the afternoon "vayechal". (Kaf Hachaim 418:2). Other cases of fasts decreed for Rosh Chodesh can be found in a list of fasts appearing in Shulchan Aruch, Orach Chaim 580. These fasts include Rosh Chodesh Nisan and Rosh Chodesh Av. The source of this list can be traced back as far as the Behag (the period of the Geonim) – (it is often incorrectly stated that this list is the last chapter of Megillas Ta'anis). The fasts on these two dates even have an application today, since a Choson and Kallah fast if they get married on Rosh Chodesh Nisan and (at least theoretically) on Rosh Chodesh Av. (Mishnah Berurah 573:9), although not on other Roshei Chodoshim.

31 October 2011

CELEBRATING ROSH CHODESH
Lines which have dropped out of Amidah!

The last paragraph of the middle berachah in the amidah for Shabbos begins with "... retzeh bimnuchoseinu, kadsheinu bemitzvosecho ..." The wording in this paragraph is to be found in every Shabbos amidah, even when any Yomtov occurs on Shabbos – with one exception! This is in musaf for Shabbos Rosh Chodesh when this wording for Shabbos is almost entirely absent from the amidah. The Aruch Hashulchan (Orach Chaim 425:2) considers that they were omitted by a printer and he personally would say the words which had been omitted when he said this amidah.

31 October 2011

CELEBRATING ROSH CHODESH
Meat instead of Fish

One of today's leading Poskim and also head of the largest non-governmental Beis Din in Israel, Rav Nissim Karelitz of Bnei Brak, each day includes fish in his daily lunch menu. However, on Rosh Chodesh meat is substituted for the fish. (Mishpacha, English edition, 13 April 2011, page 48).

1 November 2011

ADHESIVE TABS (DIAPERS AND STARK MARKS) ON SHABBOS

After using the Diaper

When a diaper is in actual use on a baby, the "sticking" of the tab could well be classed as temporary. However, after removing the diaper from the baby, resticking the tab before throwing it into the garbage is more problematic since this sticking might be considered permanent and thus not be permitted. Rav Dovid Ribiat considers that it is better to be stringent, and instead fold up the diaper and put it in a plastic bag before throwing it away. (The 39 Melachos, volume 3, page 814).

1 November 2011

SAYING L'CHAIM

Rishonim say l'Chaim

Rav Shraga Simmons gives two sources from Rishonim who specifically state that before drinking wine people say l'chaim. The first source is from Machzor Vitri (chapter 80), written nearly 1,000 years ago, and it is linked to the prohibition of speaking whilst eating, since this could lead people to choke to death. To avoid this eventuality, before a person says the berachah over wine, which under the principle of "shomea k'oneh" could also enable others to fulfil the mitzvah of saying the berachah by just listening, one asks that they agree that their mouths are empty and they answer l'chaim – and thus they won't choke to death. The second source is the Kol Bo (chapter 25) written in about the 14th century. There is a dispute whether one is obliged to bentch over a cup of wine, and one asks the others present if they hold that one should bentch over it and they answer l'chaim – it should be for life and not for the purpose of those to be put to death by a Beis Din.

1 November 2011

DISPLAYING THE ASERES HADIBROS

Lions in Shuls

In a number of shuls in the world, two model lions have been placed above or in front of the Aron Kodesh, and the question has often been asked as to whether or not it was permissible to have such lions in the shul, since there could be avodah zoroh problems. There have been numerous halachic discussions on this question and in the answers given. some permit whilst others forbid putting models of lions and other creatures on the Aron Kodesh. (see: Minhagei Hakehilos by Rav Bunim Yoel Tausig, 1:30-44).

1 November 2011

PURIM COSTUMES

Save your Money!

There is also a downside to Purim costumes. Parents, many of whom cannot really afford it, annually purchase expensive Purim costumes for their many children. Often these costumes are used just once. Who wants to wear the same costume on two Purims?! Surely it is far better to make your own costume with things found in every house and try to give this homemade costume an original caption. When my brother was at elementary school, the family put together from things found in our house, the clothing worn by a farmer. He was given a large bundle of hay to carry and he wore a caption with the word "HA(y)MAN". For this he won the fancy dress prize in his class – and the fancy dress cost us nothing!

2 November 2011

CROSSDRESSING ON PURIM
A few days before Purim

In Israel, schools are on holiday on Purim and thus often a few days before Purim, schools will arrange for their pupils to turn up in fancy dress. Would those Poskim who allow crossdressing on Purim, also allow it at the fancy dress parade held a few days before Purim?

2 November 2011

WAITING FOR TEN TO START CHAZARAS HASHATZ
Only 6 remain in the Shul

The Shulchan Aruch (Orach Chaim 124:4) writes that if 9 men don't answer "omein" to a berachah during chazoras hashatz it is close to a berachah l'vatalah. There is also a halachah that if men leave the shul during the chazoras hashatz, and only 6 men remain, the shaliach tzibur can continue until (at least) the end of the amidah (Shulchan Aruch, Orach Chaim 55:2), and this applies even if they leave during the course of the first berachah. (Mishnah Berurah 55:8). In such a case it will be impossible for 9 men to answer "omein" to even one of the berachos.

2 November 2011

WAITING FOR TEN TO START CHAZARAS HASHATZ
The Sons of Ya'akov

Although the Bavli only gives the 10 evil meraglim as the source of the number 10 for a minyan, the Yerushalmi (Megillah, perek 4, halachah 4) gives a second source, again using the word "betoch" (Bereshis 42:5). Here the number 10 is derived from the sons of

Ya'akov, (minus Yosef and Binyamin), who went down to Egypt to purchase food.

2 November 2011

✤ ✤ ✤ ✤ ✤ ✤ ✤ ✤ ✤ ✤

BESAMIM

Choose from Three

Siddurim which follow the Eidot Hamizrach, Yemenite (both baladi and shami), Persian and Italian rites, give three possible berachos which can be recited when smelling the besamim at havdalah, but the first one which they all give is "borei atzei vesamim". An extant manuscript from the Jewish community of Kaifeng in China gives only "borei atzei vesamim". However, since this community was isolated from all other Jewish communities in the world for several hundred years and their scribes recopied by hand, probably numerous times, their siddurim, it is possible that the other berachos over besamim at havdalah were, over the course of time, accidentally omitted.

3 November 2011

✤ ✤ ✤ ✤ ✤ ✤ ✤ ✤ ✤ ✤

DAVENING AND LEARNING ON THE TRAIN

Don't waste even a moment!

Not only should one learn whilst on a journey, one should also use the opportunity to do so whilst waiting in a queue at: a bus stop, a bank, a post office, a medical centre, etc. In all of these places one should be able to find a solution to the tzenius question. There was one well known Jerusalem Rav, who completed the whole of Shas (I believe even twice) whilst waiting in these various queues and on journeys.

3 November 2011

✤ ✤ ✤ ✤ ✤ ✤ ✤ ✤ ✤ ✤

195

WOMEN'S OBLIGATION IN ZIMUN

A Woman as the Tzenter!

The Mordechai (on Berachos 45b) quotes Rabbeinu Simchah who held that 9 men and 1 woman can make up a mezuman which would be able to add in the word "Elokeinu" during the zimun.

3 November 2011

PAS HABA B'KISNIN

A Piece of Cake at an Israeli Wedding

I have noticed that at an Israeli wedding, some people don't eat the roll - maybe thinking that they then won't have to say birchas hamazon! They prefer to say a berachah over each of the foods. They begin by eating the numerous salads, then the fish, then the main course of rice, potatoes and some form of meat. By that time they are almost sovea and they just have room to eat the dessert which consists of ice cream – and a piece of cake. According to the Ashkenazi practice, this piece of cake could mean that they would have to say birchas hamazon in the same way as if they had eaten the roll at the beginning of the meal! (for discussion of this subject see: Vezos Haberachah by Rav Alexander Mandelbaum, pages 31-33).

3 November 2011

KOL ISHA ON RECORDED MUSIC

Woman Chanting

Both when one is hearing the actual voice of a woman or her recorded voice, there is a definite difference between when a person speaks and when a person sings. However, there is also an "in between case"; it is difficult to find a word to describe it, but maybe "chant" can be used. One might then ask whether or not it is permitted to listen to a woman chanting, or even listen to her answering "omein" in such a manner?

7 November 2011

PAS HABA B'KISNIN

Beware of the Roll!

In a publicised ruling made by six leading Poskim in the United States regarding rolls made with fruit juice, they write that the custom to put out such rolls which are marked "borei minei mezonos" at meals such as at weddings and on airplanes, where obviously people "kovea seudah" on them, results in a "stumbling block" for a large number of people. (ruling reproduced (but without a date) in "Luach Berachos" by Rav Alexander Mandelbaum, page 50).

7 November 2011

BERACHOS ON CEREALS

Shehakol on all Cereals!!

Some time ago, I read in a religious newspaper (I think it was a paper published in England) that because of the difficulty in knowing which berachah to say over the various cereals, the writer admitted that he always said shehakol. In the next edition of this paper, a reader wrote to castigate this writer and quoted the halachah that if a person does not know which berachah to recite over a particular food, he may not say shehakol, but before eating has to go and learn which berachah to recite. (see: Vezos Haberachah by Rav Alexander Mandelbaum, page 1).

7 November 2011

WEARING WOOL TZITZIS
Silk Tzitzis

Just as the wool for tzitzis has to be spun lishmah by Jews, so does the silk for making silk tzitzis. But here there is problem. Spinning silk is a specialised activity involving extremely delicate work and almost all the silk thread in the world is spun in China by experts who are non-Jews. However, in Italy, there are Jews who know how to spin silk, and indeed there are Italian Jews who wear tzitzis made from silk threads. (see: Mishpacha, English edition, 2 November 2011, page 60).

7 November 2011

🕎🕎🕎🕎🕎🕎🕎🕎🕎🕎🕎

NER HAVDALAH
In a large Beis Hamidrash

Consider the following scenario: Havdalah is being made in a large yeshivah Beis Hamidrash and this will be the only havdalah that the bachurim will hear and they will fulfil the mitzvah of havdalah by the principle of shomea k'one. However, to fulfil the mitzvah of the berachah over the light one has to be close enough to be able to distinguish by its light, coins of two different countries. (Shulchan Aruch, Orach Chaim 298:4). Those bachurim who are too far away from the candle, as many will be in a large full Beis Hamidrash, will certainly not be close enough to be able to distinguish two such coins. In fact, it would be necessary after havdalah to leave the havdalah candle burning so that the bachurim can approach it and recite the berachah. (Mishnah Berurah: 297:13 (end), 298:13).

8 November 2011

🕎🕎🕎🕎🕎🕎🕎🕎🕎🕎🕎

SERVING AS SANDEK MULTIPLE TIMES

Both or None

The father of new born twins invited one of the Gedolei Hador to be the sandek for one of his twins. The Gadol replied that it would have to be both or none. The reason was that he had the foresight to realise that when these twins would get older, the one whose sandek had been this Gadol might taunt the other twin by saying that "my sandek was one of the Gedolei Hador".

8 November 2011

HONORING KOHANIM

The Kohen doesn't have to search!

The Kohen by having the first aliyah, also has another "plus". Before reciting the berachah over the Torah, he (or the baal koreh) does not have to search in the middle of a "paragraph" for the place where his leining will begin. It will always be at the beginning of a new "paragraph" - either a parashah pesuchah or a parashah sesumah. (The only two exceptions are parashas Vayechi, and Vayechal on a Fast Day.)

9 November 2011

TA'ANIS CHALOM

Tune without words during Duchaning

If one has had a worrying dream, there is a tefillah to recite during duchaning. (Shulchan Aruch, Orach Chaim 130:1). Since it takes time to say this tefillah, the chazzan sings a "tune without words" extending for about half a minute at the last word in each of the three verses of duchaning. (Mishnah Berurah 130:3). In Chutz La'aretz where one only duchans at mussaf on Yom Tov, this singing has to be limited to the days of Yom Tov (occurring on a weekday). However, in Eretz Yisroel where there is duchaning every day of the year, surely a case could be made for this "tune without words" to be sung every weekday, for the sake of people who have had a worrying dream on the previous night.

9 November 2011

TA'ANIS CHALOM

Leining on Ta'anis Chalom on Shabbos

The Shiurei Knesses Hagedolah (Orach Chaim 220:5) discusses the question of when a minyan of people fast a ta'anis chalom on Shabbos, whether the shaliach tzibur can say "aneinu" in the repetition of the amidah at minchah, and concludes that he had found no source to forbid it. On this basis, possibly one could also do the leining for a fast day on such a Shabbos? In such a case how would it be organised? A parallel case is a communal fast on Rosh Chodesh, when one leins the Rosh Chodesh leining at shacharis and "vayechal" at minchah. (Kaf Hachaim 418:2). Likewise here, one would lein the parashas hashavua at shacharis on the Shabbos, and at minchah "vayechal" would override the normal Shabbos minchah leining in a similar way as when Yom Kippur falls on a Shabbos.

10 November 2011

SHEVA BERACHOS

Sheva Berachos on Seder Night

According to the Rema (Shulchan Aruch, Even Haezer 62:9), one uses two cups of wine at a sheva berachos. However, if a sheva berachos were to be held on seder night, there would be a problem, since one may not add to the number of cups of wine drunk after eating the afikoman. Rav Yaakov Emden discusses this problem in his siddur (Beis Yaakov, seder hagadah, netiv 10, paragraph 25), and he states several possible solutions: 1) the participants at the seder recite birchas hamazon over their own cups of wine and the sheva berachos are recited on the birchas hamazon cup of the choson. 2) to follow the opinion of the Shulchan Aruch, which states that one always uses the same cup of wine for both birchas hamazon and the sheva berachos. 3) to use the cup of wine for birchas hamazon as the third cup and the cup of wine for the sheva berachos as the fourth cup. (see also Sha'arim Metzuyanim Bahalachah on the Kitzur Shulchan Aruch 119:15).

10 November 2011

WEARING A YARMULKA

Change in clothing styles

With today's multi-styles of clothes worn throughout almost the whole world, especially by different ethnic groups, the wearing of a yarmulka in public is nothing unusual. However, as we can see from a teshuvah of Rav David Zvi Hoffman (Melamed L'hoil, Yoreh Deah, responsum 56), that this was not always the case. Rav Hoffman reports how one day he went to visit Rav Shimshon Refoel Hirsch. Rav Hirsch's Yeshivah had a department teaching secular subjects and whose lecturers were non-Jews. Rav Hirsch told him to remove his head covering since not being bareheaded would offend the non-Jewish lecturers.

11 November 2011

THE SHEVA BERACHOS WEEK

Beware of grammen!

Mishpacha (English edition, 2 November 2011, pages 70-72) reports a true incident where at a sheva berachos, relatives of the choson, sang, with the best of intentions, grammen [rhyming songs to make people laugh] which disclosed the "not good" behaviour of the choson whilst he was still unmarried. It included a verse on how he was almost arrested for reckless driving, and a verse on how he was suspended from his Yeshivah. The kallah who was totally unaware of these incidents in her choson's life was quite shocked to hear of these incidents and it soured up the relations of the newly married couple for many weeks. The moral – be careful what one says at a sheva berachos!

11 November 2011

THE SHEVA BERACHOS WEEK

Tachanun – "In the Spirit of Purim"

There are shuls who give a sigh of relief when there is a Choson present on a Tachanun Monday or Thursday. Reading between the lines of a sarcastic article written "In the Spirit of Purim" by Rav Pinchos Jung, who is an author of many mussar books, there is a strong criticism of those who gabble off their tefillos. On the subject of Tachanun he writes: "... But of course, tachanun is a rarity; if at all, it's only tolerated on Sundays, Tuesdays or Wednesdays – and we pay Chassanim top rates here. Actually, we had a shaaloh yesterday – two Chassanim attended. Opinions varied. Celebrate the morrow as a nidche? Skip Uvo Letzion? The machmirim did both. 'If in doubt, leave it out', they said..." (Jewish Tribune London, 12 March 1976, page 9, extract has two words amended).

13 November 2011

BOWING ON THE FLOOR ON YAMIM NORAIM

Doctor's Orders

The physician of one of our recent Gedolim instructed the Gadol not to do korim. In order not to be different from all the other worshippers in his yeshivah, when the time in the service came for korim, he left his seat at the front of his Beis Hamidrash and sat by the door.

14 November 2011

✿✿✿✿✿✿✿✿✿✿

DAVENING EARLY WHEN NEITZ IS LATE

Tefillin at Night

In the German concentration camps, the inmates invariably had to get up and start work even before amud hashachar. In some cases, with great mesiras nefesh, they succeeded in smuggling in a pair of tefillin. The question was whether one could put on tefillin before amud hashachar and furthermore, whether one could say a berachah over the tefillin? This question was answered by Rav Efraim Oshri, who was Rav of the Kovno Ghetto in Lithuania, (Divrei Efraim, responsum 2), who ruled that under such circumstances one could put on tefillin and also say the berachah over them. He wrote that the concern of Chazal that one might fall asleep with the tefillin on was not relevant here, since any person doing so would endanger his life.

14 November 2011

✿✿✿✿✿✿✿✿✿✿

EXCESSIVE SINGING BY CHAZANIM

Know your Tunes!

Many people in Eretz Yisroel are not acquainted with the words which accompany Western popular tunes and this sometimes leads to undesirable results. About twenty years ago I listened to a computer teaching aid for Gemara. It was accompanied by tunes. But what were many of the tunes? Christmas carols!!! Amongst the worshippers of the shul at which I daven there are a number of Anglo-Saxons, and in the same building there is also a Talmud Torah. Throughout the day, a bell, which is a collection of tunes, rings to signal the beginning and end of lessons and it can clearly be heard even in the shul. The words of some of these tunes are close to pritsus. One year they forgot to turn off the bell for Yom Kippur. Oshamnu, bogadnu .... with the accompaniment of these tunes!!!

15 November 2011

DAVENING EARLY WHEN NEITZ IS LATE

Experiments in Yakir

It was nearly 50 years ago that the British branch of the Association of Orthodox Jewish Scientists performed practical experiments to determine the time of yakir relative to sunrise. A paper was written up on this and I think it appeared in the journal "Intercom" brought out by the American branch of this Association. The results of their experiments showed that the time for yakir depended on a number of factors, one which I remember was whether the person to be identified was facing east or west.

15 November 2011

BIRCHAS HAMAPIL

The Galach

As we can see from Rabbah (Pesachim 117a) and also from the Chasam Sofer, it is good to start a shiur or a talk with a joke.

Here is one which one can utilise on a whole variety of occasions, and it also teaches a halachah. The wife of a Jew living in Alaska gave birth to a boy. Normally a mohel would fly in to perform the bris. However, that day it was very stormy and it was impossible to fly. It happened that the local Pastor – the "galach" - had learned how to do a bris in accordance with the halachah. Some authorities rule that if a non-Jew does a bris, it is a valid bris. (Shulchan Aruch, Yoreh Deah 264:1). This Pastor therefore did the bris. The only problem was that when this boy got older and recited kriyas shema al hamita, instead of saying "hamalach hagoel..." he would say "hagalach hamohel..." (acknowledgements to R' Yisroel Goldstein z'l).

15 November 2011

✦ ✦ ✦ ✦ ✦ ✦ ✦ ✦ ✦ ✦

DALED KOSSOS WHEN WINE GETS YOU SICK

Tea sweetened with Saccharin

The use of "chamar medina" for the four cups of wine became relevant in the Kovno ghetto in Lithuania during the Second World War. When it came towards Pesach there was no wine available. In fact, the only beverage available, and even that in limited quantities, was tea sweetened with saccharin. The question was whether it could be used for the four cups of wine. On this, Rav Efraim Oshry wrote a teshuvah (Mima'amakim, volume 3, responsum 5) in which he permitted tea sweetened with saccharin to be used for the four cups, since it could be considered as "chamar medina". He added, however that, unlike wine where one says the berachah over all four cups, one should say the berachah over the tea sweetened with saccharin only on the first and third cups.

16 November 2011

✦ ✦ ✦ ✦ ✦ ✦ ✦ ✦ ✦ ✦

DALED KOSSOS WHEN WINE GETS YOU SICK
Only Water!

Baruch Duvdevani z'l, the executive director of the Jewish Agency's Aliyah department, related that in the 1950s he was in an Arab country pretending to be a non-Jew, in order to bring Jews from that country to Israel. Although he had planned to leave that country on erev Pesach, he was at the last moment delayed, and had to spend seder night in his hotel room. For the four cups of wine, all he could do was to fill a cup with water four times, at the appropriate times, and drink it. When he returned to Israel, he asked a she'elah what he should have done in the circumstances and the answer he received was to do what he had in fact done.

16 November 2011

HALLEL AFTER MA'ARIV ON THE SEDER NIGHT
Also on Erev Pesach

In addition to many shuls saying Hallel at ma'ariv on the first night(s) of Pesach, it could also be sung on the afternoon of erev Pesach. The Shulchan Aruch (Orach Chaim 458:1) based on a Yerushalmi, states that some people have the custom to bake their matzos for the seder on the afternoon of erev Pesach, namely, the same time that the Korban Pesach was being prepared. The Chidah (Moreh B'etzbah 7:205) writes that whilst baking these matzos, one sings the hallel, to commemorate hallel which was said whilst preparing the Korban Pesach. Beis Chernobyl even say the berachah over this hallel. (Piskei Teshuvos, volume 5, chapter 458, footnote 4).

17 November 2011

HALLEL AFTER MA'ARIV ON THE SEDER NIGHT

Hallel or Tachanun?

On which day of the year does one sometimes say hallel and sometimes tachanun? The answer is 3 Teves. When there are 29 days in Kislev, the 8th day of Chanukah will be on 3 Teves and so hallel will be said. If however, there are 30 days in Kislev, then 3 Teves will be the day after Chanukah and tachanun will be said.

17 November 2011

✿✿✿✿✿✿✿✿✿✿

HALLEL AFTER MA'ARIV ON THE SEDER NIGHT

Don't rely on Kiddush in Shul!!

Just as many shuls say hallel on the first night(s) of Pesach, they also, in Chutz La'aretz, say kiddush towards the end of ma'ariv every Friday night. In the past, there were visitors who would eat their meals in the shul and for this reason, kiddush was instituted in the shul service. This was based on the principle that one has to eat one's Shabbos meal at the same place as one makes kiddush and since these visitors were eating in the shul, the shul kiddush enabled them to fulfil the mitzvah of kiddush. (Shulchan Aruch, Orach Chaim, 269:1). However, there is also a downside to this shul kiddush, since some people eating their meal at home, may mistakenly think that having heard kiddush in shul, they do not have to make it when they return home.

17 November 2011

✿✿✿✿✿✿✿✿✿✿

CHALAV AKUM

Rabbi, Bless the Milk!

About 50 years ago, whilst I was living in an area of London, there was a certain occasion when there was a problem to receive cholov yisroel. Rav Morris Swift z'tl who was then a Dayan on the London Beis Din also lived in the same area, and he related to us that the milkman thought that for milk to be cholov yisroel, a Rabbi had to bless it. He therefore went to this Rav and said "You are a Rabbi. Will you bless the milk?!"

18 November 2011

🎹 🎹 🎹 🎹 🎹 🎹 🎹 🎹 🎹 🎹

BARUCH HU U'VARUCH SHEMO

Shofar – and Kiddush

In the Beis Hamidrash of the Chasam Sofer, the worshippers would answer "baruch hu u'voruch shemo" during the berachah before blowing the shofar, but the Chasam Sofer did not stop them. (Shut Maharam Shik, Orach Chaim, responsum 51). A point for consideration is whether the Chasam Sofer would distinguish in this matter on the one hand between mitzvas shofar where the berachah is bircas hamitzvah and thus not l'ikuva, and on the other hand, kiddush, where the berachah itself is the mitzvah?

18 November 2011

🎹 🎹 🎹 🎹 🎹 🎹 🎹 🎹 🎹 🎹

CHALAV AKUM

Butter from Cholov Akum

I recollect from about 40 years ago, when I lived in England, kosher butter arrived from Holland which was only supervised "mishas asiya", namely that the milk it was made from was cholov akum, yet people who would only drink cholov yisroel would use such butter. The reason is that milk from non-kosher animals cannot be made into butter. (Schach, Yoreh Deah 115:27). Such butter is however only permitted if one obtains already made butter, but should one make cholov akum into butter,

the butter would not be permitted. (Rema, Shulchan Aruch, Yoreh
Deah 115:1).

21 November 2011

🕎 🕎 🕎 🕎 🕎 🕎 🕎 🕎 🕎 🕎

CHALAV AKUM
What about a Keli Sheni?

Consider the following scenario: A person is invited to a house
which uses cholov akum, He is offered a hot drink (without
cholov akum) in a cup that has been used for hot drinks with
cholov akum. May he use this cup? According to the Maharsha
(Gilayon Maharsha, Shulchan Aruch, Yoreh Deah, beginning of
113) cholov akum does not make a keli sheni forbidden. There are
however Poskim who disagree with the Maharsha. I might add
that nearly 50 years ago when I did a course on kashrus given by
Rav Getsel Ellinson, he told us, and I have it written down in my
detailed notes from the course, that cholov akum does not make a
keli sheni forbidden.

21 November 2011

🕎 🕎 🕎 🕎 🕎 🕎 🕎 🕎 🕎 🕎

WEARING A YARMULKA
Not in Secular Classes

The Hasmonean Grammar School for Boys is an Orthodox Jewish
School in London, which was established in 1944 by Rabbi Dr.
Solomon Schonfeld z"tl. In reminiscences by former pupils,
Itzy Sabo wrote, "Hasmonean was started by Yekkes. In the
German Jewish tradition, the 'capple' was used *exclusively* in
religious contexts, e.g. praying. In the early years of Hasmo, the
school rules required pupils to wear it during religious studies
lessons, and *forbade* wearing it in secular contexts. Only pupils
(typically of eastern European extraction) who brought a note

from home saying it was their custom could wear one all the time." (see: http://melchettmike.wordpress.com/2009/10/24/hasmo-legends-xvi-1959-school-photograph/).

21 November 2011

✤ ✤ ✤ ✤ ✤ ✤ ✤ ✤ ✤ ✤

DAVENING IN A SHUL WITH A DIFFERENT NUSACH

Different Tachanuns

On Mondays and Thursdays, nusach ashkenaz begins tachanun with a very long "vehu rachum" and only after that there is nefilas apayim. In contrast, nusach sefard begins this tachanun with nefilas apayim. Consider a person who privately davens nusach sefard, but is the shliach tzibur in a nusach ashkenaz shul. Tefilos that he has to recite aloud, he would do in nusach ashkenaz, but silent things he could say in nusach sefard. Although he would say tachanun silently, it would look very out of place for him to begin tachanun with nefilas apayim.

21 November 2011

✤ ✤ ✤ ✤ ✤ ✤ ✤ ✤ ✤ ✤

DALED KOSSOS WHEN WINE GETS YOU SICK

A Nazir on Seder Night

A nazir, amongst other things, is forbidden to drink wine. Although today it is rare for a person to be a nazir, it does occasionally occur. One such case was Rav David Cohen z'tl (1887 – 1972) who was known as "Harav Hanazir". What did he do on seder night for the 4 kossos? I have been reliably informed that he used apple juice.

22 November 2011

✤ ✤ ✤ ✤ ✤ ✤ ✤ ✤ ✤ ✤

AMIRA L'AKUM

Non-Jew versus Time Switch

In the very cold weather, it is permitted to have a non-Jew light a fire on Shabbos for warmth. (Shulchan Aruch, Orach Chaim 276:5). However, today, one usually uses a time switch for this purpose, but according to a minority opinion, one should not use a time switch on Shabbos, (except possibly for lights). What is preferable in this particular case for a person who follows the opinion of not using a time switch – to have a non-Jew to light the fire or use a time switch?

22 November 2011

CHAZAN REPEATING WORDS

Mix up of Modim and Modim D'rabbonon

I was once in a shul which had both a chazan and a choir. When it came to modim on Shabbos mussaf, the chazan sang the first few words of modim and this was followed by the choir singing the first few words of modim d'rabbonon. The chazan then sang the next few words of modim and the choir then followed with the next few words of modim d'rabbonon. This then went on throughout modim and modim d'rabbonon. I must say that it was cleverly arranged musically. However, what the congregation in fact heard was a "jumble" of words. Is such a musical rendering problematic halachically?

22 November 2011

SECULAR NAMES

Alexander becomes Jewish!

Out of gratitude to Alexander the Great, who had been positively disposed towards the Jews, the Jews decided to name every boy born the following year "Alexander" (or "Sender" for short). Thus since that time till this very day, Alexander, which was a Greek name, has been the name given to many boys at their bris. (see: http://www.jewishhistory.org/alexander-the-great/).

23 November 2011

SECULAR NAMES

The Rambam's Arabic Name

The Rambam also had an Arabic name: Abū ⬚Imrān Mūsā bin Maimūn bin ⬚Ubaidallāh al-Qur⬚ubī. Another great Rav to have an Arabic name was Rav Abdullah Somech (1813 – 1889), who was the teacher of the Ben Ish Chai, and it would seem that Abdullah was the name he was given at his bris. The name "Abdullah" is of Arabic origin and means "Hashem's servant" and is a name commonly found in the Islamic world.

23 November 2011

SECULAR NAMES

Yiddisher Names

There are many Jews today who have Yiddish names. In some cases, the Yiddish name is the Yiddish translation of the Hebrew name which precedes it, for example: Yitzchok Eizik – Eizik in an Anglicised pronunciation is Isaac; Shlomo Zalman - Zalman in an Anglicised pronunciation is Solomon. There are even many people who just have the name Zalman without Shlomo. There are also cases where a Yiddish name follows a particular Hebrew name, for example: Efraim Fischel - Fischel is a little fish, and when Yaakov blessed Efraim and Menasheh, he used the phrase "v'yidgu [from the word "dag", a fish] lorov..."; Yehudah Leib – Leib is a lion, and when Yaakov blessed Yehudah he used the phrase "Gur Aryeh [lion] Yehudah".

24 November 2011

SECULAR NAMES

Don't forget your Name!

Rav Yeshayahu Horowitz (c.1565 – 1630), also known as the Shelah Hakadosh, writes that in order that we should not forget our name on the Day of Judgment, before we say the (second) "yihyu lerotzon" at the end of each amidah, we should recite a posuk from Tanach whose first letter is the first letter of our name and whose last letter is the last letter of our name. Many siddurim, after the amidah for the weekday shacharis, give a list of such pesukim for men. I also possess a Rosh Hashanah machzor with Yiddish translation (probably intended for use mainly by women), which also gives a list of such pesukim for women. Incidentally, one can see from this list that many women were given only Yiddish names.

24 November 2011

AMIRA L'AKUM

Shabbos and Yom Tov – yes; Chol Hamoed – no

There is something which is permitted on Shabbos and Yom Tov, but is forbidden on Chol Hamoed, namely having a non-Jewish contractor build a house for a Jew outside the techum. For a number of reasons, including "maris ayin" one may not employ non-Jewish workers to do work for a Jew on Shabbos, Yom-Tov and Chol Hamoed. Since one may not go outside the techum on Shabbos and Yom Tov, the question of "maris ayin" when a non-Jewish contractor builds a house for a Jew on Shabbos and Yom Tov outside the techum does not apply. However, since on Chol Hamoed, one may leave the techum, a Jew may not employ a non-Jewish contractor to build a house outside the techum on Chol Hamoed. (Shulchan Aruch, Orach Chaim 543:2, Mishnah Berurah 543:4).

27 November 2011

SEUDAS PURIM

Seudas Purim on 16 Adar

During birchas hamazon at all meals eaten on Purim one adds in "al hanisim". When however, Purim in Jerusalem (a walled city at the time of Yehoshua bin Nun and thus Purim is celebrated a day later) occurs on Shabbos, the seudas Purim is held on Sunday 16 Adar. On that day, one does not say "al hanisim" neither in the amidah nor in birchas hamazon. The question then asked is whether one should omit it even at the seudas Purim? On this, the Kaf Hachaim (688:48) writes that one should not say "al hanisim" in its usual place (between nodeh and ve'al hakol) since this would be a hefsek, but adds that it is good to say it as an additional harachamon.

27 November 2011

TRYING ON CLOTHES BEFORE CHECKING FOR SHATNES

Shaatnez and 15 Tagin

A riddle – one can learn halachah from it: What is the connection between shaatnez and 15 tagin? On seven of the letters written in a Sefer Torah, there are three tagin on each of these letters. Five of these seven letters are the five letters of the word shaatnez. (Mishnah Berurah 36:12-13). Thus on the word shaatnez as written the Sefer Torah there are 15 tagin.

27 November 2011

HAFTARAH

Same Haftarah two weeks running

There is a unique situation where the same haftarah is read two weeks running. This can only occur in a city where Purim is celebrated on Shushan Purim, and in practice the only place in the world today where this occurs is Yerushalayim. Should Shushan Purim occur on Shabbos, then the maftir is the leining for Purim, and the haftarah is that of Shabbos Zachor. (Mishnah Berurah 688:16). The previous Shabbos was Parshas Zachor and the haftarah was naturally that for Shabbos Zachor, hence the same haftarah two weeks running. The custom in places which celebrate two days Purim because of a safek, is to read the haftarah for that Shabbos, and not that of Shabbos Zachor. (Mishnah Berurah 688:16). An exception is Baghdad and it would seem that there they would read the haftarah for Shabbos Zachor on two successive weeks. (Ben Ish Chai, First year, Parshas Tetzaveh, Hilchos Purim paragraph 14).

27 November 2011

DRINKING ON PURIM

Once or all the time!

The Shulchan Aruch rules that on Purim one must drink "ad dlo yoda...". Suppose a person reaches this state on Purim and then later on the same day, he recovers from this state. Is he then obliged to drink to again reach this state? On this question there are different opinions. (see: Rav Moshe Harari, Mikroei Kodesh, Hilchos Purim, chapter 13, footnote 41).

28 November 2011

♧ ♧ ♧ ♧ ♧ ♧ ♧ ♧ ♧ ♧

KOSHER SWITCH: GLATT OR JUST KOSHER STYLE?

Use sticky tape

For six days each week, when going in and out of a room one almost automatically turns the electric lights on or off. By force of habit, one could accidentally do so also on Shabbos. A simple solution is before every Shabbos to put sticky tape over all the switches in the house.

28 November 2011

♧ ♧ ♧ ♧ ♧ ♧ ♧ ♧ ♧ ♧

SHABBOS HAGADOL

Two Sifrei Torah every Shabbos

Many shuls read a special haftarah on Shabbos Hagadol, but there is no special maftir, and so one reads from just one Sefer Torah. In contrast, in the weeks which almost precede Shabbos Hagadol, it is possible to have a situation where one reads from (at least) two Sifrei Torah on every Shabbos throughout a particular month. This occurs in Yerushalayim when 1 Adar (Adar Sheni in a leap year) occurs on Shabbos. That Shabbos will be parashas Shekalim; the following Shabbos – parashas Zachor; the following Shabbos will be Purim in Yerushalayim; the following Shabbos – parashas Poroh; and the following and last Shabbos that month will be parashas Hachodesh.

28 November 2011

♧ ♧ ♧ ♧ ♧ ♧ ♧ ♧ ♧ ♧

DRINKING ON PURIM

Ad dlo yoda in a Sofek Chomah City

In a city where there is a sofek whether it was walled at the time of Yehoshua bin Nun, one observes two days Purim (on 14 and 15 Adar). According to most opinions, all the laws of Purim should be observed on both days. (Shulchan Aruch, Orach Chaim 688:4, Mishnah Berurah 688:10). Does this include drinking "ad dlo yoda", also on the second day of Purim which is observed only because of a sofek. I have never seen this specific question discussed, but maybe because of a sfek sfeika one could answer in the negative, namely according to some opinions one does not have to reach this state on Purim in any city, and even if one does have to, then maybe Purim for that sofek chomah city is not on 15 Adar.

28 November 2011

KOSHER SWITCH: GLATT OR JUST KOSHER STYLE?

What about building an Eiruv?

Criticism of the "Shabbos Switch" have included that it is "zilzul Shabbos" or "akiras Shabbos". I have not studied the mechanics of the switch nor the halachic discussions regarding it, so I can pass no judgment on it. However, I can make the following comment. Shabbos observance is based on not performing any of the 39 melochos. By using this switch, one could argue that one is largely "removing" mavier and mechabeh from the list of forbidden melochos, and thus it could be classed as zilzul or akiras Shabbos. However, likewise by building more and more eiruvs in cities all over the world, one is "removing" the melochoh of hotzoa from the list. Has anyone classed this as zilzul or akiras Shabbos?

29 November 2011

WAITING BETWEEN MEAT AND DAIRY

Design a Clock!

It often happens that one has eaten a fleishig meal but does not note the time that one has finished eating the meat, how does one then know that 6 hours have passed so that one can now have milchig? A clock needs to be designed that one would set after eating fleishig and after 6 hours it would ring and/or show some sign that 6 hours was up!

29 November 2011

HAFTARAH

Open or Closed

The Mishnah Berurah (284:12) writes that the Tanach from which the haftarah was read should remain on the bimah whilst the after berachos for the haftarah are being recited, but does not state whether the Tanach should be open or closed. If a comparison is to be made from reading from the Sefer Torah or from Megillas Esther then it should be closed. However, in fact there are differences of opinion on whether the Tanach should be open or closed. (see: Piskei Teshuvos volume 284:13 and footnote 98).

29 November 2011

HAFTARAH

Just that Haftarah on Klaf or Printed Navi Shalem?

When reading the haftarah, if one should have to choose between a klaf which has just that haftarah written on it (but not the entire Navi), or a printed Navi shalem, which should one choose? According to Rav Ovadiah Yosef, the klaf with just that

SECTION TWO: YOU TOO MAY COMMENT!

haftarah is preferable. (Yalkut Yosef, Kitzur Shulchan Aruch, Orach Chaim 284:2).

29 November 2011

🏛 🏛 🏛 🏛 🏛 🏛 🏛 🏛 🏛 🏛

TRYING ON CLOTHES BEFORE TESTING FOR SHATNES

Kosher Clothing Stores

Here is an extract from a news item which appeared on the website of Arutz 7 on 26 November 2011: "…the Jerusalem Rabbinate will be providing certificates of 'kashrut' to clothing stores in [Jerusalem].… When people buy a suit they have no idea where it comes from … Suits today come from China, Hong Kong and various parts of the world. But even if they come from a factory in Israel they should be monitored.… Importers frequently put stamps on clothes that they are shatnez free despite the fact that no official body endorses the claim. Checking the shops we found many such 'shatnez free' garments containing shatnez.…"

30 November 2011

🏛 🏛 🏛 🏛 🏛 🏛 🏛 🏛 🏛 🏛

LECHEM MISHNAH FOR SEUDA SHELISHIS

Three Loaves

The mon in the midbar did not fall on Shabbos, but instead a double quantity fell on Friday. To commemorate this, one says hamozi over two loaves of bread on the Shabbos meals. According to some opinions the mon also did not fall on Yom Tov. (Tosafos on Beitzah 2b d.h. "vehoyoh") It could follow that if Yom Tov were to be on Friday or Sunday, then a triple quantity of mon would fall on the Thursday if Yom Tov were on Friday, or on the Friday if Yom Tov was on Sunday. One could thus possibly come to the conclusion that three loaves of bread should be used for hamotzi for the meals on such an occasion!

30 November 2011

🌳🌳🌳🌳🌳🌳🌳🌳🌳🌳🌳

SEMICHUS GEULAH L'TEFILAH

All or None

Should one come into a shul late for ma'ariv and the tzibur are about to start the amidah, one says the amidah with them and only afterwards the shema with its berachos, (Shulchan Aruch, Orach Chaim 236:3) since saying the amidah with the tzibur overrides smichus geulah l'tefillah in ma'ariv. (Mishnah Berurah 236:11). There is another halachah that even if one completely "mixes up" the order of the bircos shema, the three paragraphs of the shema and the amidah, one has still fulfilled the mitzvah of davening. (Mishnah Berurah 60:5). Now consider the following scenario which often occurs: A person arrives in shul for ma'ariv when the tzibur are in the middle of the shema with its berachos. He has time to say, (for example) the two berachos before the shema and the first paragraph of the shema but no more, before the tzibur would reach the amidah. Should he say the aforementioned, followed by the amidah together with the tzibur, and then continue onwards from the second paragraph of the shema, or should he just wait till the tzibur begins the amidah and then say it with them, and afterwards say the shema with its berachos? It would seem from the wording of the Mishnah Berurah (236:11) that the second alternative is the one to be followed.

30 November 2011

🌳🌳🌳🌳🌳🌳🌳🌳🌳🌳🌳

SEMICHUS GEULAH L'TEFILAH

Baruch Hashem L'olam in Israel

Although the almost universal custom in Eretz Yisroel is not to say "baruch Hashem l'olam" at ma'ariv, I have seen it written that at the K'hal Adas Yeshurun shuls in Bnei Brak and Beitar they do say it.
(see: www.kayj.org/forum/viewtopic.php?t=466&sid=e2e273793 182296f226fc5ceddde13d2).

1 December 2011

✿✿✿✿✿✿✿✿✿✿✿

SEMICHUS GEULAH L'TEFILAH

Aloud or Silently

In many shuls, the shliach tzibur says the words "go'al yisroel" immediately before the shacharis amidah silently, and this has been criticised as having no source. However, in contrast, there are poskim who say that it is a nice minhag to say these words silently, and Rav Moshe Feinstein is quoted as saying that he recollects from the days of his youth that this was the custom in all the yeshivas. (see: Piskei Teshuvos, volume 1, 66:10 and long footnote 86).

1 December 2011

✿✿✿✿✿✿✿✿✿✿✿

DRINKING ON PURIM

Drinking and then Sleeping

The Rema writes regarding drinking on Purim, that after drinking one should go to sleep and whilst sleeping one would be in the state of "ad dlo yoda". However, what happens if a person does the drinking on Purim, but only falls asleep when it is already night. Has he fulfilled the mitzvah of "ad dlo yoda"? This question is discussed by Rav Moshe Sternbuch (Moadim Uzmanim, volume

221

2, chapter 190), and he writes that the main thing is the actual drinking and it is therefore in order if one only falls asleep when it is already night.

1 December 2011

✿ ✿ ✿ ✿ ✿ ✿ ✿ ✿ ✿ ✿ ✿

BARUCH HU U'VARUCH SHEMO

Say it Silently

Rav Avraham Dovid ben Asher Anshel Wahrman – the Eshel Avraham Buczacz (1770 – 1840) writes (Orach Chaim chapter 66) that when he was the shliach tzibur he would say the ends of all the berachos (boruch ato...) before and after the shema silently, so that the tzibur would not answer "baruch hu u'voruch shemo" since it was forbidden to answer with these words at this part of the service.

4 December 2011

✿ ✿ ✿ ✿ ✿ ✿ ✿ ✿ ✿ ✿ ✿

DRINKING ON PURIM

Bentching whilst Shikur

Consider the following scenario. At the seudas Purim a man drinks until he is shikur, to such an extent that he cannot speak before a king. Can he in that state say bircas hamazon? Although in such a state he would not be allowed to say the amidah, the shema and its berachos, we learn from the Yerushalmi (Terumos, perek 1, halachah 4), that he would be allowed to bentch. (Shulchan Aruch, Orach Chaim 185:4). However should he have reached the state of "shikruso shel Lot", he would be exempt from all mitzvos and this includes bentching (even assuming that he was still able to do so in such a state!).

4 December 2011

✿ ✿ ✿ ✿ ✿ ✿ ✿ ✿ ✿ ✿ ✿

ASKING TWO RABBIS THE SAME SHAILA

When not to rely on your Rabbi!!

There is an occasion when should not rely on one's Rabbi – and that only occurs on a Wednesday or Thursday! When the first day of (a two day) Yom Tov occurs on Thursday or Friday, then on erev Yom Tov, namely Wednesday or Thursday, one makes eiruv tavshilin. Although the Rabbi of the city includes all the Jews in his city in his eiruv tavshilin, one should not rely on this but should make eiruv tavshilin oneself; it can even be problematic after having relied on the Rabbi on a previous occasion. So don't rely on your Rabbi on this particular Wednesday or Thursday!! (Shulchan Aruch, Orach Chaim 527:7).

4 December 2011

HAFTARAH

Only One Shabbos with Yehoshua

Although there are numerous haftarahs read on Shabbos which come from the book of Yeshayahu, there is only one Shabbos haftarah which comes from the book of Yehoshua, namely the haftarah for parashas Shelach Lecho. (There are also two Yom Tov haftarahs which come from Yehoshua, namely on the 1st day of Pesach and Simchas Torah.)

4 December 2011

HAFTARAH

Interrupting the Haftarah

There is an occasion when one interrupts the haftarah to insert a piyut. This is on the 2nd day of Shavuos (in Chutz La'aretz), when after the first verse of the haftarah, one inserts the piyut "yetziv pisgam". The authorship of this piyut is attributed to Rabbenu Tam (c1100-c1171), the grandson of Rashi.

4 December 2011

✦ ✦ ✦ ✦ ✦ ✦ ✦ ✦ ✦ ✦ ✦

TASHLICH

Tashlich Fish at Tisch

The Sadigurer Rebbe used to go to the Yarkon River in the Tel Aviv area for tashlich. Due to his advanced age, a few years ago, a pool was set up in his court into which three fish were put, and the Rebbe conducted tashlich there. Afterwards the fish were cooked and served at his tisch. (see: Mishpacha, English edition, 23 November 2011, page 57).

5 December 2011

✦ ✦ ✦ ✦ ✦ ✦ ✦ ✦ ✦ ✦ ✦

HAFTARAH

Why Gelila and not Maftir?

"What chutzpah! They promised me an aliyah and all they gave me was gelila, but Moishe who has protexia with the gabbai got maftir." This is a comment that one might well hear. But this is all wrong! Hagba and gelila are the best two mitzvos. (Shulchan Aruch, Orach Chaim 147:1; see: Piskei Teshuvos, volume 2:147, footnote 14 – Chazon Ish states that today we equate gelila with hagba). In contrast, maftir is "low" on the scale, so much so that a person receiving it is "compensated" by receiving amongst other things to be the shliach tzibur. (Megillah 24a).

5 December 2011

✦ ✦ ✦ ✦ ✦ ✦ ✦ ✦ ✦ ✦ ✦

FISH AND MEAT

Gefilte Fish only on Shabbos

When eating fish or meat on Shabbos, one must be careful not to remove the bones, since by doing this one would transgress the melochoh of borer. This is especially difficult with fish where there are numerous small bones. Therefore someone came along and invented "gefilte fish" which has become a Shabbos specialty. However, maybe on Yomtov it is not such a specialty since on Yom Tov one may remove the bones from fish, and also from meat.

5 December 2011

LECHEM MISHNAH FOR SEUDA SHELISHIS

Wine for Seudah Shelishis

According to some opinions, the Rambam holds that one should make kiddush before eating seudah shelishis. The mekubalim also hold this opinion. (Aruch Hashulchan, Orach Chaim 291:10). Because of these opinions, it is customary to drink wine during seudah shelishis. (Mishnah Berurah 291: 21). At kiddush one has to drink a certain quantity of wine – kimlo lugmov. Does it follow that since drinking wine at seudah shelishis is in place of kiddush, one has to drink the same quantity of wine as for kiddush, or is just a sip sufficient?

6 December 2011

HAFTARAH

Going Backwards in a Haftarah

In almost all haftarahs, one reads from the beginning to end without any omissions of verses. There are a few occasions where one jumps

225

forward to another place in the novi, and this is often to the following chapter. However, there is also a case where one goes backwards to the previous chapter. This is in the haftarah of parashas Mishpotim. There the haftarah begins in Yirmiyohu, chapter 34 verses 8-27, and then ones goes backwards to chapter 33, verses 25-26.

6 December 2011

HAFTARAH

Rosh Chodesh Maftir but not the Haftarah

One can have the situation where the maftir read is that for Rosh Chodesh, but the haftarah is not. This occurs when Rosh Chodesh Menacham Av falls on Shabbos. Since this is during the period of the "three weeks", each Shabbos of which has a special haftarah. (these haftarahs are known as the "shelosho d'puronusa"), the haftarah for Rosh Chodesh is overridden.

6 December 2011

NEFILAS APAYIM WHEN THERE IS NO SEFER TORAH

No Tachanun in Lederman Shul

The questions regarding nefilas apayim rarely arise at the Lederman Shul! This shul can be considered as a world-famous landmark in Bnei Brak. It was at there that the Chazon Ish z'tl and the Steipler z'tl davened, and today Rav Chaim Kanievsky davens there. When there is a ba'al bris (father of baby, mohel or sandak) present in a shul, tachanun is omitted. (Mishnah Berurah 131:22). Rav Chaim Kanievsky is a sandak almost every day of the year and so tachanun is rarely said in the Lederman Shul. (see: www. hamodia.com/inthepaper.cfm?ArticleID=569).

7 December 2011

KIDDUSH LEVANAH

In a Windowless Room

Mishpacha (English edition, 30 November 2011, page 50) wrote about a man who was incarcerated in a prison cell and could not see the moon. He asked a Rav about saying kiddush levanah and the Rav replied that "if he knows for a fact that the sky is clear and the moon can be clearly seen outside, then as long as the time for kiddush levanah has not elapsed, he can make the berachah even if he's inside." However, it is not clear what the reasoning for this is, since although the Mishnah Berurah (sha'ar hatziun 426:25) rules that one can even recite kiddush levanah looking through a closed window, he clearly adds that one must be able to see the moon through this window.

7 December 2011

MISHLOACH MANOS

Raw Foods for Mishloach Manos

Can one send an uncooked dish to somebody for mishloach manos? Rav Naftali Zvi Yehudah Berlin (the Netziv) (1816 – 1893), using a verse in parashas T'tzaveh (Shemos 29:26) shows that raw meat is called "manah", and thus by sending an uncooked dish one fulfills the mitzvah of mishloach manos. (Ha'emek She'eila on the She'iltos, 67:9).

7 December 2011

KIDDUSH LEVANAH

Fly Above the Clouds

It happened that one year during the winter it was cloudy every night and it was not possible to say kiddush levanah. The Satmar

Rebbe, Rav Yoel Teitelbaum z'tl, therefore hired an airplane and flew above the clouds in order to be able to recite kiddush levanah. (see: Meoros Hadaf Hayomi, volume 2, page 219).

8 December 2011

🕎🕎🕎🕎🕎🕎🕎🕎🕎🕎

MISHLOACH MANOS

Cross-examine the Shaliach

To fulfill the mitzvah of mishloach manos, the recipient must personally receive it before the end of Purim. (Aruch Hashulchan, Orach Chaim 695:16). Usually mishloach manos are sent by a shaliach, who is often a child. Maybe unknown to the sender, the recipient had gone away for Purim. The mishloach manos are thus left on his doorstep, and the shaliach does not inform the sender of this fact. To cover this eventuality, one should make a point of asking the shaliach whether the recipient personally (and not just a family member) had received the mishloach manos.

8 December 2011

🕎🕎🕎🕎🕎🕎🕎🕎🕎🕎

MATANOS L'EVYONIM

Don't investigate Bank Account

According to the Yerushalmi (Megillah, perek 1, halachah 4), and this is brought in the Shulchan Aruch (Orach Chaim 694:3), one does not investigate the financial situation of a person before giving them matanos l'evyonim, but one should give it to anyone who puts out their hand. Needless to say, it is at least morally wrong for a person who is not poor to go around on Purim with a cupped hand, since in this way one could deprive genuine poor people of matanos l'evyonim.

8 December 2011

🕎🕎🕎🕎🕎🕎🕎🕎🕎🕎

KITTEL ON YOM KIPPUR

Only Two Kittels

In shuls all over the world, many of the worshippers wear a kittel during the services on Rosh Hashanah and especially on Yom Kippur. However, in the Belz Shul in Jerusalem, which is probably the largest shul in Eretz Yisroel and seats many thousands of worshippers, only the Belz Rebbe and the shaliach tzibur wear a kittel. (see: Mishpacha, English edition, 28 September 2005, page 21).

11 December 2011

KIDDUSH LEVANAH

Eclipse of the Moon

Kiddush levanah may be recited each month until precisely half way between the times of two average molads. An eclipse of the moon occurs precisely when there is a full moon. Such an eclipse can occur before half way between the times of two average molads. Both the Maharil (c.1365 – 1427) (Shut Maharil, responsum 19) and the Levush (c.1530-1612) (Levush Hachor, Orach Chaim, 426:4) hold that in such a case, the time of such an eclipse will be the latest time for kiddush levanah.

11 December 2011

KIDDUSH LEVANAH

What about Motzaei Shavuos?

It is stated in maseches Sofrim (chapter 20, halachah 1), and is brought by the Shulchan Aruch (Orach Chaim 426:2) that one should say kiddush levanah only on motzaei Shabbos? Is this to the exclusion of motzaei Yomtov? One could thus ask that if Shavuos occurs on a Wednesday (and Thursday in Chutz La'aretz), should one say kiddush levanah on motzaei Shavuos, or should one wait till the following motzaei Shabbos? The Mishnah Berurah (426:5) states that the intention of maseches Sofrim is to include motzaei Yomtov, and thus one can say kiddush levanah after Shavuos and need not wait for the next motzaei Shabbos.

11 December 2011

♚ ♚ ♚ ♚ ♚ ♚ ♚ ♚ ♚ ♚

SHEMURA MATZAH

Brown Paper, no Metal nor Plastic

For many decades matzos have been hand baked in Komemius in Eretz Yisroel, and numerous chumros have always been incorporated into their preparation. These include: covering the tables with brown paper guaranteed free from starch; making sure that the flour and dough never come into contact with metal; that the jute fabric in which the wheat is delivered has undergone a thorough examination to ensure that it is free from chametz; and that no plastic utensil is to be found anywhere in the bakery. (Mishpacha, English edition, 7 December 2011, page 44).

12 December 2011

♚ ♚ ♚ ♚ ♚ ♚ ♚ ♚ ♚ ♚

GEBRUKTS

Glatt Kosher for Pesach

One often sees advertisements for holidays for Pesach which state that the cuisine is "Glatt Kosher". This term has meaning for the rest of the year, but for Pesach it is ambiguous. A place can offer cuisine with includes kneidalach and other gebrukts, and for those who follow the poskim who state this completely permitted on Pesach, it can be classed as Glatt Kosher. Furthermore, a place that follows the Sefaradi minhagim can have on their menu, rice and other kitniyos, and this can likewise be classed as Glatt Kosher. Therefore, it is important for a place offering Pesach cuisine not just to state "Glatt Kosher" but also state whether they serve gebrukts and/or kitniyos. Furthermore, prospective clients must also check this point when choosing a place to stay for Pesach.

12 December 2011

GEBRUKTS

The Vilna Gaon's Matzos

The Chafetz Chaim would not eat gebrukts on Pesach, (although he did not stop his family from doing so). When people said to him that the Vilna Gaon would eat gebrukts, he answered that were he to have the matzos of the Vilna Gaon, he would also eat gebrukts. (Ohr Yisroel (Monsey), Nisan 5759 (1999), year 4, issue 3[15], page 142).

12 December 2011

ASARA B'TEVES

Not even Water

After Yom Kippur, and Tisha b'Av when it occurs on a Sunday, one makes havdalah. Before making any havdalah during the course of the year, one is permitted to drink water. (Shulchan Aruch, Orach Chaim 299:1). This is, in particular, useful for women who are waiting at home for their husbands to come home from shul after these fasts. However, such drinking is not the case with kiddush, where even water is forbidden. (Shulchan Aruch, Orach Chaim 271:4). Therefore when Asara b'Teves occurs on

Friday, the women who are waiting for their husbands to return from shul to make kiddush, cannot even drink water.

13 December 2011

🕎🕎🕎🕎🕎🕎🕎🕎🕎🕎🕎

RETZUOS OF TEFILLIN

Narrower and Narrower

Every time one puts on tefillin, especially the shel yad, the retzuos are pulled, and over the course of many years they will, as a result, become narrower and narrower. Also the retzuos might start partially tearing across. A question to be asked is whether there is a minimum width for the retzuos and also whether the torn part can be included in such a minimum width? Some poskim rule that since no width requirement is mentioned in the Gemara, a minimum width is only a hidur, and if there are no other tefillin available, one may put them on and even say a berachah over them. (see: Sha'arim Metzuyanim B'halachah on Kitzur Shulchan Aruch 10:26).

13 December 2011

🕎🕎🕎🕎🕎🕎🕎🕎🕎🕎🕎

RETZUOS OF TEFILLIN

Writing one's Name

In, for example, a school, where numerous pupils put on tefillin, and thus mix ups between the tefillin of different pupils can occur, it is desirable to be able to identify one's own tefillin. A question can thus arise whether one may write one's name (and other contact details) on the back of the retzuos. According to the halachah, one may colour the back of the retzuos with any colour except red. (Shulchan Aruch, Orach Chaim 33:3). Maybe one can learn from this, that one may write one's name on the back of the retzuos in any colour but red.

13 December 2011

🕎🕎🕎🕎🕎🕎🕎🕎🕎🕎🕎

MISHLOACH MANOS

Don't hurry to get Drunk!

Although there is a principle to be zariz to perform a mitzvah, this could be problematic with the mitzvah of "ad dlo yoda". If a person should drink to such an extent and reach "shikroso shel Lot", he will then be potur from all mitzvos. So even if he succeeds in giving mishloach manos or matanos l'evyonim whilst in such a state, it would seem that he will not have fulfilled these mitzvos. The moral is - perform all these Purim mitzvos before drinking on Purim!

14 December 2011

AUFRUF

Check Kashrus of Sweets

It is customary at an aufruf to throw sweets (candies) at the choson, and sometimes some of those attending bring their own sweets to throw. It could be that the kashrus of some of these sweets is questionable, or even worse. As soon as the sweets are thrown, children will rush to pick them up and by that time it will be well-nigh impossible to retrieve and check them. Therefore the ba'alei simcha should try and find a tactful way to control which sweets are thrown.

14 December 2011

PRIORITIES IN TZEDAKAH

Responsibility for Tzedakah Money

When they were building an extra floor to Kollel Chazon Ish in Bnei Brak, Rav Nissim Karelitz would on every Friday climb up the scaffolding, examine the progress and then give the contractors a list of comments. When someone asked whether it was proper for a Torah scholar to engage in such activities, Rav Karelitz answered, "People have entrusted me with their money, and it is my responsibility to ensure that it is used for the purpose for which it was donated." (Mishpacha, English edition, 13 April 2011, page 46).

14 December 2011

✿ ✿ ✿ ✿ ✿ ✿ ✿ ✿ ✿ ✿ ✿

CHANUKAH GELT AND GIFTS

The Dreidel and Moshiach

It has been suggested that there is a source for the dreidel in sefer Yechezkel (37:16-17). There the Navi writes to take a stick and write on it "Yehudah" (to represent the Southern Kingdom), and on another stick write "Yosef" (to represent the Northern Kingdom), and join the two sticks together to make one stick. This is an allusion to all the tribes returning to Eretz Yisroel in the days of the Moshiach. A dreidel was originally made from wood and the gematria of the letters on it – nun, gimmel, hey, shin – is that of Moshiach. However, in Eretz Yisroel, one usually finds the letter pey instead of shin. But one can still have the gematria for Moshiach, since the gematria of nun, gimmel hey, pey, is "Menachem" or "Tzemach" which are also names for the Moshiach.

15 December 2011

✿ ✿ ✿ ✿ ✿ ✿ ✿ ✿ ✿ ✿ ✿

MINHAGIM

With a Berachah

The recital of hallel on Rosh Chodesh is a minhag and so Sefardim don't say a berachah over it. Another minhag is the lighting of Chanukah candles in shul with a berachah, and the Mishnah

Berurah (671:44) specifically compares these two minhagim with regards to berachos. However, in this latter case, Sefardim do say a berachah. Why the contradiction?! The Aruch Hashulchan (Orach Chaim 671:26) discusses this question stating that there are visitors and unmarried people who don't have a house and thus fulfill this mitzvah in shul, and even if this is not the case, then the main pirsumei nisa is today in the shul and thus one should say the berachah there.

15 December 2011

✿ ✿ ✿ ✿ ✿ ✿ ✿ ✿ ✿ ✿ ✿

TASHLICH
Where's the Body?

In Memphis Tennessee, over 50 people went near a cliff and while looking down at the river which lay about 5 metres below them, recited Tashlich. Suddenly a police car raced towards them with its lights flashing and its sirens blaring. Two policemen then rushed out of the vehicle shouting "Where's the body?" Apparently, someone had seen a large group looking at the river, and thinking that they were staring at a floating body summoned the police! (Mishpacha, English edition, 9 November 2011, page 53).

15 December 2011

✿ ✿ ✿ ✿ ✿ ✿ ✿ ✿ ✿ ✿ ✿

SHATNEZ IN MATTRESSES AND CUSHIONS
The Steipler Stands

The Chazon Ish was trying to arrange a shidduch for his brother-in-law the Steipler, and he arranged for him to meet a young woman. The Steipler before this meeting stayed up all night learning, planning to catch up on his sleep on the long train journey to this meeting. After being introduced to each other, the

235

Steipler fell asleep straight away, to the horror of the young woman. What had occurred was that on the train there were padded seats and the Steipler was worried that they might be shaatnez and therefore stood up and remained awake for the entire journey and thus arrived very tired! (see: http://ohr.edu/ask/055.htm).

18 December 2011

♜ ♜ ♜ ♜ ♜ ♜ ♜ ♜ ♜ ♜

WEARING WOOL TZITZIS
Wool Tzitzis Beged on Shabbos

Although one may leave the eiruv wearing tzitzis on Shabbos, there are some limitations. If some (but not all) of the tzitzis are posul, one may not go outside the eiruv wearing such a beged. According to some opinions, if the beged is below the minimum size, one may also not go outside the eiruv wearing it. (Mishnah Berurah 13:2). What about a garment which is not made of wool and therefore one only has to attach tzitzis mi'drabbonon? On this Reb Mottel Tenenbaum, who is an expert on tzitzis and author of the "Hadar Tzitzis" series writes, "Some people wear a wool one on Shabbos so they don't have problems of carrying because that's a real beged, no question about it." (Mishpacha, English edition, 14 December 2011, page 78).

18 December 2011

♜ ♜ ♜ ♜ ♜ ♜ ♜ ♜ ♜ ♜

THE PROCEDURE FOR GETTING AN ALIYAH
3 Year Torah Cycle – Until when?

During the course of thousands of years in the past, a person receiving an Aliyah to the Torah in Eretz Yisroel would not have the same leining as for a person in Chutz La'aretz. Unlike Chutz

La'aretz where the Torah cycle is just one year, in Eretz Yisroel until the conquest by the Crusaders at the end of the 11th century, the Torah cycle was 3 years. The Jews then fled to Fustat (Old Cairo) in Egypt and one of the shuls established there was the Eretz Yisroel shul where they continued the 3-year cycle. It would seem according to Rav Yissachar ben Mordechai ibn Susan, (Tikkun Yissachar, Venice: 5339 / 1579, page 33b), who lived in Egypt during the 16th century, that at that period, this 3-year cycle was still in force in this shul.

18 December 2011

HAFTARAH

Haftarahs for 3 Year Cycle

For every Shabbos throughout the year there is a haftarah after the Torah reading. When the Eretz Israel 3-year cycle Torah reading was in force, there had to be three times as many haftarah readings as we have today. From various sources, we today know in which navi and from where in the navi, almost all these haftarahs came from. The main sources are: a) two manuscripts which were found in the Cairo genizah. One of them gives about 70 haftarahs from Noach until the beginning of sefer Vayikra, and the other manuscript gives some of those in sefer Devarim; b) the payetan Yannai who lived in Eretz Yisroel about the 6th century (exact century not known). He composed "kerovos" for the amidah of each Shabbos in accordance with the 3-year cycle and included in these kerovos is the first verse of each haftarah. Only some of these kerovos are extant today.

19 December 2011

WEARING A GARTEL FOR DAVENING

The Snake Gartel

One morning, Rav Eliahu Hakohen Haltamari of Izmir (c.1659 -1729) got up whilst it was still pitch dark, dressed and put on his gartel. That day his gartel felt thicker and stiffer than usual and he found it more difficult to put on. He started learning when suddenly the gartel started coming loose and moving and it then slipped off and landed on the floor. He looked down and saw that it was in fact a poisonous snake. He realised that it was a great miracle that he had not been harmed at all by this venomous snake. To commemorate this miracle, he wrote the book entitled "Eizor Eliyahu" – ("eizor" is the Hebrew for gartel). (see: Mishpacha, English edition, Junior section, 18 Kislev 5772 [14 December 2011], page 3, who acknowledged that it was adapted from the book "Aleinu L'shabeiach" by Rav Yitzchak Zilberstein).

19 December 2011

🌱🌱🌱🌱🌱🌱🌱🌱🌱🌱🌱

SEUDAS PURIM

3 days Seudas Purim

Almost everybody has just one seudas Purim on 14 Adar (15 Adar in a walled city). In a "doubtful city" namely one which celebrates Purim on both 14 and 15 Adar, because of a doubt on whether it was walled at the time of Yehoshua bin Nun, one has 2 days seudas Purim. (Mishnah Berurah 688:10). When Purim of a walled city falls on Shabbos, to keep all opinions one has a seudas Purim both on the Shabbos and on the Sunday. (Mishnah Berurah, Sha'ar Hatziun 688:30). In such a case, a "doubtful city" will have a seudas Purim on the Friday, Shabbos and Sunday - namely 3 days with seudas Purim.

19 December 2011

🌱🌱🌱🌱🌱🌱🌱🌱🌱🌱🌱

THE PROCEDURE FOR GETTING AN ALIYAH

Israel Leads

A man goes to shul in Chutz La'aretz on a Monday and receives an Aliyah to the Torah and the leining is from parshas Korach. On the following day he flies to Eretz Yisroel and on the Thursday he requests and gets an Aliyah so that he may say birchas hagomel, but he notices that the leining comes from parshas Chukas! What has happened?!! The answer is that that year was a leap year and the 8th day of Pesach was on Shabbos and so the leining was that for Pesach. However, in Eretz Yisroel (where there is only one day Yom Tov) that Shabbos was the day after Pesach and so the leining was that for a Shabbos. As a result, Eretz Yisroel leads Chutz La'aretz by one parashah. The equalisation comes when the parshios Matos and Masei are separated in Eretz Yisroel, whereas in Chutz La'aretz they are joined together. (This is the most extreme example of a difference in the parshios between Eretz Yisroel and Chutz La'aretz and lasts for about three and a half months. There are also other cases which are of much shorter duration.)

21 December 2011

❦ ❦ ❦ ❦ ❦ ❦ ❦ ❦ ❦ ❦ ❦

EIRUV TAVSHILIN (PRACTICAL)

Fat on the Knife

The norm is to make eiruv tavshilin using meat, fish or an egg. But one is by no means limited to these foods. According the Gemara (Beitzah 16a) and it is brought in the Shulchan Aruch (Orach Chaim 527:6), one can even use the fat scraped from a knife. So during the days before having to make eiruv tavshilin, scrape off the fat from a knife until you have an accumulated amount of fat which is the size of a kezayis! However, needless to add, it is more respectable for this mitzvah to use meat, fish or an egg!

21 December 2011

❦ ❦ ❦ ❦ ❦ ❦ ❦ ❦ ❦ ❦ ❦

THE PROCEDURE FOR GETTING AN ALIYAH

Maximum Days

What is the maximum number of consecutive days that one can follow "the procedure for getting an Aliyah" – or in other words what is the maximum number of consecutive days that one can have Krias Hatorah? In Eretz Yisroel the answer is 10, and it occurs when Chanukah begins on a Friday or Sunday. In such a case one has the 8 days of Chanukah plus the day before and the day after the festival. In Chutz La'aretz, one can go even higher and have 11 days. When Succos begins on a Tuesday, one has the 9 days of the festival plus the day before (Monday) and the day after (Thursday) the festival.

21 December 2011

🛡🛡🛡🛡🛡🛡🛡🛡🛡🛡🛡

DRINKING ON PURIM

Bachurim - no Liqueurs

In the north-east of England is the town of Gateshead. In the Jewish world this town is famous for its Yeshivah and other Torah institutions, and the entire Jewish community there is shomrei mitzvos. The Rav of this town was concerned that the bachurim were overdrinking on Purim and he therefore made a number of takanos to solve this problem. One of them was that the bachurim were not permitted to drink anything but wine. (Mishpacha, English edition, 4 May 2011, page 43).

22 December 2011

🛡🛡🛡🛡🛡🛡🛡🛡🛡🛡🛡

EIRUV TAVSHILIN (PRACTICAL)

Put Translation on Hebrew side

When making eiruv tavshilin, one makes the declaration "bahadein eiruva yehey ..." The language of this declaration is

Aramaic, because that was the language people then spoke, and it is essential that those making this declaration in eiruv tavshilin understand what it means. (Mishnah Berurah, Sha'ar Hatziun, 529:55). In practice, however, probably the majority of people have no idea what it means! The following suggestion would surely help solve this problem for one who is using a siddur with the translation on the opposite page. In all siddurim, the translation (for example: English) of this declaration appears, as with all the prayers, on the English translation side of the siddur, and therefore a person using such a siddur will not take any particular notice of the translation of this declaration. Let this declaration appear in English on the same side as the Hebrew text, directly under the declaration in Aramaic, with a note in English stating that the person should read it in English. (A similar thing can be done with the declaration following bedikas chometz.)

22 December 2011

Section Three

Unconventional Kosher Menus

Wormy Cheese,
Cloned Pig Meat
and
Much More for
a Kosher table?

Rabbi Dr. Chaim Simons

(written in 2018)

CONTENTS

ACKNOWLEDGEMENTS

In order to write this book, I had to assemble a vast amount of material. Today, with the Internet, many of the papers and articles which I utilised in writing my book were to be found there. I acknowledge with gratitude the various authors of this material.

In particular, I must mention the writings of the following: Rabbi Dr. Ari Zivotofsky, Professor Zohar Amar, Rabbi Dr. J. David Bleich and Dr. Yisrael Meir Levinger. Their material was invaluable for my book. My sincere thanks and gratitude to these four researchers.

Another important source on the Internet is the website of "HebrewBooks." For almost every book I required, and indeed there were a large number, I was able to download the appropriate pages from their website. Those responsible for this website, have contributed an immeasurable amount for the study of Torah.

The few books (and really there were only a few!) I could not find on HebrewBooks, I found in the Israel National Library in Jerusalem, and in the Yeshivat "Nir" Library in Kiryat Arba. My sincere thanks to these two libraries.

PREFACE

Although the Headings of the various chapter and the "Bon Appétit" sections of each chapter have been written in a humorous style, this book is a serious work whose object is to teach some of the laws of Kashrut in a novel way. However, none of the foods mentioned should be eaten before consulting a Rabbinical authority.

Each chapter is divided into three sections: General Knowledge, Halachic discussion, Bon Appétit.

General Knowledge: In this section, a selection of general knowledge associated with each item is given. This information has been gleaned from a number of encyclopedias, dictionaries and other reference books. Needless to say, this information is not exhaustive.

Halachic discussion: This is by far the longest and most important section of the book. A halachic discussion is made regarding each item and this usually includes historical and geographical material.

In some cases where there is a vast amount of discussion by the Rabbis on a particular item, in order to keep the discussion to a reasonable length, only a selection of the arguments is described.

There are some items where the scope of the discussion has been broadened to incorporate associated material.

In order to avoid repetition, in cases where some of the material for different chapters are identical or nearly identical, the arguments are generally limited to just one of the items.

In this section, the references are meticulously documented. Abbreviations have been kept to a minimum and those regularly used are as follows:
SA = Shulchan Aruch

OC = Orach Chaim section of Shulchan Aruch
YD = Yoreh De'ah section of Shulchan Aruch
Rambam = Rabbi Moshe Maimonides' Mishneh Torah
OU = Orthodox Union of America

As is customary when quoting references, two Latin expressions are used:
ibid. = same as previous reference
op. cit. = refers to a previously cited work.

In order to make it easier for the reader, a detailed reference is given the first time it is mentioned in a particular chapter, even though it has been given in an earlier chapter.

In the cases where Hebrew or Greek words are used, they have been transliterated into English style letters. Likewise, in the footnotes, Hebrew words have been transliterated into English style letters. Needless to add, there are different ways of transliteration.

Bon appétit: In this section, often in a humorous manner, a suggested occasion in the year, or a method of eating the item, is given.

Don't look for the ingredients and methods of making the various items given in the Conents. You won't find them!! That is left for you to experiment with!!!

As already stated, this book is to teach halachot of kashrut. Before eating any of these items, consult with a Rabbinical authority who is proficient in this field.

Readers may put in a request to my e-mail chaimsimons@ gmail.com for original photocopied source materials quoted in this paper to be sent to their e-mails without charge.

Chapter 1
Wormy Cheese with fruit salad for Tu Bishvat

General Knowledge

Cheese is a dairy product derived from milk, which usually comes from cows and goats, although it also comes from, amongst other animals, giraffes and camels. It is usually made by coagulation of the milk protein casein. In fact, the word "cheese" comes from the Latin word "caseus." During the production of cheese, the milk is usually acidified and the enzyme rennet is added and this causes coagulation. (Rennet can be replaced by vegetarian alternatives.) The solids are then separated and pressed into their final form. In some areas, cheese is still made by allowing the milk to curdle naturally. Cheese has a longer shelf life than milk, and hard cheeses last longer than soft cheeses. There are hundreds of types of cheese, with certain cheeses being historically associated with various countries and areas. Their styles, textures and flavors depend on a number of factors: the origin of the milk, the animal's diet, whether the milk has been pasteurised, the butterfat content, the bacteria and mold, the processing and the aging. Sometimes other ingredients are added to give flavoring to the cheese.

Halachic discussion

Would the presence of worms in otherwise kosher cheese make the cheese not kosher? The answer is in the negative. Wormy cheese [often the term maggoty cheese is used] is not, according to the Shulchan Aruch, forbidden to be eaten because of the worms in it.[1] Already, about the end of the twelfth century, which was several hundred years prior to the composition of the Shulchan Aruch, Rabbeinu Eliezer ben Reb Yoel Halevi (the Ra'avyah) wrote that he heard from his father that the worms found in cheese may be eaten.[2] However, this is an exception to the halachot regarding the eating of insects, since the Torah forbids the eating of worms and almost all forms of insects. In fact, by eating them, one transgresses more prohibitions than by eating pork! These prohibitions apply to those insects who live in the sea and streams, those who fly in the air, and those who creep on the ground.[3] For such a creature to be forbidden to be eaten, it has to be visible to the naked eye. One does not have to use a microscope or even a magnifying glass to check the presence of such insects![4] Some years ago it was discovered that there were almost microscopic insects in the water in New York, which led to the question of whether one could drink the water without straining it.[5] However, the worms in cheese are not microscopic or even almost microscopic. They can reach a length of 8 millimetres.[6]

Some government health departments allow a certain number of insects in foods.[7] (One might ask whether wormy cheese would be an exception to these government rules?!) However, according to the halachah, Jews may not eat such products without removing these insects.

Some foods are so infected with insects and as a consequence great effort and time has to be expended to remove these insects.[8] A practical example is the lettuce required on the Seder night for the maror. The Mishnah Berura refers to this problem and states that a person who does not have the ability to make such a check should use horseradish for maror.[9] Today this problem has been largely solved by Gush Katif lettuce which is specially grown in conditions which will make it bug free.[10]

Another vegetable that was recently found to be infected is strawberries. Research was done by "Machon haTorah veHa'aretz" to investigate the removal of all these insects and it was found necessary to do four successive washings to accomplish this.[11]

In addition to cheese, there are instances where the consumption of visible insects is permitted. One of them concerns fish where worms are often found in some of them. Those which are in the fishes' flesh may be eaten whilst those in its intestines are forbidden since these insects had been in the sea and were recently swallowed by the fish.[12] It should be noted that due to new scientific studies, the permissibility of worms in the flesh has been questioned.[13]

It is also permitted to eat worms found in a fruit that had been detached from its source of growth and never exposed to the air. However, those worms which grew in a fruit whilst it was attached to the ground are forbidden.[14] In a case where it is difficult to ascertain how long they had been in the fruit, the fruit would be forbidden to be eaten.[15]

As stated above, worms found in cheese may be eaten. However, even with the presence of worms, the cheese might still not be kosher. There are indeed a number of factors for a cheese to be permitted to be eaten. The first question is does the cheese contain non-kosher ingredients. During the production of cheese from milk, rennet is used. Rennet is an enzyme which is produced in the stomach of a cow and it helps turn the milk into cheese. If it comes from a non-kosher animal, this in itself will make the cheese not kosher. Today there are alternative non-animal sources for rennet.[16]

Even if all the ingredients in the cheese are found to be strictly kosher, the cheese cannot necessarily be eaten. There is a Rabbinical enactment known as "gevinat akum" against the eating of non-Jewish cheese. Even a person who is lenient and drinks non-Jewish milk "chalav akum" is forbidden to eat gevinat akum.[17] To make cheese into gevinat Yisrael - "Jewish cheese," a Jew needs at least to be present when the cheese is being made and according to some opinions must himself actually add the rennet into the milk. With most Kashrus authorities, both these conditions are fulfilled in cheeses under their supervision.[18] Whether or not the law of gevinat akum applies only to hard cheese or also to soft cheeses is open to dispute.[19]

Worms might be found in cheeses which are hard,[20] aged about six months, or are prepared in a way which gives the cheese a very sharp taste.[21] If the ingredients are strictly kosher and the laws concerning gevinat Yisrael have been observed, the presence of worms will not make the cheese non-kosher![22] These worms may be eaten as long as they remain embedded within the cheese. However, if they leap off or otherwise separate from the cheese they are then forbidden to be eaten. However, there are more lenient opinions which rule that they still may be eaten so long as they have not gone further than the plate or the serving dish. Should these worms get mixed up with other food and one is unable to remove them, the food does not become forbidden since some permit them under any circumstances, although it is better to be strict unless there is a big loss.[23]

A question that can be asked is whether one may eat the cheese whilst the worms are alive and even moving around. The answer is implied by the Rema who writes about the worms jumping about on the cheese.[24] A more direct positive answer is given by Rabbi Avraham ben Mordechai who lived in Egypt in the seventeenth century, who wrote that Ashkenazi Jews eat cheese containing worms which are still alive.[25] A question which immediately then follows is whether it is permitted to eat this cheese on Shabbat since by doing so one will kill the worms, and killing living creatures on Shabbat is forbidden by the Torah. However, the answer is yes[26] and it can be compared to the killing of lice on Shabbat which is permitted.[27]

How did the worms get into the cheese? There is a cheese called Casu Marzu in Sardinia called Sardinian Sheep Milk Cheese, which has live maggots in it. To produce this maggoty cheese, whole pecorino cheeses are left outside with part of the rind removed to allow the eggs of the cheese-fly Piophila casei to be laid in the cheese. A female Piophila casei can lay more than 500 eggs at one time. The eggs hatch and the larvae begin to eat through the cheese. The acid from the maggots' digestive system breaks down the cheese's fats. The texture of the cheese becomes very soft with some liquid seeping out. By the time it is ready for consumption, a typical Casu Marzu will contain thousands of these maggots. The larvae themselves appear as translucent white worms about 8 millimetres long.[28]

Although until fairly recently, Cazu Marzu cheese could officially be made and sold, a number of years ago the European Union prohibited its manufacture for health reasons.[29] As a result, the manufacturers had to go underground and manufacture it in private houses. Dr. Zohar Amar went in search of this maggoty cheese in 2015.[30] After a lot of searching he found it in the village of Oliena Sardinia in Italy where, due to climatic conditions, it was available only during certain seasons of the year. He went to a restaurant and they took it out of the refrigerator where it was stored. It looked like a round cheese cake. After cutting off the outer layer with a sharp knife, one could see hundreds of maggots moving around,[31] as in the words of the Rema, "Jumping here and there on the cheese."[32] Wormy cheese with a hechsher can be bought at the Machane Yehudah market in Jerusalem.[33]

If the method described above of producing the maggots in the cheese is acceptable according to the halachah, then by using only kosher ingredients and following the laws of gevinat Yisrael, one can have kosher l'mehadrin Cazu Marzu cheese with maggots!

Bon Appétit

On the night of Tu bi'Shvat it is customary to eat a large number of different fruits, since it is the New Year for Trees.[34] Originally this custom was stated as an Ashkenazi custom,[35] but it has now also become a Sephardi custom which includes reading from a book entitled "Pri Etz Hadar," and conducting a "Seder Tu bi'Shvat."[36] There would seem to be no problem in making a fruit salad out of a large number of fruits and eating them together with wormy cheese!

Chapter 2

Cloned Pig Meat for Mishloach Manot

General Knowledge

Cloning is the process of generating a genetically identical copy of a cell or organism. In biomedical research, cloning is broadly defined to mean the duplication of any kind of biological material for scientific study. There are two ways of cloning an animal, such as a pig. In one of them, one takes cells from fetal pig skin and performs on them various processes in order for them to develop into embryos. These embryos are then transplanted into surrogate female pigs. The pig will be born naturally and it will therefore be no different from any other pig. The second method is a laboratory method in which the cells from the fetal pig skin is treated with various nutrients which cause it to grow into a piece of pig meat. The cloning of mammals including pigs, goats, rats, mice, dogs, horses and mules has been performed since the early 1980s. The first cloned cat was called "Copy Cat" and was born to her surrogate mother at the end of 2001.

Halachic Discussion

Would a cloned pig be kosher? Needless to say, the advent of cloning of animals has led to the question regarding their kashrut, in particular the cloning of non-kosher animal, such as pigs.

An answer to this question was widely reported in March 2018. This was after Rabbi Yuval Cherlow, a Rosh Yeshivah in Ra'anana and one of the founders of the Tzohar organization, stated in an interview with Ynet that meat from a genetically cloned pig would be kosher for consumption by Jews – including when eaten with dairy products.[37]

Rabbi Cherlow did not specifically state which of the two cloning methods he was referring to, (namely, the pig born naturally, or the pig meat grown in a laboratory), but it is thought to be the second method. His view was supported by Rabbi Dov Lior, the former Rabbi of Kiryat Arba and Rabbi Shlomo Aviner, the Rabbi of Bet-El.[38] In fact, according to the first method given above, the pig will be born naturally and there is no halachic reason why the baby pig should be any different from any other pig.[39]

There was great opposition to Rabbi Cherlow's opinion. Already, at an earlier date, namely in 5773 (2013), Rabbi David Bleich wrote a long paper on this subject. Some Dutch scientists had made a single beef hamburger in a laboratory. He immediately made the comment that one day a pork chop will be made by this method. He discussed a number of different factors on this subject and concluded that if the cells were taken from a kosher animal that had been shechted and the nutrients were kosher, the meat produced would be permitted, even with milk. However, if the cells were taken from a pig it would be forbidden.[40]

There are a number of reasons for forbidding the eating of cloned pig meat. Probably the most important one is on the question of bitul (nullifying) of a forbidden substance, namely the cells taken from the pig. As a general rule, less than one sixtieth is enough to nullify. However, in this case there is a question of davar hama'amid, namely a substance which supports or upholds the mixture. In such a case, even less than one sixtieth would not nullify the forbidden substance. For example, in cheese making, rennet is essential and only a minute quantity is required – yet non-kosher rennet will make the cheese not kosher. Similarly here, although the pig cells are miniscule compared with the nutrients, without the pig cells one would not obtain the cloned meat and thus bitul does not apply here.[41]

Another interesting argument which was mentioned was that the taking of cells from a live animal was "aiver min hachai," cutting off a limb from a living animal, and this is one of the seven Noachide laws applying also to a non-Jew. Because of these Noachide laws, even a non-Jew could not eat this cloned pig meat![42]

A person who does not follow the opinion of eating cloned pig meat has a different method to know what pig meat tastes like.

The Gemara[43] states that everything that the Torah has forbidden Jews to eat, it has permitted an equivalent. It has forbidden pig's meat but it has permitted the brain of the fish "shibutta" which has the same taste as pig's meat.

Researchers are fairly certain that the shibutta is the freshwater fish known as the shabout (scientific name: Arabibarbus grypus) which is found in the Tigris-Euphrates basin, namely the area around Iraq, Iran and Turkey.[44] According to the Gemara, it is the brain, and not necessarily the remainder of the fish, which tastes like pork. One could ask a non-Jew who eats pork and fish to taste the brain and answer whether it tastes like pork!

The shibutta was served at the "Mesorah Dinner" in Israel in 5770 (2010). In preparation for this dinner, Rabbi Zivotofsky and Dr. Greenspan journeyed to the Euphrates River in Turkey and inspected the fish. Before the dinner, they ordered 17 kilogrammes of shibutta and had it sent to Israel where it was stored in a neighbor's freezer until the dinner.[45]

The reason that it is forbidden to eat a pig is that although it has a cloven hoof, it does not chew the cud.[46] However, maybe one could find in the world a member of the pig family which does chew the cud? Since the Torah lists only ten animals that are kosher,[47] such a pig would have to be one of these ten kosher animals. This is possible since there are differences of opinion in identifying some of these ten animals.[48]

There are a number of species of the pig family, one of them being the babirusa pig, a pig which is found in Indonesia.[49] In the autumn of 1984, an article published in "Horizons" a publication of the US Agency for International Development stated that the babirusa pig had a stomach similar to that of a ruminant, namely that it had two stomachs and was thus an animal that chewed the cud.[50] This led to speculation that a kosher pig had been found![51] At the time there was only one such babirusa pig in the entire United States and it was in the Los Angeles Zoo. The zoo's director commented, "It has a modified stomach shaped like an hourglass but it does not have two stomachs and it does not chew the cud." Thus as with other species of pigs, this one was also not kosher![52]

Rabbi Bleich writes that if indeed the babirusa was kosher, the Gemara would have given this as the alternative to the pig rather than the brain of the shibutta.[53] Although all kinds of pig are not kosher today, the future will be different as Rabbi Chaim ben Attar asks, "Why is the pig called 'chazir'?" and he answers because one day it will return ("chazor") to become permitted to eat.[54] Dr. Moshe Tendler has said that if the babirusa pig is found to be kosher "I'll serve it at my daughter's wedding."[55]

Bon Appétit

One of the mitzvot of Purim is to send a fellow Jew two items of food or drink.[56] Almost all manner of foods and drink are permitted to fulfil this mitzvah. Some even permit sending a raw item which requires cooking by the recipient.[57] It seems that cloned pig meat (preferably cooked) would be permitted as one of these two items for mishloach manot!

Chapter 3
Kreplach filled with minced Swans' meat for Hoshana Rabba

―――――――――・((◍))・――――――――

General Knowledge

The Mute Swan (scientific name: Cygnus olor) is a member of the duck and geese families. Both "Cygnus" and "olor" are the Latin for "swan." This species of swans is called "mute" since it is less vocal than other swans, although it does make a variety of grunting, hoarse whistling and snorting noises and can also hiss at intruders trying to enter its territory. It grows to a height of up to 170 centimetres and it has a long neck. Its color is wholly white with an orange beak bordered in black. Swans migrate in diagonal formation or V-formation at great heights and no other waterfowl moves as fast on the water or in the air. They nest on large mounds which they build with waterside vegetation in shallow water on islands in the middle or at the very edge of a lake. They can live for 20 years in the wild and 50 years or more in captivity. The swan is one of the heaviest flying birds and has very powerful wings – but the statement that they are powerful enough to break a man's limbs has been variously claimed to be a fact or just a wives' tale!

Halachic Discussion

Is a swan a kosher bird? Unlike animals, fish and locusts, the Torah does not give a list of bodily characteristics to distinguish permitted and non-permitted birds, but just gives a list of birds which are forbidden.[58] Since it is difficult to identify the birds on this list, only birds for which there is a tradition to eat are permitted.[59] However, different communities have different traditions.

To determine whether there is a tradition for a particular species of bird to be kosher, one has to first study various physical features and actions of the bird. To this end, the Gemara[60] gives various signs, one of them being that the bird is not a bird of prey, which in Hebrew is "dores." There are a number of different opinions amongst the Rishonim[61] to explain what is meant by "dores," one of them being that it eats its prey whilst it is still alive, and this is the view of Rabbeinu Tam.[62]

What is the situation with the swan? Does it "dores"? On this question, Rabbi Yisrael Bruna, a German Rabbi and Posek (one who rules on Jewish Law) who lived in the fifteenth century, writes that he had heard secondhand that someone had seen a swan eating young birds alive and thus, according to the opinion of Rabbeinu Tam, it would be non-kosher. Either he did not accept the view of Rabbeinu Tam, or he did not regard secondhand information as reliable, since he then continued that it is obvious that all over the world, the swan is a kosher bird.[63] On his commentary on the Shulchan Aruch, entitled Darkei Teshuvah, written in the latter part of the 19th century, Rabbi Zvi Hirsch Shapira, the Muncatch Rebbe, quotes Rabbi Bruna, thus reiterating that the swan is a kosher bird.[64]

There is further evidence from a shochet named D. Yaluz, from Tiberius, who testified that in Russia he did shechitah on the swan.[65] Dr. Levinger concurs with the view that the swan is a kosher bird.[66]

In contrast, Rabbi Moshe Hanoch Berstein, who was a leading Shochet in London towards the beginning of the twentieth century, identified the swan as the "tinshemet" which is one of the forbidden birds listed in the Torah.[67] Dr. Yisrael Meir Levinger was a bit puzzled at Rabbi Berstein's identification.[68] However, the confusion could have arisen by virtue of the fact that for nearly two thousand years "tinshemet" was incorrectly translated as "swan." This seems to have begun with the Septuagint (the translation of the Torah into Greek) who translates tinshemet in both the books of Vayikra and Devarim as kyknos (in Greek letters) which in English is swan.[69] The Vulgate (translation of the Bible into Latin) similarly made such a translation, namely, cycnum,[70] and later translators obviously used these texts to translate the word tinshemet.

There is unfortunately a technical problem when researching this subject. The translators mix up the order of the names of these forbidden birds and furthermore they are sometimes moved to a different verse. It is therefore in some cases almost impossible to know which forbidden bird they are translating as swan.[71]

At the beginning of the 17th century, the British King James arranged for a team of 47 scholars to make a new translation of the Bible. The team utilised the Septuagint and Vulgate in their work. The Bible is known as the King James' Version or the Authorised Version.[72] In their translation, in the lists of non-Kosher birds in both Vayikra and Devarim, the swan appears as a non-kosher bird.[73]

However, the King James' Version was not the first English translation. There had been previous translations of the Bible into English, the first being by John Wycliffe in the 14th century. Since this was prior to the era of printing, books were then handwritten. He made a literal translation from the Vulgate and thus, as to be expected, he used the word "swan" in both lists of non-Kosher birds.[74]

In 1569 the Bishops' Bible was published. Strangely enough swan is mentioned in just one of these lists – in Devarim but not in Vayikra![75] Another translator from the 16th century was William Tyndale who was the first to translate from the original Hebrew. He did not write swan in either of the two Torah lists of non-kosher birds. His life was terminated by his execution![76] A number of subsequent translators wrote "swan" in their translations.[77]

Isaac Leeser published his translation in 5614 (1854) and used the word "swan" in both Vayikra and Devarim. However, he added a footnote: "Although this word [swan] has been left unchanged from the English version, it is not probable that the rendering 'swan' is correct."[78]

Many, (but not all [79]), of the later translations do not use the word swan.[80] In the various translations throughout the ages the word "tinshemet" has received a number of translations. They are: swan, horned owl, waterhen, lechuza blanca (Spanish for white owl), backe (meaning is unclear[81]), cycnum (Latin for swan), kyknos (Greek for swan).[82]

How could such an error of translating tinshemet as swan, which persisted for nearly two thousand years, have occurred? Dr. Yisrael Meir Levinger suggests that since the name of the bird called the stork is Cleonia, and it is similar to the name of the swan which is Cygnus, it was easy for there to have been a mix-up.[83]

Whether or not this is the reason for classing the swan as a non-kosher bird, there are kashrut organizations who specifically do so. An example is Badatz Igud Rabbonim KIR, which is one of the largest Kosher Certification organizations in Europe today.[84]

There are several species of swans. The species which Dr. Levinger states is kosher is the Mute Swan (Cygnus olor). However, he adds that it is doubtful if one can include within the tradition for a swan to be kosher, other species, such as the black swan.[85]

A person in England would have a problem if they wanted to do shechitah on a swan! They are the property of the Queen of England and since the late fifteenth century in partnership with the Vintners' Company and the Dyers' Company![86]

Bon Appétit

There are three occasions in the year when it is customary to eat kreplach, often filled with meat, for example the meat of swans. The reason is that there is some form of banging on these three days. One of them is Hoshana Rabba when one beats the aravot (willows).[87]

Chapter 4
Gefilte Turbot for Shabbat dinner

General Knowledge

The turbot (scientific name: Rhombus maximus or Scophthalmus maximus or Psetta maximus) is a large European flounder. [There are other species of turbot which are undoubtedly kosher, but this account is limited to the European turbot, which is the only one which has come under great scrutiny!] It is a flat-fish with both eyes on the left-hand side of the head. It can reach a maximum length of about one metre, has a very wide body, and a weight of about 25 kilogrammes. Its color varies with the surroundings but is usually grey brown or light brown with darker markings. It has bright white flesh that retains this appearance when cooked. Turbots are to be found in the North Atlantic, the Baltic Sea and the Mediterranean Sea. It is carnivorous and the adult turbots live mainly on fish. Spawning takes place in the Atlantic during the summer months, and in the spring in the Mediterranean. Its eggs are small and very numerous, varying from five to ten million. It has been a popular fish since the times of the Roman Empire, namely, two thousand years ago. Today it remains among the elite seafood of Master Chefs everywhere. Its production used to be limited to the European area but now turbot farming has been developed in China.

Halachic Discussion

Is the turbot a kosher fish? The Torah gives two distinguishing signs for a fish to be kosher. These are that it must have both fins and scales.[88] Almost all fish have scales. However, the books on zoology state that the turbot is scaleless, but its body is covered with conical bony tubercles.[89]

Despite this, turbot was eaten by Jews in many locations in Europe over many centuries. The cause of the confusion could have arisen since the turbot closely resembles a halibut or plaice which are kosher fish. All these fish are black on one side and white on the other, the difference being that the left side of the turbot is black whilst the right side of the kosher species is black. The question is what is the right side and what is the left side of a fish?! Rabbi David Feldman gives a simple method to ascertain this, namely by holding the fish in a certain way.[90]

It has been suggested that the dispute on whether the turbot is a kosher fish goes back about 900 years. A number of the Rishonim permitted a fish called Barba (Barbuta) whilst Rabbi Yehudah Hachasid and Rabbi Yechiel from Paris were careful not to eat it.[91] Possibly the fish under question was the turbot. Another possibility was that they were in fact referring to two different fish.[92]

However, what is known, is that in 5498/1738 two emissaries came to England and there publicly ate turbot saying that it was eaten in Venice.[93] Following this incident, there were Rabbinical discussions on the matter, by amongst others the Chief Rabbi of the Ashkenazic community of Amsterdam, Rabbi Aryeh Leib Lowenstam, who concluded that there was an uncertainty as to whether the turbot was the same fish that had been permitted in Venice, and therefore he refused to sanction the turbot as a kosher fish.[94]

Despite this, a pocket calendar published in Amsterdam in 1706-1707 and in 1725-1727 recommended the eating of turbot during two of the winter months. This calendar was published with the approbation of the Chief Rabbis of that city. It has been suggested that they did not check this part of the calendar![95]

In some locations in Europe, namely in Holland[96] and in Hamburg,[97] turbot was eaten. In the Hague it was eaten until the Second World War.[98] However, in Altona (a borough of Hamburg) it was not eaten.[99] (It has been suggested that this was as a result of the dispute at the time of Rabbeinu Tam.) There is also written signed evidence from the 18th or 19th century that the turbot was eaten by Jews in London, in Eastern countries and especially Constantinople, in Venice, and in a further unidentified place.[100]

Rabbi Lowenstam's son, Rabbi Zevi Hirsch, who was the Chief Rabbi of the Great Synagogue in London, ruled (or according to other sources, he was in favor but did go as far as to actually approve[101]) that the turbot was a kosher fish.[102]

Rabbi Hirsch's son, Rabbi Solomon Hirschell, was between the years 1802-1842, Chief Rabbi of the Great Synagogue in London. In 5582/1822, before Rosh Hashanah he received an enquiry from the north of England on whether the turbot was kosher and he answered in the affirmative. This decision was widely relied upon in England during the following 132 years.[103]

At about the same time as Rabbi Hirschell ruled permissively on the turbot, Rabbi Yisrael Lipshitz, in his commentary on the Mishnah entitled "Tiferet Yisrael" specifically wrote that the fish Steinbutten (turbot) does not have the scales required for a kosher fish.[104]

In a list of kosher fish brought out by the Berlin Center for Shechitah on erev Pesach 1937 and signed by Rabbi Munk, turbot appeared as a kosher fish. This entry was followed by "siehe [see] Steinbutt."[105] The entry for Steinbutt has a bracket around it (although the entry for Turbot did not) and on this Dr. Levinger suggests that maybe Rabbi Munk had some doubt about it.[106]

Likewise, in a list of kosher fish compiled by the London Beth Din in 5703/1943, and published in the London *Jewish Chronicle*, turbot was included.[107] However, following some scientific enquiries about the turbot, it did not appear in their list of kosher fish of 5709/1949, but still a large proportion of the Jewish population did not pay attention to this change and continued to eat the turbot.[108]

It was in October 1954 that the Anglo-Jewish Association had a dinner under the supervision of the London Kashrus Commission. Listed in the menu was *le turbot poché*. It is no exaggeration to say that this did not pass over quietly! The Chief Rabbi, Sir Israel Brodie, was present at this dinner, and he left his place at the head table to question the kashrut supervisor. It was claimed that it was a different variety of turbot which was kosher. It is reported that most of the diners ate the turbot![109]

Two weeks later there appeared in *The Jewish Chronicle* a statement by the London Beth Din pointing out that in 1949 they had made some enquiries with the Zoological Society of London regarding the anatomy of the turbot and, it was their duty to inform the public that "the turbot is not to be included in the list of kasher fish."[110]

As a result of this incident, a further enquiry was made to experts regarding the anatomy of the turbot. It was the clerk of the London Beth Din who, on 29 November 1954, wrote to the Museum of Natural History asking whether the turbot had scales. The reply sent on 8 December 1954, was that it has "small tubercles of bone scattered over its skin" adding that whether or not these were scales is a "theological matter."[111] As can be seen, this occurred after the Beth Din had publicised their ruling on 12 November 1954.

It was in 1951 that Rabbi David Feldman, the head of the Bet Din of the Machazikei Hadas of Manchester England, published his book "Shimusha shel Torah." In it he discusses the turbot. He writes that he has heard from various places that it is eaten and he does not know on what those who eat it rely on, since the books on zoology state that it has not got scales. He added that this fish is commonly found in these countries (names not given) and a lot of religious people transgress and eat it due to their lack of knowledge. He therefore published this fact in order to make it known to these people.[112]

What is the situation regarding turbot on the lists of kosher and non-kosher fish brought out at this period? The list of kosher fish prepared by Dr. James Atz, an authority in Ichthyology, and at a later date this list was brought out by the Orthodox Union (OU) Kosher Consumer Directory, includes a long list of kosher flounders followed by in heavy print: "But not including European turbot (Scophthalmus maximus or Psetta maximus)."[113] The list prepared by Dr. Moshe Tendler gives at the end "Common non-kosher 'sea foods' sold in the United States." However, turbot does not appear in this list.[114] Maybe the reason is that it was not "a common sea food sold there." In the lists of kosher fish brought out by the London and Paris Batei Din, turbot does not appear, (they did not include a list of non-kosher fish).[115] However a list brought out by the Paris Bet Din in the early 1960s did include turbot.[116]

Bon Appétit

One of the 39 forbidden works on Shabbat is "borer" separating.[117] Included in this is removing the bones from fish. Often fish are full of bones making it difficult to eat the fish in a permitted manner. It was for this reason that Jews eat gefilte fish on Shabbat, since the bones were removed prior to Shabbat whilst the gefilte turbot was in the process of being made.[118]

Chapter 5
Fried Locusts with yoghurt

General Knowledge

The desert locust (scientific name: Schistocerca gregaria) is a winged short-horned insect with long back legs. When fully grown it has a length of nearly 7 centimetres. The female locust lays eggs in an egg pod, about 3-4 centimetres in length, primarily in sandy soils, the pod containing about 100 eggs. She lays eggs at least three times during her lifetime, her total lifetime being three to five months. The locust develops in three stages. The first is the egg which after it hatches is known as a hopper. The skin of the hopper molts five times until it becomes an immature adult whose color is usually pink. Two to five generations of locusts are born annually. They are to be found mainly in the Middle East, Africa and Asia. Locusts are migratory and can travel about 100 kilometres a day, the direction often depending on the wind. These desert locusts have two phases, the solitary phase and the gregarious phase. In the former they live alone and are harmless. However, in the gregarious phase, they do not travel as individuals, but as a "cloud" of at least millions, if not more, of locusts. Billions and even twelve trillion have been known to arrive in a cloud stretching over a very large area. The locusts are not friendly visitors but they are able in a very, very short period of time to consume all the vegetation which leads to a famine in the area. A single locust can eat its weight in vegetation in a single day. Between March to October 1915, there was a plague of locusts in Eretz Israel. They consumed almost all the vegetation which seriously depleted the food supply in the area. There are photographs of a tree just before the locusts arrived and after they had stripped bare the foliage on the tree. One of the ten plagues in Egypt was these locusts and indeed as history has shown it is a serious plague.

Halachic Discussion

Are locusts kosher? The Torah forbids the eating of all insects with the exception of four named species of locusts. The Torah[119] and the Mishna[120] give various anatomical signs to help identify these locusts. However, today the identity of only one of these four locusts is known. It is the locust referred to in the Torah as the "arbe" whose scientific name is Schistocerca gregaria.[121]

Over the course of time, due to expulsions and migrations of Jews and the local availability of locusts, some countries have completely forgotten how to recognise these locusts, others have partially forgotten, whilst yet others have retained the oral traditions they had held for generations.

Spain: From the writings of the Rishonim we can see that about 800 years ago there was a tradition in some areas, but not all, of Spain to eat locusts.[122]

North Africa: Following the Inquisition in Spain, many of its Jews moved to North Africa and took with them the tradition of eating locusts. This tradition reached areas of Libya, Tunisia, Algeria and Morocco.[123] It was about 300 years ago that Rabbi Haim Ben-Atar, who lived in Morocco, came out in a very long statement in his commentary "Pri Toar" on the Shulchan Aruch, against the eating of locusts.[124] As a result, some Jews in North Africa stopped eating them. It should be mentioned that many Rabbinical authorities strongly opposed the ruling of Rabbi Ben-Atar and continued the tradition of eating locusts openly and publicly.[125] Included amongst those who opposed Rabbi Ben-Atar's opinion was Rabbi Ptachyah Birdogo, who was a prominent Rabbi in North Africa towards the end of the 18th century. He wrote a long responsum in strong language refuting Rabbi Ben-Atar's opinion point by point.[126]

Yemen: The tradition of eating locusts was accepted by all factions of Yemenite Jewry. They were experts in identifying the kosher types of locusts. In fact, they were happy when swarms of locusts arrived, despite the damage they would cause to the surroundings.[127] This tradition continued with the mass Aliyah of the Yemenite Jews to Israel in 1949, and there are a large number of accounts of this tradition by the Yemenite Jews.[128]

Europe: Since locusts are not to be found in Europe, the traditions to eat locusts was not found amongst Ashkenazi Jews and hence in modern times the reservations of the Ashkenazi Poskim to certify locusts as kosher. The Aruch Hashulchan even wrote that he had not even heard of a place who ate locusts.[129] However, the Poskim did not actually forbid them.[130]

The question is whether Jews whose direct ancestors did not have a tradition to eat locusts are allowed to eat them today? This question has been written about by many Poskim. Rabbi Yitzchak Ratzabi, a famous Yemenite Rabbi, the Av Bet Din of "Peulat Tzedek" wrote a long responsum on the subject and in it he ruled that all Jews may eat these locusts.[131] Other prominent Yemenite Rabbis, Rabbi Yosef Kafih (Kapach) and Rabbi Shlomo Korach have concurred with this ruling.[132] Amongst the Ashkenazi Rabbis there are differences of opinion on this question, with Rabbi Pinchas Scheinberg permitting Ashkenazi Jews to eat them.[133] However, various major kashrut authorities, such as OU, OK and StarK in the United States will not allow locusts under in their supervised functions.[134] Therefore, in the "Mesorah Dinners" organised by Rabbi Zivotofsky and others in the United States, the supervising body did not permit locusts on the menu. There was a substitute – chocolate in the shape of locusts![135] The dinners in Israel did have real locusts and it was reported that they were popular![136]

If one goes to a place where the tradition is to eat locusts, even if it is one's custom not to do so, one may partake of them.[137]

It is reported that locusts taste like "something between chicken schnitzel, toasted sunflower seeds and prawns.[138] Many recipes have been written for Jews which have locusts included in its ingredients.[139]

One can now purchase kosher locusts at the Biblical Museum of Natural History at a price of NIS 25 per locust,[140] but this is only individual locusts. What about the sale of kosher locusts on a large scale? It was in the summer of 5778 (2018) that Rabbi Ratzabi went with his Bet Din to visit Moshav Elifelet in Upper

Galilee, where in 2014, three men set up Hargol Foodtech, a company where they breed locusts. It is reported that this Moshav is keen in receiving the hechsher of Rabbi Ratzabi's Bet Din for their locusts, and this was the reason for their visit.[141]

From where did Rabbi Zivotofsky get the large quantity of locusts for the "Mesorah Dinner" in Jerusalem? They were at first ordered from a man who grows them for research on the roof of a girls' seminary in Jerusalem, (the girls don't know this!). However, due to the hot weather, all the juvenile locusts died. Following some research online, a company in London was found who grew them for zoos and research and sold them in packets of ten or a money saving pack of fifty. Two hundred and fifty were purchased and someone brought them by airplane to Israel.[142]

Just like fish, locust do not require shechitah[143] (but they may not be eaten whilst still alive[144]), a physical defect cannot make them treife, their blood[145] and cheilev is permitted and they are parva.[146] Even though it is written that there is a Sephardic custom not to eat fish with milk,[147] this does not apply to locusts.[148]

Bon Appétit

The berachah recited before eating locusts is shehakol.[149] Since locusts are parva and may be eaten with milk, there is no problem in picking up a locust with one's hand or with a fork and before eating it dipping it into a pot of yoghurt. Before dipping something with one's hands, into the "seven liquids," one of which is milk, one has to wash one's hands.[150] and this would thus be required when dipping a food, such as locusts, into yoghurt.[151]

Chapter 6
Giraffe's giblets as hors d'oeuvre for Yom Tov meal

General Knowledge

The giraffe (scientific name: Giraffa camelopardalis) is a long-necked mammal with long legs, the front pair being longer than the back pair. It has two short horns which are covered with skin and hair. The giraffe is the tallest of all land animals, which in a male giraffe may exceed five and a half metres which is reached after about four years. The males can weigh up to nearly two thousand kilogrammes. The giraffe has a coat pattern of irregular brown patches on a light background. They have an excellent eyesight and can see a lion, one of their predators, who is about one kilometre away. The giraffe has an enormous appetite and a large male consumes about 65 kilogrammes of food every day. The female giraffe can become pregnant after four or five years, and pregnancy lasts for about 15 months. Invariably, just one baby giraffe is born, and at birth its height is about 2 metres and its weight about 100 kilogrammes. It suckles from its mother until about 18-22 months. A giraffe can live up to about 26 years. They are to be found in East Africa south of the Sahara Desert.

Halachic Discussion

Is the giraffe a kosher animal? The Torah gives a list of 10 animals which are kosher.[152] All these animals have two identifying signs, namely chew the cud and have a cloven hoof. There is also a dispute between the poskim on whether, like in the case of birds, there has to be a tradition in order to eat these animals. There are some Ashkenazim, followers of the Chazon Ish,[153] who hold that there needs to be such a tradition.

The last animal in this list is the zemer and there is a dispute as to its identity. Both Rashi[154] and Ibn Ezra[155] cannot give a definitive answer on the identity of the zemer. However, this is not the case in the various Targumim of the Torah. According to Targum Onkelos[156] it is a "ditza" (some sort of wild goat) and in Targum Yonatan ben Uziel[157] a similar word, "ditzin," is used.

In contrast, the Septuagint[158] translates zemer as "camelopardalis" (in Greek letters); in earlier days they believed that a giraffe was a cross-bread between a camel and a pardalia (the Greek word for leopard) and they thus called a giraffe by this name. The Vulgate[159] also gives the same translation as the Septuagint for the zemer.

At a slightly later period, in his translation of the Torah known as the "Tafsid," Rabbi Sa'adia Gaon[160] translates zemer as "giraffa." Some other Rishonim, namely, Rabbi Yona ibn Ganach (also known as Abulwal d Merwan ibn Ganach),[161] Rabbi David Kimchi (the RaDak)[162] and Rabbi Shimon ben Tzemach Duran (the Rashbatz)[163] also refer to the zemer as a giraffe. A number of Acharonim likewise translate zemer as giraffe. These include Rabbi Yehosef Schwartz (who also adds that in the translation into Persian, zemer is translated as giraffe),[164] Rabbi Yitzchak Ratzabi[165] and Rabbi Yosef Kafih (Kapach).[166] However, when asked about the kashrut of giraffe, Rabbi David Lau the Chief Rabbi of Israel, answered that there was a dispute about it.[167] The Chazon Ish would probably have forbidden it, since there was no tradition amongst the Ashkenazim to eat a giraffe.[168]

A giraffe both chews the cud and has a cloven hoof. The Rambam[169] writes that the only animals in the world which have both these signs are the ten given in the Torah, thus confirming that the giraffe is the zemer. However, there are some who question whether the giraffe has the cloven hoof as required by the Torah. There is a thin layer of spongy tissue beneath the toes which attaches them together. For this reason, the camel, even though one could say its hooves are cloven, is regarded as non-Kosher. However, this tissue in the giraffe is thinner than in the case of the camel.[170]

A point made against identifying the giraffe as the zemer is that archeological evidence shows that at the time of the Bible there were no giraffes in the Middle East. Others however dispute this and have recently found evidence that there were giraffes in Egypt at the time of Moshe Rabbeinu.[171] One could ask, that even if there were no giraffes in the Middle East in Biblical times, why should their absence at a certain period prevent it from being a kosher animal!

An additional point in favor of the giraffe being a kosher animal comes from its milk. Only the milk of kosher animals can be curded. To investigate giraffe milk, in the year 5768 (2008), a group led by Professor Zohar Amar went to the Safari Park in Ramat Gan and took a routine sample of milk from a giraffe. It was examined at Bar-Ilan University and it was found that it curded in the way required by halachah. Rabbi Shlomo Mahpoud, who it seems actually accompanied this group to the Safari Park, then ruled, "The giraffe has all the signs of a ritually pure animal, and the milk forms curds which strengthen that view."[172]

A point continually made to try and prove that the giraffe is not kosher is that with such a long neck the shochet will not know where to cut! The contrary is true! With a small bird the shochet has a very limited place, just a few centimetres, in which to cut; with a giraffe it could be a span of two metres![173]

There are however a number of technical problems in obtaining a giraffe to shecht. In many countries a giraffe is a protected animal and cannot be killed for the fear that the animal might go into extinction.[174] However, in some African countries it is neither an endangered nor a protected species.[175] Even if one could obtain legally a giraffe to shecht, the shochet would require a ladder to perform the shechitah.[176] The giraffe is a very strong animal and with a kick can even kill a lion[177] - the shochet would surely not want this fate! Furthermore, the price of purchasing a giraffe is enormous - $25,000 has been asked.[178] Should after inspecting the lungs of the giraffe after shechitah, it would be found to be treife, unlike with a cow or sheep, there would be no market to sell the carcass resulting in an enormous financial loss.[179]

Despite all this, there have been rare cases of doing shechitah on a giraffe. One of these were at the Jerusalem Biblical Zoo.

The giraffe was old and would soon have died. It was therefore shechted, the lungs inspected where it was found to be kosher, and the meat was then sold as a fundraiser.[180] In 5767 (2007), it was planned to get a young giraffe for a "Mesorah Dinner," but it did not work out[181] and Rabbi Zivotofsky said that it would have to wait for the next "Mesorah Dinner."[182]

The giraffe appears on the OU list of kosher game animals,[183] and thus unlike locusts, one could serve giraffe meat at a "Mesorah Dinner" held in America.

Can one in fact go to a restaurant and order giraffe meat? The answer is positive, but they are non-Jewish restaurants, where the giraffe was killed by a method other than shechitah, possibly by a big game hunter with a high-powered rifle.[184] A restaurant in Killington Vermont in the United States, which opened about 1994, had on its menu giraffe meat. In 1997 the newspaper the "Boston Phoenix," described it as "a red meat that was served very rare, which made it extra tender. It had a melt-in-your-mouth quality." Others however claim that there is a lack of taste in giraffe meat.[185] There is also a restaurant in Johannesburg which serves giraffe meat.[186]

Bon Appétit

On an ordinary weekday one's main meal would begin with the main course or sometimes, a soup would precede it. On Yom Tov, however, to keep the mitzvah of rejoicing on a Festival one would have a more elaborate meal[187] and possibly start the meal with additional course, an hors d'oeuvre, such as giraffe giblets.

Chapter 7
Bees' Royal Jelly prior to a meal

General Knowledge

Honey Bees are winged insects. They average about one and a half centimetres in length and are light brown in color. They are usually oval shaped creatures with golden yellow colours and brown bands. The body of a honey bee is segmented into: a stinger (used as a defensive weapon and for the receiver is painful, acidic but usually harmless), legs, antenna, three segments of thorax and six visible segments of abdomen. In the wild, bees' hives are often located in the holes of trees and on rock crevices. The members of the hives are divided into three types. The "boss" of the hive is the Queen who runs the whole hive and is the largest in size of all the bees in the hive. She lays the eggs which will produce the next generation of bees. The next group are the Workers. They are all female and their job is to forage for pollen and nectar from flowers. They also have to build, protect and clean the hive, and these are the only bees seen flying outside the hive. The last group are the Drones. They are all males and their function is to mate with the Queen who can lay 2,500 eggs a day. There are several hundred in each hive during the spring and the summer. When the winter comes, the drones are kicked out the hive! Royal Jelly is a glandular secretion from the worker bees. It is an extremely nutritious thick milky white creamy substance. The bees produce this as food for the developing larva and as the unique diet for the Queen bee. Should the Queen bee die, then one of the worker bees would be fed with a large quantity of Royal Jelly to make her into a new Queen bee. All the other post-larval bees in the hive are not fed this royal jelly. Without this royal jelly, the Queen bee would fail to develop properly and this food accounts for their large size and longevity which can be as long as seven years compared with just seven weeks for the worker bees. Royal jelly is rich in protein and vitamins as well as in fatty and amino acids. It thus has a number of health benefits for humans. These include increasing of the life span, strengthening and stimulating the immune system, helping healing wounds, decreasing pain and increasing appetite. It has thus become a popular dish for humans to eat.

Halachic Discussion

Is Royal Jelly kosher? Things which come from non-kosher species such as camel milk[188] or ostrich eggs[189] are non-kosher. It could thus well be that since Royal Jelly is a secretion from a non-kosher insect, namely a bee, it could well be non-kosher.

To be able to investigate whether bees' Royal Jelly is kosher, one first has to understand why bees' honey is kosher, even though it comes from a non-kosher insect. The method of production of bees' honey is as follows: Worker bees suck nectar from flowers with their proboscis (mouth). The nectar mixes with saliva and is swallowed into the honey sac where enzymes from the saliva break down the nectar into honey. It should be noted that the nectar is never digested but just transformed into honey by the saliva.[190]

The bees do not mass produce honey. It takes up to two million flowers and 556 bees to make about half a kilogramme of honey, and a hive of bees have to fly the equivalent of twice around the world gathering nectar for such a half a kilogramme! Despite all her hard work, the average worker bee only makes one twelfth of a teaspoon in her lifetime![191]

The question that must be asked is that since honey is coming from a non-kosher insect, why is it kosher? The Gemara[192] gives two reasons. The first is that the bees do not secrete honey from their bodies, but only convert the collected nectar into honey. The other reason given is that one can learn from a verse in the Torah that specifically bees' honey is permitted. Were it just for the first reason, then honey of other insects, such as wasps, would also be kosher, which according to the majority of opinions it is not.

Honey is not the only product produced by bees. There are indeed many products, amongst them is Royal Jelly. The question is whether it can be compared with honey and thus be classed as kosher.

Some poskim argue that unlike honey, Royal Jelly is a glandular secretion and therefore forbidden as something coming from a non-kosher species. On the other hand, there are some who argue that it is honey-like and should therefore be included by virtue of the verse in the Torah which permits bees' honey. Another argument in favor of permitting it, is that it is very bitter and not fit for human consumption, although this has been challenged by those who say that admittedly it is bitter, but is by no means inedible in the raw state. A further argument in favor is that it is not a "food" such as an egg from a non-kosher bird and is therefore not forbidden.[193]

The health benefits of eating Royal Jelly very likely led to many of the contemporary poskim discussing whether or not it is kosher. In the course of their discussions they carefully analysed the wording of the subject in the Talmud and in the Rishonim. Several of them, including Rabbi Eliezer Waldenburg[194] and Rabbi Moshe Shternbuch[195] permit it for a sick person. Rabbi Isser Unterman,[196] a former Chief Rabbi of Israel would permit it even for a healthy person, but added especially for a sick person. It is suggested that from Rabbi Moshe Feinstein's[197] ruling that shellac is kosher, one could derive that he would permit Royal Jelly. Another posek who permitted it was Rabbi Padwa,[198] Rosh Beis Din of the British Orthodox Union.

On the other hand, there were a number of authorities who questioned the permissibility of eating Royal Jelly. One of them was Rabbi Shlomo Zalman Auerbach[199] who was inclined to forbid it, except in cases of great need. Rabbi Moshe Via[200] wrote that one should be strict and not eat it, but in the case of medical necessity a posek should be asked.

As can be seen, several of the poskim who specifically permitted the eating of Royal Jelly for sick people, did so because of the many health benefits, even for those who were not seriously ill.

Despite all the poskim who did not rule that it was not kosher, many of the kashrus authorities in the United States stated that it was not kosher or they did not give their hechsher for it. These include the OU,[201] Star K,[202] and Kof-K.[203] On the other hand, Triangle K[204] and KSI Kosher Supervision in Germany[205] gave their hechsher on Royal Jelly products.

In addition to honey and Royal Jelly, there are other products originating from bees. According to Star K, Propolis, Bee Pollen and Beeswax are kosher since they are not secretions of the bees. On the other hand, Bee Venom which is secreted in the venom glands of the bees, is ruled by them as non-kosher.[206]

Bon Appétit

A person has eaten something and then decides he wants to wash and eat bread. The question is does he have to recite an after berachah on what he has already eaten before washing and saying the berachah over the bread, or will birchat hamazon at the end of his meal cover also what he has eaten before eating the bread. As a general rule, he has to say an after berachah on the food he has eaten before eating the bread. However, there are some exceptions. One is eating something such a shmaltz herring which will give him an appetite for his subsequent meal.[207] One of Royal Jelly's benefits is to give a person an appetite to eat and therefore no after berachah would be required before eating the bread.

Chapter 8
Nightingale schnitzels for Chol Hamoed

General Knowledge

The nightingale (scientific name: Luscinia megarhynchos) is famous for its singing, which is done by the male bird (the only male bird that sings), and its song is regarded as one of the most beautiful sounds in nature. Nearly 200 years ago, groups of people would go outside to listen to the nightingales singing. Indeed, the old English word for nightingale is "nihtgale" which means "singer of the night." The nightingale's length is about 15 centimetres, its wingspan 24 centimetres and its weight is about 21 grammes. Its color is plain brown except for its reddish tail. It is larger than a robin with which it can be confused, especially when they are both young. The nightingale is a secretive bird who likes nothing better than hiding in the middle of an impenetrable bush, and it is therefore hard to see the singing males. It builds its nests in bushes close to the ground. It is a migratory bird which, in its southward journey from Europe, passes over Israel in the autumn, and it returns by the same route during the following spring. Although the nightingale can be seen flying in the sky in different areas of Israel, it would seem not to be a regular occurrence, since one is asked on the internet to report sightings of nightingales together with the date and location.

Halachic Discussion

Is the nightingale a kosher bird? The Torah does not give physical signs for a bird to be kosher or non-kosher. However, the Gemara[208] gives a number of signs for a bird to be kosher, one of them being that a bird does not prey. What is the situation with the nightingale? Does it prey on other living creatures? The diet of a nightingale consists largely of insects, beetles and ants, and

281

failing that caterpillars, spiders and earthworms, and on rare occasions moths and small butterflies.[209] From this it can be seen that the nightingale does prey on other living creatures. The question is whether preying on these creatures makes a bird non-kosher? One can bring a proof from a chicken which is according to all opinions a kosher bird. Like a nightingale, a chicken preys on insects. From this we can see that this eating of insects does not make a nightingale non-kosher. The following story clearly illustrates that the nightingale is not a predatory bird.

It was towards the beginning of the 14th century that Rabbi Kalonymus ben Kalonymus ben Meir translated into Hebrew a story which had been written by an Islamic sect in Arabic several hundred years earlier.[210]

In this story, a group of men were shipwrecked on an island with no human habitation. There were, however, a whole variety of animal species on this island and the shipwrecked men made these animals their slaves. The animals strongly objected and demanded a trial be held between them and the men. The judge in this case was the Spirit King. The animals were divided into six groups and each group appointed a representative to deliver their case before the judge. One of these groups was the non-predatory birds. As specifically stated in this story, they appointed the nightingale, a non-predatory bird, to present their case.[211] As stated above, one of the major factors to determine that a bird is kosher is that it is non-predatory.[212]

Dr. Levinger writes that the nightingale is a kosher bird quoting as the source of his information the book "Zivchei Kohen," a book which includes a summary of the laws of shechitah, of checking the lungs and removing the cheilev from animals. It was written about two hundred years ago by the shochet Rabbi Yitzchak Cohen of Livorno in Italy.[213]

This book includes 30 hand drawn numbered sketches of kosher birds together with the names of these birds in Italian.[214] Number 16 is named "Petti-Rosso consimili al Rosignolo" which in English is "red breasts (robins) similar to nightingales."[215] It should be mentioned that the robin and the nightingale do in fact have a number of physical and behavioral similarities.

The question can be asked is whether Rabbi Cohen is just identifying sketch number 16 as a robin and adding a comment that it is similar to a nightingale, or alternatively is stating that both a robin and a nightingale are kosher birds.

It would seem from the later literature that the second alternative is the case and both these birds are thus kosher. This can be seen from Dr. Levinger's book and paper which give these two birds as kosher utilising sketch number 16.[216]

Another indication comes from Dr. Zohar Amar's book "Masoret ha'Oaf." In it he makes a chart based on the sketches in the book "Zivchei Kohen."[217] The first column gives the names of the birds in Hebrew and for sketch 16 appears the names of both the robin and the nightingale. The second column gives the scientific names in Latin of both these birds; the third column is what appears in the book "Zivchei Kohen." The following columns give the names of the birds which appear in various manuscripts. One of them is the "Rome manuscript" which for sketch 16 gives in Italian the names of both birds, although the other manuscripts only name the robin.

Encyclopedia Judaica which reproduces the sketches by Rabbi Cohen, and underneath them gives the scientific names of the birds together with the English names, (as stated in Dr. Levinger's paper in "Sinai"[218]). For sketch 16, the Encyclopedia Judaica gives robin, but does not give nightingale.[219] Even if one would be of the opinion that sketch 16 is a robin and not a nightingale, this would not necessarily mean that nightingale is a non-kosher bird, since there are numerous kosher birds, an obvious example being chicken, which are not amongst the 30 on this sketch.[220]

Bon Appétit

There is a Torah mitzvah to rejoice on a Festival and this includes Chol Hamoed. One of the ways of rejoicing is eating more elaborate meals than during the year, and especially mentioned is meat (preferably beef) and wine.[221] Thus eating nightingale schnitzels on Chol Hamoed will be one of the methods of rejoicing on a Festival.

Chapter 9

Head of Swordfish for Leil Rosh Hashanah

General Knowledge

The swordfish (scientific name: Xiphias gladius) is characterized by a long sword, which is flat rather than rounded as in other spear-nosed fishes. This sword is about one third the length of the swordfish's body, and it extends from its snout. This sword is not used in a conventional manner, but is used to slash and injure its prey in order to make for an easier catch. It eats a whole variety of fish, the smaller ones being eaten whole. The swordfish is purplish or bluish above and silvery below and grows to a maximum length of about four and a half metres, and a maximum weight of about 500 kilogrammes. The females are larger than the males and they carry many millions of eggs. Swordfish reach maturity between the ages of four and five years, and they live until about nine years. They are found in tropical and temperate parts of the Atlantic, Pacific and Indian oceans and also in the Mediterranean. They are frequently found basking at the surface of the water, airing their first dorsal fin. Due to its popularity in restaurants, the swordfish population is decreasing and steps are being made for its conservation.

Halachic Discussion

Is the swordfish a kosher fish? For a fish to be kosher it must have both fins and scales. The Gemara[222] states that all fish which have scales have fins. Therefore, one has to just look for the scales on a fish for it to be kosher. In some cases, the existence of scales on a fish is not so clear cut and there are different Rabbinical opinions on whether the fish has scales or is scaleless.[223]

The earliest mention of the possible kashrut of a swordfish was nearly 400 years ago, when Rabbi Chaim ben Yisrael Benvenisti, known after his book, as the "Knesset Hagedolah" permitted "the fish with the sword."[224] He then gave its name as "fishei ispada," which is very similar in a number of languages to the name given to swordfish.[225] Someone then questioned him that there were no scales on this swordfish. He answered that when the swordfish came out the water, it shed its scales. (He did not answer that in its juvenile state it had scales.) To prove his point, the Rabbi took a black cloth, put it in his fishing net and after he caught a swordfish showed his questioner that it was full of scales.[226]

On the basis of this ruling of the Knesset Hagedolah, Jews would eat swordfish. One could say that it became a tradition to eat it and there are those who say that tradition to eat a particular fish, as with birds, is a relevant point.[227] There were a number of prominent Acharonim, the Pri Megadim,[228] the Kaf Hachaim[229] and others,[230] who cited the ruling of the Knesset Hagedolah as authoritative and reliable.[231] For at least 350 years, the swordfish was regarded as kosher and eaten by Jews in Mediterranean countries.[232] As can be seen in a list of kosher fish published in 1933 and in 1934 by the Agudat ha-Rabbonim of America and Canada, swordfish is included as a kosher fish.[233]

It was in 1951 that the turnabout began. This was organized by Rabbi Dr. Moshe Tendler, the son-in-law of Rabbi Moshe Feinstein. In a list of "non-Kosher sea food sold in the United States" he included the swordfish.[234] Several years later when Rabbi Isser Unterman, then Chief Rabbi of Tel Aviv (and later Chief Rabbi of Israel) permitted the swordfish, Rabbi Tendler wrote to him[235] and thus began a very public and even acrimonious debate on the subject.[236]

Rabbi Dr. Tendler's argument to forbid swordfish was that it was not the fish referred to by the Knesset Hagedolah. Then followed an exchange of correspondence between him and Rabbi Unterman, the latter maintaining that it indeed was the swordfish which was given in the ruling by the Knesset Hagedolah.[237]

Other prominent Rabbis joined in the debate, which included articles in the journals "Hamaor" and "Hapardes," generally, but not all, agreeing with Dr. Tendler that the fish referred to by the Knesset Hagedolah was not the swordfish.[238]

It was at this period that volume 7 of the "Encyclopedia Talmudit" was published. Included in this volume was an entry on dagim - fish. Photographs of 12 fish were shown with the comments of whether they were kosher or non-kosher. Included amongst them was the swordfish (and two other fish) where the comment whether or not they were kosher was omitted![239]

Also, at this period, the Conservative movement in the United States entered the picture declaring that the swordfish was kosher, bringing as support a noted ichthyologist, Dr. Bruce B. Collette, who stated that the juvenile swordfish has scales.[240] In addition, this turned the subject into a "fight" between the Orthodox and the Conservative movement.

Dr. Tendler fought strongly against anyone who challenged his opinion, and towards the end of the 1960s his opinion was finally accepted in some countries. These included America, and in parts of Israel.[241] However, countries which had a tradition to eat swordfish usually continued to eat it.[242]

A number of scientific papers have been published on the subject of scales on a swordfish. One of them is a bulletin published by the Fisheries Research Board of Canada, which states that "scales and teeth are found only on young swordfish."[243] Therefore as the fish grows older, the scales disappear and thus an adult swordfish is scaleless. Neither the Talmud nor the responsa literature discuss such a case of scales disappearing with maturity.[244] However, it would seem that the Chatam Sofer[245] and some contemporary poskim rule that such a fish is kosher.[246]

However, in two other scientific papers it can be seen that an adult swordfish has scales but they are almost "out of sight." The first is a paper published in the United States in 1952, which states: "The bases of the scales in the rows are almost connected giving a strong keeled effect. ... The rows of scales may contain two or three different stages of scale development. ... The scales of the largest specimen are strong and cover the entire body. ... The scales have degenerated conspicuously, being embedded in the skin, with their existence still traceable exteriorly."[247]

Over fifty years later in 2004, a further paper on this subject was published in the scientific journal Copeia[248] by six authors (one of them being Rabbi Ari Zivotofsky). The paper showed that as a juvenile the swordfish had scales. As the fish grew however, the scales are not shed or resorbed but become more deeply embedded within the dermis as it thickens, and as a consequence only the tips of the spines of the scales protrude through the dermis of the adult swordfish. Further unpublished research by Zivotofsky showed that some of the scales were thought to be loosely attached to the fish.[249]

The results of the research in the above two papers could answer several of the debatable points in the Knesset Hagedolah's description of the "fish with the sword" (as he called it) and explain why he saw no scales on the fish and why some were found on the black cloth he used to catch them.

Periodically, "Mesorah Dinners" are organized, (Rabbi Ari Zivotofsky being one off the main organizers). In such a dinner held in Jerusalem in the summer of 5770 (2010), swordfish appeared on the menu.[250] However, in contrast, in one held in Chicago in America a year later, there were no swordfish.[251]

Bon Appétit

It is customary on the first night of Rosh Hashana to eat certain foods as a sign for a good coming year. These include a head (preferably of a ram), and also fish.[252] Many people combine these two customs and eat the head of a fish. By using the head of a swordfish there could be a further sign. The "Untaneh Tokef" prayer recited at Mussaf on Rosh Hashanah states that it will be decided on these days who will die by the *sword*, and we pray that it will not be us.

Chapter 10
Rice Cakes for Ashkenazi Jews for Seder night

General Knowledge

Rice is an edible starchy cereal and is the seed of a grass species (scientific name: Orysa sativa). To grow this species, the seeds are sown in prepared beds and when the seedlings are 25 to 50 days old they are transplanted to a field or paddy which has been enclosed by leaves and submerged under five to ten centimetres of water and they remain submerged during the growing season. Rice is normally grown as an annual plant but it can survive a ratoon crop. [Ratooning is the practice of cutting down most of the above ground portion of the plant but leaving the roots and growing shoots intact so to allow the plant to recover and produce a fresh crop in the next season and indeed up to 30 years.] The plant normally grows to a height of just over one metre, and its leaves are long and flattened. The harvested rice kernel is enclosed by a hull, which can be removed by milling. Rice is the most widely consumed staple food for a large part of the world's human population especially in Asia (just as bread is in Western countries). Therefore, as to be expected the principal rice producing countries in the world are in this area, namely China, India, Japan, Indonesia and Myanmar (Burma). A large variety of dishes can be made using rice. One of them is rice cakes which can be made from rice which has been shaped, condensed or otherwise combined into a single object. A large variety of rice cakes exist in many different cultures in which rice is eaten.

Halachic Discussion

Is it permitted to eat rice or rice products such as rice cakes (pirchiot orez) on Pesach? The Torah forbids the eating, benefitting and possession of chametz during the Festival of Pesach.[253]

What is Chametz? The process of a food becoming chametz can only occur when, after a specific time interval, which depends on a number of external factors, water has come in contact with one of the five species of grain, namely, wheat, barley, oats, spelt and rye. Becoming chametz is the result of a series of biochemical reactions in which starch, which is a long chain polysaccharide molecule, is broken down in successive stages, to give the gas carbon dioxide. This gas causes the dough to swell (similar to blowing air into a balloon) and this swelling makes the dough chametz. Only with the five species of grain can chametz occur.[254]

During the period of the Rishonim, it became the accepted norm for certain communities not to eat kitniyot, which in general are pod products.[255] Not everyone agreed, and Rabbeinu Yerucham went as far as to call it a stupid custom ("minhag shtut").[256]

Several reasons have been given for this custom of not eating kitniyot on Pesach. Grain can easily be mixed up with the kitniyot and it requires considerable checking to remove it; a further reason is that in the same way as grain can be made into flour, so can kitniyot, and this can lead to mix ups.[257] Kitniyot themselves cannot become chametz even if one were to soak them in boiling water for an extended period.[258] The reason is that it lacks one of the components necessary for the biochemical reaction to give carbon dioxide.[259]

The communities which accepted not eating kitniyot on Pesach are all the Ashkenazi communities[260] and to a limited extent some Sephardi communities.[261] The Vilna Gaon ruled that today it is forbidden (for Ashkenazim) to eat kitniyot, even in a time of famine.[262]

What is included under the heading of kitniyot? There are numerous opinions on this question. On rice, peas and beans there is general agreement, but on other products, there are different opinions.[263] There is even an opinion that potatoes are kitniyot, since one can make potato flour from them.[264] On this, Rabbi Moshe Feinstein writes that logically potatoes should be included as kitniyot, and that the reason that they are not is that when the decree of not eating kitniyot was made, potatoes had not yet reached Europe.[265] Similarly, peanuts were not known in the Jewish communities at that period and thus he holds they are not included in the decree of kitniyot,[266] whilst in contrast the Eda Charedis in Jerusalem rules they are.[267] However, the Eda Charedis does not include potatoes as kitniyot.[268] Very recently, quinoa has come on the market and there have been discussions on whether or not it is kitniyot, with some permitting it whilst others forbid it.[269]

Another question is what about oil made from kitniyot, such as sesame oil. Rabbi Avraham Yitzchak Kook held that it did not come within the prohibitions of kitniyot and this caused a big argument in Jerusalem where the opponents said it had been forbidden hundreds of years earlier.[270] Today all such oil is marked "for those who eat kitniyot."

One product on the market today in Israel is "pirchiot orez" – rice cakes, and they are made with a hechsher for Pesach. One such manufacturer is B & D (Better and Different, located in Mishor Adumim, Israel). A few weeks before Pesach 5778 (2018), Rabbi Elyakim Levanon, the Rabbi of the Shomron, sent round a letter in which he stated that he had inspected the B & D factory during the manufacture of their rice cakes and they could be eaten by Ashkenazim during Pesach. He added that his reasoning could be found in the website of "Kosharot."[271] There he writes that the reason for him permitting it, is that no water comes into contact with the rice during the entire production of these rice cakes.[272]

This was immediately challenged by the two Chief Rabbis of Ma'ale Adumin, namely Rabbi Yehoshua Katz and Rabbi Mordechai Nagarim, who gave the hechsher to this factory. In a letter to the public at large, in response to this letter of Rabbi Levanon, they wrote that these rice cakes were only kosher for Pesach for those Jews who ate kitniyot on Pesach.[273] Furthermore, a Sephardi Bet Din who also gave a hechsher for this product wrote on the wrapper that it was only for Jews who ate kitniyot.

A few days before Pesach the Chief Rabbi of Israel, Rabbi David Lau in a questions and answers session, was asked about this ruling of Rabbi Levanon, and he replied that they were only permitted for those who ate kitniyot on Pesach.[274]

This permitting of rice on Pesach, something which had been forbidden to Ashkenazim for about 850 years was commented upon by Rabbi Refoel Goldmeier from Ramat Bet Shemesh. He wrote: "What I do not understand from what [Rabbi Levanon] says is that even those who prohibit [rice on Pesach] do not prohibit this rice. Why not? Did they differentiate in types of rice? If rice is kitniyot and prohibited, who cares how much you sift it or keep it away from water? And if keeping it away from water and sifting it is good enough to circumvent the custom against eating kitniyot, why not eat many other forms of kitniyot that are banned, as long as you sift it and inspect it and keep it away from water."[275]

Bon Appétit

On the Seder plate are placed two cooked dishes in memory of Pesach celebrated at the time of the Temple. It is customary to use a piece of roasted meat and a roasted egg.[276] But there is no problem in using two entirely different foods. The Gemara[277] gives rice and beetroot as these two cooked dishes. According to some communities, one may not eat roasted meat at the Seder.[278] However, if one were to use rice cakes instead of meat there would be no problem to eat it during the Seder meal!

Chapter 11
Fish Blood Borsht for Erev Pesach

General Knowledge

Blood is a body fluid in humans and animals that delivers necessary substances such as nutrients and oxygen to the cells and transports metabolic waste products away from those same cells. Creatures can be divided into cold-blooded and warm-blooded, fish being cold-blooded. In addition to fish, cold-blooded creatures include locusts, insects and reptiles. Warm-blooded include humans, animals and birds. The difference between the two is that warm-blooded try and keep their bodies at a constant temperature. They do this by generating their own heat when they are in a cooler environment, and cooling themselves when they are in a hotter environment. In contrast, cold-blooded creatures take on the temperature of their surroundings They are hot when the environment is hot, and cold when their environment is cold. There are both advantages and disadvantages for cold and warm-blooded creatures. How does the blood circulate within a fish? They have a closed-loop circulatory system in which the heart pumps the blood in a single loop throughout the body. The blood of fish is similar to that of other vertebrates. It consists of plasma and cellular blood cells components. The cellular components are red blood cells, white blood cells and thrombocytes.

Halachic Discussion

Is it permitted to drink blood? There is a strict prohibition in the Torah regarding the eating [drinking] of blood,[279] and in some cases the punishment is karet (the excision of the soul by Divine punishment).[280] The blood is regarded as the soul of a creature,[281] and to draw blood on Shabbat comes under the same category of forbidden work on Shabbat as killing.[282]

Blood of creatures is divided into three categories, the most severe being the blood which spouts out when the creature is killed. Eating this blood has the punishment of karet. Less severe is the blood which oozes out after the creature is killed. By eating it one transgresses a negative commandment in the Torah. The third category is blood which is contained in the flesh or muscles of the creature. This is only forbidden when the blood has left its original position.[283] Therefore, if one wants to eat the creature raw, one can just wash it and eat it without any further preparation.[284] If however, one wants to cook or roast the creature one has to perform the "salting process" to remove the blood.[285]

However, all the above only applies to animals and birds. It does not apply to fish and, according to the Torah one may eat the blood of fishes.[286] Needless to say, this is only the blood of a kosher fish, since anything which comes from a non-kosher creature is not kosher.[287]

Although fish blood is permitted, there is the problem of marit ayin, namely doing an action which can be interpreted as doing something forbidden. In this case, if someone were to see a Jew drinking a cup of fishes' blood, he might well think that he is drinking the blood of an animal or bird.[288] This applies even in the privacy of one's house.[289]

The Gemara[290] discusses this problem and forbids collecting fishes' blood into a vessel to drink. However, it then gives a permitted way to do so, namely have some fish scales in the cup of blood so that anyone seeing it will know that it is fishes' blood.[291] Strangely, the Rambam leaves out the condition of putting the scales in the cup of blood,[292] and the poskim try and understand the reason for the Rambam's omission.[293]

There is obviously no problem in eating a piece of fish with the fish blood inside it, since there is no chance of marit ayin. Similarly, if instead of putting some fish scales in the cup of fish blood, one mixes the fish blood with another substance, there is no need to add fish scales.[294] Thus in making "fish blood borsht" one would add, for example, raw eggs and sugar to the fish blood, and then one would not have to put some fish scales in the borsht.

Another question concerns the blood of a human being. Is it the same as blood of an animal and therefore forbidden, or is it like the blood of a fish which is permitted. According to most opinions, it is not forbidden by the Torah. The problem, as with fish blood, is that of marit ayin. Although one would not normally drink human blood, the question arises should one cut, for example, one's finger, or should one bite one's tongue, which will result in blood accumulating in one's mouth. In the latter case there is no problem of marit ayin and one may swallow the blood. If on the other hand, it is coming out of some external organ, there are different opinions on whether one may suck and swallow this blood. If it goes on to some food which one is eating, then that part of the food should be cut away.[295]

The drinking of blood is not just academic. All over the world, blood, albeit blood of animals and birds, is drunk or it forms an ingredient in various foodstuffs. For example, the Maasai tribe in Tanzania drink raw animal cooked blood and blood-milk mixtures (as well as other foods). Studies have shown that they are extremely healthy with no signs of heart disease and their cholesterol levels are about half those of the average American.[296] Seal blood is drunk in some Arctic regions, and a blood soup is consumed in Poland. In Europe, as well as in America and Mexico several varieties of blood sausage are made by cooking animal blood with a filler until it is thick enough to congeal when cooked. In China and southeast Asia a popular dish is made from pig's blood. In a northern region of Portugal, they have a traditional blood soup. In Finland pig's blood is used with milk, flour and molasses to make blood pancakes. There are also further examples from other areas of the world.[297] Although animal or bird blood is used in the above foods, possibly it could be replaced with permitted fish blood thus making it a kosher delicacy!

Bon Appétit

At about midday on Erev Pesach, one is limited with what one may eat. Bread may not be eaten. Matzah may not be eaten. Therefore, some have the custom to have potatoes and borsht at this meal on Erev Pesach.[298] Thus at this meal one could, at least halachically, eat borsht made using fish blood in place of beetroot water. In all probability it would not be so tasty!

Chapter 12
Deer's Kidneys for Melave Malka

General Knowledge

A deer (scientific name: Gazella) is an animal which has long and narrow legs which enable it to jump, and it can run as fast as 70 kilometres an hour. It can grow to a height of about one metre and a weight of about 450 kilogrammes. Its color is yellowy grey or brown. The male has a pair of horns, which grow from boney supporting strictures called pedicels. They are covered in velvet which is rich in nerves and blood vessels. The horns fall off each year and are then regrown. Unlike the horns of sheep which consist of a horny substance covering a bone which can be removed thus making the horn hollow, those of a deer are solid bone. Drilling throughout the length of this solid bone will not make it into a kosher shofar for Rosh Hashanah since it is not naturally hollow. The deer is a selective eater, its main diet being fruit and grass including acorns. Its habitat is the dense forests and planted areas in Europe, Asia and North America. It lives to an age of between 10 and 20 years. The length of pregnancy of a deer is about 200 days. Sometimes one needs to recognise when it is pregnant, since in some places one is not allowed to hunt a pregnant deer!

Halachic Discussion

Can one readily obtain kosher deer's kidneys, or are there problems? The Torah gives a list of ten animals which are kosher.[299] There have been discussions to identify the last seven names on this list. The fifth name in this list is "tzvi," and this word appears in the Torah on four occasions.[300] Dr. Meir Levinger, in a paper on this subject, wrote that there is general agreement that the tzvi is the gazella, namely the deer.[301]

Furthermore, the Septuagint translates tzvi as "dorkada" (in Greek letters)[302] and the Vulgate translates it as capream;[303] both when translated into English are "roe deer."

After shechitah and inspection of, especially the lungs of a kosher species of animal, there are other parts that must be removed before the animal may be eaten. These are the blood, the gid hanasheh (sciatic nerve) and in many cases also the cheilev (forbidden fats). The hardest to remove is the cheilev, and this is almost exclusively found in the hindquarters, including around the kidneys, of the animals. The process of removal of the cheilev is known as nikkur (or in English porging and in Yiddish treiben).[304]

To remove this cheilev from the hindquarters, one requires a highly skilled person trained to accomplish this,[305] and it was found that sometimes it was not done properly. Because of these problems, from the Middle Ages onwards, in some locations no nikkur was done on the hindquarters, and in other locations the custom of whether to do it or not do it periodically changed. When it was not done, the hindquarters were sold to non-Jews.[306]

From the middle of the twentieth century, Jewish butchers in Britain were forbidden to sell the hindquarters.[307] At the same period nikkur of both the forequarters and hindquarters was practiced in Jerusalem. In Israel today it is under the supervision of the Rabbanut and Sephardic Batei Din.[308] However the Eda Charedis of Jerusalem only sell the forequarters of animals.[309]

Although the generic term "animal" is used to define kosher animals, in fact the Torah divides animals into two categories, even though the list of ten kosher animals appears without any obvious sign that there are two classes. One class is beheimot, domesticated animals, and the other class is chayot, wild animals.

To know which class a particular animal is in, is not just academic. There are in fact some significant differences on the laws applying to these two groups; for example, cheilev is forbidden in beheimot whilst it is permitted in chayot.[310] Therefore, one needs to know how to distinguish which animal is a beheimah and which is a chayah. The distinguishing signs are the shape of its horns.[311] A deer comes under the class of chayot.[312]

Therefore, there is no cheilev to remove from a deer, although the prohibitions of blood and the gid hanasheh equally apply to beheimot and chayot. There is relatively no difficulty in removing them. Thus, there should be no problem in obtaining and eating deer's kidneys. In America, the OU supervises the removal of the gid hanasheh from deer.[313] Thus deer, presumably including its kidneys and the reminder of its hindquarters, is available in the United States and some other locations, as will now be illustrated.

About 1990, the restaurant Levana on the Upper West Side of New York added to its menu deer. At that time, it was mainly imported from Israel, but for some reason they were not able to continue importing it. Then Norman Schlaff, a deer farmer in Goshen New York, stepped into the breach. He raises the deer on his 100 acre farm, Musicon Farm, where they are slaughtered in a barn specially set up for this purpose, by a shochet under careful supervision and are then sold to individuals and restaurants.[314]

Another venue where venison (deer meat) is served is in Prague, in a Glatt Kosher restaurant, called the King Solomon. This restaurant has a whole variety of deer recipes including a soup, tongue, goulash and steak.[315]

On its menu, this restaurant relates an interesting historical occurrence involving deer. During the nineteenth century the Austro-Hungarian Empire permitted the Jews with the approval of Emperor Franz Joseph the First to perform a ceremony of shechting a deer. Likewise, during the time of Baron Rothschild, the Jews in Britain were permitted to observe the tradition of hunting a deer and then shechting it. However, at a later date the Jews were forbidden to continue this tradition.[316]

In the year 5774 (2014), a leaflet was published by the London Beth Din which states, "Venison is no longer available for kosher tables only because according to agricultural regulations, deer must be shot in the open field and not brought into an abattoir."[317] An identically worded statement appeared in a leaflet published by the New South Wales Jewish Board of Deputies in 5769 (2009).[318] It would seem from this that the same restriction applies in Australia.

Bon Appétit

In addition to eating three meals on Shabbat, one also has to eat a meal after Shabbat has terminated known as the Melave Malka.[319] Ideally, one should have bread at this meal, but failing that cake or even fruit will suffice.[320] The Gemara relates of a Rabbi who would shecht a calf after Shabbat in order to eat of its kidney for melave malka.[321] As stated above, it requires great skill and experience to remove the cheilev from the area of a beheimah's kidney. Since there is no prohibition of cheilev for a deer, there would not be this difficulty in obtaining and eating a deer's kidney for Melave Malka.

Chapter 13
Hard boiled Sparrows' eggs for Erev Tisha b'Av

General Knowledge

The house sparrow (scientific name: Passer domesticus) is one of the world's best known and abundant small birds. It is about 15 centimetres long and has a weight of about 30 grams. Its color is browny-grey with the male having a black bib. Its vocalisations are variations in its short and incessant chirping call. It originated in the Middle East but over the course of years has spread to most parts of the world. However, it only migrates over a limited area, and it speed of flight is about 45 kilometres per hour and it does about 15 wingbeats per second. On the ground it hops rather than walks. It can also swim short distances under water. Its diet is mainly seeds and insects, and where available, also earthworms, lizards and frogs. Until about 15 days after hatching the baby sparrows are fed mainly on insects. Sparrows are also known to eat discarded food. Nest sites are varied, though cavities are preferred, and the nests are frequently built in the eaves and other cavities of houses. In warmer climates, the sparrow may build its nest in the open on the branches of trees, especially on evergreens and hawthorns. The nests are made of course vegetation with finer materials such as feathers, string and paper for the lining.

Halachic Discussion

Is a sparrow a kosher bird? Unlike in the case of animals, fish and locusts, the Torah does not give physical signs for a bird to be kosher. The Gemara writes that It depends on tradition which is passed down from generation to generation. This is even though the Rabbis have found a common denominator of signs for a kosher bird, namely, it does not prey on other birds, and has several anatomical features, namely an extra toe, a crop and a gizzard that can be peeled.[322]

What then is the situation with the birds known as the sparrow? In his book, Dr. Levinger writes that there is tradition from almost all the various Jewish communities in the world for the house sparrow to be a kosher bird.[323] Likewise, both "Purtal Hadaf Hayami,"[324] and Rabbi Shlomo Min-Hahar[325] write that it is a tradition amongst all Jews to eat sparrows. The following are examples of this tradition in different communities.

Amongst the Ashkenazi Jews, there was a tradition that each year, or every few years, in the city of Halberstadt they would symbolically shecht one sparrow.[326] In a leaflet published by the London Beth Din in 5774 (2014), under the section of kosher birds they write that there is a Germanic tradition that a sparrow is a kosher bird.[327]

Jews from Lithuania relate that during the First World War at the time of a famine when there was nothing to eat, they would shecht sparrows. Another who gave evidence on this subject was Chacham Ezra Yair who said that the shochetim in Jerusalem shechted sparrows. Rabbi Mordechai Peretz from Morocco testified that until today he shechts sparrows, and Rabbi D. Yaluz, a shochet from Tiberias, testified on the eating of house sparrows.[328]

There is much testimony on the eating of sparrows by the Jews of Yemen. They would put out traps at the beginning of the night and by morning a large number of sparrows would be trapped. There is even a report of over a thousand sparrows which were found in the various traps put out on a particular night. They were then taken to be shechted and then after the necessary preparations would be eaten.[329] Also, at the "Mesorah Dinner," a Yemenite Rabbi vividly described trapping sparrows by the hundreds when he was a child in Yemen.[330]

Furthermore, the Septuagint in both the list of non-kosher birds given in Vayikra and in Devarim, identifies the "bat ya'anah" as "strouthón" (in Greek letters)[331] Some of those who translated the Septuagint into English, translated it as sparrow, thus indicating that the Septuagint listed a sparrow as a non-kosher bird. However, this is an incorrect translation from the Greek into English. This error occurred because strouthón is also the Greek for ostrich,[332] which everyone agrees is a non-kosher bird. There are also other translations into English of the Septuagint which correctly translate it as ostrich. Similarly, the Vulgate translates "bat ya'anah" as strutionem,[333] which is the ostrich.

There are in fact a number of species of sparrows, including the Italian Sparrow and the Spanish sparrow. The Zivchei Kohen in his book brings a sketch of the different kinds of kosher birds.[334] Under number 2, he writes the Passera which is the generic name for all the sparrows,[335] his intention being those which were known at his location.[336] Dr. Levinger comments that the Italian sparrow is a hybrid of the Spanish Sparrow and the House Sparrow, and it is reasonable to suggest that all these different sparrows are included in the tradition.[337] In his chart of kosher birds, Dr. Zohar Amar writes that in all the various hand-written manuscripts he examined, including MS London, MS Rome, MS Moscow, and MS Livorno, the sparrow appears as a kosher bird.[338]

In contrast to those permitting sparrows, there are some papers on the mitzvah of shiluach hakan (sending away the mother bird)[339] which specifically state that the sparrow is not kosher. This mitzvah only applies to kosher species of birds. What about birds who have the Rabbinically kosher signs but do not have a tradition to be eaten? On this the American Kashrut organization Star-K writes that one may perform this mitzvah with them but they may not be eaten, and they give a short list of such birds which includes sparrows, namely, in practice, they regard sparrows as non-kosher.[340] Likewise in a question on shiluach hakan submitted to Rabbi Ya'akov Ariel, he writes that a sparrow is non-kosher.[341]

Anything coming from a non-kosher creature, such as eggs or milk, is not kosher.[342] Therefore, the eggs of a sparrow, which is generally accepted as a kosher bird, are kosher. The eggs of a house sparrow are white, bluish white or greenish white, spotted with brown or gray. They are subelliptical in shape, about two centimetres in length and one and a haf centimetres in breadth, surface area nine square centimetres and they weigh about three grammes.[343] In each clutch the bird lays about four to five eggs and there at least two clutches per year. The period of incubation is between 11 and 14 days.[344]

After these eggs have been laid, and there is no embryo or blood in them, they may be eaten.[345] Eggs which are completely formed and are found in a kosher bird are parva.[346] If, on the other hand, partially formed eggs are found in the bird after it has been shechted, they are fleishig (meaty).[347]

Sparrows were served at the "Mesorah Dinner." They were in the soup course together with other birds, namely dove and pigeon.[348] However, there is no record of sparrows' eggs being on the menu!

Bon Appétit

At the meal before the fast of Tisha b'Av there are limitations on the food which may be consumed, namely no meat or wine and no more than one cooked dish.[349] It is a custom to eat at this meal just a hard-boiled egg plus bread dipped in ashes.[350] Normally one uses a chicken's egg but one could use a different kosher bird's egg, such as a sparrow's egg.

Chapter 14
Pig Bone Gelatin coating on Chanukah Latkes

General Knowledge

Gelatin is a translucent, colourless, brittle (when dry) flavorless food derived from collagen. Collagen is a fibrous, insoluble protein that makes up a major portion of bone, skin and connective tissues of animals such as cattle, chicken, pigs and fish. The word "gelatin" comes from the Latin word "gelatus," meaning stiff or frozen. Gelatin is manufactured as a powder or in thin sheets. For practical reasons, about ninety per cent of gelatin is made from the skin of young pigs. Gelatin is used in various ways during the manufacture of numerous foodstuffs. These include jelly-like confections, toffees, bakery glazes, cake mixes, meringues, spreadable frostings, creams, yoghurts, ice creams and fluffy marshmallows. A practical example of using gelatin is by adding it to a candy since it can make it last longer, since gelatin does not break down as quickly as sugar. Gelatin is also used in various medications such as making a gelatinous coating to hold in the contents of pills and also to make them easier to swallow.

Halachic Discussion

Is there any kashrut problem in incorporating gelatin in food products? Although history shows that gelatin has been used since the 1400s, and it was originally made by boiling cattle hoofs for six hours,[351] the first discussion on its kashrut status was only about one hundred year ago.

The various Rabbinical responsa on this question have generally revolved around the question of whether the dry bones of a non-kosher animal (namely, a non-kosher species, or one not slaughtered by shechitah, or one found to be treife after an inspection) may be eaten by a Jew.[352] Another relevant point is whether after the various processes utilised in making the gelatin, the dry bones are fit for eating.[353]

It can be derived from the Gemara[354] that animal bones do not have the status of meat on a Torah level. However, on a Rabbinical level they are forbidden, but if in gelatin they are completely unfit for human consumption, there is a leniency to allow one to eat them.[355]

The first recorded source on the kashrut of gelatin is a responsum by Rabbi Chaim Ozer Grodzinski, who was the Rabbi of Vilna just before the Second World War. He held that there was no problem whatsoever in eating dry bones of non-kosher animals.[356] In 1953, Rabbi Yechezkel Abramsky, who was a Dayan in the London Beth Din, wrote a responsum on the subject where he argued that since the Torah only prohibits the flesh of non-kosher animals, and of animals which are treife, there is no prohibition to eat gelatin which is from the bones of such an animal.[357] Despite this, however, he was reluctant to permit gelatin, the reason being that up to then it had been forbidden, and by now permitting it, might make people lax in observing other halachot.[358] Rabbi Ovadiah Yosef also permitted the eating of gelatin.[359]

However, there are those who take the opposite opinion with regards to eating gelatin from any non-kosher animal. Amongst them are Rabbi Aharon Kotlar. He argued that were gelatin to be unfit for human consumption it would be permitted to eat it, but because it has now been processed to make it edible it has become forbidden.[360] There are also other contemporary Acharonim[361] who hold similar views.

In April 1972 (5732), Rabbi Gavriel Krausz, a Dayan in the Manchester Beth Din in the north of England, delivered a lecture on the subject of gelatin. He concluded that it was forbidden to eat it. However, in the case of medicaments containing gelatin, he said that one could be lenient especially if they are tasteless or preferably have an unpleasant taste.[362] It thus follows that capsules made from pig skin gelatin may be consumed. In contrast, the OU holds that for those who are not "desperately sick" it might be better to avoid such medicines.[363]

However, the production process for the making of gelatin has since then changed. Today gelatin is made from fresh, namely soft, bones instead of dry bones and thus the leniency of permitting gelatin made from dry bones no longer applies.[364]

Today most kashrut organizations in America do not permit gelatin and will only give their approval if it is made from kosher fish or from animals which have been killed by shechitah.[365] The London and Manchester Botai Din do not certify or approve products containing gelatin from a non-kosher source.[366] There are conflicting opinions of the situation in Israel, regarding permitting or forbidding gelatin, depending on whether the product is mehadrin or regular kashrut.[367] A former Chief Rabbi of Israel, Rabbi Bakshi-Doron said that although the Rabbanut would certify as kosher the gelatin taken from the bones of non-kosher animals, they required the product to be labelled as such.[368] However, the number of products on the market labelled "Kosher for those who eat gelatin" has considerably decreased over the last decades.[369] A further question is what is the situation regarding gelatin made from kosher but non-glatt animals? It was ruled that such gelatin could be used in glatt products.[370]

Another question which arises when manufacturing gelatin from kosher animals is whether the gelatin is then parva or fleishig (meaty). There are those who state it is parva, whilst others state it is fleishig.[371] There is also a discussion on whether one may eat it with fish, since meat-fish mixtures are forbidden because of a danger to health.[372]

The laws concerning eating meat and milk do not apply to a non-kosher species of animal, such as a pig.[373] Therefore, by eating pig meat with milk one does not transgress the prohibition of eating meat and milk together. Thus, those who permit the eating of gelatin, and also hold that one may not eat gelatin from a kosher species of animal together with milk, could not likewise hold this for pig bone gelatin.

There are today gelatins which originate from kosher species of fish, and gelatin originating from vegetable matter such as agar-agar. Here kashrut problems are avoided, but these gelatins are inferior to that of animal origin gelatin.[374]

Bon Appétit

There are several foods mentioned by the poskim which it is customary to eat on Chanukah. Some of them are milk-based foods whose source is the book of Yehudit in the Apocrypha,[375] and there are also sufganiyot (donuts), which are mentioned in the writings of Rabbi Maimon ben Yosef (the father of the Rambam).[376] These foods include cheese blintzes. The cheese sometimes oozes out, especially during transport, and since pig bone gelatin is parva, a thin coating of it over the surface of these blintzes might prevent this oozing.

Chapter 15

Caviar from Sturgeon for Seudah Shlishit

General Knowledge

Sturgeons (scientific name: Acipenser) are large cartilaginous fish which are found in the temperate waters of the Northern hemisphere. Their average length is about 3 metres and their weight is of about 270 kilogrammes. The basic diet of the sturgeon consists of crayfish, shrimp, snails, plants, aquatic insects, larvae, sludge worms and clams. They are long-living, late maturing fish having an average lifespan of 50 to 60 years. They migrate upstream to spawn but spend most of their lives feeding in river deltas and estuaries. A female can lay from 100,000 to three million eggs, but not all will be fertilized. The fertilized eggs become sticky and it takes between 8 and 15 days for the embryos to mature into larval fish. During this period, they are dependent on their yok sac for nourishment. Sturgeons are famous for caviar which is processed from their roe. One method used to extract this roe from the sturgeon is by stripping it from ripe females who are subsequently released. As a result of the popularity of caviar, the sturgeons are overfished and their numbers are decreasing, resulting in a risk of extinction.

Halachic Discussion

Is a sturgeon a kosher fish? To be kosher, the Torah requires fish to have both fins and scales.[377] However, neither the Torah nor the Talmud make conditions regarding the scales. It was the Ramban (Nachmanides) in his commentary on the Torah who ruled that for a fish to be kosher one must be able to remove the scales by hand, namely they are not stuck to the underlying skin. He brings a proof from Targum Onkelus[378] who translates the word for scales as "kalfin" something which can be peeled off.[379]

The Ramban's opinion is accepted in the Shulchan Aruch as halachah.[380]

Zoologists give a classification of the various type of scales on fish.[381] Some scales are easily removable; others the skin is torn, and with others the scales can only be removed without tearing the skin by the application of various treatments such as hot water. With this latter class of fish, there are various opinions as to whether or not they are kosher.[382]

One of the fish coming into this latter category is the sturgeon and others of the same family such as the sterlet.[383] It is from the roe of this fish that caviar, a great food delicacy which is grossly expensive (50 grammes costing $470[384]) is made. It is reported that some of the best caviar in the world is made in Israel and then exported to New York.[385]

The first recorded report on the possible kosher status of the sturgeon was given by the Ramban. On this, Rabbi Shmuel ben Meshullam Gerondi, who was a scholar in Gerona Catalonia in Spain in the early fourteenth century, writes in his book of dinim "Ohel Moed": "The fish called the sturgeon is permitted. ... The Ramban checked it and soaked it in boiling water and the scales then came off it, and therefore it is permitted."[386]

It is significant that the Ramban who was the Rabbi who forbade scales which were not easy to remove allowed as kosher a fish which requires boiling water treatment to remove its scales.

The Ohel Moed also stated that Rabbeinu Tam ruled that the sturgeon is a kosher fish. In addition, he wrote that there were those who forbade ("yesh sheosrim") the eating of the sturgeon but gave no names of those who forbade it.[387] The son of the Nodah b'Yehudah wrote that the use of this expression means that there was only a single opinion who forbade its consumption. It does not say, as some others have suggested, that the Ohel Moed agreed with those who forbade eating sturgeon.[388]

At a later date, the Pri Chadash in his commentary on the Shulchan Aruch quotes verbatim the Ohel Moed, but makes no comment that he disagrees with it.[389]

Several hundred years later a fish was sent to the Noda b'Yehudah by Rabbi Tzvi Hirsch, the Rabbi of Temesvar, in order for him to rule whether or not it was kosher. The Noda b'Yehudah did not state the name of the fish, (it has been suggested that it was the sterlet, which is of the same family as the sturgeon) but it required the same processes as the sturgeon for the removal of its scales. The Noda b'Yehudah ruled that the fish which had been sent to him was kosher.[390]

This ruling of the Noda b'Yehudah caused an enormous controversy in Europe. Rabbi Mordechai Banet, the Chief Rabbi of Moravia, in one of his responsa, argued that one could not remove the scales of this fish without tearing the skin underneath, and also that for hundreds of years Jews had not eaten this fish.[391] However, it is reported that the Jews of Turkey did eat this fish.[392]

In contrast, one of the Noda b'Yehudah's students, Rabbi Aharon Chorin published a book in defense of the Noda b'Yehudah's ruling.[393] (Ironically, at a later date, Chorin became a member of the Reform movement.)

In 5559 (1799), Rabbi Yitzchak Grishaber, the Rabbi of Paks published a book (which contained the approbation of nine great Rabbis) against the ruling of the Noda b'Yehudah.[394] In his book, Rabbi Chorin wrote that Rabbi Grishaber claimed that the Noda b'Yehudah had retracted his ruling on the kosher status of the sturgeon, and that the Noda b'Yehudah had written a letter to this effect for Rabbi Grishaber to hand over to Rabbi Hirsch, who had originally asked the Noda b'Yehudah this question.[395] However, he added that Rabbi Grishaber had claimed that this letter had got lost[396] and he could not even find the copy he made for himself![397] However, this was not true. The Noda b'Yehudah's son Shmuel wrote two responsa which have been published amongst the Noda b'Yehudah's responsa[398] which in strong and direct language called Rabbi Grishaber a liar saying that no such letter ever existed. If his father had reversed his decision, he would have sent it direct to Rabbi Hirsh in the fastest possible way, publicised the fact, kept a copy of the letter and deleted the original responsum from his book.[399] Likewise, one of the Noda b'Yehudah's leading students, Rabbi Eleazer Fleckeles wrote in a similar style to Rabbi Grishaber.[400]

In mitigation of Rabbi Grishaber's spreading this false information about the Noda b'Yehudah's retraction of the ruling permitting this fish, the Noda b'Yehudah's son magnanimously wrote that Rabbi Grishaber did this with the best intentions to prevent Jews from eating this fish.[401]

Which opinions were later followed regarding the sturgeon? In the lists of kosher fish published by the Agudas ha-Rabbonim in America in April 1933, and in December 1934, sturgeon appears as a kosher fish.[402] Furthermore, the 1934 list is followed by letters received from the Washington Bureau of Fisheries, and the American Museum of Natural History, in which their experts write that the sturgeon has the scales required by Jewish law to be kosher.[403]

However, these lists are now history. The lists of fish produced by Dr. Moshe Tendler,[404] by Dr. James Atz[405] and by the Chabad organisation[406] also give lists of non-kosher fish and in these lists sturgeon is included as a non-kosher fish. The lists published by the Batei Din in London and Paris[407] don't specifically give lists of non-kosher fish, but their lists of kosher fish do not include the sturgeon.

If today in Britain one catches a sturgeon, one has to ask the permission of the Queen of England to keep this fish! Even with this permission, selling it can lead to one to be arrested![408]

Bon Appétit

There is a custom to eat fish at all three meals on Shabbat.[409] To avoid problems of "borer" (selecting) on Shabbat,[410] fish without bones are the preferred type.[411] In caviar there are no bones and so this problem of selecting does not arise. Thus caviar is an ideal food for a Shabbat meal!

Chapter 16

Milk dessert following a Meat meal for Shavuot

General Knowledge

Milk is a fluid secreted by the mammary glands of females and is the primary source of nutrition for infant mammals. The origin of the word "milk" is from the Old English "meolc" and from the Anglian "milc." Milk is extracted from farm animals, almost entirely cows (about 85 percent) but also from goats and other animals, during or soon after pregnancy. Some milk is converted into milk powder. In 2011, dairy farms worldwide produced about 730 billion kilogrammes of milk from 260 million dairy cows, the largest producer of milk being India. Throughout the world more than six billion people consume milk and milk products. *Meat* is animal flesh that is eaten as food. The word "meat" comes from the Old English word "mete" which refers to food in general. Meat is mainly composed of water, protein and fat, and is edible raw but is usually eaten after it has been cooked. As far back as thousands of years ago, hunters would go after and kill animals and meat was of a considerable portion of their diet. Today, many animals have been domesticated and are slaughtered in abattoirs using various methods. The nature of the animals killed often depends on the country and there are even locations in the world where dogs and cats are eaten.

Halachic Discussion

What are the restrictions regarding mixtures of meat and milk? On three occasions the Torah forbids the cooking of a domesticated kosher animal (beheimah) with the milk of such an animal.[(412)] From this, one learns that there are three Torah prohibitions regarding milk and meat mixtures, namely, cooking, the subsequent eating, and the subsequent deriving benefit.[(413)]

311

The Rabbis have added the prohibition of eating a kosher wild animal (chaya) and a kosher bird with milk.[414] Furthermore, the Rabbis forbade the eating of milk products after meat for a certain period of time.[415]

The question is how long is this period of time? The Gemara[416] quotes a statement by Mar-Ukba that the time period is from one meal to the next meal. This can be interpreted in two different ways. One of them is the time a person waits between partaking of two meals. The other interpretation is that of a new meal which is consumed immediately after finishing a previous meal.

According to the first interpretation, one needs to investigate what is the accepted interval of time between two meals, and to this there are various opinions. The Gemara[417] refers to a scholar having his meal at midday, and his next meal will be at the beginning of the night – namely a space of six hours. (The Vilna Gaon[418] implies that this is the source for the Shulchan Aruch giving a waiting time of 6 hours.) The Rambam[419] and the Shulchan Aruch[420] both quote a figure of six hours and this is the figure accepted by Sephardi Jews, with no room for divergent opinions. However, in practice there are reports (but almost invariably without the original sources being quoted) that some Sephardi Jews who lived in European countries waited less than six hours. These included those living in Greece, Amsterdam and Italy.[421] Also, the Jews of Tunisia, although after eating meat would wait six hours, after eating bird would wait only three hours.[422]

To be precise, the Rambam writes *about* 6 hours and this word "about" has halachic ramifications. There are Jews who interpret it as five and a half hours or even five plus (even one minute!) hours. Rabbi Aharon Kotler ruled five and a half hours, whilst Rabbi Yosef Shalom Eliashiv ruled five hours plus.[423] There are Yeshivot who serve a milky supper five hours (or five and a half) hours after a meaty dinner.[424] One might well ask that since the Rambam writes *about* six hours, why go down to five - instead go up to seven!

There is a yekke (German) custom to wait three hours.[425] This opinion is quoted by one of the Rishonim, Rabbeinu

Yerucham[426] (although in another book he writes "at least six hours" when writing about the meat of beheimah[427]). Three hours is also quoted by Rabbi David Pardo (born in Venice in 1718).[428] Rabbi Tzvi Hirsch Shapira quotes Rabbi Pardo and comments that this is the custom in a number of places and on this there is what to rely.[429] A number of reasons have been put forward to justify the waiting of just three hours.[430] Rabbi Tzvi Krakhour has an interesting explanation. A person is awake for fifteen hours and in Germany ate five meals during that time, namely three hours from meal to meal.[431]

The custom in Holland is to wait just one hour.[432] Also, the Rema writes that in the place where he lived, Krakow, the custom was to wait one hour.[433] On this period of time of one hour, the Terumat Hadeshen[434] writes that there is no basis for this and it is a compromise between six hours and zero waiting time. However, one could bring some support for the opinion of one hour from the Zohar[435] which mentions one hour.

The Rema[436] quotes a number of opinions on this question. He begins by stating that Birchat Hamazon and clearing the table is sufficient, namely, according to the letter of the law, no waiting time is required. There are a number of Rishonim[437] who support this interpretation of "one meal to the next," namely, immediately beginning a further meal, and this, according to these opinions, is the halacha. (The Rema goes on to also mention six hours.)

Thus, if one were to eat a meaty meal, then say Birchat Hamazon and clear the table, one could immediately have cheese cake for the dessert! In practice one does not do this, but today people usually follow an opinion of a greater interval of time between meat and milk, usually six hours.

So far, the discussions have been regarding the required time interval between meat and milk. Two cases will now be brought regarding the theoretical eating of meat and milk *together* during a meal. The first is regarding udders of kosher cattle. After they have been shechted it is very likely that milk will be found in their udders. By Torah law this milk is fleishig (meaty) and the udders could thus be eaten together with the milk which is inside it. However, the Rabbis have ruled that the udders should be cut and smacked against a wall to remove all the milk.[438] Dr. Moshe Tendler who was present at a "Mesorah Dinner" knew how to do this and before the meal he did this and the udders were then served.[439]

The second case involves a ben pekuah. If after shechting (for example) a cow and opening it, one finds inside it a live baby calf just ready to be born, this baby is known as a ben pekuah. According to some opinions the laws regarding milk and meat do not apply to it and it can therefore be eaten with milk.[440]

Bon Appétit

On the Festival of Shavuot it is customary to eat milk foods.[441] Being Yom Tov one should also eat meat. There is then the technical question of how to arrange one's timetable of meals in order to wait the appropriate time (according to one's custom) between the meat and the milk. It is reported that it was customary to shorten this period on Shavuot,[442] but this is not regarded as acceptable.[443] However, those who follow the opinion to just recite birchat hamazon and clear the table, could immediately following their meat meal by having a dessert of milk ice cream, milk chocolate, cheese cake, cheese blintzes etc.

Chapter 17

Zebu meat in Shabbat cholent

General Knowledge

The zebu (scientific name: Bos indicus) is a species of cattle characterized by a fatty hump on its back, and indeed the name "zebu" comes from the Tibetan word "ceba" which means "hump." It is also characterized by its hanging skin and this enables it to survive for long periods of time in very hot climates without food or water. Zebus are one of the smallest breeds of cattle, with some adults being only one metre tall at the shoulder. They are also about half the weight of other cattle, reaching a weight of up to 200 kilogrammes. The color of their fur can be black, white and brown. The zebu can run up to 40 kilometres per hour. The diet of zebus is, as with other cattle, grass, seeds, leaves and flowers. It has a life span of between 12 to 16 years. The zebu originated in the Indian subcontinent and today they are to be found in Africa, Asia and to a lesser extent in the American continents. It is the only cattle species that can easily adapt to life in the hot tropics and it is mainly used for lighter agricultural work.

Halachic Discussion

Is a zebu a kosher animal? The Torah gives two signs for an animal to be kosher. It must chew the cud and also have a cloven hoof.[444] The zebu definitely has these two signs. According to the Rambam,[445] the Shulchan Aruch[446] and other Rishonim, one just requires these two physical signs for an animal to be kosher. This is unlike the case of a bird, where one requires a tradition for it to be kosher.[447]

However, at a later date, one of the commentators on the Shulchan Aruch, Rabbi Shabtei Cohen (17th century), known as the Shach,[448] added that a tradition is also required for an animal to be kosher. Rabbi Avraham Danzig (late 18th century), the author of Chochmat Adam[449] agreed with the Shach. On the other hand, Rabbi Yosef Teomim, the "Pri Megadim" (18th century)[450] disagreed, claiming that it would be contrary to the Gemara[451] and that there was no mention of such a requirement in the earlier sources. There are those who interpret the words of the Shach and the Chochmat Adam differently, and state that their intention is that one needs to be able to distinguish between a kosher beheimah (a domesticated animal) and a kosher chaya (a wild animal). The reason for this is that there are some different practical halachot between these two species of animals, and one thus needs to know to which of these two categories an animal belongs.

In the case of the zebu there is some uncertainly in this matter and thus if one would allow the shechting of zebu one might not do kisui hadam (the mitzvah of covering the blood of a chaya)[452] thinking a zebu was a beheimah.[453]

However, as can be seen below, the Chazon Ish had a different understanding of the Shach and the Chochmat Adam.

It was in 1950, soon after the establishment of the State of Israel, that there was a shortage of food. Zebu meat is eaten throughout the world, and it was thus suggested to shecht zebus in Madagascar and bring their meat to Israel.[454] A question was submitted to the Israeli Chief Rabbi Yitzchak Herzog on whether the zebu was a kosher animal.[455] He answered that it was kosher since it had the required two physical signs, and whether or not it was a beheimah or a chaya would have no bearing on the permissibility to eat it.[456] In the course of his research on the subject, he approached Rabbi Avraham Yeshaya Karelitz, the Chazon Ish, for his opinion. The Chazon Ish was of the opinion that the zebu was a non-kosher animal since there was no tradition to eat it, and one had to follow the opinions of the Shach and the Chochmat Adam.[457] There then followed an exchange of correspondence on the subject between these two Rabbis.[458]

In one of his later letters, the Chazon Ish accepted that technically the zebu was kosher but reiterated that one needs a proper tradition to permit it to be eaten.[459] However, in contrast, Rabbi Herzog held that there was a tradition for Jews to eat zebu.[460]

Indeed Iraqi Jews who had been living in India for hundreds of years ate the zebu.[461] The elderly experienced shochetim in Jerusalem testified that zebus were shechted in Jerusalem.[462] Furthermore, Rabbis from Yemen stated that they would shecht zebus.[463]

The followers of the Chazon Ish thought that his opinion to forbid the zebu had been accepted.[464] However, this was not the case and zebu meat was imported from several locations in Ethiopia under the supervision of the Israeli Chief Rabbinate, and this continued until the Yom Kippur War. The shechitah was then continued in Israel (where they had by then started breading zebus) and also in the Diaspora, and it was marketed as mehadrin.[465]

It was in the spring of 5764/2004 that this subject flared up in Israel and the religious press was full of it. According to one report, what caused the flareup was the following incident. A shochet in a south American country revealed that almost all the animals shechted there and certified as glatt were from the zebu. A Rabbi from Har Nof in Jerusalem took the matter to Rabbi Yosef Shalom Eliashiv who said he would investigate the matter but meanwhile it should not be publicised.[466]

However, as often happens in these incidents, the matter was leaked to the press. The first paper to publish it was the Hebrew edition of Mishpacha weekly, who printed an enormous size headline, "The Great Meat Scandal."[467] Other religious papers then followed suit.[468]

As a result of all this publicity many families did not cook the meat they had bought for Shabbat, others koshered their saucepans (although afterwards it was announced that this was unnecessary[469]), whilst some yeshivot threw away hundreds of portions of cholent they had prepared.[470] Even wedding menus were changed at the last moment.[471]

After all the dust had settled and the matter could be looked at rationally, it was found that zebus had been shechted in Jerusalem and Tiberius for years without anyone raising an objection, and that it was acceptable to everyone as mehadrin shechitah.[472] In contrast, it was reported that there were some Botei Din and Kashrut organizations in Israel (the names were not specified) who did not shecht the zebu;[473] perhaps these followed the opinion of the Chazon Ish. However, Rabbi Shmuel Halevi Wozner[474] said it was permitted as did the various chareidi non-state Batei Din.[475] Even in Bnei Brak, the city where the Chazon Ish had lived, they would every year shecht zebus and no one objected to it.[476]

Bon Appétit

On Shabbat it is forbidden to cook, but it is proper to eat hot food and this includes the daytime of Shabbat.[477] Thus cholent was "invented." On erev Shabbat various beans, vegetables and pieces of meat are placed into a saucepan. This is left on the Shabbat platter from before Shabbat until it is required during the Shabbat day meal.[478] Different meats can be used including that of the zebu.

References

(1) SA YD 84:16
(2) Rabbeinu Eliezer ben Reb Yoel Halevi, *Sefer haRa'avyah*, (Mekitsei Nirdamim Jerusalem, 5698/1938), para.1089; this permission to eat such wormy cheese also appeared in the *Kolbo* (author unknown) chap.101 whose first printing was in 1519
(3) Rabbi Moshe Via, *Bedikat Hamazon Kahalachah*, (Hamachon lehanhalat hahalachah, Jerusalem, 5758/2008), pp.97-98
(4) Via, op. cit., pp.56, 100
(5) "New York City Tap Water Statement," OU Kosher, (Internet)
(6) Professor Zohar Amar, "Kashrut Hamazon, Al tolaim kesheirot sheb'gevina v'kinim shemutar laharog b'Shabbat," (Internet); an almost identical paper by Zohar Amar appeared in *Emunat Itecha*, (Machon haTorah veHa'aretz: Kfar Darom 5777/2017), issue 116, pp.115-19
(7) Via, op. cit., pp.49-50
(8) e.g. books by Rabbi Moshe Via
(9) Mishnah Berura 473:42
(10) Via, op. cit., pp.65, 272
(11) Rabbi Yehudah haLevi Amichai, "Al Bedikot Tut Sadeh 5776," *Emunat Itecha*, (Machon haTorah veHa'aretz: Kfar Darom), Nissan 5776/2014, issue 111, pp.154-55

(12) SA YD 84:16
(13) "What's Going on with the 'Bugs' in the Fish?" OU Kosher Certification, (Internet)
(14) SA YD 84:6
(15) SA YD 84:7
(16) "Kosher Cheese," OU Kosher Certification, (Internet)
(17) SA YD 115:2 and Rema
(18) "Kosher Cheese," op. cit.
(19) Ibid.
(20) Taz SA YD 89:4
(21) Rabbi Ari Enkin, "Kosher Worms and Insects," Orthodox Union, (Internet)
(22) Ibid.
(23) SA YD 84:16 and Rema
(24) Rema YD 84:16
(25) Rabbi Avraham Halevi, *Ginat Veradim*, (Constantinople, 5476/1716), YD klal aleph chap.3
(26) Rabbi Yitzchak Yosef, *Yalkut Yosef,* issur v'heter vol.2, 84:53; Rabbi Yisrael Lifschitz, *Mishnayot im Peirush Tiferet Yisrael,* (Vilna 5673/1913), Kalkelet Shabbat 26 (hashochet); Rabbi Binyamin Aryeh Hakohen Weiss, *Even Yekorah al Arba'ah Chelkai haShulchan Aruch*, (Druck von F Badnarski: Lemberg, 5654/1894), responsum 174; Rabbi Gavriel Zinner, *Nitei Gavriel, Hilchot Chag Hashavuot,* (Jerusalem, 5759 /1999), chap.29 para.14 and fn.24.
(27) Lifschitz, op. cit.
(28) Casu marzu, (Wikipedia)
(29) Amar - Al tolaim, op. cit.
(30) It was for academic purposes and not for eating since it might contain non-Kosher ingredients and be gevinat akum!
(31) Amar - Al tolaim, op. cit. A far more detailed account of a successful attempt to obtain casu marzu cheese in 2017 was written by Matt Collangelo in "A Desperate Search for Casu Marzu, Sardinia's Illegal Maggot Cheese," (Internet)
(32) Rema SA YD 84:16
(33) Information from Rabbi Ya'akov Blau, Kiryat Arba, 2 Elul 5778/13 August 2018
(34) Rabbi Yissachar ben Mordechai Sasson, *Ibur Shanim - Tikun Yissachar,* (Venice, 5339/1579), e.g. p.22b
(35) Ibid.
(36) Rabbi Shlomo Yosef Zevin, *Hamoadim b'Halachah*, (Avraham Tzioni: Tel Aviv, 5724/1963), p.187
(37) "Rabbi: Genetically Cloned Pig Meat is Kosher, even with Milk," JTA [Jewish Telegraphic Agency], 22 March 2018, (Internet); "Rabbi says meat from genetically cloned pig could be eaten by Jews – including with milk," JTA [Jewish Telegraphic Agency], 22 March 2018, (Internet)
(38) "haRabbanim Lior, Cherlow v'Aviner: basar m'turbat yiyeh kasher...," Netanel Lipa, forum "Kipa," 17 May 2016 (5776), (Internet)

(39) "Cloned Pigs Aren't Kosher," Rabbi Gil Student, "Torah Musings," 9 April 2018 (5778), (Internet)
(40) Rabbi J. David Bleich, "Stem-Cell Burgers," *Tradition,* no.46 issue 4, 2013, (Rabbinical Council of America), Survey of Recent Halachic Periodical Literature, pp.48-62
(41) Rabbi Yair Hoffman, "Tzohar Rabbi Is Incorrect: Cloned Pig Meat Is Not Kosher," *Halachic Musings,* reprinted from "The 5 Towns Jewish Times," 5 April 2018, (Internet)
(42) Gil Student, op. cit.
(43) Talmud Bavli, Chulin 109b
(44) Shabout, (Wikipedia); Ari Zivotofsky and Zohar Amar, "Identifying the Ancient Shibuta Fish," (originally appeared in *Environmental Biology of Fishes,* March 2006, vol.75, issue 3, pp.361-363), (Internet)
(45) Ari Zivotofsky and Ari Greenspan, "Quail, Blue Eggs and Shibuta," *Mishpacha* Jewish Family Weekly, Jerusalem, 28 Tishri 5771/6 October 2010, p.45
(46) Chumash: Vayikra 11:7, Devarim 14:8
(47) Chumash Devarim 14:4-5
(48) Dr. I. M. Levinger and Dr. M. Dor, "Sheva ha'Chayot ha'Tehorot" (The Seven Clean Wild animals), *Torah u'Mada,* vol.4 no.2, Elul 5735/ September 1975, (Association of Orthodox Jewish Scientists in Israel), pp.37-50
(49) Babirusa, (Wikipedia)
(50) Rabbi David Bleich, "The Babirusa: A Kosher Pig?" *Contemporary Halachic Problems,* vol.3, (Ktav Publishing House: New York), p.66
(51) "Israeli Farmers Say They've Found a Pig whose Meat is Fit for a Rabbi," Hugh Orgel, Tel Aviv, 17 July 1990, (Internet)
(52) This Little Piggy Not Likely to Be on Kosher Menus," John Dart, Times Religion Writer, 19 February 1985, (Internet)
(53) Bleich – Babirusa, op. cit., p.74
(54) Rabbi Chaim Ben-Attar, *Ohr Hachaim al Chamishah Chumshai Torah – sefer Vayikra,* (Zolkiew, 5559/1799), Chumash Vayikra 11:3
(55) "This Little Piggy ...," op. cit.
(56) SA OC 695:4
(57) Rabbi Naftali Tzvi Yehudah Berlin (Netziv), *Ha'amek She'eila al Sheiltot d'Rav Achai Gaon,* (Vilna, 5621/1861), Parashat Vayakhel 67:9
(58) Chumash: Vayikra 11: 13-19, Devarim 14: 12-18
(59) SA YD 82:2-3
(60) Talmud Bavli, Chulin 59a, 65a
(61) e.g. Rashi on Talmud Bavli, Chulin 59a; Tosafot "hadores" on Talmud Bavli, Chulin 61a; Rambam, Peirush Hamishnayot, Chulin 3:6
(62) Tosafot "hadores" on Talmud Bavli, Chulin 61a
(63) Rabbi Yisrael ben Chaim Bruna, *Teshuvot Mahari Bruna,* (Saloniki, 5558/1798), responsum 145, p.56
(64) Rabbi Tzvi Hirsch Shapira, *Darkei Teshuvah* on SA YD vol.3, 2nd edition, (Vilna, 5652/1892), YD 82:13

(65) Dr. Yisrael Meir Levinger, *Mazon Kasher min Hachai* (Modern Kosher Food Production from Animal Source), (Institute for Agricultural Research According to the Thora: Jerusalem 5740/1980), p.71. fn.187

(66) Ibid., p.71; Meir Levinger, "Oaf tahor ne'echal bamasoret," *Sinai*, vol.64, Tishri-Adar 5729/1969, (Mosad Harav Kook, Jerusalem), p.265 (8)

(67) Rabbi Moshe Berstein, *Olam hatoshia*, (London 5710/1950), p.72

(68) Levinger - mazon kasher, op. cit., p.71

(69) *Septuagint*: Levitikón 11:18, Defteronómio 14:16

(70) *Vulgate*: Leviticus 11:18, Deuteronomium 14:16

(71) Kosher animals, (Wikipedia)

(72) King James Version of Bible, (Wikipedia)

(73) *The Holy Bible, King James Version*: Leviticus 11:18, Deuteronomy 14:16

(74) John Wycliffe's translation of Bible: Leviticus 11:18, Deuteronomium 14:17

(75) *The holie Bible* - the Bishops' Bible: Deuteronomy 14:17

(76) The Tyndale Bible. At about the same period a translation of the Bible was made into German and this was known as the "Luther Bible" and in both Leviticus and Deuteronomy appears "swan" (den Schwan), Levitikus 11:17, Deuteronomium 14:17

(77) e.g. Noah Webster Bible, (mid-19th century); Darby Bible, (late 19th century)

(78) *Holy Scriptures* translation by Isaac Leeser, (Philadelphia, 5614/1854), p.229 fn.a

(79) Jubilee Bible published in 2000 writes "swan": Leviticus 11:18, Deuteronomy 14:16

(80) e.g. *Holy Bible*, New International Version (1970s); *Holy Bible*, New King James Version (1982); *Holy Bible*, English Standard Version (2001); *The Holy Scriptures*, Jewish Publication Society of America, 5677 (1917)

(81) "backe" cannot be another name for swan since in the Bishops' Bible in the list of non-kosher birds in Devarim appears *both* "swan" and "backe"

(82) "Disclaimer About Bible Version Usage," Lee, 28 February 2012, (Internet)

(83) Levinger - Mazon Kasher, op. cit., p.71 fn.189

(84) "What Does Kosher Mean?" Badatz Igud Rabbonim KIR, (undated), (Internet)

(85) Levinger - Mazon Kasher, op. cit., p.71

(86) Swan Upping, (Wikipedia)

(87) "Kreplach: A look beneath the dough," foodhistoryreligion, "Schoolchanger," 8 October 2015, (Internet)

(88) Chumash: Vayikra 11:9, Devarim 14:9

(89) *Encyclopædia Britannica* 1911: Turbot

(90) Rabbi David Feldman, *Shimusha shel Torah*, (Hamadpis: London, 5711/1951), p.19

(91) Rabbi Yitzchak ben Yosef of Corbeil, *Sefer Mitzvot Katan (haSmak m'Tzorich)* part 2, (Jerusalem 5737/1977), mitzvah 209 fn.135; Rosh and Yisrael of Krems, Hagahot Asheri Avodah Zarah 2:41

(92) Dr. Meir Levinger, "Al zihui hadag hanikra Barbuta," _Hamayan,_ (Jerusalem), vol.22, issue 2, Tevet 5742/1982, pp.17-18

(93) M. Levinger and M. Negin, "l'iyun b'shailat dag haturbot," _Sridim,_ (Standing Committee of European Rabbis), no.5, Iyar 5744/1984, p.15

(94) Rabbi J. David Bleich, "Kashrut – Turbot," _Contemporary Halachic Problems_, vol.3, (Ktav Publishing House: New York, 1989), p.63

(95) Ibid., p.63 fn.8; _Sridim,_ op. cit., p.15

(96) Rabbi David Tzvi Hoffmann, _Melamed Leho'il_, vol.2 YD, (Hermon Press: Frankfurt am Main, 5687/1927), responsum 19

(97) Rabbi Meir Lerner, Hadar _Hacarmel_, vol.2 YD, (London, 5731/1971), responsum 28

(98) Levinger - _Hamayan_, op. cit., p.18

(99) Lerner, op. cit.

(100) Dr. C. Duschinsky, _The Rabbinate of the Great Synagogue, London, from 1756-1842,_ (Oxford University Press, 1921), pp.292-93

(101) Bleich - Turbot, op. cit., p.64

(102) Duschinsky, op. cit., p.292

(103) Hyman A. Simons, _Forty Years a Chief Rabbi: the Life and Times of Solomon Hirschell,_ (Robson Books: London, 1980), p.68

(104) Rabbi Yisrael Lipschitz, "Tiferet Yisrael Yachin" on Mishnah Chulin chap.3 fn.96

(105) Dr. Yisrael Meir Levinger, _Mazon Kasher min Hachai_ (Modern Kosher Food Production from Animal Source), (Institute for Agricultural Research According to the Thora: Jerusalem 5740/1980), p.205

(106) Levinger - _Hamayan_, op. cit., p.18

(107) "Kasher Fish – List Issued by [London] Beth Din," _The Jewish Chronicle_ (London), 14 May 1943, p.18

(108) _Sridim,_ op. cit., p.16

(109) "Incidentally ... Fishy Business," _The Jewish Chronicle_ (London), 29 October 1954, p.6

(110) "Confusion over Turbot – Statement by Beth Din," _The Jewish Chronicle_ (London), 12 November 1954, p.5

(111) Anne J. Kershen, ed., _Food in the Migrant Experience,_ (Centre for the Study of Migration, University of London, 2002(?)), pp.90-91, and fn.42

(112) Feldman, op. cit., p.19

(113) "Kosher and Non-Kosher Fish," list published by Kashrut.com, updated 19 July 2017, (Internet); Levinger, op. cit., p.211; lists brought out by other kashrut organizations make a similar comment following their list of permitted flounders.

(114) Levinger – Mazon Kasher, op. cit., p.208

(115) Ibid., p.220

(116) Kershen, op. cit., p.91

(117) SA OH 319

(118) Rabbi Zushe Blech, "The Fortunes of a Fish," (reprinted by Kashrut.com. from MK Vaad News & Views, February 2000), (Internet)

(119) Chumash Vayikra 11:21

(120) Talmud Bavli, Chulin 59a

(121) Zohar Amar, "The Eating of Locusts in Jewish Tradition After the Talmudic Period, *The Torah u-Mada Journal,* (Association of Orthodox Jewish Scientists in Israel), volume 11, 2002-2003, p.188

(122) Ibid., pp.190-91

(123) Ibid., pp.191-92

(124) Haim Ben-Atar, "Peri Toar" on *Peirot Ginosar,* (Amsterdam, 5502/1742), SA YD 85:1

(125) Amar - Locusts, op. cit., pp.193-95

(126) Rabbi Petachya Mordechai Birdugo, *Nofet Tzufim,* (Casablanca, 5698/1938), YD responsum 13

(127) Rabbi Amram Korach, *Sa'arat Teiman,* (Jerusalem, 5714/1954), p.94

(128) Amar - Locusts, op. cit., pp.195-96

(129) *Aruch Hashulchan* YD 85:5

(130) "The Desert Dessert Locust," Biblical Museum of Natural History, Bet Shemesh Israel, (Internet)

(131) Rabbi Yitzchak Ratzabi, "Achilat Chagavim Haksherim al pi haMasoret" part 2, *Tenuvat Sadeh,* (Hamachon Lemitzvot Hat'luyot Ba'aretz: Bet Uziel), no. 23, Nisan-Iyar 5759/1999, pp.33-39

(132) Dessert Desert Locust, op. cit.

(133) Ibid.

(134) "Can insect powdered food be Kosher?" Rabbi Alex Shandrovsky founder of "L'chaim Foods – Artisan Kosher Cuisine," San Francisco California, 23 August 2016, (Internet)

(135) "Adventurous Kashrus," Amy Spiro, "The New York Jewish Week," 26 July 2011, (Internet); Shallots Bistro, menu for "Mesorah Dinner" held in Chicago on 24 July 2011, (Internet)

(136) "Eating locusts: The crunchy kosher snack taking Israel by swarm," Cordelia Hebblethwaite PRI's The World, "BBC News Magazine," 21 March 2013, (Internet)

(137) "Why are locusts kosher?" Meir Lipnick, 8 September 2014, (Internet)

(138) Eating locusts, op. cit.; prawns are a non-kosher sea creature and it is reported that "When Australia was hit by a swarm of locusts in 2004 they were renamed 'sky-prawns'."

(139) e.g. "Matconnei arbe lo l'Taimanim bilvad," News from Walla, 7 March 2013, (Internet)

(140) Dessert Desert Locust, op. cit.

(141) "Haposek Hataimani biker b'chavat gidul chagavim," Menachem Kolodski, Altualia olam hayahudut," 25 June 2018, (Internet); "Kasher l'ma'achal? Tiud: Maran haRav Yitzchak Ratzabi siyar b'chavat chagvim," Kalman Teller, "Chadashot Chareidim," 2 Tammuz 5788/25 June 2018, (Internet)

(142) Ari Zivotofsky and Ari Greenspan, "Quail, Blue Eggs and Shibuta," *Mishpacha* Jewish Family Weekly, Jerusalem, 28 Tishri 5771/6 October 2010, p.49

(143) SA YD 85:2

(144) Rema SA YD 13:1

(145) *Aruch Hashulchan* YD 85:7

(146) SA YD 87:3

(147) Bet Yosef on Tur YD 87 "dagim"; Rabbi Ovadia Yosef, *Yechave Da'at* vol.6, (Jerusalem, 5744/1984), responsum 48; Rabbi Yitzchak Yosef, *Yalkut Yosef – Kitzur Shulchan Aruch,* (Machon Chazon Ovadia: Jerusalem, 5757/1997), YD 86:1 "din achilat dagim im chalav o basar"; Rabbi Eli Mansour wrote "the custom in Halab (Syria) was to avoid eating fish with milk," (Daily Halachah), (Internet)

(148) SA YD 87:3; Rabbi Yitzchak Ratzabi, *Shuchan Aruch Hamekutzar,* YD vol.1, (Bnei Brak, 5760/2000), 136:8

(149) SA OC 204:1

(150) SA OC 158:4

(151) Ba'er Heteiv OC 158:9; According to Rabbi Ben-Zion Abba Shaul, *Ohr LeZion,* (Machon Ohr LeZion: Jerusalem, 5753/1993), responsa part 2, chap.11, responsum 5 and fn.) with frozen yoghurt (presumably almost frozen!) one would not have to wash one's hands

(152) Chumash Devarim 14:4-5

(153) Rabbi Avraham Yeshaya Karelitz, *Chazon Ish,* YD, (Bnei Brak, 5754/1994), YD 11:4

(154) Rashi on Talmud Bavli, Chulin 80a

(155) Ibn Ezra on Chumash Devarim 14:5

(156) Targum Onkelos, Devarim 14:5

(157) Targum Yonatan ben Uziel, Devarim 14:5, (according to other opinions it is Targum Yerushalmi)

(158) *Septuagint,* Defteronómio 14:5

(159) *Vulgate,* Deuteronomium 14:5

(160) Rabbi Sa'adia Gaon, *Tafsir* (Judeo-Arabic translation of Torah), Devarim 14:5

(161) Rabbeinu Yona (Abulwalid Merwan ibn Ganach), *Sepher Haschoraschim,* lexicon, (Druck von H. Itzkowski: Berlin, 5656/1896), "zemer," p.134

(162) Rabbi David ben Yosef Kimchi (RaDak), *Sefer Haschoraschim,* lexicon, (Impensis G. Bethge: Berolini, 5607/1847), "zemer," p.89 col.177

(163) Rabbi Shimon ben Tzemach Duran (Rashbatz), *Yavin Shmuah,* (Levorno 5504/1744), Hilchot Teraiphot

(164) Rabbi Yehosef Schwartz, *Tevuot Ha'aretz - Totzaot Ha'aretz,* (J. M. Stand: Lemberg 5625/1865), p.2

(165) Rabbi Yitzchak Ratzabi, *Shuchan Aruch Hamekutzar,* YD vol.1, (Bnei Brak, 5760/2000), 134:1 fn.6

(166) *Sefer Zicharon l'Rav Yosef ben David Kafih (Kapach),* ed. Zohar Amar and Hananel Seri, (Bar-Ilan University: Ramat Gan, 5761/2001), p.73; Zohar Amar, "Ibud Ohr Giraffa l'ketivat Stam," *Masorah l'Yoseph* (Moreshet of Rabbi Yosef Kafih (Kapach), vol.9, (Machon Mishnat HaRambam: Netanya, Israel, 5776/2016), fn.2

(167) "Shal et Harav – Kashrut," answer by Rabbi David Lau – Modi'in, 3 Tevet 5765/2005, "Moreshet," (Internet)

(168) Rabbi Eliezer Melamed, "Bein habeheimah hatahorah l'temeiah," "Revivim" (weekly column in newspaper "B'sheva" by Rabbi Eliezer Melamed), 24 Nisan 5773/4 April 2013, (Internet)

(169) Rambam, Ma'achalot Asurot 1:8

(170) "Kashrut of a Giraffe," "Torah Learning Resources" under the direction of The Edmond J. Safra Synagogue, (Internet)

(171) Dr. Oded Shveirman, "leparashat Re'ah – Zemer l'Giraffer - al Kashrut Ba'alei Chaim," (Internet)

(172) "Giraffe is Kosher, rabbis rule in Israel," Tim Butcher in Jerusalem, *Telegraph* (England), 6 June 2008, (Internet); "Rabbi decides it's OK for Jews to eat giraffe after declaring the animal's meat kosher," reporter, *Daily Mail online*, 6 June 2008, (Internet)

(173) Avi Zivotofsky, "What's The Truth About ... Giraffe Meat!" *Jewish Action*, (Orthodox Union of America), Fall 2000/5761; Rabbi Yirmiyahu Ullman, "Kosher Giraffe," letter to Ben in Baltimore from Ohr Somayach, (Internet)

(174) "Giraffe," Lory Herbison and George W. Frame, *Britannica online*, (Internet); Ullman, op. cit.

(175) "Kosher Conundrums," Gil Stern Stern Hoffman, *Jerusalem Post Magazine*, 30 July 2010, (Internet); "Quail, Blue Eggs and Shibuta," *Mishpacha* Jewish Family Weekly, Jerusalem, 6 October 2010, p.48

(176) "Has a Giraffe ever been slaughtered for its kosher meat," Pete Zeman, "Quora" (an online question and answer site based in Mountain View California), 21 December 2015, (Internet)

(177) "Eating Giraffe Meat, Why is it common practice not to eat Giraffe meat?" "Mi Yodeya," 4 July 2010, edited 29 November 2011, (Internet); Ullman, op. cit.

(178) "Has a Giraffe ever been slaughtered for its kosher meat," op. cit., Zev Sero, 29 December 2015, Ibid.

(179) Ibid.

(180) Ibid.

(181) Ibid.; Quail, op. cit.

(182) Quail, op. cit.

(183) "Stalking kosher game (Hold the Giraffe)," Kara Newman, 19 October 2005, *The New York Times*, (Internet)

(184) "The Jewish Giraffe," Larry Kaplan, 11 June 2008, *The Atlantic* (USA), (Internet)

(185) Hoffman, *Jerusalem Post*, op. cit.

(186) "What does Giraffe Meat Taste Like?" Adam Martin, 10 February 2014, *New York Magazine*, (Internet)

(187) Mishnah Berura 529:11

(188) SA YD 81:1

(189) SA YD 86:1

(190) "Do Bee don't Bee – A Halachik guide to Honey and Bee Derivatives," Rabbi Dovid Heber Star-K Kosher Certification, Baltimore Maryland, Fall 2010, (Internet)

(191) "Honey Interesting Facts," Dr. Yvette Alt Miller, 16 September 2017, Aish Hatorah, (Internet)

(192) Talmud Bavli, Bechorot 7b

(193) Sources for above arguments are given below; for summary see paper by Rabbi Zushe Yosef Blech, BDK Sao Paulo Brazil, (Internet)

(194) Rabbi Eliezer Waldenberg, *Tzitz Eliezer*, vol.11, (Jerusalem, 5733/1973), chap.59

(195) Rabbi Moshe Sternbuch, *Teshuvot ve-Hanhagot,* vol.4, (Jerusalem, 5762/2002), YD 188

(196) Rabbi Isser Yehuda Unterman, "lishaylat 'Tuny Royal" - badin 'J'ila Royal' hayotsei m'devorim," *Kol Tora,* (Slomon: Jerusalem), year 13 issue 6, 5719/1959, p.5

(197) Rabbi Moshe Feinstein, *Igrot Moshe,* YD vol.2, (New York, 5733/1973), responsum 24

(198) Rabbi Chanoch Dov Padwa, *Cheishev haEphod,* vol.2, (London, 5737/1977), responsum 104, (pp.122-23)

(199) Rabbl Shlomo Zalman Auerbach, *Minchat Shlomo,* vol.2, (Jerusalem, 5760/2000), responsum 64

(200) Rabbi Moshe Via, *Bedikat Hamazon Kahalachah*, (Hamachon L'hanchalat haHalachah: Jerusalem, 5758/1998), p.149

(201) "Halachos of the Hive," OU Kosher Certification, (Internet); "Royal Jelly in Raw Honey," Council of Orthodox Rabbis of Greater Detroit, 1 March 2018, (Internet)

(202) "The Bee Folks," statement put out by The Bee Folks Company of Maryland, (Internet)

(203) "The Kashrus and Halachos of Honey," Kof-K Kosher supervision Teaneck New Jersey, (Internet)

(204) Advertisement of "Fruitful Yield Health Foods," Bloomingdale Illinois for Royal Jelly stating it is supervised by Triangle K, (Internet)

(205) Kosher certification for Royal Jelly by Rabbi T. Hod-Hochwald of KSI Kosher supervision Bad Kissingen Germany, (Internet)

(206) "Bee Folks," op. cit.

(207) Mishnah Berura 176:2

(208) Talmud Bavli, Chulin 65a

(209) "Nightingale – Birds," what-when-how - in Depth Tutorials and Information, (Internet)

(210) Rabbi Kalonymus ben Kalonymus, *Igeret Ba'alei Chaim,* (Vilna, 5634 /1874); Prior to this book, there was no word in Hebrew for "nightingale" and when Rabbi Kalonymus made his translation he created the word "zamir" for a nightingale. This word occurs in Shir Hashirim 2:12, but there it means a song or pruning a vine.

(211) Kalonymus, op. cit., p.53a; *The Animals' Lawsuit Against Humanity*, English translation by Anton Laytner and Dan Bridge, (Fons Vitae: Louisville Kentucky, 2005), pp.42, 50

(212) SA YD 82:2

(213) Rabbi Yitzchak ben Meir haKohen, *Zivchei Kohen,* (Livorno, 5592/1832) Frontispiece

(214) Ibid., between pp.12-13

(215) Ibid., p.13

(216) Dr. Yisrael Meir Levinger, *Mazon Kasher min Hachai* (Modern Kosher Food Production from Animal Source), (Institute for Agricultural Research According to the Thora: Jerusalem 5740/1980), p.85; Meir Levinger, "Oaf

tahor ne'echal b'masoret," *Sinai,* vol.64 subvols.1-6 (366-391) Tishri-Adar 5729/1969, (Mosad Harav Kook: Jerusalem), p.274 (17) no.11

(217) Zohar Amar, *Masoret ha'Oaf* - kovetz ma'amarim, (Tel-Aviv, 5764/2004), pp.52-53

(218) Levinger - *Sinai,* op. cit., pp.263-276

(219) *Encyclopedia Judaica* vol.6 - Dietary Laws, (Keter Publishing House: Jerusalem), pp.29-30

(220) see Levinger - *Mazon Kasher,* op. cit. and Levinger - *Sinai,* op. cit.

(221) Rambam, Hilchot Yom Tov 6:17-18

(222) Talmud Bavli: Chulin 66b, Niddah 51b

(223) *Encyclopedia Talmudit* vol.7 – Dagim, (Talmudic Encyclopedia Institute: Jerusalem, 5713/1956), col.208

(224) Rabbi Chaim ben Yisrael Benvenisti, *sefer Knesset Hagedolah,* (Constantinople, 5471/1711(?)), YD dinei dagim, chap.83

(225) Ari Z. Zivotofsky, "The Turning of the Tide -The Kashrut Tale of the Swordfish," *B.D.D* (Bekhol Derakhekha Daehu), 19 January 2008, (Bar-Ilan University, Ramat Gan 2008), p.21 and fn.41

(226) *Knesset Hagedolah,* op. cit.

(227) Zivotofsky - *BDD,* op. cit., p.20

(228) Rabbi Yosef ben Meir Teomim, *Pri Megadim,* YD Siftei Da'at, (Amsterdam, 5588/1828), YD 83:2

(229) Rabbi Ya'akov Chaim Sofer, *Kaf Hachaim,* YD 83:9

(230) see Zivotofsky - *BDD,* op. cit., p.22 for list

(231) Zivotofsky - *BDD,* op. cit., p.22

(232) "Kosher Conundrums," Gil Stern Stern Hoffman, 30 July 2010, *Jerusalem Post Magazine*

(233) "Et ze tochlu micol asher bamayim," *Hapardes,* (Chicago Illinois), vol.7 no.1, Nissan 5693/April 1933, p.17; "Et ze tochlu mikol asher bamayim, kol asher lo snapir v'kaskeset tocheilu," *Hapardes,* op. cit., vol.8 no.9, Kislev 5698/December 1934, p.19

(234) Zivotofsky - *BDD,* op. cit., p.24

(235) possibly the letters reproduced in *Hapardes,* op. cit., vol.40 no.4, Tevet 5726/January 1966, pp.16-18

(236) Zivotofsky - *BDD,* op. cit., pp.5, 25

(237) *Hapardes,* op. cit., vol.40 no.4, Tevet 5726/January 1966, pp.16-19, includes exchange of letters between Rabbi Unterman and Dr. Tendler from Adar II 5722 (1962)

(238) Zivotofsky - *BDD,* op. cit., pp.28-33

(239) *Encyclopedia Talmudit* vol.7 – Dagim, op. cit., between columns 208-209

(240) "Swordfish," *Proceedings of the [Conservative] Rabbinical Assembly* (USA), year 30, 1966, prepared for the Committee on Jewish Law and Standards, pp.111-115

(241) Zivotofsky - *BDD,* op. cit., p.45, p.46 fn.107, p.48 fns.112, 113

(242) Ibid., pp.48-49 and fn.113

(243) "The swordfish (Xiphias gladius L.) its life-history and economic importance in the northwest Atlantic," *Bulletin,* no.130, "The Fisheries Research Board of Canada," 1961, p.4

(244) "Why Swordfish is Unclean," based on an article by Cecil E. Maranville, (Internet)

(245) Rabbi Moshe Sofer, *Chatam Sofer*, YD responsum 75

(246) Zivotofsky - *BDD*, op. cit., p.19

(247) George F. Arata Jr., "A Contribution to the life history of the swordfish Xiphias gladius Linnaeus, from the south Atlantic coast of the United States and the Gulf of Mexico," *Bulletin of Marine Science of the Gulf and Caribbean,* vol.4 no.3, 1954, p.215

(248) J. J. Govani et al., "Ontogeny of Squamation in Swordfish, Xiphias gladius," *Copeia*, (The American Society of Ichthyologists and Herpetologists), vol. 2004 no.2 (May 5 2004), pp.391-96

(249) Zivotofsky - *BDD*, op. cit., p.44 fn.102

(250) "Locusts, Swordfish and Doves: All the Fixings for a Gourmet Kosher Meal," The Associated Press: Jewish World – Haaretz – Israel News, 29 July 2010, (Internet)

(251) Shallots Bistro, menu for "Mesorah Dinner" held in Chicago on 24 July 2011, (Internet)

(252) Ba'er Heteiv SA OC 583:4; *Kitzur Shulchan Aruch* 129:9

(253) Rambam, Hilchot Chametz uMatzah 1:1-2

(254) Chaim Simons, *Ma ze Chametz?* (Nehemiah Institute: Kiryat Arba, 5753/1993), pp.3-4, 12

(255) Amongst those who mention this, but do not necessarily agree are: Mordechi masechet Pesachim 588; Maharil Hilchot Pesach; Tur OC 453

(256) Rabbenu Yerucham ben Meshullam, *Sefer Toldot Adam v'Chava,* (Venice), Adam, chap.5 para.3

(257) Mishnah Berura 453:6

(258) Ibid., 453:5

(259) Simons, op. cit., p.7

(260) "What is Kitniyot?" Kashrut.com, authored by the OU, 2008, (Internet)

(261) Kitniyot, (Wikipedia)

(262) Vilna Gaon (the Gra), *Ma'aseh Rav,* para.184

(263) "What is Kitniyot?" op. cit.

(264) Rabbi Avraham Danzig, *Nishmat Adam,* (Warsaw, 5632/1872), responsum 20

(265) Rabbi Moshe Feinstein, *Igrot Moshe,* OC, (New York, 5733/1973), responsum 63

(266) Ibid.

(267) Beth Din Tzedek Eda Charedis (Jerusalem), *Madrich haKashrut lechag haPesach,* vol.69, 5778/2018, p.17

(268) Ibid. Potato flour was under their supervision for Pesach, p.63; however, at a much earlier period (including the 1960s) they stated it was only for young children (although it cannot be excluded that it was for some other reason.)

(269) Rabbi Yehuda Spitz, "Pesach - The Quinoa-Kitniyos Conundrum," Ohr Somayach, 5775/2015, (Internet)

(270) This is described at length in footnote 13 to "The Quinoa-Kitniyos Conundrum," op. cit.

(271) Letter to the general public from Rabbi Elyakim Levanon, the Rabbi of Shomron, headed "pirchiot orez – 'kasher le'Pesach,'" 28 Adar 5778 (2018), (Internet)

(272) "Bama l'Kashrut – Pirchiot Orez – B & D – l'Ashkanazim," para.5, Rabbi Elyakim Levanon, Kosharot, (Internet)

(273) Letter to the general public from the two Chief Rabbis of Ma'ale Adumim headed "hoda'ah b'nosei pirchiot orez," erev Pesach 5778 (2018), (Internet)

(274) "Pirchiot Orez b'Pesach," Question submitted to the Chief Rabbinate of Israel on the question of pirchiot orez, and the subsequent answer, Yeshiva website – Ask the Rabbi, 5 Nissan 5778 (2018), (Internet); "Harav David Lau: Im kol hakavod l'Rav Levanon, ossur le'echol pirchiot orez b'Pesach," Guy Ezra, Chadashot Srugim, 13 Nissan 5788/29 March 2018, (Internet)

(275) "Interesting Psak: B & D rice cakes are not kitniyot," life in Israel. blogspot, 15/18 March 2018 (5778), posted by Rafi G., (Internet)

(276) SA OC 473:4

(277) Talmud Bavli, Pesachim 114b

(278) SA OC 476:1-2

(279) Chumash Vayikra 7:26

(280) Chumash Vayikra 7:27

(281) Chumash Devarim 12:23

(282) Mishnah Berura 316:29

(283) SA YD 67:1

(284) SA YD 67:2

(285) *Chochmat Adam* 30:1

(286) SA YD 66:1

(287) Rambam, Ma'achalot Asurot 6:1

(288) SA YD 66:9

(289) *Kaf Hachaim,* YD 66:43; Rabbi Yitzchak Yosef, *Yalkut Yosef – Kitzur Shulchan Aruch,* (Machon Chazon Ovadia: Jerusalem, 5757/1997), YD 66:6

(290) Talmud Bavli, Kritut 21b; SA YD 66:9

(291) Ibid; ibid.

(292) Rambam, Ma'achalot Asurot 6:1

(293) *Aruch Hashulchan* YD 66:34

(294) Rema SA YD 66:10; *Kaf Hachaim* YD 66:50; *Yalkut Yosef,* op. cit., YD 66:6

(295) SA YD 66:10; *Aruch Hashulchan* YD 66:35; Rabbi Avraham-Sofer Avraham, *Nishmat Avraham,* 2nd expanded edition, vol.2, YD, (Jerusalem, 5767/2007), YD 66:1

(296) "Traditional Maasai Food: Blood and Milk," Thomson Safaris, 16 January 2014 (5774), (Internet)

(297) Blood as food, (Wikipedia)

(298) "Chasal Sidur Pesach k'hilchato," *Yisrael Hayom*, 3 April 2015 (5775), (Internet)

(299) Chumash Devarim 14:4-5

(300) Chumash Devarim: 12:15, 12:22, 14:5, 15:22
(301) Dr. Meir Levinger and Dr. M. Dor, "Sheva hachayot hatehorot," *Tora u'Mada,* vol.4 no.2, Elul 5735/September 1975, (Association of Orthodox Jewish Scientists in Israel), pp.43-44
(302) *Septuagint,* Defteronómio 14:5
(303) *Vulgate,* Deuteronomium 14:5
(304) Ari Zivotofsky, "What's the Truth About ... Nikkur Achoraim?" *Jewish Action,* (Orthodox Union of America), Fall 2006
(305) Dayan Dr. Isidor Grunfeld, *The Jewish Dietary Laws,* vol.1, (Soncino Press: London, 1972 (5732)), pp.66-67
(306) *Jewish Action,* Fall 2006, op. cit.
(307) Grunfeld, op. cit., p.67 fn.1
(308) *Jewish Action,* Fall 2006, op. cit.
(309) Beth Din Tzedek Eda Charedis (Jerusalem), *Madrich haKashrut lechol Hashanah,* vol.69, 5778/2018, p.76
(310) SA YD 80:1
(311) Ibid.
(312) *Encyclopedia Talmudit,* vol.14 - Chayah, (Talmudic Encyclopedia Institute: Jerusalem, 5733/1973), col.744
(313) *Jewish Action,* Fall 2006, op. cit.
(314) "Stalking Kosher Game (Hold the Giraffe)," Kara Newman, 19 October 2005, *The New York Times,* (Internet); "From Venison to Addax Kosher Game," Aaron Kagan, 17 February 2011, *The Forward* (New York City), (Internet)
(315) "Tafrit Basar Hatzvi b'Misedet King Solomon hakasheirah Prague," menu publicised by this restaurant, (Internet)
(316) Ibid.
(317) "Kosher. What is Kosher?" London Beth Din, 5774/2014, (Internet)
(318) "Kosher Food," New South Wales Jewish Board of Deputies (Australia), 5769/2009, (Internet)
(319) SA OC 300:1
(320) Mishnah Berura 300:1
(321) Talmud Bavli, Shabbat 119b
(322) SA YD 82:2
(323) Dr. Yisrael Meir Levinger, *Mazon Kasher min Hachai* (Modern Kosher Food Production from Animal Source), (Institute for Agricultural Research According to the Thora: Jerusalem 5740/1980), p.80
(324) "mashal leadam shemosar tzipur dror l'avdo – dror habayit," *Purtal hadaf hayomi,* 13 Av 5766 (2006), (Internet)
(325) Rabbi Shlomo Min-Hahar, "Kashrut habayit – hatamei vehatahor," "Haskel," Michlelet Herzog, Gush Etzion 5747, (Internet); he writes that "ankor" is sparrow
(326) Levinger – Mazon Kasher, op. cit., pp.80-81; Ari Zivotofsky and Ari Greenspan, "Quail, Blue Eggs and Shibuta," *Mishpacha* Jewish Family Weekly, Jerusalem, 6 October 2010, p.50
(327) "What is Kosher?" London Beth Din, 5774/2014, (Internet)
(328) Levinger - Mazon Kasher, op. cit., p.81

(329) Zohar Amar, "Achilat tziporei dror b'masoret yehudai Taiman," *Afikim –* l'techia ruchanit v'chevratit l'haganat zechuyot u'lmizug goluyot, (Tel Aviv), vol.123-124, Nisan 5763/2003, pp.51-52

(330) Quail, op. cit.

(331) *Septuagint:* Levitikón 11:15, Defteronómio 14:15

(332) Kosher animals, (Wikipedia)

(333) *Vulgate*: Leviticus 11:16, Deuteronomium 14:15

(334) Rabbi Yitzchak ben Meir haKohen, *Zivchei Kohen,* (Livorno, 5592/1832), between pp.12-13

(335) Ibid., p.12

(336) Levinger - Mazon Kasher, op. cit., p.81

(337) Ibid.

(338) Amar, op. cit., p.52

(339) Chumash Devarim 22:6-7

(340) "Shiluach Hakan," Rabbi Zvi Goldberg, Kashrus Kurrents 2017, Star-K, (Internet). This is in contrast to the OU in America who certifies sparrow as a kosher bird, ("OU position on Certifying Specific Animals and Birds, OU Kosher, (Internet))

(341) "Shiluach Hakan b'Tzipor Dror," Rabbi Ya'akov Ariel, Yeshivah website, (Internet)

(342) SA YD 81 title of chapter; Rambam, Ma'achalot Asurot 3:1

(343) House Sparrow, Eggs and young, (Wikipedia). For comparison purposes size of an average chicken's egg: length 59 cm, breadth 44 cm, surface area 74 square cm, weight 50 gm. (Chicken egg sizes, (Wikipedia))

(344) House sparrow, op. cit.

(345) SA YD 86:5

(346) SA YD 87:5

(347) Ibid.

(348) "At Kosher Feast, Fried Locusts for Dessert," Nathan Jeffay, Jerusalem, 28 July 2010, *The Forward*, New York City, (Internet)

(349) SA OC 552:1

(350) *Kitzur Shulchan Aruch* 123:3

(351) *Encyclopedia of Food and Culture –* Gelatin, The Gate group, 2003

(352) "Getting into the Thick of Things: Gelatin," Rabbi Avrohom Mushell, Spring 2013, Kashrus Kurrents 2013, Star-K Kosher certification, (Internet)

(353) "Kashrus, Food and Chemicals," Dayan Gabriel Krausz of Manchester Beth Din, 3 April 1972 (5732), p.3; *Emunat Itecha,* issue 97, Tishri 5773/2002, chap.37, Gelatin, (Machon haTorah veHa'aretz: Kfar Darom), p.41

(354) Talmud Bavli, Chulin 114a

(355) "Gelatin in Halacha: Recent Developments," David Roth, 9 July 2014, *Torah Musings*, (Internet)

(356) Rabbi Chaim Ozer Grodzinski, *Achiezer*, (Vilna), YD chap.33, para.5

(357) This responsum is brought in the introduction to volume 4 of *Tzitz Eliezer* by Rabbi Eliezer Waldenberg, (Jerusalem, 5715/1954), p.10

(358) Ibid., p.12

(359) Rabbi Ovadia Yosef, *Yabia Omer*, vol.8, (Jerusalem (new edition), 5775/2015), responsum 11

(360) Rabbi Aharon Kotler, *Mishnat Rebbi Aharon*, vol 1 OC YD, (Machon Yerushalayim: Jerusalem, 5745 /1985), YD chap.17

(361) e.g. Rabbi Moshe Feinstein, *Igrot Moshe*, YD, (New York, 5720/1960), YD responsum 37; Rabbi Yitzchak Ya'acov Weiss, *Minchat Yitzchak*, vol.5, (Minchat Yitzchak: Jerusalem, 5753/1993), responsum 5

(362) Krausz, op. cit., p.7

(363) "What is Kosher Gelatin Revisited," OU Kosher certification, (Internet)

(364) *Torah Musings* – Gelatin, op. cit.

(365) Ibid.

(366) Readers' Comments to *Torah Musings* – Gelatin, op. cit., including a notice from the London Beth Din, (Internet)

(367) *Torah Musings* – Gelatin, op. cit., fn.27

(368) Ibid.

(369) "Who determines the kosher status of "new" foods?" "Mi Yodea," 4 July 2012, (Internet)

(370) "What is kosher gelatin revisited," op. cit.

(371) Kashrus Kurrents - Gelatin, op. cit.

(372) SA YD 116:2; Kashrus Kurrents - Gelatin, op. cit.

(373) Rambam, Ma'achalot Asurot 9:3

(374) Kashrus Kurrents - Gelatin, op. cit.

(375) Rema SA OC 670:2

(376) "The "Hole" Truth About Sufganiyot," Carol Green Ungar, *Jewish Action*, (Orthodox Union of America), Winter 2012

(377) Chumash Vayikra 11:9

(378) Targum Onkelus, Vayikra 11:9

(379) Ramban on Chumash Vayikra 11:9

(380) Rema SA. OC. 83: 1

(381) e.g. Amna Jalil, "Types of Scales in Fishes," 21 February 2015, *Education* (further identification not specified), (Internet)

(382) "All About Kosher Fish," Aryeh Citron, Parashat Shemini. Chabad.org, (Internet)

(383) Yisrael Meir Levinger, *Mazon Kasher min Hachai* (Modern Kosher Food Production from Animal Source), (Institute for Agricultural Research According to the Thora: Jerusalem 5740/1980), p.106 fn.2

(384) "New York's Finest Caviar: All the Way From a Socialist Kibbutz in Northern Israel," Haim Handwerker, 27 April 2010, *Haaretz* online, (Internet)

(385) Ibid.

(386) Rabbi Shmuel ben Meshullam Gerondi, *Ohel Moed*, part 1, (Shmuel Halevi Tzukerman: Jerusalem, 5646/1886), sha'ar issur v'heter, derech rishon, netiv daled, p.14

(387) Ibid.

(388) Rabbi Yechezkel Landau, *Noda b'Yehudah*, section OC/YD, 2nd edition, YD 29 (written by his son Shmuel)

(389) Rabbi Chizkiah da Silva, *Pri Chadash*, (Amsterdam, 5451/1691), YD 83:26

(390) *Noda b'Yehudah,* op. cit., YD responsum 28
(391) Rabbi Mordechai Banet, *Har Hamor,* (Vienna, 5622/1862), responsum 12
(392) Rabbi Yitzchak Grishaber, *Makel Noam,* (Vienna, 5559/1799), p.8a
(393) Rabbi Aharon Chorin, *Imrei Noam,* (Prague, 5558/1798)
(394) Grishaber, op. cit.
(395) Chorin, op. cit., pp.12b-13a
(396) Ibid., p.16b
(397) Ibid., p.19a
(398) *Noda b'Yehudah,* op. cit., YD responsa 29-30 (written by his son Shmuel)
(399) Ibid., YD responsum 29 (written by his son Shmuel)
(400) Rabbi Elazar Fleckeles, *Teshuvah m'Ahava,* vol.2, (Prague, 5581/1821), Responsum 329
(401) *Noda b'Yehudah,* op. cit., YD responsum 29 (written by his son Shmuel)
(402) "Et ze tochlu mikol asher bamayim," *Hapardes,* (Chicago Illinois), vol.7 no.1, April 1933, p.17; "Et ze tochlu mikol asher bamayim, kol asher lo snapir v'kaskeset tocheilu," *Hapardes,* (Chicago Illinois), vol.8 no.9, December 1934, p.19
(403) *Hapardes* 1934, op. cit., pp.20-21
(404) List is in Dr. Yisrael Meir Levinger, *Mazon Kasher min Hachai* (Modern Kosher Food Production from Animal Source), (Institute for Agricultural Research According to the Thora: Jerusalem 5740/1980), p.208
(405) List in Levinger – Mazon Kasher, op. cit., p.219
(406) Citron, op. cit.
(407) Both lists appear in Levinger – Mazon Kasher, op. cit., p.220
(408) "Police inquiry over sturgeon sale," BBC News, 3 June 2004, (Internet)
(409) *Kitzur Shulchan Aruch* 72:7
(410) SA OC 319
(411) Gefilte fish, (Wikipedia in Hebrew); "The Truth about Gefilte Fish," Jewish Treats, Juicy Bits of Judaism, *Daily,* 24 April 2009, (Internet)
(412) Chumash: Shemot 23:19, Shemot 34:26, Devarim 14:21
(413) SA YD 87:1
(414) SA YD 87:3
(415) SA YD 89:1 and Rema
(416) Talmud Bavli, Chulin 105a
(417) Talmud Bavli, Shabbat 10a
(418) Vilna Gaon (the Gra) SA YD 89:2
(419) Rambam, Ma'achalot Asurot 9:28
(420) SA YD 89:1
(421) "Where do the different traditions for hours of waiting between meat and milk come from?" "Mi Yodea," asked 29 November 2011, edited 1 May 2012, (Internet)
(422) "Hamtana bein basar l'chalav," (Wikipedia in Hebrew)
(423) "Dairy After Meat: How Long A Wait?" Parshas Shlach, Rabbi Doniel Neustadt, torah.org fn.10, (Internet)
(424) "Hamtana bein basar l'chalav," op. cit.
(425) Neustadt, op. cit.; "Hamtanah bein basar l'halav," op. cit.
(426) Rabbenu Yerucham ben Meshullam, *Issur v'Heter,* chap.39 para.1

(427) Rabbenu Yerucham ben Meshullam, *Sefer Toldot Adam v'Chava*, (Venice), sefer Adam, chap.15 para.5 subpara.28

(428) Rabbi David Pardo, *Mizmor l'David*, (Livorno, 5578/1818), Hilchot basar b'chalav, YD 89 (p.61)

(429) Rabbi Tzvi Hirsch Shapira, *Darkei Teshuvah* on SA YD, 2nd edition, (Vilna, 5673/1912), YD 89:6

(430) "Where do the different traditions...," op. cit.

(431) Ibid.

(432) Neustadt, op. cit.; "Hamtana bein basar l'chalav," op. cit.

(433) Rema SA YD 89:1

(434) Rabbi Yisrael ben Petachia Isserlein (author of "Terumat haDeshen"), hagahot on *Sha'arei Dura hashalem* (written by Rabbi Yitzchak ben Meir Dueren), part 2, (Vernov, 5700/1940), dinei issur achilat basar achar gevinah, fn.50

(435) *Sefer haZohar*, Parashat Mishpatim 125a

(436) Rema SA YD 89:1

(437) Tosafot "lis'udata" on Chulin 105a; Mordechi in the name of haRa'avyah, Chulin chap.8 para.689; hagahot Asheri, Chulin chap.8; hagahot Maimani on Rambam Ma'achalot Asurot 10:3

(438) SA YD 90:1

(439) Ari Zivotofsky and Ari Greenspan, "Quail, Blue Eggs and Shibuta," *Mishpacha* Jewish Family Weekly, Jerusalem, 28 Tishri 5771/6 October 2010, p.47

(440) Rabbi Yitzchak ben Moshe Nunes Belmonte, *Sha'ar haMelech*, parts 3 and 4 (S. L. Flecker: Lemberg, 5619/1859), Hilchot Isurei Mizbeiach chap.3

(441) Rema SA OC 494:3

(442) Ba'er Heteiv OC 494:8

(443) *Aruch Hashulchan* OC 494:5

(444) Chumash: Vayikra 11:4, Devarim 14:6

(445) Rambam, Ma'achalot Asurot 1:2

(446) SA YD 79:1

(447) Talmud Bavli, Chulin 63b

(448) Rabbi Shabtei Cohen (the Shach) SA YD 80:1

(449) *Chochmat Adam* 36:1

(450) Rabbi Yosef ben Meir Teomim, *Pri Megadim*, YD Siftei Da'at, (Amsterdam, 5588/1828), YD 80:1

(451) Talmud Bavli, Chulin 59a

(452) Chumash Vayikra 17:13

(453) "Are Zebus Kosher," Rabbi Yechiel Teichman quoting Rabbi Shlomo Miller the Rosh Beis Din of Kollel Toronto, Kashruth Council of Canada (COR), (Internet)

(454) Rabbi Tzvi ben Moshe Yibrov, *Ma'aseh Ish* (Chazon Ish), (Bnei Brak, 5759/1999), p.122

(455) Rabbi Yitzchak Halevi Herzog, *Psakim v'Katavim*, vol.4, (Mossad Harav KooK: Jerusalem, 5750/1990), chap.20, "Kuntras P'nai Shor," p.57

(456) Ibid.

(457) Rabbi Avraham Yeshaya Karelitz, *Kovetz Igrot,* (Jerusalem, 5715/1955), letter 99; Yibrov, op. cit., p.122

(458) Zohar Amar, "Hazebu b'Eretz Yisrael: Bakar im Chatoteret," *Katedra* (Cathedra), (Yad Yitzchak Ben-Tzvi: Jerusalem), no.137, Tishri 5776/2015), pp.17-20

(459) Rabbi Avraham Yeshaya Karelitz, *Pa'er Hador*, vol.4, (Netzach: Bnei Brak, 5733/1973), "pirtzah goreret pirtzot," p.229; Rabbi Avraham Yeshaya Karelitz, *Kovetz Igrot,* vol.3, (Bnei Brak, 5750/1990), letter 113, p.135

(460) "The Zebu Controversy," Zoo Torah, (Rabbi Nosson Slifkin), 5773/2013, (Internet)

(461) Yibrov, op. cit., p.122

(462) Amar - Hazebu, op. cit., p.25

(463) Ibid, p.27; Zebu controversy, op. cit.

(464) Amar - Hazebu, op. cit., p.20

(465) Ibid.

(466) Ibid., p.21

(467) Ibid., p.21, on p.31 is a photocopy of this front page of *Mishpacha* Jewish Weekly Hebrew edition, 18 Adar 5764 /11 March 2004

(468) Ibid. pp.21-22, some news clippings reproduced on p.22

(469) Ibid. p.22 fn.80

(470) Ibid. p.22

(471) Zebu controversy, op. cit.

(472) Amar - Hazebu, op. cit., p.25

(473) Zebu controversy, op. cit.; Amar - Hazebu, op. cit., p.26

(474) Rabbi Shmuel Halevi Wozner, *Shevet Halevi,* vol.10, (Bnei Brak, 5762/2002), responsum 114; he does not specifically mention the zebu but rules that the physical criterion given in the Torah are sufficient to permit eating the animal

(475) Amar - Hazebu, op. cit., p.26

(476) Ibid., p.27

(477) Hamaor Hakatan on Rif Masechet Shabbat Perek Hakira, p.16b

(478) "Cholent! A Guide to Proper Enjoyment," Rabbi Moshe T. Schuchman, Kashrus Kurrents, Star-K Kosher Certification Baltimore Maryland, Spring 2011, (Internet)

Section Four

Beware of the smell!

UNPLEASANT ODOURS AS DISCUSSED IN RABBINIC LITERATURE WITH ACCOMPANYING SCIENTIFIC BACKGROUND

Rabbi Dr. Chaim Simons

(written September 2019)

Readers may put in a request to my e-mail chaimsimons@ gmail.com for original photocopied source materials quoted in this paper to be sent to their e-mails without charge.

It is written in the Torah "And you should cover that which comes out of you [faeces] ... your camp should be holy."[1] From this we learn that it is forbidden according to the Torah to recite any tephillot (prayers) or berachot (blessings) in the presence of human faeces, and in addition, in the surrounding area of their odours.

In this paper we shall attempt to look at the various halachot (Jewish laws) concerning a whole variety of unpleasant odours and examine the associated scientific material.

Odours

It is first necessary to understand general information on odours and especially on their intensity and tone. The Almighty gave man five senses, one of them being the sense of smell. There are some smells, including those of spices, trees, flowers, and fruits, which are so pleasant that one is obliged to recite a berachah when smelling them.[2]

In order for something to have a smell, it must be able to give off molecules which are generally light volatile chemicals, in the main organic compounds, sulphides and ammonia, which then float through the air until they enter the nasal orifices. These molecules then stimulate the sensory cells in the nose, which pass on an electrical impulse to the brain. The brain then interprets patterns in electrical activity as specific odours.[3] The molecules leave the source and float through the air by a process of "diffusion." Diffusion is the movement of molecules from a region of high concentration to a region of low concentration.[4] Hence, it is possible to detect an odour at a distance from its source. In 1855 Adolf Fick formulated in mathematical terms his laws of diffusion which enable one to measure the amount of a substance that will flow through a unit area during a unit time interval.[5] There are two factors, (relevant to this paper) relating to odours. They are the intensity and the tone of the odour. The intensity of an odour can range from "very faint and not annoying" to "[very strong and] extremely annoying."[6] This subject has been researched quantitatively and from the law of Stevens[7] (based on the Weber-Fechner law[8]) there is (in simplified terms) a proportionality between the intensity of an odour and the concentration of the molecules making up this odour. The tone of an odour, (as given in the Hedonic tone assessment) has a scale rating an odour from "pleasant" to "unpleasant."[9] An odour can thus be unpleasant but of low intensity so that it does not annoy an average person.[10]

Following this scientific introduction, we can now start to understand the halachot concerning unpleasant odours.

Human Faeces

The Torah forbids reciting any tephillot or berachot or learning Torah, even in a non-Hebrew language, in the vicinity of human faeces.[11] The definition of "vicinity" is as far as one can see to the front, and four amot (about 2 metres) both to the sides and behind.[12] It is also forbidden in an area where one can smell the odour from the faeces plus a further four amot in any direction.[13]

What is the origin of the odour of human faeces? In the latter stages of digestion, which occurs in the digestive tract, there are countless micro-organisms. These produce a number of odourant volatiles, namely, hydrogen sulphide, mercaptans, indole and skatole, which then pass out of the body together with the faeces and give it the unpleasant odour.[14] The longer the food remains in the digestive tract, the greater will be the concentration of these odourant volatiles and thus according to Stevens' law, the intensity of the odour. The time food spends in the digestive tract depends on the nature of the food.[15] For example, fruits and vegetables have a short transit time, whilst beef, lamb and hard cheese have a much longer one.[16]

We can see from the Torah that davening (praying) is only prohibited in the presence of uncovered faeces.[17] Thus, if the faeces were in a glass container (even though transparent) or in a hole in the ground covered by a foot, it would not then be forbidden to daven in that area.[18] Since the faeces were then covered by the glass or the foot, the molecules of the odourous volatiles would not be able to escape and there would therefore be no odour in the area, thus permitting one to daven there. If, however, the faeces were not hermetically sealed off and the molecules could escape producing an odour in the area, the prohibition of davening in the area would still apply.

Should the human faeces have dried to such an extent that when thrown they would become desiccated, they would then be regarded as dust and one may then daven beside them,[19] since, due to the desiccation, the microbial action stops very quickly and there is therefore no longer an unpleasant odour.[20]

Baby's Faeces

There is a chapter in Shulchan Aruch on baby's faeces, which gives the stage in the life of the child at which one must distance oneself from its faeces and urine. This stage is reached when the child is able to consume a quantity of grain (namely, wheat, barley, spelt, oats, rye) the size of an olive in a short span of time.[21] Different Rabbinical opinions give this span of time a range of from 2 to 9 minutes.[22]

The reason for distancing from the faeces of a child only from the stage when he can consume grain under such conditions is that the intensity of the odour of faeces depends on the child's diet.

How does all this fit in today with the current practice of feeding babies? So long as the baby is fed exclusively on mother's milk, his faeces will be of a yellowish colour and almost odourless and even have a sweetish smell,[23] and there is therefore no problem in davening even in the presence of his faeces.

However, in some cases the baby is not being breast fed, but instead is being bottle fed with formula. In such a case it is more difficult for the baby to digest this formula and this results in his faeces being a paler yellow and having a more intense odour.[24]

The next question is for how long a baby should be breast fed? The halachic sources give a specific length of time. This is written about by Rabbi Efraim ben Shmuel Danvil haKasher in his book entitled "Adnei Paz,"[25] where he rules that it is forbidden to stop breast feeding before a child is 24 months.[26]

One could mention that the minimum age for weaning - 24 months plus – as given by the "Adnei Paz," is today given by the World Health Organization (WHO), and is adopted by many mothers, some of whom even continue breast feeding (together with complementary foods) well beyond the child's second birthday.[27]

A question which arises from this ruling of the "Adnei Paz" is, does this mean that the child is fed *exclusively* on mother's milk until the age of 24 months, or is this milk complemented with solid foods. The difference is that if the mother's milk is complemented by other foods, the faeces could have an unpleasant odour and thus require a distancing before davening in the vicinity of this odour.

What is the present practice regarding complementing the mother's milk with other foods? In other words, at what age does a baby start eating solid food? Until about the 1920s, babies were usually fed exclusively on mother's milk and it was considered harmful by many pediatrics to give them any other food before the age of one year.[28] It would thus seem that under such conditions there were no problems with odourous faeces. At a later period, views changed and it was proposed that from the age of six months solid food should gradually be added to the baby's diet,[29] and this seems to be the general practice today. However, there have been many discussions and trials on feeding babies until the age of one year (or even above that age) on mother's milk exclusively.[30]

At the other extreme, there is a paper from the 1950s which reports on the feeding of babies who are just a few days old on cereal.[31] Another paper refers to giving solid food to babies just a week or two after birth.[32] There is also a report of giving desiccated steak to babies at one to three weeks of age.[33] Thus such babies by this age might well have odourous faeces.

What are the solid foods which are today given to the baby and at what age? One of the first foods is a cereal[34] – sometimes but not always a grain – and this causes the faeces to have a greater odour intensity. Being a grain, this coordinates well with the halachah of when to distance from a baby's faeces.

One should mention that the term "cereal" is not limited to grain but includes rice cereal and soya cereal.[35] Such cereals are not included in the halachic definition of grain, and one might thus be able to argue that if a baby could eat such cereals in the quantity and time stated above, there would be no obligation to distance oneself from their faeces. Could this mean that the odour from their faeces is less intense than that from grain fed babies?

Cereal given to the baby is usually mixed with a liquid and is thus somewhat fluid. In halachah there is a difference between solids and liquids, regarding the time span and quantity that must be consumed for a berachah acharonah (blessing recited after eating food) to be recited.[36] Does this mean that if the baby can consume an "olive size" of this fluid cereal in the allotted span of time then one must distance oneself from his faeces, or that since the cereal is fluid this criterion is not relevant? The Poskim (Rabbinical authorities) of today are divided on this question. Rabbi Yosef Shalom Eliashiv held that it is regarded as a liquid and hence one would not have to distance oneself, whereas in contrast, Rabbi Nissim Karelitz held that if one could drink the "size of an olive" of the liquid in the time taken to drink a "revi'it" (average opinion: about 120 mls), one would have to distance oneself.[37]

Food given to a baby is not limited to a grain cereal; it could well be various other foods such as pureed sweet potatoes, bananas, peaches and pears. These foods will cause the baby's faeces to be more like an adult's and thus the intensity of the odour of the faeces will increase, hence one would have to distance oneself from the baby.[38] So why should the Gemara specifically mention a "grain." Maybe this was the basic food then given to a baby, or alternatively, perhaps even if the eating of the grain in this period of time did not make the faeces have an unpleasant odour, one would still have to distance oneself from the faeces, in the same way as one may not daven in the vicinity of certain chamber pots even if they are completely clean and odourless.[39]

The Shulchan Aruch does not give the actual age of a baby as to when it becomes forbidden to daven in the vicinity of its faeces. However, a number of Poskim do give various ages. Rav Yaacov Emden in his book Migdal Oz gives the age of one year.[40] At a later date the Misgeret Hashuchan on the Kitzur Shulchan Aruch states that in places where they give the baby grain with milk, the age is three months old,[41] whereas the Shulchan Melachim[42] decrees an even lower age of ten weeks, and in the case where the mother is unable to breast feed the baby, one should be strict as to its faeces from the age of four weeks. These Poskim obviously came to these conclusions after a practical examination of the odour of the baby's faeces, and the reasons for their different quoted ages very likely arose from the different diets given to babies at different periods and locations.

Finally, the most extreme opinion was that of the Magen Avraham who writes that it is proper to distance oneself even from the faeces of an eight day old baby.[43] Could this mean that, unlike during the period of the Gemara, an exclusively breast fed baby's faeces had an unpleasant odour, possibly due to the mother's diet, or, that as we have seen above, even babies of a few days old were fed on cereals, possibly grain cereals?

Human Urine

According to the Torah, it is forbidden to daven in the vicinity of human urine whilst it is still leaving the body.[44] However, once it reaches the ground, the prohibition is only Rabbinic.[45] However, if the urine has an odour which would disturb people,[46] it is forbidden by the Torah to daven in its vicinity.

Urine is a liquid produced by the kidneys to remove waste products from the bloodstream, and it is yellowish in colour. Its chemical composition consists primarily of water plus urea and trace amounts of many things including enzymes, carbohydrates and fatty acids.[47]

What gives urine its usually unpleasant odour? Fresh urine has only a very slight odour. However, if it is allowed to stand for period of time at room temperature, the bacteria in the urine will break down the urea present to form ammonia which has a strong odour.[48] The eating of certain foods, including asparagus,[49] onions and garlic, or suffering from certain illnesses, will also give an odour to urine.[50] One must even distance oneself from urine even if it has no odour.[51] However, since this is only a Rabbinic restriction, one can nullify the urine by pouring a "reviyit" (average opinion: about 120 mls) of water on it.[52] However, should the urine have an unpleasant odour, one would have to pour a sufficient quantity of water on it in order to nullify the smell.[53] Obviously, the more intense the odour, the more water that is required to reduce the odour. This can be seen from Stevens' law, since as concentration of the urine will then be less, so will be the intensity of the odour. It has been ruled that one could also use a liquid other than water to nullify the smell.[54]

Flatulence

It is estimated that everybody passes gas between 10 and 20 times a day.[55] This gas is normally formed in the colon when the bacteria there acts on the undigested foods and produces a number of gases.[56] The non-odourous gases produced comprise nitrogen, hydrogen, carbon dioxide, methane and oxygen.[57] The odourous part of these gases is less than one per cent and comes from a combination of volatile sulphur compounds, mainly hydrogen sulphide. Smelling these compounds can be an extremely unpleasant experience.[58] The more concentrated the sulphur compounds, the greater the intensity and unpleasantness of the odour.[59] (It should be noted that it was originally thought that the cause of the smell was from compounds such as indole, skatole and ammonia.[60]) Both the odourous and non-odourous gases are expelled from the body via the rectum. The quantity of gas produced depends on a number of factors. One of them is the food which has been consumed. Foods such as, beans, broccoli, cabbage, cauliflower and soy products will produce a large amount of gas.[61] Experimental studies have shown that the amount of gas emitted in a single emission varies among individuals, probably because different people have different sensitivities to gaseous distention of the rectum. This study also showed that more gas was released during the day than when the individual was asleep.[62]

Needless to say, for many reasons, it is advisable to reduce the quantity of gas passed. For this purpose, there are many medications, some of which can be purchased without a physician's prescription.[63] There are also medications to reduce the odour from the emitted gases, and these include tablets of bismuth subgallate and bismuth subsalicylate.[64]

The passing of gas has halachic ramifications. One of them concerns Tephillin. One is not allowed to pass gas when wearing Tephillin and people who have problems in this respect are strictly limited as to the time they may wear Tephillin.[65] One of the reasons for not sleeping with Tephillin, or not wearing them at night is that one might pass gas whilst wearing them.[66] It would seem that even if there is no odour from these expelled gases, their emission would still be forbidden whilst wearing Tephillin.

So long as there is a smell arising from the passing of gas, there are limitations in the recitation of tephillot (even without Tephillin) and the studying of Torah.[67] The recitation of tephillot would have to stop until the smell had passed away. However, apart from the person who caused the smell, the others in the room could continue learning.[68]

In a short responsum, Maharil Diskin writes that it is possible that if three people learning Torah together all pass gas at the same time giving a resultant unpleasant odour, they can all continue learning Torah, since the majority of the intensity of the smell is not from any particular one of them.[69] However, this assumes that the intensity of the smell from each of them is identical. This is not always the case. The intensity of the odour depends on the concentration of the sulphides emitted during the gas emission. Thus, if from one of them, the gas intensity is more than from the other two put together, it could be seen from Maharil Diskin's ruling that these two would be able to continue learning since the majority of the smell is not from them, and only the one whose intensity of odour was greater than that of the other two put together, would have to stop learning until the smell had completely dispersed.

Although the odour from flatulence is unpleasant and has halachic ramifications, it has recently been found by research at the University of Exeter in England, that hydrogen sulphide could be beneficial in small quantities to people suffering from certain diseases.[70]

Animal Faeces and Urine

Unlike human faeces and urine from which one must distance oneself when davening, the same prohibitions do not apply, with a few exceptions, to the faeces and urine of animals and birds.[71] However, if their faeces have an unpleasant odour, the same halachah will apply as for human faeces.[72] The reason for the difference is that the diet of many animals and birds is comprised of grass and similar vegetation, which results in odourless faeces and urine.[73] Now for the exceptions:

Donkeys: The Talmud Yerushalmi states that the soft faeces of a donkey that has come in from a journey will have a strong smell.[74] It is also written that the urine of a donkey which has come in from a journey will have a strong smell.[75] The Shulchan Aruch brings both these statements as halachah.[76] One might well ask: Why soft faeces and why a journey?

The greater the number of molecules associated with smell which reaches the nose, the greater is the intensity of the odour. When the faeces are soft, namely more liquid, the transfer of the molecules will obviously occur more readily and hence the faeces will be more odourous. Although under normal circumstance, the faeces of donkeys are hard, there are several things which can cause them to be soft. One is the eating of different or poor-quality food, which could have occurred on its journey. Another is stress which could also be the result of a journey. Regarding the strong odour of the donkey's urine, the issue of coming in from a journey could indicate that the donkey had been working or exercising, and it could also be dehydrated which would cause its urine to be more concentrated and thus have a stronger odour.[77]

Tarngolim aduma: Another species according to the Talmud Yerushalmi where one must distance oneself from their faeces is "tarngolim aduma."[78] There are differences of opinion as to its identification, and the bird "turkey" has been suggested,[79] although turkey was apparently unknown in the Middle East at the period of the Talmud Yerushalmi.[80] Due to the fact that the diet of birds generally consists of less meat and more fruits and vegetables,[81] birds' faeces generally do not smell, unless the bird has some sort of infection or illness.[82]. However, a change, such as feeding the chickens whole grains (an excellent dietary choice[83]) could (as with a baby) give the faeces an unpleasant odour. Indeed in 2014, a case was brought against a person in California for dumping chicken manure in a public place due to the offensive odour of the manure.[84]

Marten: The Talmud Yerushalmi[85] writes that one must distance oneself from the faeces of the marten. The Peirush Mibaal Sefer Charadim[86] notes that the reason that the marten was specifically mentioned was that it could be raised in one's house. The Shulchan Aruch quotes this Talmud Yerushami as halachah.[87]

The marten is an agile member of the weasel family. There are a number of species of martens. They have bushy tails and large paws with semi retractable claws. They are omnivorous animals whose diet consists of squirrels, mice, rabbits, birds, fish, insects, and fruit.[88]

During the latter part of the twentieth century research was done in Poland on the diet of martens that lived in the wild. The results showed that the available foods depended on the seasons. In the summer and autumn months their diet was mainly plant food, whilst in the winter and spring it was mainly animal food.[89] Thus the faeces of the marten would have a more unpleasant odour in the winter and spring. However, this might well be different when, according to the Talmud Yerushalmi, martens were raised in the house. If they were given a meat diet throughout the year, their faeces would always have an unpleasant odour, since meat takes a longer time to digest than plant food.[90]

Cat: The Shulchan Aruch[91] states that the faeces of a cat (as with several other animals) is like that of human faeces. The Be'er Hagolah brings the source as the Talmud Yerushalmi,[92] although, in fact, our editions of the Yerushalmi do not mention a cat. Rabbeinu Yonah writes that the odour of cats' faeces is unpleasant as that of the marten, and the reason that the Yerushalmi mentioned marten is that at that period they would raise martens in their houses in the same way as today we raise cats in our houses.[93]

What makes the odour of cats' faeces considerably more unpleasant than that of many other animals? The reason is the different diet of cats compared with many other animals. The main diet of herbivorous such as cows, sheep and rabbits is grass and other plants which are quick to digest and thus do not result in odourous faeces. In contrast, cats are obligate carnivores, they must eat meat. Cats, particularly those in the wild, therefore catch birds, rabbits, mice, squirrels, weasels, hares, and other small animals for their diet. The digestion time of protein containing products, such as meat, is long and so the food remains for a lengthy time in the large intestine. The longer it remains there, the greater the time the bacteria have in which to produce the various sulphides etc. which result in very odourous faeces. It should be mentioned that the cause of the foul-smelling faeces of cats is similar to that of human faeces.[94]

Dogs and Pigs: The Shulchan Aruch states that one must distance oneself from the faeces of dogs and pigs, if one has put the skins of animals into these faeces.[95] Such a mixture will have a particularly unpleasant smell.

This mixture used to be employed in the tanning of animal skins and was used in the process of treating skins and hides of animals to produce leather. (These processes comprise several of the Avot Melachah of Shabbat.[96]) The first stage was to clean the skins to remove any flesh and hair adhering to them, often using a lime solution. The next stage was "bating" the skins, namely softening the material, which was done by pounding faeces into the material. Bating was a fermentation process which relied on enzymes produced by bacteria found in the faeces. Among the faeces commonly used were those of dogs. Sometimes the faeces were mixed with water in a large vat, and the prepared skins were kneaded in the dung water until they became supple from bacterial enzyme action.[97] At a later stage in the preparation of the skins, alkaline dressings, whose ingredients amongst others included dog and pig faeces, were applied to the hides.[98]

It is unnecessary to add that skins of an animal have a very unpleasant smell and with the addition of animals' faeces, the smell would be unbearable! So much so, that the tanneries were located outside the towns.[99]

What is the situation if these skins are not mixed with the faeces of pigs and dogs? Both the Talmud Yerushalmi[100] and the Talmud Bavli[101] discuss the question, and the Shulchan Aruch[102] then rules that if the skins are mixed with these faeces one must distance oneself from them. If on the other hand they are not mixed with faeces, one need not do so provided the skins do not have a bad odour.

Rabbi Avraham Yosef (the son of Rabbi Ovadiah Yosef) writes that the food consumed by dogs today will result in smelly faeces.[103] An expert on clinical pet nutrition elaborates on this and writes that a change in a dog's diet can result in less smelly faeces. The expert explains that firm faeces with a light smell and brown colour is the norm for healthy dogs. To achieve this, the dog should be fed a raw diet, which is easy for the dog to digest.

However, in contrast, meat byproducts and grain are very hard for dogs to digest and the longer food remains in the dog's digestive tract, the greater will be the sulphur, which is formed as a result of the bacteria breaking down the food, and hence the faeces will be more odourous.[104]

Conclusion: It is advisable to look at one's surroundings before davening, otherwise in some situations one would have to daven a second time![105]

References

(1)   Chumash Devarim 23:14-15
(2)   Shulchan Aruch, Orach Chaim [henceforth: SA OC] 216
(3)   Gloria Rodriguez-Gil, M.Ed., "The Powerful Sense of Smell," *reSources,* (California Deaf-Blind Services), spring 2004, vol.11 no.2, pp.1-3
(4)   The Editors of Encyclopædia Britannica, "Diffusion," (Internet)
(5)   Steven L. Jacques et al, "Diffusion theory, Fick's 1st law of diffusion," (Oregon Graduate Institute, 1998, (Internet)
(6)   Morris Forman Wastewater Treatment Plant Community Odor Survey, (MSD & Webster Environmental Associates Inc.), 1999-2000, slide no.6
(7)   Steven M. LaValle, "Stevens' power law," Virtual Reality, (Internet)
(8)   R. D. Portugal et al, "Weber-Fechner Law and the Optimality of the Logarithmic Scale," *Minds and Machines, Journal for Artificial Intelligence, Philosophy and Cognitive Science,* (Springer/ Kluwer Academic Pub: Dordrecht, Netherlands), February 2011, pp.73-81
(9)   Kirsten Sucker et al., "Odor frequency and odor annoyance. Part 1: assessment of frequency, intensity and hedonic tone of environmental odors in the field," *International Archives of Occupational and Environmental Health,* May 2008, vol.81, issue 6, pp.671-682
(10) Morris Forman, op. cit.; One could mention in passing that the intensity and tone of an odour have merited much world-wide research and attention since there is a general objection to noticeable odours, such as from faulty sewage, chemicals and petroleum.
(11) Mishnah Berurah [henceforth: MB] 76:2
(12) SA OC 79:1
(13) Ibid.
(14) The Editors of Encyclopædia Britannica, "Feces – Biology," (Internet)
(15) Healthwise Staff, "Bowel Transit Time," (Michigan Medicine, University of Michigan), 28 March 2019, (Internet)
(16) "Digestion Time of various foods in the stomach," Wednesday 20 June 2012, (Internet); "How Long Different Foods Take to Digest and Why It's Important to Know," (Bright Side), (Internet). [There is a similarity here with the time one must wait between meat and milk and vice versa.]

(17) Chumash Devarim 23:14

(18) SA OC 76:1-2; MB 76:1

(19) SA OC 82:1

(20) Question submitted to Wikipedia Reference Desk – Science, 2 March 2016, Odor of Human Feces

(21) SA OC 81:1

(22) Shiurai hamitzvot - "kedai achilat pras," *Encyclopedia Yehudit,* (Michlelet Herzog, Da'at, Limudei yahadut v'Ruach)

(23) BabyCenter staff, "Introducing solids," (BabyCenter: San Francisco, California), September 2017, (Internet); BabyCenter Editorial Team, "Baby poop guide," (BabyCenter: San Francisco, California), August 2019, (Internet)

(24) Tommee Tippee, "Baby poop – color, texture and smell, Baby poop when Bottle Feeding," (Mayborn Group, Newcastle-upon-Tyne, England), 2019, (Internet)

(25) Rabbi Efraim ben Shmuel Danvil ha Kesher, *Adnei Paz,* (Altona, 1743), chap.87 dibur hamatchil: "ulda'ati"

(26) It is not forbidden to breast feed a child over 24 months old, and the Shulchan Aruch states that under certain circumstances a healthy child breast feeds until the age of 4 years and a weak child till the age of 5 years. (SA YD 81:7).

(27) "Nutrition - Exclusive breastfeeding," (World Health Organization), (Internet)

(28) Report by the Committee on Nutrition "On the Feeding of Solid Foods to Infants," *Pediatrics,* (American Academy of Pediatrics), April 1958, vol.21, [henceforth: *Pediatrics 1958*], p.685

(29) Report by the Committee on Nutrition "On the Feeding of Supplementary Foods to Infants," *Pediatrics,* op. cit., June 1980, vol.65 no.6, pp.1178-1179

(30) "My one-year-old is exclusively breastfed. Are there other mothers that still exclusively breastfeed at this age?" (Quora, an American question-and-answer website), September 2014, (Internet); Thread: Exclusive Breastfeeding for a Year, May 2010, (Internet)

(31) *Pediatrics 1958,* p.686

(32) Robert Deisher et al, "A study of early and later introduction of solids into the infant diet," *The Journal of Pediatrics,* (University of Washington Child Health Center), August 1954, vol.45 issue 2, p.191

(33) *Pediatrics 1958,* p.687

(34) *Pediatrics 1980,* p.1179

(35) Ibid.

(36) Rabbi Alexander Aryeh Mandelbaum, *Vezot Haberachah,* (Jerusalem, 5760), p.43

(37) Dirshu on SA OC vol.1, (Dirshu Hashem v'uzo: Jerusalem, Kislev 5774), chap.81 para.2

(38) Introducing solids, op. cit.

(39) SA OC 87:1; MB 87:1

(40) Rabbi Yaakov Emden, *Migdal Oz,* (Zhitomir, Ukraine, 5634), Birchot Horai, peleg 9, 2 achar shena'aseh ben shana

(41) Rabbi Chaim Yeshaya Hakohen, *Misgeret Hashulchan on Kitzur Shulchan Aruch Hashalem,* part 1. (Eshkol: Jerusalem), chap.5, Misgeret Hashulchan para.3

(42) Rabbi Moshe Tzvi Landau, *Shulchan Melachim,* (Kleinwardein, 5691), Kitzur Shulchan Aruch, chap.5, Halachah l'Moshe para.35

(43) Magen Avraham SA OC 81:1: He chose 8 days because that is the date of the Brit Milah, but he could have specified even younger than 8 days old. (What would he write about a baby girl?!)

(44) SA OC 77; MB 77:2

(45) MB 77:2

(46) Dirshu, SA OC, op. cit., chap.77 para.6; MB 77:2

(47) *The World Book Encyclopedia,* (Field Enterprises Educational Corporation: Chicago), vol.17, Urine, p.8393

(48) Patricia Potter et al, *Fundamentals of Nursing,* ninth edition, (Elsevier Mosby: Missouri USA), p.1112

(49) C. Richer et al, Letters to the Editor, "Odorous urine in man after asparagus," *British Journal of Clinical Pharmacology,* 1989, vol.27, pp.640-41, [There are also a number of other papers on the effect asparagus has on the odour of urine]

(50) Josh Baum, "Foods that Affect the Odor of Urine," (Livestrong Foundation: Austin, Texas), (Internet); Mayo Clinic Staff, "Symptoms, Urine odor, Causes," (USA), (Internet)

(51) SA OC 77:1; MB 77:2

(52) Ibid.

(53) MB 87:2

(54) Dirshu, SA OC, op. cit., chap.77 para.5

(55) Dr. Michael D. Levitt et al, "Evaluation of an extremely flatulent patient: Case report and diagnostic and therapeutic approach." *Journal of Gastroenterology,* 1998, vol.93, pp.2276-2281

(56) F. Azpiroz, "Intestinal gas dynamics: mechanisms and clinical relevance," *Gut,* 2005, vol.54 issue 7, pp.893-895

(57) F.L. Suarez, "Identification of gases responsible for the odour of human flatus and evaluation of a devise purported to reduce this odour," *Gut,* 1998 vol.43, pp.100-104

(58) Xu Beixi, "How do I stop making smells/neutralise digestive system?" (Quora, an American question-and-answer website), 24 January 2014, (Internet)

(59) Suarez, op. cit.

(60) Ibid.

(61) Azpioz, op. cit.; Harold McGee., *On Food and Cooking,* (Scribner: New York, 2004), p.486

(62) J. Tomlin et al, "Investigation of normal flatus production in healthy volunteers," *Gut,* June 1991, vol.32 (6), pp.665-669

(63) Gwen B. Turnbill, "The Ostomy Files: The Issue of Oral Medications and a Fecal Ostomy," *Ostomy Wound Management (OWM),* (Health

Management Publications: Pennsylvania USA), March 2005, vol.51 issue 3

(64) Ibid; Dr. Justin Bailey et al, "Effective Management of Flatulence," *American Family Physician*, (American Academy of Family Physicians: Leawood, Kansas), 15 June 2009, vol.79 (12), pp.1098-1100

(65) SA OC 38:2; MB 38:2

(66) SA OC 30:2; MB 30:4

(67) SA OC 79:9

(68) Ibid.

(69) Rabbi Moshe Yehoshua Yehudah Leib Diskin, *Shut Maharil Diskin,* (Jerusalem, 5671), acharon, chap.5 para.4

(70) Science daily, "Rotten egg gas holds key to healthcase therapies," *Science News,* (University of Exeter, England), 9 July 2014, (Internet)

(71) SA OC 79:4

(72) MB 79:4; MB, Biur Halachah OC 79, dibur hamatchil: tzoar chamor

(73) Why do human feces smell so bad compared to other mammals' feces?" (Quora, an American question-and-answer website), December 2014, (Internet)

(74) Talmud Yerushalmi, Masechet Berachot, perek 3 halachah 5; SA OC 79:5

(75) SA OC 79:6

(76) SA OC 79:5-6

(77) e-mails from Dr. David Hadrill, FAO Myanmar [Burma] ECTAD Country Team Leader, 24 February 2016, and Dr. Faith Burden, Head of Research and Pathology, The Donkey Sanctuary, UK, 24 February 2016

(78) SA OC 79:6

(79) MB 79:26; Dirshu, SA OC, op. cit., chap.79 para.38

(80) Rabbi Israel Meir Levinger, *Modern Kosher Food Production From Animal Source (Mazon Kasher min hachai)*, (Instuitute for Agricultural Research According to the Thora: Jerusalem, 1980,) p.47

(81) Nikki Moustaki, "All You Ever Wanted to Know About Bird Poop, Why doesn't Bird Poop Smell?," (From the Pages of Birds USA), 28 April 2015, (Internet)

(82) Alyson Kalhagen, "Bird Poop 101, Odors," (The Spruce Pets), 3 February 2019, (Internet)

(83) The Pet Bird Health Handbook, "Vegetables, Grains and Fruits," (Carolina Veterinary Specialists: North Carolina), p.7

(84) Harry Jones, "Chicken manure stink could be costly," *The San Diego Union-Tribune*, 14 April 2014

(85) Talmud Yerushalmi, Masechet Berachot, perek 3 halachah 5

(86) Peirush m'Baal sefer Chareidim on Talmud Yerushalmi, Masechet Berachot, perek 3 halachah 5 dibur hamatchil: "mitzoat nemiya"

(87) SA OC 79:5

(88) Editors of Encyclopædia Britannica – Marten, (Internet)

(89) Jacek Goszczynski, "Composition of the Food of Martens," *Acta Theriologica*, 1976, vol.21 36: pp.527, 534; Jacek Goszczynski, "Diet of foxes and Martens in Central Poland," *Acta Theriologica,* 1986 vol.31 36: pp.491-506

(90) The research by Goszczynski also included the diet of the fox which was almost entirely meat, could make its faeces even smellier than that of the marten.

(91) SA OC 79:5

(92) B'eir Hagolah 30 (on SA OC chap.79) writes "Yerushalmi [Berachot] 6d" - this is an older printing of the Talmud Yerushalmi

(93) Rabbeinu Yonah on the Rif, Berachot chap.3, (p.32) dibur hamatchil: "v'tzoat"

(94) Margaret Gates, "The Benefits of a Raw Meat Diet for Your Cat," (Feline Nutrition Foundation, Fairfax, Virginia, USA), 4 October 2015 (Internet); Dr. Mike Paul, "Why do My Cat's Stools Smell so Bad?" (Pet Health Network, IDEXX, Westbrook, Maine, USA), 27 August 2014, (Internet); Susan Leisure, "Dog Food That Helps With Smelly Stools," (The Nest), (Internet) (a similar principle applies to other creatures); Quora, Why do human feces, op. cit.

(95) SA OC 79:4

(96) *Chayei Adam*, Hilchot Shabbat, klalim 32-36

(97) *The World Book Encyclopedia,* op. cit., vol.10, Leather, p.4346

(98) Ibid.; Tanning in the Seventeenth Century, (Historic Jamestowne), (Internet)

(99) Tanning, Ancient methods of tanning, (Leathernet,) (Internet)

(100) Talmud Yerushalmi, Masechet Berachot perek 3 halachah 5

(101) Talmud Bavli, Masechet Berachot 25a

(102) SA OC 79:4

(103) Rabbi Avraham Yosef, Tzoat k'lavim, (Sheal et Harav) Moreshet, 22 Tevet 5771, (Internet)

(104) Susan Leisure, op. cit.

(105) SA OC 76:8

Section Five

An Etrog with Fingers

THE CHINESE ETROG [1]

Rabbi Dr. Chaim Simons

(Written September 2008)

Readers may put in a request to my e-mail chaimsimons@
gmail.com for original photocopied source materials quoted
in this paper to be sent to their e-mails without charge.

Introduction

It is written in the Torah "And you shall take for yourselves on the
first day the fruit of a goodly tree...."[2] What is the identity of this
fruit? From the translation of the Torah by Onkelus[3] and from
discussions in the Talmud,[4] we can see the identity of this fruit to
be an etrog. We shall begin by examining the botanic identity of
the etrog.

Botanists have made a detailed classification of flora, in which
every different "subspecies" has a unique name, which is
traditionally in Latin. The "kingdom" of flora is divided into
"divisions" which are divided into "classes" which are divided
into "subclasses" which are divided into "orders" which are
divided into "families" which are divided into "genera" which are
divided into "species" which are finally divided into "subspecies."
(Further divisions are also known.)

The citrus fruit is a member of the Rutaceae family. This is a
family of dicotyledonous plants, which mainly consists of shrubs
and trees. The Rutaceae family has about 144 genera and 1,600
species, and is found in temperate and tropical regions. In addition
to citrus fruits, this family includes, for example, rue (a woody
and bushy herb), satinwood, shrubby trefoil or wafer ash, and
prickly ash.[5]

One of the 144 genera of the Rutaceae family is the citrus fruit, which includes citrons (etrogim), lemons, oranges, grapefruits and pomelos. Even those citrus fruits which are botanically close to the citrons cannot be used as etrogim on the Festival of Sukkot. Not even lemons which are very close to the etrog, (and are regarded as the same species in the laws of kilayim), can be used.[6]

The genus citrus is divided into a number of species, one of them being citrons, in Hebrew etrogim, and these are further divided into subspecies which include, the Eretz Israel (Baladi) etrog, the Diamante (Italian/Calabria/Yanova) etrog, the Moroccan etrog, the Corfu (Greek) etrog, the Yemenite (Taimani) etrog, the Florentine etrog, the Corsican etrog and the Chinese etrog.[7] As is to be expected, they are called by these names, since this is the locality where they grow, even if in the distant past they originated from different parts of the world. Most of these species are or have been used by various groups of Jews around the world.

Today almost all these different species have been transplanted and grow in Israel. Some Jews still use the same species as they were accustomed to use in the Diaspora. For example, Yemenite Jews in Israel tend to use the Yemenite etrog and Chabad use Diamante (Calabria) etrogim.[8]

The usual reason for disqualifying a particular species of etrog is the problem of grafting[9] and not any suggestion that the species is not an etrog. Even a seed from an etrog grown on a tree which had been grafted in the distant past, would according to most opinions still be regarded as grafted.[10] Therefore the pedigree of a particular etrog tree has to be investigated thoroughly.

In this paper, we will make a study of the Chinese etrog, which until now has rarely been used as an etrog for the mitzvah on Sukkot. It should be stressed that the purpose of this paper is not to make a Halachic ruling on the use of this etrog. That is the function of the Rabbinical authorities.

About the Chinese Etrog

The official name given by the botanists to the species called citrons is *Citrus medica*. The Chinese etrog which is one of the citron subspecies, is known as *Citrus medica var. sarcodactylis*.[11]

The tree on which the Chinese etrog grows is shrubby and reaches a height of about two metres. It has long irregular branches which are covered in long thorns. The leaves of this tree are large, oblong, crinkled and leathery and are coloured pale green. They are about 10-15 centimetres (cms) long. The tree also has blossoms with clusters of white or pale purple fragrant flowers.[12]

The lower part of the fruit of this tree looks like any other etrog. The upper part is however noticeably different from other species of etrogim, in that it is segmented into finger-like sections whose length can reach 30 cms.[13] However, the fruit is usually about 15-30 cms in length.[14] It has a very thick peel,[15] with no, or only a small amount of flesh or juice,[16] resembling the Yemenite Etrog in this respect.

The Chinese etrog is seedless[17] and in this respect resembles the Moroccan etrog. A citrus flower is considered a perfect flower, which means that the male flower and the female flower are found as parts of the same single flower, the male part being the stamens, namely the organs bearing the pollen, and the female part the ovary, namely the organ which bears the seed. The pollen is transferred to the ovary by the wind or by insects, and this produces etrogim which will be seedy. If however the temperature is very high, the pollen will not be viable, and it will not germinate or grow and will therefore be unable to fertilise the egg. In such a case the fruit will be parthenocarpic and the etrogim will be seedless. Therefore in areas of Morocco which are very hot, the etrogim are seedless.[18] The Shanghai area has almost as high temperatures as Morocco[19] and this could be the reason why the Chinese etrog is likewise seedless.

At the beginning of the development of this etrog, the fingers are closed. As time progresses they may open up to different extents, alternatively, depending on the growing conditions they could remain closed.[20] In a shop selling Chinese etrogim, one might find a mixture of those where the fingers are completely closed and those where they are open.[21]

One should mention that most of the other species of etrogim, namely those which have some flesh inside, (and even more so with other types of citrus fruit), are segmented into finger like sections internally, but their peels are totally fused together and thus there is no external sign of segmentation. However, the Chinese etrog "is indeed a citron but lacks the gene which causes the sections of the fruit to fuse."[22]

This etrog is widely cultivated in China, Japan, Indo-China and India.[23] From a wall painting from El-Kab[24] in ancient Egypt, it can be seen that the Chinese etrog was also known in ancient Egypt.[25] The tree cannot be planted in every part of the world since it is sensitive to frost and various other climatic conditions. It grows best in temperate conditions. In addition to the Far East, a suitable area for growing is, for example, the coast of Southern California.[26] Just as with other species of etrogim from different parts of the world which grow in Israel, it would seem that the cultivation of the Chinese etrog should pose no difficulties in the appropriate areas of Israel.

In general, Chinese etrog trees can be grown from cuttings taken from branches two to four years old. These cuttings replete with foliage must be buried deep in the soil.[27] Since it has been reported that the Chinese etrog tree will give fruit even in the first year of growth,[28] in the event of these trees producing fruit before the three years required by the laws of orlah are up,[29] care must be taken not to transgress the laws of orlah both when eating and when using the fruit for the mitzvah.

As with other species of etrogim, the peel of the Chinese etrog can be candied into succade. For this purpose, etrogim have an advantage over other citrus fruits in view of the fact that their peel is extra thick and their inner rind less bitter.[30] The zest of the Chinese etrog can also be used in salads. The fingers are cut off and sliced longitudinally and the pith is then removed.[31]

In China[32] and Japan this etrog is well-known and highly esteemed for its fragrance and beauty and is used for perfuming rooms and clothing.[33]

The Chinese etrog is also known as "Buddha's hand citron." One of the religions practiced in China is Buddhism. The etrog is offered up as a religious offering in Buddhist temples. According to Buddhist tradition, Buddha prefers the fingers of the etrog to be in a position where they resemble a closed rather than an open hand as closed hands symbolise to Buddha the act of prayer.[34] Since this is clearly an act of idol worship, the use for the mitzvah of a particular etrog which had been utilised for Buddhist offerings would require a Halachic ruling.[35]

Laws of Etrog with reference to the Chinese Etrog

Size: The minimum size for an etrog is the volume of an egg.[36] A Chinese etrog is certainly above this minimum size.[37]

Colour: The ideal colour for an etrog is yellow.[38] When it first grows it will be green and it will then turn yellow.[39] There are discussions by the Rabbis as to whether a green etrog which will eventually turn yellow can be used for the mitzvah.[40] As with other species of etrogim, the Chinese etrog is first green and then turns yellow.[41] Also as with other etrogim, the juxtaposition of apples with Chinese etrogim will turn the etrogim yellow quicker.[42]

Black spots: A black spot can sometimes make an etrog pasul, especially if it is on the "chotem."[43] There are different opinions as to which area of an etrog is called the chotem. The strictest opinion is the top portion of the etrog after it begins narrowing.[44] The question is how one defines the "chotem" for a Chinese etrog, which opens up like the fingers of a hand. However, before it opens up, this etrog is shaped similar to other etrogim and one can easily identify where the chotem is. If however the etrog has already opened, it would seem that the area of the chotem would become far more problematic.

Pitam: The pitam is the upper tip of the etrog which protrudes beyond the etrog. If it is missing, the etrog is often pasul.[45] Since it seems that there never was a pitam on a Chinese etrog, would this make this etrog pasul? A similar question arises with a Yemenite etrog which also does not have a pitam and there the Rabbis have ruled that the Yemenite etrog is not pasul, since this is way it normally grows.[46]

Oketz: The oketz is the portion of the etrog with which it is connected to the tree, namely the stem of the etrog. If the oketz has fallen out, and a cavity is left, then the etrog is pasul.[47] Naturally, as with all fruits, the Chinese etrog has an oketz and obviously a similar law will apply.

Part missing: If even a minute part of the etrog is missing, the etrog is pasul (on the first day of Sukkot),[48] and this would of course apply likewise to a Chinese etrog. It can often happen that one of the many thorns on an etrog tree can scratch the etrog. If however such a scratch on an etrog, has become encrusted, then the etrog is not pasul.[49] This can also arise with a Chinese etrog, the tree of which has long thorns.[50]

Seedless: A problem which has been discussed and researched at length regarding the Moroccan etrog, is the fact that it is seedless and there are those who therefore say that it is pasul. However this argument has been rejected and the Moroccan etrog is thus not pasul.[51] The Chinese etrog does not have seeds either[52][53] and as with the Moroccan etrog, this lack of seeds should not pasul the Chinese etrog.

Grafted etrog: According to almost all opinions, a grafted etrog is pasul, even if the grafting had been done many generations earlier to the ancestor of that particular etrog tree.[54] For this reason there have been disputes on etrogim which have originated from many different parts of the world.[55] Some authorities try to give signs that indicate a non-grafted etrog. These include a non-smooth outer skin, a sunken in oketz, only a little flesh and juice, (and some add, the direction of the seeds being vertical).[56] These indeed are the signs found on a Chinese etrog.[57] However today, due to the advances in agricultural technology, it is possible to reproduce these signs even in grafted etrogim.[58] Furthermore, even before these advances in agricultural technology, there were discussions as to whether or not one could rely on these signs, or if there had to be a tradition that the etrog was ungrafted.[59]

Smell: As with other etrogim, the Chinese etrog has a very strong smell.[60] The main function of any fruit, and this includes the etrog, is to be eaten, and the smelling of it is only secondary. Thus the particular etrog which is being used for the mitzvah may be smelled during Sukkot.[61] This would likewise apply to the Chinese etrog.

Trumot and Ma'asarot: If a Chinese etrog were to be grown in Eretz Israel, the same rules for these mitzvoth would apply as with other species grown in Eretz Israel.[62]

Is there a Tradition for using the Chinese Etrog?

To look into this question, one needs to look into the history of the Jews of China which goes back nearly a thousand years, and some say even longer. Around the year 1100 a group of Jews settled in the large city of Kaifeng in northern China[63] at the invitation of the Emperor of that city,[64] (although some give the date as about 100 years earlier,[65] and according to some Arab reports even a further 150 years earlier.[66]) In Kaifeng they managed to maintain their Jewish identity, despite being cut off from all other Jewish communities for roughly seven centuries.[67] In addition to the Kaifeng community, there have been Jewish communities in other Chinese cities including Beijing (Peking), Hangchou, Ningpo, Ningxia and Canton, but very little is known about them.[68]

In 1163, the Jews began to build a Synagogue in Kaifeng.[69] Possibly they rented a place as a house of worship even before that date.[70] During the course of the next five hundred years, this Synagogue was repaired or rebuilt nine times, in some cases after a natural disaster.[71]

As already stated, for hundreds of years, the Jewish community in Kaifeng was isolated from all other Jewish communities in the world and when its Rabbi died around 1800-1810[72] there was no successor. Hence the community was left without a religious leader. Synagogue services and observances of the Festivals might have lasted a little longer but by about 1850, the Jews had assimilated amongst the Chinese.[73] In 1854 the Synagogue became a ruin.[74]

Although the community was isolated from world Jewry, a lot is known about its history.[75] Much of what we know about the community comes from inscriptions found on steles (stone pillars) in the courtyard of the Synagogue dating from the years 1489, 1512 and 1663 and a further stele from 1679 built into the wall of a nearby house,[76] on which were engraved the history of the Jewish community, Jewish rituals and observances of the community and moralistic teachings.[77] In addition, portions of prayer books for Sabbaths and Festivals, and Hagaddot for Pesach are extant.[78] From this we can see that the liturgy was certainly Talmudic and Rabbinic, in common with other Jewish communities in the world.[79] There are also lengthy reports by western visitors, usually Christian missionaries, from about the year 1600 onwards.[80]

From the steles we know that the Synagogue had 13 Sifrei Torah,[81] and held three services every day.[82] The order of the service was identical with that laid down by the Rambam, which is also followed by the Yemenite Jews.[83] Furthermore, many of the rites of the services were similar to those practiced by other Jewish communities in the world.[84] The annual cycle of the Reading of the Torah was almost identical with that followed in the West, a small difference being that it was divided into 53 Parashiot[85] rather than 54. The Kaifeng community knew how to accurately calculate the Jewish calendar[86] (which is not a simple thing to do!). Unlike the Karaites, the Chinese Jews also knew about and observed festivals and other notable days which were of Rabbinic origin, such as Chanukah, Purim and Tisha b'Av.[87] They also had hakafot on Simchat Torah.[88]

In this paper, we are particularly interested on what occurred on Sukkot and especially with regards to the Arba'at Haminim.

In one of the manuscripts from the community there is a list of Readings from the Torah for the festival of Sukkot.[89] There the readings are identical[90] to those read by other Jewish communities. (The Torah readings for Shemini Atzeret *and* Simchat Torah are also given.[91] This shows that the community observed two days Yom Tov, in common with other Diaspora communities).

Also amongst the manuscripts is one which includes handwritten portions of the prayers for Sukkot. These are the berachot preceding the amidah, the amidah for Yom Tov of Sukkot followed by the entire Hallel,[92] but there is no mention of the Arba'at Haminim. However, in another handwritten manuscript there is included a *list* of the prayers said on Yom-Tov of Sukkot, Shabbat Chol Hamoed Sukkot and weekday Chol Hamoed Sukkot. In the last mentioned, amongst the list of prayers is found the word "lamed-vav-lamed-bet-vav" ("lulavo"?),[93] which is almost certainly referring to taking the lulav sometime during the morning service of Chol Hamoed Sukkot. If one takes the lulav, one takes it together with the other three species, which of course includes the etrog. But unfortunately, nothing further was found in this, or indeed in any other manuscript.

In addition to these manuscripts, from the works of the historians, we can see that the Chinese Jews were fully aware of the Festival of Sukkot. A Sukkah was built in the courtyard of the Kaifeng Synagogue.[94] Father Jean Domenge, a Jesuit, who visited the community writes of how he attended Sukkot services in the Synagogue during the Sukkot of 1722.[95] He does not mention seeing any Arba'at Haminim in the Synagogue, but this is not surprising since he writes "I went to the Synagogue on the *Saturday* during the week of their feast of Tabernacles."[96] *(emphasis added)* The Arba'at Haminim are not taken on the Shabbat during Sukkot.[97]

James Finn, who wrote on Jewish life in the interior of China, noted in his book published in 1843, regarding the Chinese Jews, "They observe circumcision, passover, tabernacles, the rejoicing of the law, and, perhaps, the Day of Atonement, for it is said that on one day of the year they fast and weep together in the synagogue."[98]

Even after the Jewish community had effectively assimilated, reports given by outside visitors strongly indicate that Sukkot had been observed in former generations. One of these is in a report given by a Christian visitor, Rev. W. A. P. Martin, who went there in 1866. Rev. Martin writes, "They remember the names of the Feast of Tabernacles, the Feast of Unleavened Bread, and a few other ceremonial rites that were still practiced by a former generation; but all such usages are now neglected."[99] Another report, although possibly less reliable, by J. L. Liebermann, the first western Jew to visit Kaifeng, writing in 1899 about past generations (of a hundred years earlier?) states, "The Jews keep the sabbath, and hold weekly services in the Rabbi's house. They celebrated Passover, Tabernacles etc., but use the Chinese tongue instead of Hebrew."[100] [101]

Apart from this sole reference in the above mentioned manuscript, nothing has been found regarding the Arba'at Haminim. The fact that they read on the first days the portion in the Torah which includes this mitzvah confirms that they knew about it. Since they were isolated from world Jewry and world Jewry almost certainly did not even know of their existence, they obviously did not import etrogim from other parts of the world. Further study would thus be required to determine from where they obtained their etrogim.

In the mid-19th century following the First Opium War of 1839-1842 between Britain and China, a smallish number of Baghdadi Jews moved to Shanghai in China, and built several synagogues there.[102] These Jews were scrupulous in the observance of mitzvoth,[103] and they imported their etrogim from Eretz Israel.[104]

Does the fact that they imported etrogim indicate that their Rabbis did not accept the Chinese etrogim as kasher? A specific answer to this question is reported for a year when the *only* etrogim available were the Chinese etrogim. The Rabbis prohibited their use.[105] It is not reported in which year this occurred or whether it was Rabbis from Baghdad or Shanghai who pronounced this prohibition.

Possibly these Rabbis followed the opinion of Rabbi Yoseph Chaim (who disagreed with his teacher Rabbi Abdullah Somech) and did not want to accept the Chinese etrog as kasher for the mitzvah.[106]

One might ask why the Jews in Shanghai waited for a year when only Chinese etrogim were available to ask this question. The answer could be that they may have wanted to continue with the traditions that they had in Baghdad and use the same species of etrog as they had been accustomed to use there.

Alternatively, they may have asked their Rabbis as soon as they arrived in Shanghai, and been told they could not use the Chinese etrog, but should use species of etrog brought from abroad. However, in a year when importing etrogim was not possible, they may in view of the changed circumstances, have again asked the question but again been given a negative answer.

The Baghdadi Jewish millionaire David Abraham arrived in Shanghai in about 1880 and at some later date planted an etrog tree (obviously of the species the Baghdadi Jews were accustomed to use) in the garden of his mansion in Shanghai,[107] together, it would seem, with the flora for the lulavim, hadassim and aravot.[108] He employed a whole team of Chinese gardeners to tend these plants.[109]

Towards the beginning of the 20th century, there were both Sepharadi and Ashkenazi Jewish communities in Kobe in Japan. Relations between these two communities were cool. However, the Ashkenazim went to the Sepharadi Synagogue on Sukkot to perform the mitzvah on the Arba'at Haminim and then returned to their own Synagogue for the continuation of the service. The Arba'at Haminim in Kobe were brought to Japan each year just before Sukkot from the Abraham family gardens in Shanghai.[110] This would indicate that the only Arba'at Haminim available at that period in Shanghai were from the Abraham gardens.

Hence it would seem that the tens of thousands of Ashkenazi Jews from Eastern Europe, who arrived in China at this period, forming fairly extensive communities,[111] also had no alternative but to use these Arba'at Haminim from the Abraham gardens.

At the start of the Second World War, Jews fleeing from Hitler, including the entire Mirrer Yeshiva reached Shanghai. What they did about the etrog is described in detail later in this paper.

It is reported that after the Second World War, the Rabbis ruled that Jews in Shanghai could use the Chinese etrog on Sukkot, but without a berachah.[112] It is not reported in which year, or to which Jews in Shanghai this ruling was given, or who the Rabbis were.

Chinese Etrogim in the Responsa

There is very little in the Halachic literature on the question of the acceptability of the Chinese etrog for the mitzvah. The Gemara does not directly mention an etrog with fingers. The closest is the case of the twin etrog (t'yom in the language of the Gemara[113]) – which on the face of it would be two etrogim fused together – like Siamese twins.

On this "t'yom" etrog, the ruling of the Rambam[114] (and others[115]) is that it is kasher. But what does the Rambam mean by "t'yom"? About a hundred years after the Rambam, there lived in Eretz Israel, Rabbi Tanhum ben Yoseph Yerushalmi (c.1220-1291) who subsequently went to Egypt, where he died.[116] One of his books was "Al-Mursid al-Kafi" which was a lexicon giving in alphabetical order the etymologies of all the words found in the Rambam's Mishneh Torah. Rabbi Tanhum translates this word "t'yom" when used in connection with the etrog, to refer to the Chinese etrog,[117] and hence, according to this, the Rambam holds that the Chinese etrog is kasher for the mitzvah.

One might well ask how the Rambam, who lived in the Middle East, knew about etrogim which grew in the Far East. The Rambam, apart from his phenomenal knowledge of Judaica, was also a very famous medical practitioner and physician to the Sultan, the Grand Vizier and other members of the court. At that period there were Arabs who travelled to the Far East and it is quite possible that they returned with samples of the Chinese etrog which they showed or even gave to the Rambam. It has even been suggested that well before the period of the Rambam, the Romans and the Greeks brought these Chinese etrogim from the Far East to the Mediterranean area.[118]

During the course of the Rambam's lifetime, there were Rabbis in Spain who considered him to be a heretic and they wrote to Germany saying that he deserved to be excommunicated. A Rabbi Meir from Germany came to investigate and when he arrived, the Rambam's servant brought in food that looked like human hands. The Rambam saw the reluctance of this Rabbi Meir to eat this food and the Rambam then informed him that it was an edible plant.[119] Could this item have been a Chinese etrog?

About the middle of the 19th century, a question regarding the permissibility of the Chinese Etrog was sent from the city of Hangchow (or possibly Hongkew) in China[120] to Rabbi Abdullah

Somech, who was one of the leading Rabbis in Baghdad at that period. The questioner asked about etrogim growing in his city and said that they were like those in Baghdad in their shape and identification marks but with one difference. This was that the upper half of the etrog resembled the hand of a man with about 10 or 15 fingers, some being long whilst others were short. The questioner wanted to know (in view of the fact that etrogim sent from Egypt often arrived blemished due to the long journey, or arrived only in the middle of the Festival), whether these Chinese etrogim could be used and if so, could a beracha be said over them.

Rabbi Somech began his responsum by making a comparison between the Chinese etrog and an etrog grown in an unnatural shape using a mould. Such an etrog would be pasul. However he discounted this comparison, since the hand shape is the natural way that etrogim grow in China. He then went on to compare it to an etrog grown in a mould, retaining the general oval shape of an etrog, but looking like the rungs of the wheels of a water-mill. Such an etrog would be kasher. However again he discounted the comparison, since there is a much greater difference between a Chinese etrog and a "conventional" etrog, than there is between an etrog looking like the rungs of the wheels of a water mill and a "conventional" etrog. His next comparison was with a twin-etrog which the Shulchan Aruch rules is kasher. If a twin etrog which is like two separate etrogim is kasher, how much more so, rules Rabbi Somech, must the Chinese etrog which only differs from other etrogim by its finger like upper portion, be kasher.[121]

However, Rabbi Somech's pupil, (who was also his brother-in-law), Rabbi Yoseph Chaim (the Ben Ish Chai) disagreed with him on the matter. He held that for an etrog one cannot rely on identification marks alone. There has to be a tradition that a particular fruit is an etrog, or that it is similar to an etrog from another city. But in contrast, any tree which has not got a tradition of being indeed an etrog tree and whose fruits are not really similar to the etrogim of another place for which we have a tradition, cannot be used for the mitzvah. Rabbi Yoseph Chaim also brought a proof from the fruit called dibdib, which was found in Baghdad and had the identification marks of the etrog, looked like an etrog but was sour. The tradition in Baghdad was that it could not be used as an etrog, even in a case of extreme necessity, even though the majority of etrogim in the world were also sour. He went on to argue that the reason that a twin etrog is permitted is that on the same tree are to be found etrogim which are not twin etrogim. This he said is in contrast to the Chinese etrog where all the etrogim on the tree are the same. Furthermore, no-one had ever heard that there exist etrogim which have fingers coming out of them.[122]

Mirrer Yeshiva in Shanghai

Towards the beginning of the Second World War the Mirrer Yeshiva fled from Eastern Europe, travelling by train across Russia and then by ship to Japan. After a number of months, they moved on to Shanghai where they remained for over five years.

One of the most difficult things to obtain in a place like Shanghai is an etrog. The remaining three species for the mitzvah are easier to obtain since they grow in a variety of climates.

In his book "Operation: Torah Rescue," Rabbi Yecheskel Leitner explains what the Jews in Shanghai did to obtain etrogim during the period of the Second World War.[123]

He writes that for several decades prior to the Second World War, the Jews of Shanghai had obtained their etrogim from a tree which had been planted in the garden of the Jewish millionaire David Abraham who lived with his family in a mansion in Shanghai. However, after the attack on Pearl Harbour in December 1941, which brought the United States into the war, the Abraham family, being British subjects, were arrested and interned in a civilian prisoner of war camp, and their mansion was confiscated by the Imperial Japanese Army.

Prior to the following Sukkot, someone arranged for a Chinese to climb the tall walls surrounding this mansion and pick some etrogim. In retaliation the Japanese cut down the etrog tree.

Before the approach of the following Sukkot, two Jews from Shanghai together with a Chinese guide went on an expedition in search of etrogim. They had been informed that there were certain regions where etrog trees were alleged to grow. They finally found them on a vacation site for wealthy Chinese businessmen, near the city of Hangchow, which is situated about 160 kilometres south-west of Shanghai. These etrogim, however, had an extension growing out from the main fruit that bore a similarity to the fingers of a human hand.

They brought back a number of these Chinese etrogim to Shanghai. Some of the Jews used them but without making the beracha, others just used them as a symbolic commemoration of the mitzvah, whilst others refused to use them at all, saying that they were not etrogim.

On reading Rabbi Leitner's book, it was not clear to me what the source was for the Jews of Shanghai to come to the three different decisions on whether or not to use these Chinese etrogim. Rabbi Leitner is not just an author who has researched a book on the Mirrer Yeshiva in Shanghai. He himself was present at the Yeshiva in Shanghai at that period[124] and so he saw things firsthand.

I therefore wrote Rabbi Leitner a letter asking him "Was any material written on the *halachic* aspects of this Chinese esrog and the reasons that the experts in halacha came to different conclusions."[125] He replied,[126] "The pertinent discussion of such a problem is found in the Shulkhan Orukh" giving the references to the comments of the Mishnah Brurah[127] and the B'eer Hettev,[128] arguing that "the decisions regarding the use of such an Esrog (or non-Esrog evtl. *(sic)*) are clearly expounded in those explanations."

On looking up these references, I found that they were general comments on the correct procedure in a time of hardship when a kasher set of Arba'at Haminim was unavailable. Here the authorities differentiate between having a valid species which has a blemish which makes it pasul and having a different species, such as a grafted etrog. In the case of the latter, it should not be taken under any circumstances to avoid any error in future years.

I replied to Rabbi Leitner that what I had had in mind was not a general reference "but details of the *specific discussions* on this question between the Rabbis of the Mirrer Yeshivah which led to at least three different conclusions."[129] In reply[130] he answered quoting a different chapter in Shulchan Aruch[131] but not specifying which paragraph. It would seem that he was referring to two paragraphs[132] which dealt with the case when a particular species is not available, at which time an alternative may not be taken. He added in this letter that to the best of his recollection "new points were not added" to this reference in the Shulchan Aruch and "no additional material was published then on it nor deposited in the various libraries of the Mirrer Yeshivah."

I was puzzled as to why the Rabbis in Shanghai were not prepared to rely on the ruling of Rabbi Somech, considering the very extreme wartime circumstances, and why even those who used this Chinese etrog, refrained from making a beracha over it. Possibly, the responsa of Rabbi Somech on the Orach Chaim was not available in wartime Shanghai.

It seems that when the members of the Mirrer Yeshiva fled to Japan and then China, they managed to take very few books with them. In Shanghai hundreds or even thousands of copies of books[133] such as the Talmud were lithographed by Chinese printers.[134]

However it is reported that when the Jewish Sepharadi millionaire, Silas Hardoon, built the magnificent "Beth Aharon" (Museum Road) Synagogue in 1927,[135] he included a large Jewish library.[136] (Rabbi Leitner when describing the Synagogue complex does not mention the existence of such a library.[137]) The other Synagogues also had libraries.[138] However there are no catalogues available of the books in these libraries and so we don't know whether they had the responsa of Rabbi Somech on the Orach Chaim. If they had, Rabbi Leitner would have probably mentioned it in his correspondence with me.

There is a further possible reason for the Mirrer Yeshiva's reluctance to use the Chinese etrog. If the etrogim which were brought to them had open fingers they would have looked completely different from the etrogim that they were used to in past years. For this reason the Yeshiva may have had serious doubts as to whether they were in fact etrogim.

Conclusion

With today's methods of rapid international transport, it is unlikely that in any place in the world where there is a congregation of Jews, the only etrog available will be the Chinese etrog. However, it is possible that a Jewish traveler to the Far East who happens to be far from a Jewish settlement on Sukkot, could find the only etrog available to him to be the Chinese etrog.[139] In such a case, it would be advisable for him to telephone a Rabbinical authority and ask whether he could rely on the opinions which permit the use of this Chinese etrog.[140]

References

(1) This etrog is also known by many other names, e.g. fingered citron, flesh-finger citron, Buddha's hand citron, foshou (in Chinese), Indian citron. However, in this paper the name "Chinese etrog" has been chosen, since the various Halachic questions on its possible permissibility were sent from China or occurred in China.

(2) Leviticus chap.23 verse 40.

(3) Targum Onkelos on Leviticus chap.23 verse 40.

(4) Babylonian Talmud, Sukkah 35a; Jerusalem Talmud, Sukkah chap.3 halachah 5.

(5) "Rutaceae," Encyclopædia Britannca, vol.19, (Chicago: Encyclopædia Britannica Inc, 1963), p.769.

(6) Rabbi Avraham Yeshaya Karelitz, Chazon Ish - Zeraim, (Bnei Brak, 5719 - 1959), Kilayim, chap.3 par.7.

(7) Wikipedia, "Citron," (Internet: en.wikipedia.org/wiki/Citron). It is reported that in the UC Riverside Citrus Variety Collection in California there are 35 kinds of etrogim. (Julie Gruenbaum Fax, "The secret life of etrogs," The Jewish Journal, 27 September 2007, Internet: www.jewishjournal.com/food/article/the_secret_life_of_etrogs_20070928).

(8) Shulchan Aruch Harav, Orach Chaim, additions, p.72 (725).

(9) e.g. Rabbi Eliahu Weissfish, Arba'ath HaMinim HaShalem, (Jerusalem, 5735 - 1975), pp.185-208.

(10) Ibid., pp.259-60.

(11) Walter T. Swingle, "The Botany of Citrus and Its Wild Relatives," The Citrus Industry, revised edition, (University of California, 1967-89), vol.1 chap.3, p.372, (Internet: lib.ucr.edu/agnic/webber/Vol1/Chapter3.html). Some botanists call it Citrus medica var sarcodactylus. These names are used interchangeably in the scientific literature.

(12) Wikipedia, "Buddha's hand," (Internet: en.wikipedia.org/wiki/Fingered_ citron ; Bay Flora, "Buddha's Hand Citron Tree," (Internet: www.bayflora. com/ buddhahand.html); Practically Edible, "Buddha's Hand Citron,"

(Internet: www.practicallyedible.com/edible.nsf/list/Fingered%20 Citron!opendocument& BaseTarget=Right).

(13)   Practically Edible, op. cit.

(14)   Citrus Variety Collection, "Buddha's Hand citron," (Internet www. citrusvariety.ucr.edu/citrus/buddha.html).

(15)   Wikipedia, "Buddha's hand," op. cit.

(16)   Swingle, op. cit.; Bay Flora, op. cit.

(17)   Wikipedia, "Buddha's hand," op. cit.; Bay Flora, op. cit.; Practically Edible, op. cit.

(18)   Two letters from Professor W. P. Bitters of the University of California to Rabbi B. Polatsek, 30 October 1980, 4 June 1981, (reproduced in Rabbi Yisrael David Harpenes, *Pri Etz* Hadar, (Brooklyn, New York: 5746 – 1986), pp.125-27).

(19)   The Best of Morocco, Weather in Morocco, (Internet: www.morocco-travel.com/morocco/TemperaturesWeather ; Wikipedia, Geography of Shanghai, (Internet: en.wikipedia.org/wiki/Geography_of_Shanghai).

(20)   Citrus medica "Sarcodactylis," (Internet: www.homecitrusgrowers.co.uk/ citrusvarieties/BuddhasHandCitron.html).

(21)   Flickr, "Buddha hands," photograph, (Internet: www.flickr.com/photos/ ian_riley/51333444/in/set-72157594568450939).

(22)   e-mail from Rabbi Dr. Ari Zivotofsky, 3 August 2008.

(23)   Swingle, op. cit.

(24)   El-Kab is the present name of the ancient site of Nekheb, which was situated in the third nome of Upper Egypt, on the right bank of the Nile. It is a very ancient site with a lot of graffiti probably, dating from the Biblical period, on the walls of the wadis. (The Site El Kab, Internet: www. osirisnet.net/tombes/el_kab/e_el_kab.htm).

(25)   Shmuel Tolkowsky, *Citrus Fruits (Pri Atz Hadar)*, Jerusalem: Bialik Institute, 1966), pp.43-44. Tolkowsky writes that he doesn't believe that this drawing can be but the Chinese etrog.

(26)   Wikipedia, "Buddha's hand," op. cit.

(27)   Ibid.

(28)   Exotic plants in Mexico, "Citrus Medica var. sarcodactylus," (Internet: www.xplanta.com/?p=63).

(29)   Shulchan Aruch Yoreh Deah, chap 294; Rabbi Weissfish, op. cit., p.90.

(30)   Wikipedia, "Succade," (Internet: en.wikipedia.org/wiki/Candied rinds).

(31)   Wikipedia, "Buddha's hand," op. cit.

(32)   Much research has been done on this etrog by Chinese researchers, and this has been published, most of the publications being in Chinese. (For list of published papers see: Citrus Variety Collection, op. cit.)

(33)   Swingle, op. cit.

(34)   Wikipedia, "Buddha's hand," op. cit.

(35)   cf. the various rulings on sheitels after it was discovered that the hair from which they were made may have come from Hindu women who had offered the hair up in their temples. Collection of Documents on the Sheitel Shailah, (Internet: www1.cs.columbia.edu/~spotter/sheitel).

(36)   Shulchan Aruch Orach Chaim, chap.648 par.22.

(37) Citrus medica "Sarcodactylis," op. cit.; Practically Edible, op. cit.
(38) Rabbi Yaacov Emden, *Mor V'ktzizh*, (Altona, 5521 – 1761), chap.648.
(39) Shulchan Aruch Orach Chaim, chap.648, Mishnah Brurah, par.65.
(40) Ibid.; Rabbi Yechiel Michal Stern, *Kashrut Arba'at Haminim*, (Jerusalem, Machon Imrei David, 5752 – 1993), pp.196-97.
(41) Practically Edible, op. cit.
(42) Flickr, photograph, op. cit.
(43) Shulchan Aruch Orach Chaim, chap.648 par.16.
(44) Rabbi Stern, op. cit., pp.79-80, 188-89.
(45) Shulchan Aruch Orach Chaim, chap.648 par. 7.
(46) Rabbi Weissfish, op. cit., p.270.
(47) Shulchan Aruch Orach Chaim, chap.648 par.8.
(48) Ibid., par.2.
(49) Ibid., Rema; Rabbi Stern, op. cit., p.43.
(50) Fingered citron, photograph. (Internet: insideskills.com/album/flowers/pages/fingered%20citron.html).
(51) Rabbi Harpenes, op. cit., pp.97, 137.
(52) Practically Edible, op. cit.; Exotic Plants in Mexico, op. cit.
(53) There is another clone where the seeds hang free in the locules. Robert Willard Hodgson, "Horticultural Varieties of Citrus," *The Citrus Industry*, revised edition, (University of California, 1967-89), vol.1 chap.4, p.556, (Internet: lib.ucr.edu/agnic/webber/Vol1/Chapter4.html).
(54) Rabbi Weissfish, op. cit., pp.259-60.
(55) e.g. Rabbi Weissfish, op. cit., pp.185-208.
(56) Rabbi Moshe Isserlis, *Sheilot Uteshuvot Rema*, (Cracow, [n.d.]), chap.126; Shulchan Aruch Orach Chaim, chap.648, Mishnah Brurah par.65.
(57) Bay Flora, op. cit.; Practically Edible, op. cit.; Flickr, "Buddha hands," photograph, op. cit.; PlantWorld" photograph, (Internet: plantworld.org/gallery2/main.php/key/Fruit?g2_itemId=7476).
(58) Rabbi Stern, op. cit., p.75.
(59) Rabbi Moshe Sofer, *Chatam Sofer – Orach Chaim*, (New York, 5718 – 1958), chap.207; Rabbi Schneur Zalman Fradkin, *Torat Chesed*, (Warsaw, 5643 – 1883), chap.34.
(60) Wikipedia, "Buddha's hand," op. cit.
(61) Shulchan Aruch Orach Chaim, chap.653 par.1 and Mishnah Brurah chap. 653, par.1.
(62) Rabbi Weissfish, op. cit., pp.91-92.
(63) Eric Zurcher, "Eight Centuries in the Chinese Diaspora: The Jews of Kaifeng," *Sino-Judaica*, (Sino-Judaic Institute), vol.3, (2000), p.11.
(64) Professor Tang Yating, "Kaifeng Jewish Community," paper for the SIMS Melbourne, 2004, (Internet: www.hebrewsongs.com/kaifeng.htm).
(65) Ibid.
(66) Donald Daniel Leslie, "The Kaifeng Jewish Community," *Studies of the Chinese* Jews, compiled by Hyman Kublin, (New York: Paragon, 1971), p.196.
(67) Zurcher, op. cit., p.11.

(68) Xu Xin, *The Jews of Kaifeng, China*, (New Jersey: Ktav, 2003), pp.151-60.

(69) 1489 stele, 1663 stele, (reproduced by William Charles White, *Chinese Jews*, second edition, (University of Toronto press: 1966), part 2, pp.11, 88).

(70) Xin, *Jews of Kaifeng*, op. cit., p.78.

(71) 1489 stele, 1512 stele, 1663 stele, 1679 stele, (reproduced by White, op. cit., part 2, pp.12, 13, 43, 46, 62, 64, 88, 97-100); Jews *in Old China*, trans. and ed. Sidney Shapiro, (New York: Hippocrene Books, 1984), pp.40-41).

(72) Donald Daniel Leslie, *The Survival of the Chinese Jews*, (Leiden: Brill, 1972), p.54.

(73) Xu Xin, "Jewish Identity of the Kaifeng Jews," *From Kaifeng ... to Shanghai*, ed. Roman Malek, (Nettetal: Steyler Verlag, 2000), p.127; Leslie, *Survival of Chinese Jews*, op. cit., pp.54, 56.

(74) Yating, op. cit.

(75) For a list of primary sources, etc. on the Jews of Kaifeng, see: Leslie, "Kaifeng Jewish Community," op. cit., pp.195-97.

(76) A translation into English of all the texts written on the steles together with many footnotes is given in White, op. cit., part 2, pp.7-103.

(77) Ibid.

(78) Donald Daniel Leslie, *Jews and Judaism in Traditional China – A Comprehensive Bibliography*, (Sankt Augustin: Monumenta Serica Institute, 1998), p.33. There are 30 manuscripts of these prayers in the Hebrew Union College, Cincinnati, and in a few others in other libraries.

(79) Leslie, *Survival of Chinese Jews*, op. cit., p.86.

(80) Leslie, "Kaifeng Jewish Community," op. cit., p.196.

(81) 1663 stele, (reproduced in White, op. cit., part 2, pp.65, 89).

(82) 1489 stele, 1663 stele, (reproduced in White, op. cit., part 2, pp.9, 59).

(83) Marcus N. Adler. *Chinese Jews*, Lecture given on 17 June 1900 in London, (Oxford: Horace Hart), p.16.

(84) 1489 stele, 1512 stele, 1663 stele, (reproduced in White, op. cit., pp.10, 11, 44, 46, 59, 60, 61).

(85) 1489 stele, 1512 stele, (reproduced in White, op. cit., pp.9, 43).

(86) Xin, *Jews of Kaifeng*, op. cit., pp.83-84.

(87) This is known from the various extant manuscripts in the Hebrew Union College, Cincinnati. see: Leslie, Jews *and Judaism in Traditional China*, op. cit., p.33.

(88) Jean Domenge, documents 2a, 7a, (reproduced in Joseph Dehergne and Donald Daniel Leslie, *Juifs de Chine*, (Rome: Institutum Historicum, 1980), pp.147, 167).

(89) MS 932 Hebrew Union College, Cincinnati, Hebrew Manuscripts from China no.13, folios 37-39, (Jewish National Library, MS 19224).

(90) With the exception of the maftir for Shabbat Chol Hamoed Sukkot, where the portion "v'hikravtem" is given. This is the maftir read on Shabbat Chol Hamoed *Pesach*. It would seem that a writing error occurred when copying this manuscript.

(91) MS 932 Hebrew Union College, op. cit., folios 40-41.
(92) MS 935 Hebrew Union College, Cincinnati, Hebrew Manuscripts from China no.16, (Jewish National Library MS 19227).
(93) MS 932 Hebrew Union College, op. cit., folio 39.
(94) Domenge, document 3, description of the Kaifeng Synagogue, (reproduced in Dehergne, op. cit. p.154); James Finn, *The Jews in China*, (London: Wertheim, 1843), p.18.
(95) Domenge, document 7a, (reproduced in Dehergne, op. cit., p.166).
(96) Ibid.
(97) Shulchan Aruch Orach Chaim, chap.658 par.2.
(98) Finn, op. cit., p.23.
(99) Leslie, *Survival of Chinese Jews*, op. cit., pp.61-62, 88.
(100) Ibid., p.64 fn.1.
(101) There is a further reference to Sukkot brought by Domenge document 2a: "Bibles, written entirely by hand with good ink that they make themselves and renew every year after the feast of Tabernacles." (reproduced by Dehergne, op. cit., p.147).
(102) *The Jews of China,* vol.2, ed. Jonathan Goldstein, (New York: M.E.Sharpe, 2000), pp.86-87.
(103) Maisie J. Meyer, *From the Rivers of Babylon to the Whangpoo*, (Langham, Maryland: University Press of America, 2003), p.81.
(104) Ibid., p.85.
(105) *The Jewish Journal*, op. cit.
(106) The differing opinions of Rabbi Somech and the Ben Ish Chai are discussed later in this paper.
(107) Rabbi Yecheskel Leitner, *Operation: Torah Rescue*, (Jerusalem: Feldheim Publishers, 1987), p.108.
(108) Aviva Shabi, "Baghdadi Jews in Shanghai," *The Scribe*, (London, The Exilarch's Foundation), no.72, September 1999, p.41.
(109) Ibid.; Ezra Yehezkel-Shaked, "The Ohel Shelomo Synagogue in Kobe, Japan," *Nehardea – Journal of the Babylonian Jewry Heritage Center*, (Or-Yehuda: The Babylonian Jewry Heritage Center), no.10, November 1997, p.10.
(110) *Nehardea*, op. cit., p.10.
(111) Goldstein, op. cit., p.87.
(112) *The Jewish Journal*, op. cit.
(113) Babylonian Talmud, Sukkah 36a.
(114) Rambam, Mishneh Torah, Hilchot Lulav, chap.8 halachah 8.
(115) e.g. Shulchan Aruch Orach Chaim, chap.648 par.20; Aruch Hashulchan Orach Chaim, chap.648 par.41.
(116) "Tanhum ben Joseph (Ha-)Yerushalmi," *Encyclopedia Judaica*, vol.15, (Jerusalem: Keter Publishing House, 1971), col.797.
(117) *Al-Mursid al-Kafi – The Lexicon of Tanhum ben Yosef Hayerushalmi to Mishne Tora of Maimonides*, with translation from Judaeo-Arabic into Hebrew by Hadassa Shy, (Jerusalem: The Israel Academy of Sciences and Humanities, 2005), pp.638, 639.
(118) Wikipedia, "Buddha's hand," op. cit.; Exotic Plants in Mexico, op. cit.

(119) *Allerlei Geschichten Maasse-Buch*, (Frankfurt am Main: J. Kauffmann Verlag, 1929), pp.242-45; *Ma'aseh Book*, translated into English by Moses Gaster, (Philadelphia: Jewish Publication Society of America, 1934), pp.461-66. This book of moralistic stories in Yiddish was first published in Basel in 1602 and has been translated and reprinted numerous times, sometimes with additional stories.

(120) The words in Hebrew used by Rabbi Somech transliterated are "from the country of Gin from the city of Hanchan." It is known that there was a Jewish community in nearby Shanghai and in this same area, the Chinese etrog was to be found. It is very reasonable to assume that the reference of Rabbi Somech was to the country of China – (what other country could it be?!) and the city Hangchow, or Hongkew which was an area of Shanghai. In his paper dealing with the kashrut of unusual etrogim (Techumin vol. 24, 5764 (2004) p.345, published by Tzomet, Alon Shevut), Rabbi Dr. Avraham Ofir Shemesh suggests that what Rabbi Somech meant by Gin was Ujjain, a holy city in central India. It is hard to accept this since Ujjain is a city and Rabbi Somech writes about the COUNTRY of Gin.

(121) Rabbi Abdullah Somech, *Zivchei Tzedek*, part 2, Orach Chaim, (Baghdad: Bechor Chutzin, 5664 – 1904), chap.37.

(122) Rabbi Somech, op. cit., reply by Rabbi Yoseph Chaim, the Ben Ish Chai to Rabbi Somech.

(123) Rabbi Leitner, op. cit., pp.108-10.

(124) see p.123 of Rabbi Leitner's book where a photocopy of his ghetto pass is reproduced.

(125) Author of paper to Rabbi Leitner, 6 November 1994, (from files of author of this paper).

(126) Rabbi Leitner to author of paper, 23 November 1994, (from files of author of this paper).

(127) Shulchan Aruch Orach Chaim, chap.649, Mishnah Brurah, pars.53, 54.

(128) Ibid., Be'er Heteiv, par.14.

(129) Author of paper to Rabbi Leitner, 1 December 1994, (from files of author of this paper).

(130) Rabbi Leitner to author of paper, 16 December 1994, (from files of author of this paper).

(131) Shulchan Aruch Orach Chaim, chap.651.

(132) The paragraphs are 12, 13.

(133) Yaakov Edelstein, "The Mirrer Yeshiva in Shanghai during the Second World War," *Kivunim*, no.19, May 1983, (Jerusalem: World Zionist Organisation), p.131.

(134) David Kranzler, *Japanese, Nazis & Jews*, (Hoboken, New Jersey: Ktav, 1988), p.434.

(135) Shanghai Jewish Center, (Internet: www.chinajewish.org/jewishsites.htm).

(136) *Kivunim*, op. cit., p.129.

(137) Rabbi Leitner, op. cit., p.92.

(138) Kranzler, op. cit., p.434.

(139) *Techumin*, op. cit., p.344.

(140) Grateful Acknowledgments are due to (in alphabetical order): Rabbi Yecheskel Leitner (during the year 1994); Librarians at the Jewish National and University Library, Givat Ram, Jerusalem together with the staff of the Microfilm department; Ms. Asia Nawe of Sasa-da; Librarians at Kiryat Arba Municipal Library; Users of Wikipedia Reference Desk who answered my questions; Librarians at Yeshivat "Nir" Kiryat Arba Library; Rabbi Dr. Ari Zivotofsky.

Section Six

Good Shabbes
Mother Earth

HETER MECHIRAH OR IMPORTED VEGETABLES WHICH SHOULD ONE CHOOSE?

Rabbi Dr. Chaim Simons

This paper was written in 2007 in preparation
for the Shemittah year 5768

Introduction

A few weeks before Shavuot 5767 [2007], Eliezer Barat, the Managing Director of "Alei Katif" wrote: "Otzar Ha'aretz suggests possible solutions for the supply of fruit and vegetables which are Mehadrin for Shemittah, without having to use non-Jewish produce and without utilising the Heter Mechirah."[1] About a month and a half later, "Otzar Ha'aretz" modified this position and stated that when non Heter Mechirah vegetables from Jewish sources are finished, "Otzar Ha'aretz" will place "two alternatives before the buyers: imported produce from the Diaspora or Heter Mechirah. The Bet Din of Otzar Ha'aretz, (which is composed of four well-known Rabbis[2]), will not decide on this question but will leave it to the decision of the consumer."[3] In answer to a question, Rabbi Yehudah Amichai of "Otzar Ha'aretz" answered that "vegetables which are Heter Mechirah will be clearly and prominently labeled."[4]

In this paper, I, a *consumer* of "Otzar Ha'aretz" produce will discuss in depth the choice between Heter Mechirah produce and imported produce. The discussion will include the question of whether the Heter Mechirah has, according to the consensus of Rabbinic opinion, any halachic validity today and, indeed whether it ever had such validity in the past. (It is not the purpose of this paper to enter into the lengthy and complex Halachic arguments for and against the Heter Mechirah.) Furthermore, even according to those who give Heter Mechirah halachic validity, does it have ideological acceptability? A further question is: can one take seriously the sale of Eretz Yisrael to a non-Jew? According to those who hold that the Heter Mechirah is not halachically acceptable, what is the status of Heter Mechirah agricultural produce – is it kosher or not, and is there a difference between fruit on the one hand and vegetables on the other? After delving into all these questions, I will attempt to answer the question as to whether to use Heter Mechirah or imported produce.

Early history of Heter Mechirah

In a paper written by Rabbi Kalman Kahana, he summarized the observance of Shemittah throughout the generations until the period of the "First Aliyah." He wrote, "For thousands of years Jews of Eretz Yisrael kept the Mitzvah of Shemittah with trust in the kindness of the Almighty. ... This was even in periods when there were no non-Jewish owned fields in Eretz Yisrael and all the food came from Jewish owned fields and also in periods when it was not easy to import such produce."[5]

In the 1880s when, what is popularly known today as the "First Aliyah" began, many of the new Jewish immigrants worked in the production and export of wine and citrus fruits. As the Shemittah year 5649 (1888-89) approached, the Rabbis of Jerusalem, Rabbi Yehoshua Yehudah Leib (Maharil) Diskin and Rabbi Shmuel Salant, forbade work on the land during the Shemittah.[6] The men of the "First Aliyah" then began a propaganda campaign in which "they falsely stated in a loud voice that observance of the Shemittah would be life threatening, and as a result of this there were some Rabbinical authorities in the Diaspora, who living far away [from Eretz Yisrael] gave a lenient decision on this matter."[7]

In fact, the colonists had a different reason for the non-observance of Shemittah – they were concerned about creating a precedent. Moshe Leib Lielienblum, one of the secular Zionist leaders of the time wrote, "If the colonists stop work for this first

Shemittah, it will create a precedent in accordance with those who are strict ... and then there will be no future possibility of permitting work during Shemittah ... therefore we must from the outset not accept the opinion of those who are strict and not permit any cessation of work."[8]

Some Rabbis in Eastern Europe were contacted and three of them[9] gave a Heter, for that Shemittah alone, subject to the approval of Rabbi Yitzchak Elchanan Spektor of Kovno, to sell the land to a non-Jew. Rabbi Spektor, gave his agreement in a very guarded manner and stressed that this was valid solely for that Shemittah.[10] However, on this approval, some Rabbis of that generation wrote that the colonists had used "trickery and deceit on the Rabbi [Spektor]."[11] and that "he was not conversant with the situation."[12]

The Sepharadi authorities in Eretz Yisrael represented by Hacham Yaacov Shaul Elyasher gave their approval.[13] However the Ashkenazi Jerusalem Rabbinate, headed by Rabbi Diskin and Rabbi Salant strongly disagreed and issued a proclamation that "there is no Heter whatsoever to plough, to sow, to reap and to plant whether by themselves [the colonists] or by a non-Jew."[14] Later a further similar proclamation was issued in Jerusalem by about twenty Rabbis.[15] One of these Rabbis, Rabbi Tuvia Rosenthal, wrote a book in which he clarified the laws of Shemittah. In the introduction to this book he wrote, "It is obvious that had they [the colonists] not found someone to give the Heter [Mechirah], they would have observed the Shemittah in accordance with the Halachah."[16]

At that period, there were also a number of renowned Rabbis in Europe who came out strongly against this Heter. These included Rabbi Yoseph Dov Soloveichik (the Bet Halevi), Rabbi Naftali Tzvi Yehudah Berlin (the Netziv), Rabbi Shimshon Refoel Hirsch (a leading Rabbi in Germany), Rabbi David Friedman of Karlin (a leading Rabbi in Lithuania), Rabbi Eliezer Gordon (Rosh Yeshivah of Telz), the Admor of Radzin (who is famous for his work on Techelet), Rabbi Yoseph Stern (Av Bet Din of Shavli) and Rabbi Yechiel Michel Epstein (the author of the "Aruch Hashulchan").[17] The last named described this Heter as an "insult to our Holy Torah and our Holy Land."[18] In contrast Rabbi Yoseph Engel[19] and Rabbi Avraham Bornstein of Sochochov[20] came out in favour.

There were some colonists who observed the Shemittah. However, it was not easy for them since great pressure was put on them from various sources. One of these sources was the overseers of Baron Edmond Rothschild who was helping to financially support the new settlers.[21] A further source of compulsion was the leaders of "Hovevei Zion" who stopped giving financial support to the Shemittah observers. On this Dr. Leon Pinsker, one of the founders and leaders of "Hovevei Zion" wrote, "I gave an order to stop supporting the community of Gedera if they do not work during Shemittah."[22] There were even people "who were not ashamed to involve the [Turkish] government in this matter and they went and informed against them [the Shemittah observers] to the authorities saying that the Jews were not working and would thus harm the treasury."[23] Only a few of the colonists were able to withstand this pressure.[24]

In the year 5664 (1904), Rabbi Avraham Yitzchak haKohen Kook came on Aliyah and soon after was appointed Rabbi of Jaffa. Whilst he was in Russia, he had opposed this Heter – "my opinion then inclined towards those who oppose this Heter."[25] Approaching the Shemittah year 5670 (1909-10) a lot of pressure was put on him to give a Heter Mechirah – the pressure was so much that he said that "if a Yeshivah in Jerusalem were to give him... [a stipend] each month he would leave his position [as the Rabbi of Jaffa] because of the Shemittah problem, and go and learn in the Yeshivah."[26] However, because of the critical economic situation of the colonists, he finally gave a Heter.[27] We can see from his letters that it was given with great reluctance[28] and "my heart aches continually because of this priceless Mitzvah,"[29] He called it a "heter given in strained circumstances"[30] and that it was only a "temporary measure."[31] However, he also wrote, "that anyone who wishes not to work the land at all during the Shemittah year is to be praised."[32] He also declared that "every Jew who is in a position to observe the Shemittah even in strained circumstances, and in the following year will be able to work his land, and not be forced to abandon it [his land] and depart to the Diaspora, is in duty bound to observe the Shemittah in accordance with the law, and this would be a great merit for the whole Jewish people."[33]

This Shemittah – 5768

In our generation for every successive Shemittah, fewer Rabbis support the Heter Mechirah. This Shemittah, there were a number of official city Rabbis who refused the give a hechsher to those establishments which utilized the Heter Mechirah. This refusal was made with the consent of the Chief Rabbinate who decided "that each city Rabbi should have the sole right to decide on his city's policy regarding Shemittah in accordance with his own individual interpretation and opinion on the laws of Shemittah."[34]

Furthermore, the Chief Rabbinate Council decided "to encourage the observance of Shemittah. In a case where it is possible to decrease the use of the Heter Mechirah, it will be done in accordance with the circumstances…. The need for the use of the Heter by a particular farmer will be investigated."[35] Chief Rabbi Yona Metzger went as far to announce that they planned to discontinue the use of the Heter Mechirah after the current Shemittah.[36]

To combat the situation where the "local Rabbinate was not prepared to allow organizations to purchase Heter Mechirah products,"[37] a group of "Religious Zionist Rabbis" in the organization "Rabbis of Tzohar" "established their own new Kashrut organization."[38] They brought out an advertisement for "owners of businesses" who "have had difficulties in receiving a Kashrut certificate in the Shemittah year" to apply for their "Teudat Hashgacha" (supervision certificate)[39] and they then started "to distribute them."[40] (For legal reasons they could not use the term "Teudat Kashrut" and so they had to call it "Teudat Hashgacha."[41]) A sample of their "Teudat Hashgacha" was reproduced in the Israeli press[42] and also displayed on the Internet[43] and it is headed "The National Supervisory Committee for Shemittah" with the names of the four Rabbis who comprised the Presidium.[44]

However, some organisations who market agricultural produce took more decisive action and took the Chief Rabbinate to the Supreme Court claiming "that for many years, the policy was to recognize the Heter Mechirah, and we are thus dealing with a change in policy for a stricter one, which will cause immeasurable damage to agriculture."[45] In their lengthy ruling written largely by Judge Elyakim Rubinstein who is an observant Jew, the Court ruled that "in any instance where the local Rabbi is not prepared to give a Kashrut certificate based on 'Heter Mechirah', the [Chief] Rabbinate must use its powers... and appoint Rabbis who will do this."[46] (Even though this ruling was based on administrative considerations, it caused strong negative reactions from Knesset members of the 'Yahadut haTorah" party. [47]) Following this ruling, the Chief Rabbinate authorized five Rabbis to grant such Kashrut certificates.[48]

Are the early rulings on Heter Mechirah relevant today?

There are today some leading Rabbis in Israel who still utilise the Heter Mechirah. It goes without saying that even if one personally disagrees with their ruling, one must not talk disparagingly of these Rabbis and their ruling on this question.

Those supporting the Heter Mechirah today, often adduce support (in particular) from Rabbi Kook's ruling. However, the question is whether Rabbi Kook's ruling is still relevant today. As we have seen above, nearly one hundred years ago he himself described it as a "temporary measure."

In a lecture he gave over forty years ago, Rabbi Shlomo Goren said that Rabbi Kook's ruling no longer applied and any such sale had no validity.[49] At a later date, he published an article in "Hatzofe" reiterating this point. In it he wrote that "after the establishment of the State of Israel, when most of Eretz Yisrael is in Jewish hands, there is no validity to the Heter Mechirah according to the writings of Rabbi Kook himself,[50] or the Heter has been completely weakened and one cannot rely on it, especially as one is speaking of the sale of all Eretz Yisrael to non-Jews in order to nullify its sanctity."[51]

A similar conclusion, but for economic reasons, was reached by Rabbi Moshe Ushpizai who was Chief Rabbi of Ramat Gan and at a later date, Chairman of the Board of Rabbis of Hapoel Hamizrachi. Over forty years ago he wrote, "Now there has been a great change in the economy of the State of Israel. The economy is increasingly being based on industry and not on agriculture. Industry is taking first place in the country. Even the kibbutz economy is increasingly being based on industry. ... We are also, time and time again witnessing a sad phenomenon where excess fruit and vegetables are being thrown on the dung-heap." He very strongly suggested that the original protagonists, and especially Rabbi Kook, would not agree to the Heter Mechirah today.[52]

This same point was made during the month prior to this Shemittah, when a list of fifteen of the leading Rabbis in Israel,[53] including both Ashkenazi and Sepharadi Rabbis, issued a proclamation regarding this Shemittah. In it they stated, "As is well known, about a hundred years ago, at a time of great necessity and in life threatening situations, there were great Rabbis who permitted as a temporary measure relying on the Heter Mechirah, but it is absolutely clear that even those who then permitted it would not do so today."[54]

In contrast to this, those who today are in favour of Heter Mechirah try to adduce support by quoting the names of the prominent Rabbis who a century ago gave their consent, but they fail to mention that these Rabbis said that it was only for that particular Shemittah that they gave the Heter. Incidentally, one of the names they mention is Rabbi Yehoshua Yehudah Leib (Maharil) Diskin. But this is inaccurate. Rabbi Diskin was strongly against the Heter Mechirah. What he supported was the one-time suggestion by the Rabbi of Jaffa, Rabbi Naftali Herz that for that particular Shemittah (5656 / 1895-96) one could sell the fruit trees and even this had very strict limitations placed on it.[55]

Heter Mechirah viewed ideologically

Is it ideologically right (even according to those who hold that halachically the Heter Mechirah is valid) to sell Eretz Yisrael to non-Jews? The Almighty gave Eretz Yisrael in its entirety only to the Jewish people and now we want to sell it to avoid observing a Mitzvah in the Torah! Just as the Jewish people have been Divinely given the Shabbat, the holy soil of Eretz Yisrael has likewise been given its Shabbat.

Rabbi Ze'ev Vitman, the Chairman of the Shemittah Committee of the Chief Rabbinate, wrote that "Heter Mechirah is based on completely nullifying the Mitzvah of Shemittah" and "thus there are essential and basic differences between Heter Mechirah and other heterim," such as Mechirat Chametz [sale of Chametz], Heter Iska [method used to avoid infringing the prohibition against taking interest] and Pruzbul [document allowing collection of debts after the end of the Shemittah year].[56] In a similar vein, Rabbi Moshe Levinger, who (before he re-established Jewish settlement in Hebron) was Rabbi of Kibbutz Lavie, (a kibbutz of the "Kibbutz Hadati"), wrote an article entitled "A proposal to limit the sale [of land] to a non-Jew in the Shemittah year." In this article he stated that "it is difficult for the populace to take upon themselves the instructions of the Chief Rabbinate who obligate them to observe some of the laws of Shemittah even after the sale. It is indeed found that these instructions are barely implemented, and thus the practice has shown that with the sale of the land based on the Heter Mechirah, one sells the whole of the Shemittah."[57]

In is written about the "Netziv" "that his entire soul was filled with devotion and immeasurable love for Eretz Yisrael, which was in the process of being resettled, so that every small brick in a [new] building gave him spiritual joy." In addition to opposing the Heter Mechirah on halachic grounds, he also did so on ideological grounds as he saw this as "a blemish on the holiness and purity of Eretz Yisrael."[58] He wrote in connection with the Mitzvah of Shemittah, "Eretz Yisrael is different from other countries. Its existence does not rely on natural causes as with other countries, but on Divine providence.... [which includes] the observance of the Shemittah as explained in the Torah."[59]

Another person to realise the importance of not trying to avoid Shemittah observance was the Director of "Neot Kedumim"

[The Biblical Landscape Reserve in Israel], Nogah Hareuveni, who, prior to the last Shemittah (5761), was asked whether he would include Neot Kedumim in the Heter Mechirah. He replied that "Eretz Yisrael is not for sale." All the activities at that location during the Shemittah year were done in accordance with the Shemittah laws.[60]

How genuine is the Heter Mechirah?

This Shemittah a non-Jew, bought all the Jewish farmland in Eretz Yisrael for seventy billion shekels with a post-dated cheque![61] Two questions immediately come to mind: The first is: Does this non-Jew have, or is he likely to have, cover for this sum, by the time his cheque is due?! The second is: What if he refuses to sell this land back after the Shemittah year?!

Those who are involved in implementing the Heter Mechirah will obviously argue that these questions do not disqualify the sale. However, there are contrary opinions. Rabbi Vitman writes that "I heard from Rabbi Yosef Elyashiv and Rabbi Shlomo Zalman Auerbach that in their opinion the genuineness of the sale is the biggest problem with Heter Mechirah."[62] Even Rabbi Moshe Levinger, who fully accepts the validity of Heter Mechirah, comments that "one cannot hide from the fact that the populace do not understand and are unable to understand the Heter Mechirah in its present form of selling all the Land of Israel to one Arab."[63]

The "Minchat Yitzchak" goes further and writes that "the sale has no validity since everyone knows that it is not a genuine sale of all the Land to a non-Jew."[64] Likewise, Rabbi Elazar Teitz, the Av Bet Din of Elizabeth, New Jersey, and Rabbi of the Congregation Adath Yeshurun, argues that the sale is not a true one but an "asmachta" namely, a matter agreed to in anticipation of its never being realised, and this renders the sale halachically invalid.[65]

There are those who argue that if Mechirat Chametz is in order, so is Heter Mechirah. However, this argument has a serious flaw. If at the end of Pesach, the non-Jew does not want to sell back the Chametz, he pays for it and takes it.[66] The Jew can easily then buy fresh Chametz. This is certainly not the case with all the farmland in Eretz Yisrael!

Abolishing the Heter Mechirah

The question which is asked with increasing frequency with every successive Shemittah is whether the Heter Mechirah should be discontinued?

By actively supporting those who want to use the Heter Mechirah, one is assisting in perpetuating this Heter forever, whilst the intention of its proponents a hundred years ago was that it was to be a temporary measure to be dispensed with as quickly as possible. If those supporting the Heter Mechirah - an ever-decreasing minority opinion – were to see that the market for Heter Mechirah products was vanishing, an alternative solution would have to be found.

Such a solution could hopefully be found if the Government of Israel had the serious intention of working as a team together with agriculturists and Rabbis.

The question to be asked is how much it would cost the Israeli economy if the agricultural sector were to cease to do work forbidden during the Shemittah year. A study of this was made by Rabbi Professor Yehudah Levi and Rabbi Dr. Gershon Metzger at the "Jerusalem College of Technology – Machon Lev." They studied the agricultural situation in Israel and the profitability of agricultural exports, and then concluded that if farmers ceased forbidden work during Shemittah, did not engage in other work and were recompensed for all their losses, spread out over seven years, it would increase the government budget by 50 agorot for every 1,000 shekels annually.[67] The suggested Israeli government total budget for 2008 is just over three hundred billion shekels,[68] thus making the annual cost of keeping Shemittah, about 150 million shekels annually.

One could mention here, that the Finance Ministry announced that there was a budget surplus during the first eleven months of 2007 of 7.7 billion shekels.[69] This could easily pay off the entire cost of observing the Shemittah 5768 (2007-2008).

The study by "Machon Lev" goes on to propose advanced professional courses for agriculturists during the Shemittah year in which the participants would learn about new developments in the agricultural field. The knowledge gained from these courses would definitely improve the efficiency of the workers in the years following the Shemittah year and thus increase their productivity level and hence their income, and this could well offset losses incurred as a result of observing the Shemittah year.[70]

Furthermore, new agricultural techniques could be utilised to assist with the observance of Shemittah.[71] To accomplish this, an infrastructure would be built up with a onetime initial outlay. This infrastructure would also assist agriculture in the non-Shemittah years. The infrastructure would consist of extensive facilities for keeping vegetables in cold storage, building hothouses for growing vegetables detached from the soil and developing land in the southern Arava part of Israel (where the laws of Shemittah do not apply) for massive agriculture. In addition, there could be large scale planting of vegetables before Rosh Hashanah of a Shemittah year. Land could also be rented in Jordan, (as is already being done this Shemittah), and this would also give employment to Jewish agronomists.[72] The proximity of Jordan would keep transport charges to a minimum. Possibly land in Sinai and Egypt could also be utilized.

Where to shop?

In order to understand where one can shop during the Shemittah period, one needs to understand the various laws concerning different types of agricultural produce.[73]

Things which grow from the ground can broadly speaking be divided into fruit and vegetables. There is a crucial difference between fruit and vegetables regarding the laws as to what may and may not be eaten. Because there were Jews who secretly planted things during the Shemittah year and then claimed that they sprouted by themselves, the Rabbis made a decree that things which had an annual planting – in practice, mainly vegetables – which began to sprout during the Shemittah year in a Jewish owned or Jewish worked field, were classed as "sefichim" and were forbidden to be eaten.

In the case of fruit there is no such prohibition, since fruit trees are not planted annually. However, there is the question of fruit trees which are illegally worked on during Shemittah (ne'evad) and fruit which the owner has not made "ownerless" (shamur) as required. Is it permitted to eat such fruit? This question has been in dispute for many hundreds of years – some permitting whilst others forbid eating "shamur v'ne'evad." Today opinions are still divided. The Eda Charedit of Jerusalem states, quoting the opinions of Rabbi Chaim Berlin and the Ridbaz, that it is forbidden, adding that "this has been the accepted practice of all the Batei Din of the different communities,"[74] whereas the Chazon Ish[75] and Rabbi Shlomo Zalman Auerbach[76] permit "shamur v'ne'evad" produce, the former b'dieved [post facto].

This question – where to shop – was asked during the previous Shemittah (5761 / 2000-01) and was answered by Rabbi Shlomo Aviner, the head of the Ateret Kohanim Yeshiva and Rabbi of Bet El. In his answer he comes out strongly in favour of buying Heter Mechirah produce from Jews. "If someone buys from Arabs and financially hurts Jewish agriculturalists can this be called a stringency?! On the contrary. It is a Mitzvah to buy from Jews. .... Is destroying Jewish agriculture a stringency?! Is strengthening the hold of Arabs on our Holy Land a stringency?! On the contrary. It is more stringent to buy from Jews relying on the Heter Mechirah."[77]

These comments came under very strong criticism from the Av Bet Din, Rabbi Teitz, who commented that Rabbi Aviner had left the realms of "halachic analysis" and was utilising "arguments based on rhetoric and emotion."[78] Rabbi Teitz also pointed out that most of the profit from Arab agricultural produce does not go to the Arab farmer but to those who handle it from the farm to the consumer. All these middle men are Jewish and buying Arab produce will thus add to the Jewish economy.[79]

Rabbi Mordechai Eliahu, a former Chief Rabbi of Israel and Rishon Lezion, who with some hesitation, accepts the validity of the Heter Mechirah[80] lists in his book, published this Shemittah, an "order of preference in purchasing agricultural produce during the Shemittah." Unlike Rabbi Aviner, he places imported products from Jordan, Egypt and Gaza (and presumably other Diaspora countries) above Heter Mechirah produce.[81]

Of course, ideally one would prefer to buy products from Jews. However, one has to be bound by the restraints of the Halachah and the practicalities of day-to-day living. We must remember that the majority of authorities hold that today the Heter Mechirah is invalid and this accordingly makes "sefichim" non-kosher. The Ridbaz goes as far as to write, "and every Jew should know that produce which is sown in the Shemittah year and fruit and vine from a vine which is pruned in the Shemittah year are as forbidden to a Jew as is pork."[82]

In a further article brought out by Rabbi Aviner for this Shemittah, entitled "I Choose Heter Mechirah," he gives a list of reasons for eating Heter Mechirah produce. In addition to those he gave in the previous Shemittah, he states that "if someone uses the expression 'it is forbidden' regarding produce provided in accordance with Heter Mechirah, he is libeling the great Rabbis who followed it," and also "undermining Rabbinic authority."[83] However, Rabbi Aviner is incorrect. The Heter was not given as a permanent institution but only as a temporary one to be reviewed every Shemittah and, as already stated above, the Rabbis who originally gave the Heter would not give it today.

It is relevant to mention that with no connection to Shemittah, every year a noticeable percentage of agricultural produce which is found in the Jewish sector is grown by Arabs. In the case of cucumbers, the majority are grown by Arabs. Agricultural produce which is sold under the sign "Heter Mechirah" includes this produce grown by Arabs.[84]

In order to supply those who wish to observe Shemittah with agricultural produce, many settlements have Shemittah shops. However, unfortunately not every settlement has a Shemittah shop and for those living in such places, a partial solution has been proposed by Rabbi Moshe Heiman in his book "Hamitbach b'Shemittah." Under such circumstances, he writes one can rely on those permitting "shamur v'ne'evad" and buy from any shop in the community (even those who have Heter Mechirah produce or no supervision at all in connection with Shemittah[85]), with the following proviso. In the case of fruit: until no more of that species is found in the fields ("zeman biur"). In the case of vegetables: during the first weeks of the Shemittah year, when the vegetables reaching the shops are those where the vegetables began to sprout before Rosh Hashanah. After this period, they will be sefichim and forbidden to be eaten, and likewise after "zeman biur." In the case of vegetables this period extends to about a year but for fruit it is much shorter, and during this period one would thus have to travel outside one's town for one's shopping.[86]

Heter Mechirah or imported produce?

The object of this paper is to help me, a *consumer* make a decision between using Heter Mechirah produce and imported products when all the vegetables from all the non-Shemittah sources are exhausted.

Here is my answer:

As stated right at the beginning of this paper, the Managing Director of "Alei Katif" said: "Otzar Ha'aretz suggests possible solutions for the supply of fruit and vegetables which are Mehadrin for the Shemittah, without having to use non-Jewish fruits and without utilising the Heter Mechirah." If they could adhere to this principle throughout the Shemittah year and during the subsequent months when the laws of Shemittah produce are in practice still in force, then they would of course have found the ideal solution. However, they already admit that in practice after the winter of the Shemittah year, the consumer will have to decide between Heter Mechirah and imported vegetables.

As we have already seen, the majority of Rabbinical authorities rule that today the Heter Mechirah is invalid (and many have ruled so from its inception!). The proclamation by the fifteen leading Rabbis (referred to above) states that "anyone who gives support to the 'Heter Mechirah' uproots a Mitzvah. And our ruling is that it is forbidden to rely on this 'Heter' and there is no room for a difference of opinion between the different communities and therefore every Jew is obligated to observe the Shemittah and anyone who gives a ruling to abolish the Shemittah by the 'Heter Mechirah' is guilty of causing a desecration of G-d's name (Chillul HaShem) by giving the appearance of making a big joke of this important and holy commandment."[87]

It thus follows that this will make vegetables grown in the Shemittah year non-kosher and as with other non-kosher food forbidden to be eaten.

Even many of those Rabbis who today accept the validity of the Heter Mechirah consider it praiseworthy to avoid utilising it. For example, such an answer was given by Rabbi Yehudah Amichai of the "Otzar Ha'aretz" Bet Din in answer to a question posed to the "Machon haTorah v'ha'Aretz." He wrote, "and anyone who is able to go through Shemittah without utilising the Heter Mechirah is to be praised."[88] These Rabbis will also certainly admit that one cannot class Heter Mechirah produce as Mehadrin. Let us give an example of this. Before the last Shemittah, the Chief Rabbi[89] of Ramat Gan, Rabbi Yaacov Ariel, who is one of the members of the "Otzar Ha'aretz" Bet Din, was asked whether the Mehadrin restaurants in that city utilized Heter Mechirah products. He answered that if they gave a "Mehadrin Hechsher," the products used were not Heter Mechirah.[90]

In the case of fruit however there is no question of "sefichim." There is the question of "shamur v'ne'evad" but many great authorities allow this, at least b'dieved. There is therefore a strong case to prefer such fruit from Israeli Jewish sources rather than imported fruit, when no "Otzar Bet Din" [produce storehouse of Bet Din that provides Shemittah fruit to the public] fruit is available in one's locality.

The question of what to eat in the Shemittah year is of course not a new question and it was already put to Rabbi Moshe di Trani, the "Mabit" nearly five hundred years ago. Amongst the list of products which he gave was "vegetables of non-Jews."[91] As stated above, Rabbi Mordechai Eliyahu gives priority to imported vegetables over Heter Mechirah produce.

Thus, when my choice as a consumer is between Heter Mechirah or imported vegetables, I would use the imported ones.(92)

References

(1)   Kommemiyut, (Bet El), no. 50, Parashat Bahar-Bechukotai, 23 Iyar 5767 – 11 May 2007, p.4.
(2)   Rabbi Yehudah Amichai, Rabbi Yaacov Ariel, Rabbi Nechemiah Goldberg and Rabbi Dov Lior.
(3)   B'sheva, no. 247, 5 Tammuz 5767 - 21 June 2007, p.35.
(4)   "How will I know how to identify vegetables which are Heter Mechirah?" Answer by Rabbi Yehudah Amichai, Otzar Ha'aretz, (Internet: 212.199.215.132/otzar/answer9.asp).
(5)   Rabbi Dr. Kalman Kahana, "The Sabbatical Year During the Generations," Torah u'Mada, vol.2, no.2, Elul 5732 - September 1972, p.101.
(6)   Mordechai Diskin, Divrei Mordechai, (Jerusalem, 5649 - 1889), pp.16-17.
(7)   Open letter from Mordechai Gimpel Yaffe, Ketavim l'Toladot Chibat Zion v'Yishuv Eretz-Yisrael, [henceforth: Ketavim], vol.3, (Tel Aviv: Achdut, 5692 – 1932), letter 1322, col.891.
(8)   Moshe Leib Lielienblum, Derech la'avor Gulim, (Warsaw: Achiasaf, 5659 -1899), pp.131-32.
(9)   Rabbi Shmuel Mohilever, Rabbi Yisrael Trunk and Rabbi Shmuel Zanvil Klepfish.
(10) Rabbinical ruling, Hameliz, (St. Petersburg), no.58, 19 Adar II 5649 – 10 (22) March 1889, pp.2-3.
(11) Rabbi Yaacov David Willowski, Bet Ridbaz, Introduction to Pe'at Hashulchan, (Jerusalem, 5672 – 1912).
(12) Letter by Rabbi Moshe Nachum Wallenstein, Av Bet Din of Jerusalem, Habazeleth, (Jerusalem), no.46, 24 Sivan 5670 – 1 July 1910, p.297 (3).
(13) Rabbi Yaacov Shaul Elyashar, Dvar haShemittah, Hazewi, (Jerusalem), no.16, 11 Nissan 5648 – 23 March 1888, pp.7-10; Rabbi Yaacov Shaul Elyashar, Simcha La'ish, (Jerusalem 5653 – 1893), Yoreh Deah, chap.26, pp.107-109.
(14) Public announcement, Habazeleth, (Jerusalem), no.6, 21 Marcheshvan 5649 – 26 October 1888, p.44 (4); Hora'at Rabanan Kashishai to Pe'at Hashulchan, op. cit., Introduction.
(15) Hora'at Rabanan Kashishai to Pe'at Hashulchan, op. cit., Introduction.
(16) Rabbi Tuvia Rosenthal, Halachah M'voreret, (Warsaw, 5655 – 1895), Introduction, p.4.
(17) Dayan Dr. Isidor Grunfeld, The Jewish Dietary Laws, vol.2, (London: Soncino Press, 1972), pp.115-18, 124. The Bagatz ruling (referred to later) p.10, incorrectly states that the Netziv and the Bet Halevi gave their agreement to the Heter Mechirah.
(18) Rabbi Yechiel Michel Epstein, Aruch Hashulchan Ha'atid, part 1, (Jerusalem: Mossad Harav Kook, 5729 – 1969), chap.15, para.9 (end).

(19)   Rabbi Yoseph Engel, Otzrot Yoseph - part 2, Shvi'it bazman haze, (Vienna, 5688 – 1928), pp.90-102.

(20)   Rabbi Avraham Bornstein, Avnei Nezer, (Warsaw, 5673 – 1913), Yoreh Deah, part 1, chap.458.

(21)   Rabbi Kahana, op. cit., p.108.

(22)   Letter from Dr. Leon Pinsker to the Netziv, 17 Adar I 5649 – 1889, Ketavim, vol.2, (Tel Aviv: Hapoel Hatzair, 5685 – 1925), letter 874, col.657.

(23)   Letter from Yechiel Michel Pines to Rashi Pin, 9 Shevat 5649 – 1889, Ketavim, vol.2, op. cit., letter 866, cols.639-40.

(24)   Rabbi Kahana, op. cit., p.109.

(25)   Rabbi Avraham Yitzchak Hakohen Kook, Igrot haReiyah, vol. 1, (Jerusalem: Mossad Harav Kook, 5722 – 1962), letter 207, p.258.

(26)   Bet Ridbaz, op. cit.

(27)   Igrot haReiyah, op. cit., letter 177, pp.226-29.

(28)   Ibid., vol.2, letter 555, p.184.

(29)   Ibid., vol.1, letter 255, p.296.

(30)   Ibid, letter 236, p.283, vol.2, letter 400, p.57.

(31)   Ibid., vol.1, letter 177, p.227, vol.2, letter 555, p.184.

(32)   Ibid., vol.1, letter 236, p.283.

(33)   Open letter from three farmers from Ekron, Habazeleth (Jerusalem), no. 25, 21 Tevet 5670 – 2 January 1910, pp.127-28 (1 – 2).

(34)   Israel Supreme Court, Bagatz 7120/07, Bagatz 7628/07, Ruling given 11 Marcheshvan 5768 – 23 October 2007, [henceforth: Bagatz], pp.4, 22.

(35)   Ibid., pp. 20-21.

(36)   "Rabbi Metzger Against Heter Mechira," Arutz Sheva News Brief, 19 Tishri 5768 – 1 October 2007, (Internet: www.israelnationalnews.com/News/Flash.aspx/133995).

(37)   Tzohar "Hashabbat" no.166, Parashat Noach, 1 Marcheshvan 5768, p.6.

(38)   Ibid.

(39)   Ibid., no.168, Parashat Vayera, 15 Marcheshvan 5768, p.5.

(40)   Ibid., no.169, Parashat Chaye Sara, 22 Marcheshvan 5768, p.2.

(41)   Ibid., no.166, op. cit., p.6.

(42)   Hatzofe, 21 Marcheshvan 5768 - 2 November 2007, p.6; Jerusalem Post, 2 November 2007, p.14.

(43)   "Tzohar's alternative kashrut apparatus launched," Ynet Jewish World, 30 October 2007, (Internet: www.ynetnews.com/articles/0,7340, L-3465743,00.html).

(44)   Rabbi Tzefanya Drori, Rabbi Yaacov Ariel, Rabbi Dov Lior and Rabbi Chaim Druckman.

(45)   Bagatz, p.6.

(46)   Ibid., p.34.

(47)   Yated Ne'eman, (Bnei Brak), 13 Marcheshvan 5768 - 25 October 2007, p.2; Hamodia, (Jerusalem),13 Marcheshvan - 25 October 2007, p.2.

(48)   "Chief Rabbinate ordains substitute kashrut supervisors," Ynet Jewish World, 4 November 2007, (Internet: www.ynetnews.com/articles/0,7340, L-3467466,00.html).

(49)   Lecture delivered by Rabbi Shlomo Goren to Jewish students at London University at Hillel House London in the 1960s (prior to July 1966). The author of this paper was present at this lecture.

(50)   Possibly, Rabbi Goren's source is Igrot haReiyah, op. cit., vol.1, letter 177, p.226.

(51)   Rabbi Shlomo Goren, "Validity of the Heter Mechirah for Shemittah after the establishment of the State of Israel," Hatzofe, (Tel Aviv), 12 Marcheshvan 5747 - 14 November 1986, p.8.

(52)   Rabbi Moshe Ushpizai, Amudim, (Kibbutz Hadati), nos. 226-227, Adars 5725 – March 1965, pp 143-44.

(53)   Rabbi Yosef Elyashiv, Rabbi Yehuda Shteinman, Rabbi Shmuel Vosner, Rabbi Michal Lefkowitz, Rabbi Pinchas Scheinberg, Rabbi Nissim Karelitz, Rabbi Chaim Kanievsky, Rabbi Shmuel (the son of Rabbi Shlomo Zalman) Auerbach, Rabbi Yehudah Shapira, Rabbi Yitzchak Sheiner, Rabbi Gershon Edelstein, Rabbi Meir Bergman, Rabbi Nissim Toledano, Rabbi Yehuda Ades, and Rabbi Natan Finkel.

(54)   "Kriat Kodesh," Yated Ne'eman, 10 Elul 5767 - 24 August 2007, p.1.

(55)   Rabbi Yoseph Tzvi Halevi, Hora'ot Sha'a, (Jerusalem, 5669 - 1909), pp.115-116, 124-25.

(56)   Rabbi Ze'ev Vitman, Likrat Shemittah Mamlachtit b'Medinat Yisrael, (Alon Shevut: Tzomet. 5760 – 2000), p.29.

(57)   Rabbi Moshe Levinger, Amudim, (Kibbutz Hadati), no. 224, Shevat 5725 – January 1965, p.115.

(58)   Eliyahu Ganchovsky, Harav Mordechai Elishberg, (Jerusalem, 5697 – 1937), p.78.

(59)   Rabbi Naftali Tzvi Yehuda Berlin ("Hanetziv"), Meishiv Davar, part 2, (Jerusalem, 5728 – 1968), chap.50.

(60)   Related to the author by one of the guides of Neot Kedumim.

(61)   "Heter Mechirah is launched," Ynet News, 5 September 2007, (Internet: www.ynet.co.il/articles/0,7340,L- 3446165,00.html).

(62)   Rabbi Vitman, Likrat Shemittah…, op. cit., p.45 fn.9; Rabbi Ze'ev Vitman, "Shemittah 5747 in Kfar Etzion," (Kfar Etzion: Hamayan, 5748-5749 – 1988-89), p.76 fn.85a.

(63)   Rabbi Levinger, op. cit., p.115.

(64)   Rabbi Yitzchak Weiss, Minchat Yitzchak, vol.8, (Jerusalem, 5753 – 1993), Orach Chaim, chap.96, pp.184, 328.

(65)   Rabbi Elazar Teitz, "Heter Mechira," Mail-Jewish vol.34 no.28, 11 February 2001, (Internet: www.ottmall.com/mj ht arch/v34/mj v34i28.html).

(66)   There have actually been cases of this occurring. One was in Sha'alavim. The Rabbi of the community was very happy about this since it proved the sale to be valid, [related to the author of this paper by a Rabbi at the Yeshivah Tichonit Sha'alavim in the summer of 5753].

(67)   "Behar – The Blessing of the Shemittah Year in our Time," Jerusalem College of Technology Machon Lev, [n.d.], (Internet: www.hra.jct.ac.il/judaica/dvarTorah/dt34.html).

(68)   Israel Government, Suggested Budget for the Financial Year 2008, (Internet: www.mof.gov.il/budget2007/docs2008/12.pdf).

(69)   "Finance Ministry announces budget surplus of NIS 7.7 billion for 2007,"
        Haaretz.com, 4 December 2007, (Internet: www.haaretz.com/hasen/
        spages/931092.html).

(70)   Machon Lev, op. cit.

(71)   Jonathan Rosenblum, "Shmita is our test of faith, "Jerusalem Post,
        30 November 2007, p.10.

(72)   "Shmita year: Jordan farmers to the rescue," Ynet Jewish World, 14 July
        2007, (Internet: www.ynetnews.com/articles/0,7340,L-3423793,00.
        html).

(73)   These laws can be found in the many excellent books which bring the laws
        of Shemittah. (74) Dvar haShemittah, Kashrut guide for the whole year,
        no.57, 5768, (Va'ad haShemittah/ Va'ad haKashrut of the Eda Charedis,
        Jerusalem), p.43.

(75)   Rabbi Avraham Yeshayahu Karelitz, Chazon Ish, Zeraim, (Bnei Brak,
        5719 – 1959), Shevi'it, chap.10 para.6.

(76)   Rabbi Shlomo Zalman Auerbach, Minchat Shlomo, vol.1, (Jerusalem:
        Sha'arei Ziv, 5746 – 1986), chap.44.

(77)   Rabbi Shlomo Aviner, Iturei Kohanim, (Jerusalem: Yeshivat Ateret
        Kohanim), no.192, Marcheshvan 5761 – 2000, Igrot k'tsarot, p.13.

(78)   Rabbi Teitz, op. cit.

(79)   Ibid.

(80)   Rabbi Mordechai Eliyahu, Ma'amar Mordechai - V'shovta Ha'aretz,
        (Jerusalem: Darchei Hora'ah Lerabanim, [n.d. 5768 – 2007]), p.118.

(81)   Ibid. In the course of this book, this list is brought on a number of
        occasions but with differences. (pp. 65, 71-72, 190, 191, 194, 195). In the
        majority of the cases brought, imported products have priority over Heter
        Mechirah.

(82)   Bet Ridbaz, op. cit.

(83)   Rabbi Shlomo Aviner, "I choose Heter Mechirah," B'ahavah uve'emunah,"
        no.639, Parashat Vayera 5768, 15 Marcheshvan 5768 - 2007, (Machon
        Meir), p.8.

(84)   Statistical Abstract of Israel 2004, no.55, (Central Bureau of Statistics),
        Agriculture 19-10, table 19.5, (after the year 2004, this Abstract did not
        differentiate between Jews and non-Jews); personal conversation with
        Rabbi Yehudah Amichai, 24 December 2007.

(85)   Obviously one has to check for Terumot and Ma'asarot and Orlah.

(86)   Rabbi Moshe Heiman, Hamitbach b'Shemittah, (Bnei Brak, 5753 –
        1993), p.49.

(87)   Kriat Kodesh, op. cit.

(88)   Rabbi Yehudah Amichai, Answer to question received by the Rabbis of
        "Machon haTorah v'ha'aretz" on Heter Mechirah, 26 Shevat 5767 –
        2007, (Internet: www.moreshet.co.il/Webs/moreshet/shut/shutMachon.
        asp? codeClient=1555&codeSubWeb=0&id=84234).

(89)   or possibly his representative.

(90)   Question was put to him by the author of this paper.

(91)   Rabbi Moshe di Trani, Responsa of Mabit, part 3, (Lvov, 5621 – 1861),
        chap.45.

(92)   Grateful acknowledgements to: Yeshivat "Nir" Kiryat Arba Library;
Kiryat Arba Municipal Library; Jewish National and University Library
Jerusalem; Rabbi Yehudah Amichai; the staff of Kommemiyut (Bet El); R'
Zvi Shpak.

*(On seeing my above paper which was originally written in
Hebrew, I was asked if it could be published in the yearly journal
of Yeshivat "Nir" Kiryat Arba. I readily agreed and it appeared in
issue 121 summer 5768 (2008). In the same issue, Smaryahu
Gershoni and Eitam Henkin wrote their comments on this paper,
and in the following year in issue 122 summer 5769 (2009) I
answered their comments.)*

*[Eitam Henkin and his wife Na'amah hy'd were both murdered in
an Arab terrorist attack in the Shomron in October 2015.]*

ANSWER TO COMMENTS MADE TO MY ABOVE PAPER

Let me begin by thanking Shmaryahu Gershoni (henceforth SG) and Eitam Henkin (henceforth EH) for studying my paper and writing their comments on it. In particular I wish to congratulate EH who thoroughly researched and wrote an excellent paper on the *history* of the Heter Mechirah controversy. However as far as a criticism of my paper goes, this article is totally irrelevant.

I clearly stated both at the beginning and at the end of my paper what the purpose of my paper was. It was to answer a question posed by Otzar Haaretz to the consumer, namely, whether one should choose imported produce or Heter Mechirah produce. The Bet Din of Otzar Haaretz did not rule on this question and left it up to the consumer to make the choice, namely, what is the opinion of the consumer on Heter Mechirah *today* – for the Shemittah year 5768?

EH tried so hard to show that towards the Shemittah year 5649 the number of Rabbis forbidding or permitting the Heter Mechirah was almost equal, (from his language it seems that there were more against than for!) But in fact, all his work was in vain. Really it is of no importance today whether a minority of Rabbis or a majority of Rabbis, or even if all the Rabbis in the world, *then* gave the Heter Mechirah. Furthermore, it is of no relevance today whether or not Rabbi Yitzchak Elhanan Spector began looking into the questions of Heter Mechirah before or after he was approached by three Rabbis, or when the book "Aruch Hashulchan Ha'atid" was published. All this is history. The question today is how would *those Rabbis* rule *today*, in light of the dramatic improvement of the living conditions.[1]

One cannot overstress the sentence which appears in my paper, *"the agreement of these Rabbis* [who gave the Heter

Mechirah more than one hundred years ago] *was only for that Shemittah* [and these Rabbis specifically said this].[2] (I wrote this sentence in the *text of my paper*, but the editorial board downgraded it to *just a footnote!*)

In order to answer the question as to whether the Rabbis who *then*, gave the Heter Mechirah would still give it today, namely for the Shemittah 5768, I showed that not only did 15 "Charedi"[3] Rabbis, which include the recognised gedolei hador [great Rabbis of the generation], such as Rabbi Yoseph Shalom Eliashiv and Rabbi Shmuel Vosner, give a clear and binding ruling stating that today the matter is perfectly obvious that also those Rabbis who one hundred years ago gave the Heter Mechirah, would not give it today. In addition, I showed how Rabbi Shlomo Goren and Rabbi Moshe Ushpizai, who come from the "Dati Leumi camp," have said that the Heter given by Rabbi Kook and others is not applicable today. Furthermore, Rabbi Yaakov Ariel, the Chief Rabbi of Ramat Gan, and a member of the Bet Din of Otzar Haaretz will only give a Mehadrin Kashrut certificate to establishments in his city to places which don't use Heter Mechirah. In addition, there are an ever-decreasing number of City Rabbis who rely on the Heter Mechirah. Chief Rabbi Metzger has stated that Shemittah 5768 is the last time that the Heter Mechirah will be used.

SG and EH question my statement that one cannot compare Heter Mechirah for Shemittah to Mechirat Chametz. I refer them to what Rabbi Ze'ev Vitman wrote on this subject. He states that there is a fundamental difference between Heter Mechirah and other Heterim which utilise sales. Heter Mechirah is done to prevent observing a Mitzvah, whereas in Mechirat Chametz the purpose is not to prevent observing a Mitzvah since the observance of this mitzvah requires the removal of chametz from our possession.[4]

Contrary to what both SG and EH wrote about me, I did not rule that the Heter Mechirah which is practiced today does not have "gemirat da'at" [genuineness]. It is the ruling of the gedolei hador, such as Rabbi Yoseph Shalom Eliashiv, Rabbi Shlomo Zalman Auerbach and Rabbi Yitzchak Weiss (the "Minchat

Yitzchak"). In addition, the fact is that many farmers sign the "Heter Mechirah" form and then go on working in their fields as usual![5]

SG and EH described as "impertinence" my comment that the Almighty gave Eretz Israel in its entirety solely to the Jewish people and thus how is it possible for us to sell it in order to avoid observing a Mitzvah from the Torah. In fact, the Netziv's comments on his ideological objections to the Heter Mecirah are of a similar nature.[6]

One would expect that Jews who, with a large amount of self-sacrifice, fight to establish Jewish settlements in Yehuda and Shomron, and at every opportunity set up new outposts, and who fight to prevent their demolition, and class themselves as "dati leumi" would be the *last* ones to sell Eretz Israel to non-Jews, but to our sorrow this is not the case! They will surely argue that it is done to help the Jewish farmers.[7] The Rambam rules that to give a Jew employment is the highest level of charity.[8] But would the Rambam agree that the way to do this is by "abolishing a Mitzvah given in the Torah"[9] or by "selling the whole Mitzvah of Shemittah"? [10]

The solution is to find an alternative method to observe the mitzvah of Shemittah. In my paper I referred to the research by "Machon Lev" on this subject, in which they recommend that the farmers would receive compensation. In addition, they would attend during the Shemittah year professional courses in farming, and as a result of their studies, their efficiently in farming would improve in the years following the Shemittah. This would yield an increase in their annual production and hence their income would also increase. However, SG and EH did not so much as even refer to this research and recommendations in their comments to my paper.

Of course, to put such a programme into practice will cost a lot of money. But the answer that there is no money in the kitty is not acceptable, since we well know that if we want something we will find the money. If the Government needed several hundred millions of shekels each year in order to respond to the requests of certain political parties to join the coalition, the money would immediately be found! If they needed similar sums to open ten additional Ministries, together with their secretarial staff, clerks, tea-boys and Volvos, money would appear without delay! If, G-d forbid, the government required money to expel 100,000 Jews from Yehudah and Shomron, there is no doubt whatsoever that such a government would immediately put this money on the table! With this money one could observe 50 - 100 Shemittahs!

All that is required is pressure on the Government to pay for the observance of Shemittah. However, as long as those working in the agricultural sector or those marketing their products are able to receive a kashrut certificate for Heter Mechirah produce, there won't be such pressure to find an alternative solution. Heter Mechirah will continue forever and this is completely contrary to the opinions of Rabbi Kook and other Rabbis who in the past implemented the Heter Mechirah. If one would stop giving kashrut certificates for Heter Mechirah produce, an alternative solution would speedily be found![11]

SG and EH ask why I did not state that when Rabbi Goren was the Chief Rabbi of Israel, he utilised Heter Mechirah. They could have likewise have added that when he was Chief Rabbi of the Army, he also utilised it for the army kitchens. My answer to this is that when one holds a public and national office one is subject to all sorts of pressures, and thus one sometimes has to rely on lenient and minority opinions, even if they contradict one's personal views. We must also remember that all this occurred *over 30 years ago* and one cannot use the fact that because Rabbi Goren used the Heter Mechirah when he was then Chief Rabbi, one can automatically use it today.

I wish to state an additional fact. In a lecture given by Rabbi Goren, at which I was amongst those present, he stated clearly and firmly that Rabbi Kook's Heter Mechirah is not valid today. He added that he himself does not eat Heter Mechirah produce. When asked after the lecture how one could override Shabbat and defend Israel during the Shemittah year when the land had been sold to non-Jews, he laughed and added "if indeed it had been sold!"

SG and EH quoted a number of leading Rabbis, who after the establishment of the State supported the Heter Mechirah. However, we can see that most of these were at least fifty years ago, in the early days of the State, when there was a gross shortage of food. I recollect my parents in those days sending their relatives in Israel one small tin of sardines for Yom Tov, which was received with great pleasure. Today this seems laughable when there is no room on the shelves of the supermarkets for all the food they stock. One therefore cannot compare a Shemittah of then with a Shemittah of today.

They also referred to articles written by three Dayanim who today sit on the Bet Din Hagadol. These articles were not written for the Shemittah 5768 but they appeared between 13 and 22 years ago, and this was before these Rabbis were Dayanim of the Bet Din Hagadol. Do these three Dayanim still hold these same opinions today? Why don't SG and EH mention the opinions of the other Dayanim who today sit on the Bet Din Hagadol and also the 100 Dayanim of the various regional Rabbinical courts. It is worthwhile for them to investigate how many of them support Heter Mechirah.

They also quote word for word various Torah Rulings that the gedolei hador published during the past four years on the prohibition on selling land in Eretz Yisrael to non-Jews, and also of the non-validity today of the Heter Mechirah, but every time they omitted the heading "Torah Ruling" which appeared at the top of these documents, and instead described them as "paskivillim" [bill-board notices] (which in my opinion is very disrespectful to these Rabbis who signed them). They also argue that the bringing out of these Torah Rulings two years before the Shemittah is "weird timing" and asked "what is the urgency to proclaim this matter on the notice boards in Jerusalem specifically at that period." Precisely the opposite – making these announcements at that date gives those involved in agricultural production and marketing sufficient time to plan ahead for the Shemittah of 5768. If these Rabbis had made their ruling close to the Shemittah year, a justifiable argument would have been "why have you waited until the last moment?" SG and EH keep referring to the fact that these Torah Rulings were given at the time of the expulsion of the Jews from Gush Katif, but these Torah Rulings don't refer to this expulsion and I therefore don't see why SG and EH did so. Furthermore, SG and EH *stressed* that Rabbi Nehemiah Goldberg (who is on the Bet Din of Otzar Haaretz) signed the first Torah Ruling which was dated Iyar 5765 only in the middle of the year 5767. I can see nothing in this Torah Ruling to *substantiate* this claim of SG and EH.

EH wrote that I erred and even gave no source whatsoever when I stated that Rabbi Shimshon Refoel Hirsch opposed the Heter Mechirah. A glance at my article will immediately show that I did give a source – footnote number 18 - which was the book in English by Rabbi Isidor Grunfeld, who was a Dayan of the London Beth Din, and one of the world's authorities on the writings of Rabbi Shimshon Refoel Hirsch.

EH repeatedly asks why I did not mention the name of this or that Rabbi who was in favour of Heter Mechirah. However, he *never* asks why I did not mention the names of Rabbis who were *against* it, and indeed there were plenty of them, such as Rabbi Yisrael of Kotzk, Rabbi Shneiur Zalman Fredkin (the "Torat Chesed"), Rabbi Nahum Weidenfeld, Rabbi Shalom Mordechai Schwadron, Rabbi Avraham Mendel Steinberg of Brody and Rabbi Meir Arik. Even if the purpose of my paper had been only to give a history of the Heter Mechirah controversy, one obviously cannot quote in 3 pages the same number of Rabbis that EH mentions in his article which is 22 pages long!

EH also asks why I quoted Rabbi Kook saying that when he lived in Russia he was against this Heter but did not give the continuation. However, if one reads the continuation of what I wrote, one would immediately see that I summarised the continuation of Rabbi Kook's words.

SG and EH mention the writings of Rabbi Mordechai Eliahu. In his book, Rabbi Eliahu clearly states on pages 72 and 191 that one should prefer imported products *including from Gaza*, rather than Heter Mechirah. On page 195 he prefers imported products over Heter Mechirah, although here he adds one should avoid vegetables from Gaza. Only on pages 65 and 194 does he prefer

Heter Mechirah. Thus in the majority of cases in his book, he prefers imported products over Heter Mechirah but SG and EH decided that there is a "printer's error"! In addition, Rabbi Mordechai Eliahu was one of the signatories on the Torah Ruling that strictly forbade the sale of land in Eretz Israel to non-Jews. However, SG and EH add after they mention his name "(!)" and add the comment, "it is hard to believe that Rabbi Eliahu signed this text in connection with Heter Mechirah." Are they suggesting that also here there is a "printer's error"?!

I could add and write much more, but I trust that with what I have written sufficiently answers the comments of SG and EH.

References

(1)   I began my paper by giving just a *brief* synopsis of the early history of Heter Mechirah, *only i*n order to show that right from the outset there were many Rabbis who opposed the Heter.

(2)   Another example of this could be on the question of kitniot on Pesach. Even though today there is a prohibition for Ashkenazi Jews and some Sepharadi Jews on eating kitniot on Pesach, there have been situations of famine where the Rabbis have allowed them for a particular Pesach. However, this permission was only for that Pesach and did not extend to all future Pesachs!

(3)   I myself do the best to avoid using expressions such as Charedi, Dati, Dati Leumi, Chiloni. I see everyone as Jews and any categorisation as unnecessary. However, since the editorial board like to use these expressions, I shall use them in my answers to their comments. I should add that the word "Charedi" that occurs before the "15 Rabbis" in the "conclusion" of my paper, is an addition by the editorial board. It is unfortunate that there are those who class those who accept the Heter Mechirah as "Dati Leumi" whilst those who don't as "Charedi." From people I know in Kiryat Arba this is in many cases incorrect.

(4)   Rabbi Ze'ev Vitman, Likrat Shemittah Mamlachtit b'Medinat Yisrael, (Alon Shevut: Tzomet, 5760 – 2000), p.29.

(5)   Rabbi Moshe Levinger, Amudim, (Kibbutz Hadati), no. 224, Shevat 5725 – January 1965, p.115.

(6)   Rabbi Naftali Tzvi Yehuda Berlin ("Hanetziv"), Meishiv Davar, part 2, (Jerusalem 5728 – 1968), chap.50.

(7)   One might mention that amongst the leaflets which are distributed to the various Shuls in Israel towards every Shabbat, there are those *produced by "data leumi"* groups. Week by week one will find in them, sometimes on as many as four pages, and even sometimes full page of advertisements, enticing people to go on holiday to China, Thailand, Italy, Turkey and

even the *Arab countries* of Morocco and Tunisia. What about the livelihoods of the Jewish hotel owners and the Jewish hotel staff in Israel? What about the livelihoods of the Jewish tour guides in Israel? And all this is apart from the prohibition of taking a holiday outside Israel.

(8) Rambam, Mishnah Torah, Hilchot Matanot Aniyim, chap.10 halachah 7.

(9) Expression used by Rabbi Ze'ev Vitman.

(10) Expression used by Rabbi Moshe Levinger.

(11) Needless to say, this is not a personal criticism of those giving these hechsherim, but an ideological criticism. It is forbidden to insult any Rabbi even if one disagrees with his opinion on certain matters.

Section Seven

By the River Mersey

JUST AS RELEVANT TODAY!

Sermons delivered by Rabbi Dr. Chaim Simons at the

Childwall Synagogue Liverpool England in the 1970s

INTRODUCTION

For nearly seven years during the 1970s, I was Director of Jewish Studies at the King David High School in Liverpool. During this period, I was sometimes invited to give a sermon or a Shabbos Hagadol derashah at the Childwall Synagogue in Liverpool.

On reading over these sermons today, I see that they are just as relevant today as they were when they were given. I have therefore decided to publish these sermons.

I have in my possession the text of these sermons etc. either in almost verbatim form or as very detailed notes. In the former case, I have reproduced them with just some stylistic changes and in the latter case, I have had to reconstruct the sentences.

The two main themes of these sermons are Jewish education and Eretz Israel. Since I left Liverpool, the size of the Jewish community of Liverpool had radically decreased. In order to prevent further decrease it is important to strengthen the Jewish education in the city. Should the numbers decrease even further, let it only be as a result of the members of the community coming on Aliyah to Eretz Israel.

Note: There is a universal problem of how to transliterate Hebrew words into English letters. This is further complicated by the fact that some words are conventionally transliterated in a particular way. For these reasons, I wish to point out that I have not followed a consistent pattern in this booklet.

Since it was not possible in this book to print words in Hebrew letters, it was necessary for me to delete them (especially in the Shabbos Hagadol Derashah) from my text. In addition, on some occasions, I translated them into English, or on a few cases, transliterated them.

🏵 🏵 🏵 🏵 🏵 🏵 🏵 🏵 🏵 🏵

Sermon delivered
on the second day of Shavuos - 20 May 1972

On the morrow after the Pesach, the Children of Israel went out with a high hand in the eyes of all Egypt. *[quote from Parashas Masei]*

On the 15 Nissan we left Egypt. We went through the Sinai desert, arrived at Mount Sinai, made various preparations, and 52 days after leaving Egypt we received the Torah.

Today, 7 Sivan - the second day of Shavuos, is 52 days after 15 Nissan, and is therefore the anniversary of receiving the Torah.

On 10 Nissan, of the year of the Exodus from Egypt, we were commanded to take a lamb to offer up as a Passover sacrifice. Although this was the animal the Egyptians worshipped, they were powerless to stop us. This was therefore the beginning of the miracle and by tradition it was a Shabbos, namely, Shabbos Hagadol. We thus left Egypt on a Thursday, and by calculation we can see that 52 days later, the day we received the Torah, was a Shabbos.

Therefore, both in day and date, we today celebrate the anniversary of giving of the Torah - Shabbos 7 Sivan.

What a wonderful Shabbos it was. The Torah was given in 70 languages simultaneously. The blind saw, the deaf heard and everyone paid attention. However, the best achievement of the day was that every Jew in the world observed that Shabbos - an occurrence which has unfortunately never reoccurred.

The Gemara in Shabbos states that if every Jew observed two Sabbaths we would be redeemed. Therefore, just one more Shabbos like that at Mount Sinai and we will be redeemed!

When on this historic day we were asked whether we would accept the Torah we answered "we will do and we will listen." Note the order: "we will do" and only then "we will listen." The normal thing is that when a person is asked if he will accept something, he says: "Let me hear it first and then I will decide."

Before giving the Torah to the Jewish people, G-d asked the nations of the world whether they would accept it. They asked what was written in it. When they heard that it contained such prohibitions such as killing or robbing, they answered that they were unable to accept it. However, we answered: "All that G-d has spoken we will do."

We made an oath on Mount Sinai that we will always observe the Torah. If a Jew were to make an oath not to observe a certain commandment, such as not eating Matzah on Seder night, then such an oath would not hold, because one cannot make an oath to counteract the oath we made at Sinai.

The reason for us making an oath at Sinai that we will always observe the Torah is obvious, "G-d's Torah is perfect," it needs no amendment.

The acceptance of the Torah advanced us from an era of lawlessness and idol worship to an era of civilisation. Nations who continued living without law and order disappeared since they had no system of civilisation to guide them on the correct path.

Having already seen how G-d's law is eternal and that today is the anniversary of both day and date of this great day when we received the Torah, we should give serious consideration of how we can pass on the Torah to our children. The Torah uses the expression "and you shall teach it to your children" when phrasing the important law of studying Torah. We can thus see that the answer is by education and example to our children.

In this complex of buildings in this area of Childwall, we are striving to do this. Let us look at what this complex contains. There is the Primary School, the High School, this Shul, Chedarim, and soon to be built, a Mikvah. This is an entire complex devoted to education and Torah observance. But wait a moment! - there is also a telephone exchange. What is a telephone exchange doing in this complex of buildings?

Everything in this world is arranged for a definite purpose. What does a telephone exchange signify? The answer is contact. For the school to contact the Shul, it must go through the telephone exchange. For the a Cheder to contact the school, it must go through the telephone exchange.

A telephone exchange signifies contact. From all this we learn an important lesson, namely, there must be contact between the various units.

Even through statistics show that the percentage of Jewish pupils in Liverpool attending Jewish Schools is the largest in the country, we must not be complacent. The standard of learning and observance of Yiddishkeit has much room for improvement.

We must not be satisfied with pupils attending the King David Schools but not coming to Shul or vice versa. There is an excellent Youth Service for the boys to participate in - they must be encouraged to do so.

We also must not be satisfied with the Torah education received at the School alone - we must supplement it with Cheder or Talmud Torah or at a higher level with the Yeshivah. Once again, we can see the contact signified by the telephone exchange.

In this context it is necessary to mention education for girls. Above the age of about 12, there is nothing outside the school. This is a serious problem to which the community must give thought.

Let us return to the telephone exchange. It also signifies contact between school, Cheder, Shul and the homes of the individual children.

An integral part of Jewish education is what the children receive at home. It is no good to see one thing at the school and another at home. This just causes conflicts in the minds of the children.

A lot of parents did not have the opportunity themselves to experience traditional Judaism in their houses. This was possibly due to the war, evacuation and a whole variety of causes and as a result, today they don't observe the practices of Judaism.

I am sure that all parents want to do the best for their children. Therefore I ask you to give your children the opportunity to experience traditional Judaism at home. Ensure that your home is Kosher, that Shabbos and Festivals are traditionally observed. At first it may be hard but as time progresses, I assure you that it will become natural and hence easier.

Let us resolve on this anniversary of receiving the Torah that we will give our children a full Jewish education, and hence we will pass on the eternal values of Judaism to our successive generations.

🕎🕎🕎🕎🕎🕎🕎🕎🕎🕎

Sermon delivered
on Shemini Atzeres - 30 September 1972

And you shall rejoice in your feast, you, and your son, and your daughter and your man-servant and your maid servant and the Levite and the stranger and the fatherless and the widow that are within your gates. Seven days shall you keep a feast unto the L-rd your G-d in the place where the L-rd shall choose, because the L-rd your G-d shall bless you in all your increase and in all the work of your hands and you shall be altogether joyful. *[quote from the Leining of Shemini Atzeres – Parashas Re'eh]*

From these verses the Rabbis learn that it is a positive commandment to rejoice on the Chagim - the Festivals.

In particular, the Festival of Sukkos was in Temple times a period for special rejoicing. From the verse in Isaiah "and you shall draw water in joy," our Sages deduced that the Water Drawing ceremony is accompanied by rejoicing. As we know, on Sukkos the world is judged for rain and the water libation ceremony formed an important part of the Temple service.

The Mishnah in Sukkah tells us that at the conclusion of the First Day of Sukkos (namely, the beginning of Chol Hamoed in Israel) they would put up a ladies' gallery on the Temple Mount to prevent levity between the sexes during this rejoicing. Large candelabras with golden bowls at the top of each were placed on the Mount and these were filled with oil and lit by the young priests. The resulting light was so intense that every courtyard in Jerusalem was illuminated. Men of piety and good deeds would dance before them with lighted torches in their hands. The Gemara tells us that during this rejoicing, Rabbi Shimon ben Gamliel would take eight lighted torches and throw them into the air so that no torch touched another one during this juggling act.

Levites with their harps, lyres, cymbals and trumpets were on the fifteen steps leading down from the court of the Israelites to the court of the women - the fifteen steps corresponding to the fifteen Shir Hama'alos - the Songs of Degrees.

Is it therefore any wonder that the Rabbis said that "He who has not seen the rejoicing at the place of the water drawing has never seen rejoicing in his life."

Let us return to our verse "and you shall be altogether joyful." What is the significance of the Hebrew word "ach" which apparently appears superfluous? The Vilna Gaon gives the following explanation. On Sukkos we have a number of commandments - Sukkah, Arba'as Haminim - the willows, the water libation ceremony and rejoicing. When Shemini Atzeres arrives, all these commandments finish with the exception of rejoicing and we can then understand this part of the verse as "you shall have only [ach] rejoicing."

On this second day of this Festival of Shemini Atzeres, namely, Simchas Torah, we have a further cause for rejoicing - we finish reading the Torah and in Jewish tradition, the completion of study of a particular work is a sign for a celebration.

Let us look at the last words in the Torah which we will read tomorrow "in the presence of all (kol) Israel". We can translate the Hebrew word "kol" as "all" or as "every" - that is to say "in the presence of all Israel" implying the Jewish people as a collective unit and "in the presence of every Israelite" implying each Jew is an individual.

We can learn an important lesson from this, namely, that whereas every Jew is an individual, he is also a member of the congregation of Israel and shares in communal responsibility. This communal responsibility can be illustrated with reference to the Festivals which we have just celebrated.

On Rosh Hashanah we have the important Mitzvah of blowing the Shofar. There is a law in Shulchan Aruch that a person who has already fulfilled the Mitzvah of hearing the Shofar is still able to blow for somebody else, the reason being that Jews are responsible for one another, and hence, even though a person has already fulfilled a particular Mitzvah, he can act to enable a fellow Jew to fulfill it.

Coming to Yom Kippur, the integral part of repentance is the confession of sins. If we look through the vidui, what do we notice? We are guilt-laden. We have robbed. For the sin we have committed, etc. The confession of sins is in the plural. The reason for this was given by the Ari, who explained that all Israel is one body and every individual Jew is a member of that body and hence there is a mutual responsibility among all the members.

We can learn a similar lesson of mutual responsibility from the Mitzvah of Arba'as Haminim. The esrog has both taste and fragrance and represents the Jew who is both learned and has good deeds. The lulav bears tasty fruit (dates) but had no fragrance and represents the Jew who is learned but does not do good deeds. The hadas bears no fruit but has fragrance and represents the Jew who is not learned but does good deeds. Finally, there is the arovo which bears no fruit and has no fragrance and is like a Jew who is neither learned nor does good deeds.

Now if even one of these species is missing, the remaining three species become worthless and one cannot perform this Mitzvah at all.

There was a case of a Shul which ordered beautiful Arba'as Haminim for its members and at the last moment discovered that the arovos were missing. Without these arovos, all these beautiful esrogim, the long lulavim and the leafy hadassim were quite useless and it was fortunate that they managed to obtain the arovos at the last moment.

What a wonderful lesson we can learn from this analogy - the Jew who is neither learned nor does good deeds is an integral part of the Jewish people and his brethren bear responsibility for him.

We will learn our final lesson on mutual responsibility from the Mitzvah of Sukkah. With regard to this Mitzvah, the Torah states "every Jew shall live in a Sukkah" which we can metaphorically understand that "every Jew shall dwell under one roof" - once again we have the concept of communal responsibility.

We have now seen a number of examples of communal responsibility existing between Jews and we must ask ourselves how can we use this important principle in our communal life in Liverpool. The answer is in Jewish Education and as we so sadly know, we have much room for improvement in this field in Liverpool.

A few weeks ago, we had the privilege to have the Chief Rabbi in Liverpool. Amongst his many engagements was an educational conference in which the Chief Rabbi reiterated the view that we must consider the problem on a communal basis.

Let us not allow the excellent suggestions made by the Chief Rabbi to be filed away and forgotten, but let us use our communal responsibility and consider the ways and means to implement these suggestions.

In a few minutes time, we will be saying prayers for rain. As we all know, without rain we cannot live. Similarly, without Torah education we cannot live.

Let us therefore resolve that this year 5733 will mark a turning point in the Torah education of our Community.

🌴🌴🌴🌴🌴🌴🌴🌴🌴🌴🌴

Sermon delivered
on 23 December 1972

The angel who has redeemed me from all evil, bless the lads and let my name be named in them and the name of my fathers Abraham and Isaac, and let them grow into a multitude in the midst of the earth. *[quote from the Sidra of that Shabbos – Parashas Vayechi.]*

This verse which forms part of today's Sidrah, is the verse which we read after calling up the boys on Simchas Torah.

The reason for calling up the boys under Barmitzvah who stand under the Tallis and recite Birchas HaTorah together, is to train them in the performance of Mitzvos. This Shabbos, Parashas Vayechi which contains this posuk, is therefore a most appropriate day for the young men of Liverpool to conduct the service and leining in this Synagogue. For these boys it is not a once-a-year show put on to impress the town, but services are fully conducted by them throughout the year. Every Friday night and Shabbos morning, their services take place in a room in this building and on weekdays they take place in the Bes Hamedrash of the King David School. We must not be complacent about this, however. The young people who attend and conduct these services only represent a small percentage of our young people in Liverpool, although happily this percentage is slowly increasing.

We know that people tend to take a pride and care in things which are their own and perhaps if these young people would organise all their services in the framework of a constituted Minyan with its own name (for example "Zeirei Liverpool"), more young people would be attracted to come and participate.

When the boys are called up to the Torah on Simchas Torah, we hold a tallis over their heads, and we learn a lesson from this. On the four corners of this tallis are tzitzis. The numerical value of tzitzis is 600 and this together with the five knots and the eight threads on each of the tzitzis makes 613, corresponding to the Taryag Mitzvos which we are teaching these boys to observe. To observe these mitzvos one must "go and learn" and to do this we require a Torah education framework. The roof which this tallis makes over these boys' heads is symbolic of this Torah education framework.

The establishment of places of Torah education is not a new idea. The Gemara in Megillah tells us that between the time that Jacob fled from his brother Esau and his arrival at the house of his uncle Laban, he spent 14 years studying at the Yeshivah of Eiver. It is important to note that whereas Jacob was later punished for not being able to keep the commandment of Honour to Parents whilst he was staying at Laban's house, he was not punished for not observing this commandment whilst he was studying at Yeshivah. This illustrates the importance of Torah learning.

We also learn from Rashi on last week's Sidrah that Jacob arranged for the first Yeshivah in the Diaspora to be established in Goshen. From then on, throughout the generations, wherever we have resided, we established places of Torah study.

In this city of Liverpool, we have a very good record for the establishment of Torah institutions. The Yeshivah which has an honoured history used to be one of the foremost Yeshivas in the country. In fact, the Liverpool Yeshivah sent about a dozen of its students to start off the Yeshivah in Gateshead which, today, has become probably the best Yeshivah in Europe, and we in Liverpool can take some of the credit for this. Although our Yeshivah has in the past had its ups and downs, we are very pleased to see that in the last few years the number of boys attending has sharply increased.

Another Jewish institution providing Torah education in Liverpool is the King David Schools, and, only a couple of weeks ago we commemorated the one hundred and thirty second anniversary of the setting up the original Jewish Day School in Liverpool, and we must pay tribute to these men who in 1840 had the foresight to set up an institution which would provide a Torah education to the community at large.

The Gemara tells us that the sanctity of a Bes Hamedrash is greater than that of a Synagogue, since the former is a place which is specially set aside for the study of Torah. We have a principle "one goes up in holiness but does not go down," and we are thus able to elevate a Synagogue to a Beis Hamedrash. I am happy to say that this has now happened in the School's Synagogue. Until recently it was just used as a place for davening and for the rest of the day, the sound of Torah was not heard between its walls. Today, however, it is transformed to a Beis Hamedrash and Gemara and Halachah Shiurim take place in it throughout the week.

What is perhaps most encouraging is that we have boys at the top of the school - boys who do not attend the Yeshivah and are fully occupied with their A-level studies, but who come along voluntarily to learn Gemara and one can see that they derive great simcha from their learning.

In the book of Bereshis, we on several occasions encounter conflicts between Jacob and Esau. The first conflict occurred even before they were born: "And the children struggled in her." The Midrash explains this that whenever Rebekah passed by the doors of a Yeshivah, Jacob struggled to be born, and, whenever she passed by the gates of a pagan temple, Esau struggled to be born. Thus the struggle between Jacob and Esau personifies the struggle which occurs between Torah and anti-Torah forces.

The final struggle occurred when Jacob's sons came to bury him in the Cave of Machpelah in Hebron. As we know this was the place where Abraham and Isaac and three of the Matriarchs had already been buried. Jacob had during his lifetime anticipated that Esau would try and be buried in this Cave instead of him, and so he had purchased all Esau's possible rights to the Cave. A document to this effect had been written and sealed and deposited in safe keeping in Egypt.

Despite all this, however, when Jacob's sons who had come up from Egypt to bury him, arrived in Hebron, Esau appeared at the entrance to the Cave and claimed that the one burial recess remaining in the Cave belonged to him.

Jacob's sons reminded Esau that he had given up his rights to the Cave and the relevant documents were in Egypt. Esau then demanded that they produce this document, and Naphtali who was a fast runner was dispatched post-haste to Egypt to bring it.

Meanwhile Hushim the son of Dan, who was deaf, and could not follow the proceedings saw that Esau was delaying the burial and so he chopped off Esau's head which then rolled into the Cave.

This Midrash, in which we saw how the wicked Esau tried to obtain by force a burial place amongst the righteous Patriarchs and Matriarchs is an illustration of anti-Torah personalities trying to obtain a position in a Torah community.

We thus see that the struggles and fights between Jacob and Esau are not just fights between individuals but fights between Torah and anti-Torah forces. Sadly, these fights are not just limited to bygone days but occur today even more so.

We must therefore be on our constant guard and do all in our power to strengthen Torah in our Community. The conducting of the entire service by our young men is an important step in this direction, for the young men of today are our leaders of tomorrow.

Today we finished reading the book of Bereshis and, as is customary, when we finish a book, we add the words "Be strong, be strong and let us strengthen one another." Let us take away with us today this motto - we must all do our utmost to fight and strengthen Torah education in Liverpool and in this way we will strengthen one another. If we fight for Torah, we can be sure that G-d will help us and we will be victorious.

🐜🐜🐜🐜🐜🐜🐜🐜🐜🐜

(From about 1973 to 1977, Childwall Synagogue had its own Rabbi, and it was he who delivered the sermons.)

🐜🐜🐜🐜🐜🐜🐜🐜🐜🐜

Sermon delivered
on 28 January 1978.

In the third month after the children of Israel were gone forth out of the land of Egypt, the same day they came into the wilderness of Sinai. *[quote from the Sidra of that Shabbos – Parashas Yisro.]*

A few weeks ago, we read about, the Exodus from Egypt. Following the Exodus, our ancestors went through the Sinai desert and in the third month arrived at Mount Sinai to receive the Torah.

Tradition tells us that the Torah was given on a Shabbos. What a wonderful Shabbos it was when the Torah was given simultaneously in 70 languages. The blind saw, the deaf heard and everyone paid attention. But the best achievement of the day was that every Jew in the world observed that Shabbos - an occurrence which has unfortunately never happened again.

When on this historic day, we were asked whether we would accept the Torah, we answered "we will do and we will listen." Note the order – "we will do" and then "we will listen." This seems a strange order, since normally when a person is asked whether he will accept something he says, let me hear it first and then I will decide.

Before giving the Torah to the Jewish people, G-d asked the nations of the world whether they would accept it. They asked what it contained. When in answer, one of the nations was told "Thou shalt not kill," they replied that they were killers and could therefore not accept the Torah. When another was told "Thou shalt not steal," they replied that they were robbers.

The Jewish people, however answered, all that G-d has spoken we will do."

The acceptance of the Torah advanced us from an era of lawlessness and idol-worship to an era of civilisation. Nations who continued living without law and order disappeared since they had no system of civilisation to guide them on the correct path.

The receiving of the Torah was not an isolated incident in our history, but part of a general pattern. The first part was the Exodus from Egypt - physical freedom. The second part was the Revelation - receiving of the Torah. The third part was the conquering and settling of the Promised Land - lead us up in joy into our land.

These three themes: "freedom," "receiving the Torah" and "joy," correspond with the three Foot Festivals

This pattern did not just happen, but as we see from earlier verses in the Torah, was predetermined.

G-d said to Avrom, "Your seed will be a stranger in a land that is not theirs and they shall serve them, and they shall afflict them four hundred years," and this is immediately followed by G-d's promise, "Unto your seed I have given this Land from the river of Egypt unto the great river, the river Euphrates."

Furthermore, at the beginning of the Book of Shemos, G-d promises Moshe: "And I am come down to deliver them out of the land of the Egyptians and to bring them out of that land into a good and large land flowing with milk and honey," and a few verses later: "when you bring forth the people out of Egypt, you will serve G-d on this mountain" - which is Mount Sinai.

The Torah is not a story book - it is a book of law and as such should logically begin with Shemos chapter 12. Why then the Book of Bereshis and the first 11 chapters of Shemos? This is answered by the first Rashi in the Torah which asks the very same question. The answer given is that if the Torah did not begin with Bereshis, the nations of the world would say to the Jewish people: "You are robbers because you took by force the lands of the seven nations of Canaan." The Jewish people would then reply to them: "All the earth belongs to G-d. He created it and gave it to whom he pleased."

We therefore see that Eretz Israel is the land of the Jewish people, whose claim to sovereignty over all of it is clear and as ancient as G-d's decision to grant that sovereignty. Over the rest of the world the Jewish people have no claim. Conversely, no other people in the world can establish a claim to Eretz Israel.

Our rights were not conferred by the Balfour Declaration or the League of Nations Mandate - they only confirmed our Divine given title. As Ben-Gurion summed it up before the British Royal Commission in 1936, "The Bible is our Mandate."

Recently a pupil was giving me his ideas for a Jewish Studies programme: "Phase out Bible, phase out Mishnah, phase out Gemara. Instead, teach facts all about Modern Israel and all about people such as Moshe Dayan." My answer to him was that without our Torah, we would have no claims or rights whatsoever to Eretz Israel. Only by a study of these books can Israel become meaningful to a Jew.

Our borders are clearly defined in the Torah. If we question our rights to live in Yamit in Northern Sinai, we similarly question our rights to live in Tel-Aviv.

We often hear the criticism that our Rabbis are still living in the Middle Ages. Anyone reading contemporary responsa will see that this is not the case, and that they are abreast with all the developments in the world. In 1937, when the Peel Commission proposed the partition of Eretz Israel, the Moetzes Gedolei HaTorah - the Council of Sages - ruled that the "boundaries of the Holy Land have been established by the Creator and recorded in the Torah for all time to come. The Jewish people cannot possibly compromise these borders." Two years ago, a special Beis Din of 72 Rabbis unanimously gave an identical ruling.

Despite all the difficulties, persecutions, massacres and expulsions, Jews have maintained a continuous presence in Eretz Israel. Great works such as the Jerusalem Talmud, the Zohar, the Shulchan Aruch, Rabbi Bartinura's commentary on the Mishnah, were all written in our Land whilst under foreign domination. The Kabbolas Shabbos service was compiled by the Kabbalists in Safed.

In every generation there was Aliyah to Israel encouraged by such great people as Yehudah Levi, the Vilna Gaon and the Baal Shem Tov.

Even those not fortunate enough to go on Aliyah, remembered Eretz Israel several times a day, every day of their life. An Amidah or Birchas Hamazon would not pass without a mention of Eretz Israel. In a few minutes time we will be saying in Mussaf: "To lead us up in joy into our Land and to plant us within our borders."

Wherever in the world a Jew prayed, he would face Eretz Israel - whether it was in a Marrano Synagogue in Spain, in a bunker in the Warsaw Ghetto, behind an outhouse in Auschwitz, or in a salt mine in Siberia. Everywhere there was this great yearning to return to Eretz Israel.

Soon after the Six Day War, Jews started arriving in Israel from Russia. One of the first groups was met at Vienna by Rabbi Kirshblum of the Jewish Agency. The first thing that these Jews said to him was: "Don't give away the West Bank; it's for us to live in when we arrive." From this incident we can see that despite Soviet attempts over half a century, to eradicate all vestiges of Judaism, Russian Jews still had Eretz Israel in their hearts, and a deep concern that parts of it should not be given away to non-Jews.

The Exodus from Egypt, the Revelation at Sinai, and the settling of Eretz Israel, all have a special lesson for young people.

With regard to the Exodus from Egypt, when Moshe stood before Pharaoh to state his demands as to who will go out of Egypt, he began with "our young ones." If our young ones remain enslaved, then the Jewish people have no future. Enslaved does not only mean actual slavery. Today, young people are enslaved to ideas completely alien to Torah, and we must do our best to ensure that they return to the ways of the Torah.

On the Revelation at Sinai, The Midrash tells us that when G-d was about to reveal the Torah to the Jewish people, he asked for guarantors. The Jewish people offered Avrohom, Yitzchok and Ya'acov, but they were told that they can be no security for later generations. They then offered their children and G-d accepted them as guarantors saying: "It is only through the young generation that the future of the Jewish people is assured."

On the Settling the Land of Israel, our children must be in the forefront. Even if we cannot settle in Eretz Israel ourselves, we must ensure that our children settle there.

The miraculous events witnessed in the Six Day War, liberated large areas of Eretz Israel and has given a great challenge to the Jewish people in settling our Holy Land. Your children will have a far greater spiritual satisfaction pioneering and living, during the first stages of settlement, in a one roomed house without modern amenities, in Shechem or Jericho, than by living in a 3 or 4 bedroomed house in Liverpool with all its mod. cons. and trappings.

Let us not pretend this is easy. There will be pressures by those who for their own selfish ends pretend to be our friends and offer us advice, namely advice that is to suit them and not us. But remember the Pirkei Ovos: "They appear as friends when it is to their own advantage, but they stand not by a man in his hour of need."

Our so-called friends are only concerned with their self-preservation. There is the story of the worm called Jimmy who used to live on peanuts and now survives by licking boots coated with oil.

To fortify us against any pressure, let us not forget that Eretz Israel belongs to us not by right of might but by might of right. Any attempt to knuckle under, would not only be a betrayal of the Torah, but also a betrayal of Jews who in the Warsaw ghetto, Auschwitz, and Siberia never forgot Eretz Israel. It would also be a betrayal of Russian Jews who are planning to settle on the West Bank when they are released from the prison called the Soviet Union.

The Gemara states: "If Israel merits the redemption by repentance and faith in HaShem, then He will hurry the redemption before its time. But even if Israel does not merit it, it will surely come in its appointed time."

Let us pray that we will merit the Moshiach to come speedily and bring all our people home to Eretz Israel and create a land that will be a light unto the nations.

🐝 🐝 🐝 🐝 🐝 🐝 🐝 🐝 🐝

Sermon delivered
on 22 July 1978
(Three days before going on Aliyah)

"Come now therefore, I pray you, curse me this people, for they are ˎtoo mighty for me, perhaps I shall be able to bring it about that we deal him a blow and that I may drive them out of the land, for I know that he whom you blessest is blessed and he whom you cursest is cursed." *[quote from the Sidra of that Shabbos – Parashas Bolok.]*

In this week's Sidra, we find that Balak the king of Moab is persistently trying to persuade the heathen prophet Bilam to curse the Jewish people.

Instead of cursing them however, Bilam is swept away in admiration of the Israelite encampments that he proclaims: "How goodly are your tents O Jacob, your dwellings O Israel."

At this stage of history, the Jewish people were about to enter upon the last stage of their journey to the Promised Land. If we extract the narrative passages of the Torah, we find that it directed towards the goal of entering and conquering Eretz Israel.

Eretz Israel was not just an arbitrary piece of land on the face of the globe which happened to become the Jewish homeland. Right back to the creation of the world, it was imbued with a unique destiny. Consequently, our Rabbis were most concerned to use opportunities which superficially had nothing to do with Eretz Israel in order to bring out our link with the land.

Our Written Torah begins with a general statement: "In the beginning G-d created the heaven and the earth."

Our great commentator Rashi uses the opportunity to quote from the Midrash Tanchuma, to tell us that G-d as creator of the world is its owner and he assigned a portion to be known as Eretz Israel to the Jewish people.

The Oral Torah begins with the question: "When do we read the Shema in the evening?" We would normally expect the answer to be, "when the stars come out." But we don't find this. Instead, we find the answer, "At the time when the Kohanim go out to eat their Terumah." The Shema is a law which applies to Jews all over the world. Terumah, however is a law linked with the holy soil of Eretz Israel.

We can therefore see how the Rabbis have made a special point of identifying Eretz Israel with the beginnings of both the Written and Oral Torahs.

And this has gone on throughout every generation. Whether in golden ages or in pogrom ages, Eretz Israel was always woven into the Jewish fabric. Even during the years of the holocaust, the cry "Next year in Jerusalem," was on Jewish lips.

This unparalleled holocaust was preceded by the decade of the 1930s, when the Nazis came to power in Germany and introduced their Nuremberg laws which were to severely restrict the rights of the non-Aryans, particularly the Jews.

The places where Jews could live were severely ₍curtailed. Judenrein, the Nazi term for an area cleansed from Jews, were created. The cat-call "Juden raus" became the expression of the day.

Today we see a concerted attempt by the National Front to reenact Germany's Nazi Nuremberg laws. To combat this, the Board of Deputies Defense Committee is taking special action. Millions of leaflets are being printed and Synagogue levies are being increased to meet the expense, in order to be prepared for any eventuality that may arise from the National Front gaining popular support.

However, at the same time as precautionary measures are being taken against a possible resurgence of the National Front in this country, the nations of the world are trying to dictate to Israel not to make settlements in parts of Eretz Israel, our eternal homeland. This amounts to nothing less than the application of the Nuremberg laws of the Nazis to the Jews in Israel. They are saying: "You can only settle on the West Bank if you are not Jewish." They want to make Judea and Samaria, a Judenrein, an area cleansed of Jews. Any Jews already living there should dismantle their settlements and get out. We have the situation of "Juden raus" once again, but this time not in a foreign land, but in our own State.

In the U.S.A. in the state of Pennsylvania, there is a place called Bethlehem; in the state of Nebraska, a place called Hebron; and in the state of Tennessee, a place called Shiloh. Could you imagine the outcry if Jews were barred from living in any of these places? There would follow speeches in the Congress, cases in the Supreme Court, invocations of the Constitution, and charges of discrimination. Yet the very same people who would make all this fuss against discrimination against Jews in the United States, quite happily condemn Jewish settlement in the original Bethlehem, Hebron and Shiloh in our Holy Land.

Suppose a new suburb were to be built in Liverpool and it was to be decided that Jews would not be allowed to live there. The Rep. Council would go into continuous session, the Board of Deputies would be alerted, M.P.s would be lobbied, Chanukah candles would be lit outside Lewis's, the Shofer would be blown outside the Town Hall, Sifrei Torah would be paraded through St. John's Market - in fact all steps would be taken to nullify such a decision.

But what happens when the nations of the world try to dictate to Israel that Jews be barred from parts of Eretz Israel, when they try to reactivate the Nazi Nuremberg Laws, when they want to set up a Judenrein in our own country, when they scream out the Nazi cry "Juden raus" to Jews who have already made their homes in Eretz Israel. There is almost a total silence from world Jewry.

How can we explain this difference in reaction? When there is just a chance of a National Front emergence in the Diaspora, massive preparations are made, yet when nations want to apply Nazi ideas to Jewish settlement in Israel, there is no action.

At a Jewish function we sing in the Hatikvah that our hopes and dreams for two thousand years of resettling Eretz Israel is now possible. Why are we then silent when the nations of the world try to thwart it?

My friends, the answer is simple. Our trust and confidence is in the wrong place. This can be summed up by an incident which happened a few months ago, after the U.S.A. decided to sell fighter planes to the Arabs. A member of the community came to me and said, "Israel's existence depends on America." "No," I replied, "it depends on the Almighty. Behold, he who guardeth Israel shall neither slumber nor sleep."

We only have to look at miracles during the last 30 years to realise that they cannot be explained in military terms. On its birthday in 1948, Israel almost unequipped, was attacked simultaneously by seven Arab nations, yet she defeated them all. A parallel to the Six Day War would be the Allies going from Dunkirk to Berlin in six days - it in fact took them five years! On Yom Kippur 1973, the Arabs made a surprise attack with a task force equal to that of N.A.T.O., yet within weeks, Israel defeated them. Even Israelis calling themselves "non-believers" acknowledged the miracles they witnessed during these wars.

We must always remember that the nations of the world think of their own self-interest: "They appear as friends when it is to their own advantage, they stand not by a man in his hour of need."

When Jimmy Carter was a Sunday school teacher, he surely taught the verse from Koheles: "A good name is better than precious oil." He now seems to have inverted it to read that "Precious oil is better than a good name."

If the State of Israel were to decide to give all their land, including Tel-Aviv, to the Arabs to form a Palestinian Arab State and the Jews would move into the sea, would the world praise them for such a decision? Nothing of the sort - they would be condemned for wanting to cause ocean pollution!

On the other hand, however absurd a proposal Sadat would put forward, it would earn him world praise for his initiative. The latest example is Sadat's latest proposal that Jewish settlements on the West Bank, including Jerusalem, need only be removed after five years. He is very kindly giving us five years grace before establishing a Nazi Judenrein in Eretz Israel. In mitigation for Sadat, we must remember that he was a Nazi agent during World War II, and even in the 1950s when the Nazi atrocities were well known, Sadat publicly praised Adolf Hitler.

After the destruction of the second Temple, when the situation was very bleak for the Jewish people, Rabbi Akiva took great comfort and inspired hope from the words of the Prophets. The Gemara relates how Rabbi Akiva was walking up to Jerusalem with some other Rabbis when they saw a fox emerging from the Holy of Holies. The Rabbis starting weeping, but Rabbi Akiva began to laugh. Seeing that his comrades were perplexed by his behaviour, Rabbi Akiva then explained why he laughed. Prophecies are given on both the ploughing up of Jerusalem and also on its rebuilding: "So long as the prophecies concerning Jerusalem's ploughing up had not been fulfilled," explained Rabbi Akiva, "I had misgivings that the prophecies about its rebuilding would not be fulfilled. Now that I can see that the prophecies concerning the destruction of Jerusalem have been fulfilled, I am certain that the prophecies concerning its rebuilding will also be fulfilled." The Rabbis thereupon replied: "Akiva, you have comforted us! Akiva, you have comforted us!"

Surely, we can apply the same lesson to today's situation. We find promises of peace in the land, given by the Torah and the Prophets, but we must earn them: "If you walk in my ways and keep my commandments and do them..." and then the Torah continues "I will give peace in the land."

The road to peace in Israel is not to rely on the nations of the world but to observe the Mitzvos of the Torah. To keep Shabbos, to observe Kashrus and family purity, to lay Tephillin every weekday morning, to keep the Mitzvos towards one's fellow man.

If we all do this, we can be sure that instead of the nations of the world cursing Israel, they will find themselves emulating Bilam, who came to curse Israel, but found himself praising them.

435

Let us pray for a speedy fulfillment of the words of the Prophet Zechariah: "the fast of Tammuz (which we commemorate tomorrow), together with the fast of Av, the fast of Gedaliah and the fast of Teves will be to the house of Judah for joy and for gladness." Amen.

Shabbos Hagadol Derashah delivered at the
Childwall Synagogue, Liverpool, England
on 10 April 1976

The Shulchan Aruch begins the laws of Pesach by quoting from the Gemara: "One asks on the laws of Pesach 30 days before Pesach."

There are a number of explanations of what this statement means. For example, the explanation of the famous commentator, the Ran is that if two students ask their teacher a question, one on the subject currently being taught and the other on another subject, the teacher must first answer the question on the subject being taught. However, if during the 30 days before Pesach, one of them asks a question on the subject being taught and the other concerning Pesach, then the teacher must first answer the question on Pesach.

I don't tell my pupils this explanation until just before Pesach, otherwise they could sabotage every lesson from Purim onwards by continually asking questions on Pesach!

From this statement from this Gemara, the "Magen Avraham" a famous commentator on the Shulchan Aruch" explains that the Rabbi gives a Derashah on Shabbos Hagadol.

In a few days' time, we shall be performing the Mitzvah of "relating to your son on that day," which is the Mitzvah of the Seder.

The purpose of the Seder is not to rush through it as quickly as possible until one reaches the meal - the meal is probably the least important part of the Seder! We can clearly gauge the purpose of the Seder by the wording used by the Torah for this Mitzvah "and you shall relate it to your son on that day." It is incumbent upon the father to explain and discuss with his children

436

the Exodus from Egypt. As one goes through the "relating" part of the Seder, one should analyse and find deeper meanings and explanations of the contents of the Haggadah. Every Seder should be unique.

Therefore, in preparation for your Sedarim, I shall go through portions of the Haggadah and illustrate them with explanations. Needless to say, there are numerous commentaries on the Haggadah in both Hebrew and English and the explanations I shall bring are far from being exhaustive.

🕎🕎🕎🕎🕎🕎🕎🕎🕎🕎

"Avodim hoyinu": This afternoon we began our reading of the Haggadah with "we were slaves to Pharaoh in Egypt."

This paragraph ends with the words: "the more a man tells of the coming forth from Egypt, the more he is to be praised."

The Gemara relates of a Reader who said: "O G-d, the great, mighty, terrible, majestic, powerful, awful, strong, fearless, sure and honoured." When he had finished, Rabbi Hanina said to him: "had Moshe not said the first three praises in the Torah and the "Men of the Great Synagogue" not incorporated them into the prayers, we should not be able to say even these. Since we cannot give G-d all his praises, it is an insult to give him a few. It is like a king who owns a million pieces of gold; if we praise him as possessing silver, it would be an insult."

Furthermore, the Gemara says that we must not dwell in excess on the praises of G-d. This is an example of familiarity breeding contempt.

From all this it is difficult to understand the line that "the more one relates on the Exodus from Egypt, the more one is to be praised," since by doing so, we are praising G-d in excess.

The Rashba in the name of Rabbi Hai Gaon explains that this only applies to prayer - otherwise it is permitted. In contrast, the Rambam in his "Guide to the Perplexed" says it applies even outside prayer. However, the relating of the Exodus from Egypt is not in this category.

In addition, we can learn an important lesson from this. A person might think that he is clever enough not to have to discuss the Exodus from Egypt. Hence the paragraph states "and even if we are all wise, all men of understanding" and this is immediately followed by the story of the five great Sages of the age who studied the entire Seder night.

What a wonderful lesson to learn from this incident. Even the wisest man can learn. The Pirkei Avos says: "Who is Wise? One who learns from everybody."

🏵 🏵 🏵 🏵 🏵 🏵 🏵 🏵 🏵 🏵

"Ma'aseh b'Rabbi Eliezer": It happened that Rabbi Eliezer, Rabbi Yehoshua, Rabbi Elazar ben Azaryah, Rabbi Akiva and Rabbi Tarfon were reclining in Bnei Brak and discussing the Exodus from Egypt all that night.

A number of interesting problems arise from this incident. To understand them we must first look at the laws of reclining at the Seder.

Pesach is "the season of our freedom" and we know from the Mah Nishtanah about reclining at the Seder. The source of this reclining is found in the Gemara. Even the poorest man must recline. However, a pupil in his teacher's presence does not recline, since the fear of your teacher is as the fear of Heaven.

Rabbi Akiva was a pupil of Rabbi Eliezer and Rabbi Yehoshua. How then could he recline? The answer is that the Seder took place in Bnei Brak. Rabbi Akiva was the Rabbi of that city and was therefore permitted to recline in his own city.

A further problem is that Rabbi Eliezer and Rabbi Elazar ben Azaryah hold that the Paschal lamb sacrifice must be eaten before midnight. It follows that the Haggadah must be finished by midnight. Why then did they discuss it throughout the entire night?

There are two aspects - one is discussing the Haggadah and the other is the relating of wondrous things of G-d bringing us out of Egypt. The first only applies to midnight, the second always applies. Therefore, until midnight they discussed the Haggadah, and after midnight they discussed the wondrous things of G-d bringing us out of Egypt.

If "Reading of the Shema" were not a Mitzvah which had a fixed time, they would not even have stopped discussing the going out of Egypt when morning arrived!

🕎🕎🕎🕎🕎🕎🕎🕎🕎🕎

"Omar Rabbi Elazar ben Azaryah": I am like seventy years of age - it does not say 70 years but like 70 years. We learn from the Gemara that Rabban Gamliel was originally head of the Sanhedrin. However, after he publicly insulted Rabbi Yehoshua he was removed from this post. Rabbi Elazar ben Azaryah was appointed in his place but he was only 18 years old at the time. That night 18 rows of his hair became white and he thus looked like a 70-year-old.

The Torah in addition to the Mitzvah "relating to your son on that day" there is also the Mitzvah "remember the day you went out of Egypt all the days of your life." We observe the latter every day when we read the third paragraph of the Shema

It is interesting to note that the Rambam does not list the Mitzvah of "remembering the day you went out of Egypt all the days of your life" in his enumeration of the 613 commandments. An explanation of this omission has been given by Rabbi Chaim Soloveitchik of Brisk. To understand his explanation, we must consider the dispute between Ben Zoma and the Rabbis.

The Rabbis understand the words "the days of your life" to mean "in this world" and the words "all the days of your life" to mean "in the days of the Moshiach." On the other hand, Ben Zoma understands the words "the days of your life" to mean "the daytime" and the words "all the days of your life" to mean "the nighttime." Thus according to Ben Zoma, in the days of the Moshiach, there will not be the Mitzvah to remember the going out of Egypt.

At the beginning of his "Sefer Hamitzvos," the Rambam lists the principles for his identification of the 613 Mitzvos in the Torah. One of these principles is that the Mitzvah must apply in all generations. (For example - laws concerning the collecting of the Manna are not listed by the Rambam amongst the 613 commandments.)

The Rambam holds the halachah is like Ben Zoma. Hence this Mitzvah will only apply in the days prior to the coming of the Moshiach.

According to the Rabbis, what will be the position regarding the Exodus from Egypt in the days of the Moshiach? The answer is that the deliverance from other kingdoms will take first place - the deliverance from Egypt will only take second place.

This may be compared to the parable of a man who encounters a wolf but manages to escape. He will then relate of this escape. He then encounters a lion but escapes. From then on, he will relate of his escape from the lion. He later encounters a snake but escapes. He then relates this incident, forgetting his previous escapes. Likewise with Israel. The later troubles make them forget the earlier ones.

🏛️ 🏛️ 🏛️ 🏛️ 🏛️ 🏛️ 🏛️ 🏛️ 🏛️ 🏛️

"Kneged Arba'ah Bonim": From the four sons of the Haggadah, one can make an analogy of the four different types of people who come to live in a town.

The wise son asks: "What mean the testimonies and statutes?" His intention is where is the Bes Hamedrash, the House of Study - Torah is his first consideration.

The wicked son asks: "What is all this work?" His immediate intention is where can he do business - money is his first consideration.

The simple son receives an answer: "With a strong hand" – namely "superman!" The simple son wants the cinema – entertainment is his first consideration.

The son who does not know how to ask: This son does not know what to do when he arrives in a town.

If we carefully analyse the questions of the wise and the wicked sons, we find something very interesting. Why is the wicked son called wicked? Because he says "you" he excludes himself. But the wise son also says "you"?!

There are several answers to this problem:

(1) the wise son includes the Divine name in his question proving he has not excluded G-d.

(2) In the book of Joshua, the term "Oschem" is used, meaning "I and you."

(3) The Jerusalem Talmud and one version of the Rambam's Haggadah have "us" instead of "you," thus disposing of this difficulty.

(4) The Torah is talking to the generation which went out of Egypt. Because of this, the wise son wishes to learn and be instructed and therefore says: "You father, heard the voice of G-d; teach me the testimonies, statutes and ordinances that I may learn to obey them."

The answer we give the wise son seems strange: "We may not eat anything after the Pesach Afikomon." The following explanation can be given for this answer: In the Gemara it states that we distribute nuts to the children so that they will notice a difference and ask about other things at the Seder table. Normally a child keeps nuts for after the meal. So that he should not do on that night, we tell him to eat them immediately because we may not eat anything after the Pesach Afikomon.

"Yachol m'rosh Chodesh": One might think that one should start to relate the going out from Egypt from Rosh Chodesh Nisan. Why should one think this, and why from Rosh Chodesh Nisan? The previous month is Adar - Adar has a link with Nisan by virtue of "redemption." (Adar - the redemption from Haman, and Nisan - the redemption from Egypt.)

The Talmud Yerushalmi states that one can already read the Megillah from the beginning of Adar and it learns this from the verse in the Megillah: "The month which was turned for them from sorrow to rejoicing." Similarly, one might think that the verse "Remember the month of Aviv and do the Paschal sacrifice" - namely, one can observe Pesach from Rosh Chodesh. Hence the Torah says "and you shall relate to your son on that day."

"Mitchilah ovdei Avodah Zarah hoyu avoseinu": In the beginning our fathers were worshippers of strange gods but now G-d has brought us to his service

The story is related of Rabbi Yitzchak Elchanan from Kovno, who was very popular amongst all Jews, even the Reformers, because of his giving lenient decisions (within the framework of the Halachah). One day he was passing through Vilna on a train and a Reformer saw crowds of Jews going towards the train. The Reformer asked why and on hearing the reason ran to see the Rabbi. When he saw him with his beard and peyos and wearing tallis and tephillin, the Reformer was petrified. He said to the Rabbi: "I thought you were a modern Jew, not an old-fashioned type." Replied Rabbi Yitzchak Elchanan: "I am a modern Jew - you are an old-fashioned type 'in the beginning our fathers were worshippers of strange gods but now G-d has brought us to his service.'"

The moral is quite clear. The Jew who observes the Torah is the modern Jew. Those who wish to abolish Mitzvos in the Torah are old-fashioned and have retrogressed to the days when our ancestors (such as Terach) were idol-worshippers.

🌹🌹🌹🌹🌹🌹🌹🌹🌹🌹

"Vehi sheanu lavoseinu": This faithfulness it is that has stood by our fathers and us. The Ari says that this refers to the Divine presence, which has stood over our fathers and us. Of this there is a proof from the Gemara: Rabbi Shimon bar Yochai taught. Come and see how beloved are Israel in the sight of G-d, in that to every place to which they were exiled the Divine presence went with them - Egypt, Babylon - and when they will be redeemed in the future the Divine presence will be with them.

In the book of Bereshis appears a list of the names of the 70 people who went down to Egypt. However only 69 names are listed. The Midrash says that the remaining one is G-d and brings a proof from the verse which reads, "I will go with you to Egypt."

Let us therefore always remember that where ever we are exiled to, until we return to Eretz Yisroel we are in exile, whether in England, Russia, U.S.A., the Divine presence is with us and when we return to Zion, it will accompany us.

✦ ✦ ✦ ✦ ✦ ✦ ✦ ✦ ✦ ✦

"Tzei ulmad": Come and learn what Laban sought to do to Jacob our father. Pharaoh issued his edict only against the males but Laban sought to uproot all.

How can we conceive that Laban wanted to kill everyone? We know he was wicked, but to kill everyone?

The following explanation has been given. The Rabbis teach that a man should never pick a favourite from among his children. As a result of the coat of many colours given by Yaacov to Yosef, Yosef was sold to Egypt and consequently there was the slavery in Egypt.

However, the Torah gives the first-born a double inheritance. If Yosef had been the first-born, there would have been no jealousy from his brothers and hence no going down to Egypt.

Why was Yosef not Yaacov's firstborn? Because Laban deceived Yaacov and gave him Leah instead of Rachel. Thus Laban was the cause of the Jews going down to Egypt.

✦ ✦ ✦ ✦ ✦ ✦ ✦ ✦ ✦ ✦

Let us end by looking at the wording of the section of the Haggadah called "Korech," incorrectly translated "Hillel's sandwich." Before eating it, we say in order to observe what is stated in the Torah that you should eat "the Paschal lamp sacrifice with matzah and bitter herbs." In fact, these words in the Torah are used in connection with Peasch Sheni. Surely it would be more logical to use words in connection with Pesach (namely Pesach that we observe today).

We might suggest that the answer is that on Pesach we hope that the Temple will be rebuilt by Pesach Sheni and we will then offer up the Paschal Lamb sacrifice.

This however is not relevant today, because if the majority of the people are spiritually unclean on Pesach, then the Paschal Lamb sacrifice is still offered on Pesach, and therefore Pesach Sheni does not apply.

However, the Talmud Yerushalmi brings the opinion of Rabbi Yehudah is that we still offer it on Pesach Sheni, and hence the wording in "Korech" is thus in accordance with Rabbi Yehudah.

Let us pray that the Temple will be rebuilt by Pesach, or at the very latest by Pesach Sheni, and then and we will eat in Jerusalem the Paschal lamb sacrifice.

🛐 🛐 🛐 🛐 🛐 🛐 🛐 🛐 🛐 🛐

VALEDICTORY SPEECH
(Speech delivered in July 1978 on leaving the King David High School in Liverpool, immediately before returning to Israel)

Mr. Chairman, Parents, Friends and Pupils

In his play "As You Like It," Shakespeare talks of the seven ages of man. Nearly 1,500 years before Shakespeare, the Rabbis in the Ethics of the Fathers also divided up the life of man. *Ben shlosh esrei lemitzvot* - 13 is the age when it becomes incumbent for a boy and 12 for a girl to observe all the Mitzvot in the Torah. Prior to this age, boys and girls are in training.

At the Barmitzvah ceremony, the father recites the Berachah, *Baruch sheptarani mayonsho shel ze*, Blessed be he who hath freed me from the responsibility for this child.

Unfortunately, many parents take this Berachah too literally and Bar and Bat Mitzvah become the age when they lose all interest in their children's religious education. If we look at this more closely, however, we find that although a boy is fully obligated for Mitzvot at 13, and a girl at 12, it is only after the age of 20 that a person becomes *bar onshin*, liable for punishment for the non-observance of these Mitzvot. The fact that a teenager had not reached the age of punishment shows that he still requires parental guidance and interest in these informative years.

About three years ago, the Minister of Education set up a Committee under the Chairmanship of Councillor Taylor to review the arrangement for the management and government of primary and secondary schools in England and Wales, including the composition of the bodies of managers and governors.

This committee was composed of people from all walks of life; Professors of education, Education Officers, Headmasters, Ministers of Religion, Directors of Industries and Parents. Two years later they submitted their report. In it they concluded that for a school's success, all parties should be brought together; namely, the local education authority, the staff, the parents and the local community. Significantly they called their report "A New Partnership for our Schools."

It is especially important for parents to be partners in the Religious Education of their children. Religion is the teaching of a way of life. A child is only at a Jewish day school for part of a day, five days a week, term time only. For the remaining time, he is under parental influence.

It therefore follows that parents need to take at least as much interest in their children's Jewish Studies as in their secular subjects. However, we found that it was rare for a parent to ask for an appointment with a Jewish Studies' teacher at the Parents' Consultation Evenings. A few months ago, we initiated an experiment for holding a special consultation evening for Jewish Studies and Modern Hebrew for parents of pupils in years 1 and 2. Just over one third of the parents attended. This was certainly an improvement, but where were the other two thirds?

In order to try and strengthen this partnership and increase parental interest, we have made this Barmitzvah / Eshet Chayil presentation in the evening. This ceremony is a culmination of a two-year course followed by an examination.

During this course, the boys learn to sing any unseen Haftarah and cover a detailed knowledge of Tephillin, Tzitzit and Reading the Torah. For the girls, the course covers Kashrut and the home and the preparation of a house for Shabbat and Yom-Tov. The practical aspects are stressed in these courses.

At the end of this two-year course, there is an examination on this work. Naturally, the ability of pupils varies considerably and therefore in assessing who *passes* this examination, the ability of a particular pupil is taken into consideration. To obtain *distinction*, however, the pupils must reach a definite high standard, irrespective of their ability.

This year, our results are better than ever before. No fewer than *thirteen* boys and *eleven* girls have achieved *distinction*. In addition, a number of pupils came within a handful of marks of receiving a distinction.

We consider that this Barmitzvah / Eshet Chayil course is one of four ways in which this school leads all other Jewish schools in this country.

The second way is by our use of audio-visual aids. We have made a special study and then integrated the most up-to date filmstrips, slides, cassette tapes and models into our Jewish Studies courses, including this Barmitzvah / Eshet Chayil course. We are regularly consulted by other Jewish schools and institutions regarding the best audio-visual aids available.

The third way in which we lead other Jewish schools concerns the 4th and 5th years. Here we have written Jewish orientated syllabuses in Scripture Knowledge for both O-level and CSE which have been accepted by the respective external examination boards. We are the only school to have accomplished this and other Jewish schools and classes in Manchester, Leeds, Sheffield and Cardiff take our O-level syllabus. Were it not for the geographical boundaries imposed by the external examination boards, it is very probable that centres in London would also be taking the examination. Our results in these examinations have been steadily rising and last year 87% of *all* the Jewish pupils in the 5th year gained a pass in either O-level or CSE.

Finally, the fourth way involves the sixth forms. As we all well know, there has been a massive increase in the anti-Israel activity on the University campuses and to our regret we have found that our Jewish students are not equipped to counter this activity. We have therefore introduced for our sixth forms a course called "How to answer anti-Israel propaganda" and have written our own accompanying booklet. This course has now completed its second year, and pupils who left the school last year, have successfully defended anti-Israel motions on the campuses. We have also received requests from different parts of the country for copies of our booklet on this subject.

As you will observe, these four ways in which we lead other Jewish schools cover the entire spectrum of the school - from the first form to the sixth forms. Parents! Whatever form your child will be in, you have something in his Jewish Studies programme to take a special and we hope active interest in.

Next week this time, *im yirtzeh Hash*em, I will be on the plane to Israel with my family going on Aliyah (or knowing El-Al, still in the departure lounge of Heathrow!). I would like to leave thinking that as a result of this evening's ceremony, you will take a greater interest in your child's Religious education right up the school.

(Two articles I wrote for the King David
High School Liverpool
Jewish Studies magazine)
Tishri 5737/1976

WELL OVER THE FAST

At this time of the year, we continually see New Year cards and greetings with the words "Happy New Year and well over the Fast." We are so used to seeing these words that we do not give them a second thought. But what in fact are the words "Well over the Fast" meant to convey?

Surely we do not want to say that we wish to be well over Yom Kippur? (i.e. we wish it were the day after Yom Kippur!) The Mishnah in Ta'anit (chap. 4 Mishnah 8) states: "There were no happier days for Israel than 15th Ab and Yom Kippur." Obviously then, we do not want such a happy day to be well behind us.

The suggestion that this greeting means that we should not get ill as a result of fasting on Yom Kippur is also untenable, since if there is any possibility of danger by a person's fasting, then he is forbidden to fast. What then do the words "Well over the fast mean? We put forward the following two suggestions.

447

1. The word "fast" refers to the Fast of Gedaliah (which occurs the day after Rosh Hashanah), and not to Yom Kippur. The Fast of Gedaliah is one of the four fasts connected with the fall of Jerusalem, and concerning these fasts the prophet Zechariah (chap. 8 verse 19) says: "The fast of the fourth month and the fast of the fifth and the fast of the seventh and the fast of the tenth shall be to the House of Judah joy and gladness". This means that in the Messianic days these fasts will become days of happiness. Therefore, we look forward to the Messianic era when Tzom Gedaliah will become a day of joy and gladness and we will hence be well over the Fast of Gedaliah.

2. The expression should be "Well over the **Past**" instead of "Fast". We begin the service for the first night of Rosh Hashanah with the Pizman entitled "Achot Ketanah." Each verse ends with the words: "May the (old) year and its misfortunes now cease altogether." The last verse however ends with the words: "May the New Year and its blessings now commence together." We can now understand our New Year greeting to mean the following: "Happy New Year" – may blessings now commence with the New Year. "Well over the Past" – let us be well over the past year with all its misfortunes.

A HAPPY NEW YEAR AND
WELL OVER THE FAST OF GEDALIAH
and
WELL OVER THE PAST

DO-IT-YOURSELF SHOFAR

Today, do-it-yourself things are becoming fashionable. So why not a do-it-yourself Shofar? Actually, it is quite simple – on paper at least.

First of all, as with D.I.Y. things, you require the materials. The most important is, of course, a horn .... Any horn? .... No, a cow's horn is no good (remember the golden calf). You need a sheep's horn. It's unlikely that your Kosher butcher will have one – and you don't want to be seen going into a Treife butcher (do you?) although they probably also won't have one. Instead ask a Shochet nicely, or maybe go to an abattoir. Try and get a few spare horns – you are sure to mess up the first one.

Having got the horns (they will probably smell a bit – so put a peg on your nose), you will need to use the kitchen stove, (buy your mother a bouquet of flowers and ask her nicely whether you can use her stove "just for a few minutes"). Also ask her for a discarded saucepan – do not use a Kosher one.

If you mother has agreed, (she doesn't know what she is in for), you are now ready to start.

As you will notice, the horn has a bone in it and this must first come out to make the horn hollow (the word Shofar comes from Shefoferet meaning tube). Take the horn, put it in your saucepan, fill with water and boil for a few hours. (Don't do it just before dinner – you may lose your appetite. Most important, watch it carefully, someone may unknowingly serve it up as your soup for dinner!) Then take the horn, tap it gently on the floor and if you are lucky, the bone should now come out.

You then take the horn and heat it over a flame. Don't hold it too near the flame, you will probably melt it and cause pungent odours to percolate all over the house. When the horn is hot, you should be able to straighten it out. You may need some strength for this – so practice your Mr. Universe exercises – in – out – in – out ......

You will notice that the other end of the horn is solid and needs to be drilled. If your father has not yet seen your activities in the kitchen, he may loan you his drill and you must then carefully drill the solid part until you reach the hollow portion. However, if your activities in the kitchen have already made you a persona non grata and you cannot get a drill, take a 6-inch nail (15 cms on the foreign metric system), hold the head in a schmatter, heat up the other end and keep pressing it on the solid portion. After doing this several hundred times you should reach the hollow portion.

Carefully shape the mouth-piece, how you do this will "make or break" your Shofar. Finally polish the Shofar.

Now try and blow your Shofar. Maybe you will be lucky – otherwise, hard luck, mate – try again.

Section Eight

Mishpacha receives Letters

MY LETTERS TO THE WEEKLY JOURNAL "MISHPACHA" ENGLISH EDITION

The English edition of the weekly journal "Mishpacha" begins with a section entitled "Letters to the Editor." Readers are invited to send up their letters whose comments invariably refer to recent previous articles and other material appearing in "Mishpacha." In the past I sent up many such letters, some of which were published in this journal.

Sent to "Mishpacha" 2 January 2017

The article "Danny in the Lions' Den" (issue 641) on the infamous United Nations Security Council Resolution 2334, was excellent; I would, however, like to elaborate on a few points.

The resolution refers to Judea and Samaria as being "occupied Palestinian territory," the occupier being Israel. It is utterly and completely incorrect to use such an expression for the following reasons:

1. The area of Judea and Samaria ("West Bank") belonged to no country, and thus Israel is not occupying territory which belongs to another country. Indeed, many renowned international lawyers state that the State of Israel has a better title to this area than any other country in the world.
2. Resolution 2334 conflicts with UN Security Council resolution 242 which only demands that Israel withdraw to "secure and recognized boundaries". Leading military authorities have ruled that the 1949 Armistice lines are by no means secure boundaries, and the various Armistice agreements signed with the Arab neighboring countries clearly state that these Armistice lines are not recognized boundaries.

3. In accordance with Article 80 of the United Nations Charter, Jews have every right to settle, even if organized by the Israeli Government, anywhere in Judea, Samaria and the Gaza strip.
4. The existence of a "Palestinian" Arab nation is one of the greatest hoaxes of the 20th and 21st centuries and even Arab historians admit that it is a myth.

A number of years ago, I wrote a meticulously documented paper which greatly elaborates on the above points. This paper has over 120 references and it is accompanied by about 40 photostats of the appropriate extracts of documents quoted in the paper.

Rabbi Dr. Chaim Simons

✿ ✿ ✿ ✿ ✿ ✿ ✿ ✿ ✿ ✿ ✿

Published in "Mishpacha" issue 642 dated 4 January 2017

Rabbi Zevi Trenk's practical teaching methods (reported in "Lessons You Can Touch" – issue 640) took me back about 40 years to when I was Director of Jewish Studies at the Jewish High School in Liverpool England, a school where the majority of the pupils came from non-observant homes.

I made a point of having courses entitled Practical Dinim in which actual objects were used to teach the dinim. One such course was on Tephillin which I gave to a class of the Barmitzvah year. For this course, I "dissected" the batim of old Tephillin, (including separating a bayit of a shel rosh into its four sections), so that pupils could see the component parts. I also showed the pupils the different parshios in the Tephillin and gave them pieces of parchment and feathers to make quill pens which they then used to write some Hebrew letters on the pieces of parchment.

The pupils enjoyed this course and in the written examination which followed the results were on the whole excellent.

I heard that one of these pupils had put on Tephillin on the Shabbos of his Barmitzvah before going to Shul. I afterwards spoke to him about it and he said that he knew that one does not put on Tephillin on Shabbos but he regarded the Shabbos of his Barmitzvah as a special day. In a way I was happy about this incident, since it showed that he appreciated the importance of Tephillin.

When I came to live in Israel, I brought most of the teaching tools with me and a few months ago I mentioned it to a teacher of the Talmud Torah "Kinyan Torah" in Kiryat Arba who was teaching his class of 12-year-olds about Tephillin. He asked me to give a lesson using these props to his pupils, which I did to the great enjoyment and excitement of the boys.

Rabbi Dr. Chaim Simons

❦ ❦ ❦ ❦ ❦ ❦ ❦ ❦ ❦ ❦

Published in "Mishpacha Family First" issue 534, dated 29 March 2017

The excellent article by Brachi Blumenberg entitled "Lost & Found" (Family First) reminded me of my research a few years ago for my book "Carmel College in the Kopul Era – 1948-1962" (Urim Publications – Jerusalem). Carmel College was an Orthodox Jewish Boarding School for boys, established in the south of England by Rabbi Kopul Rosen in 1948, and managed by him until his early death in 1962.

Whilst researching for this book, I learned that the Carmel alumni knew almost nothing about the biographies of their teachers (the majority of whom were non-Jewish) – not even their first names. By extensive research, since contact had been lost with them for over half a century, I was able to build up biographies of almost all the teachers, in some cases with gaps in their lives, and I included this information as the second part of the book.

My methods included tracking down relatives of the teachers (not an easy undertaking after so long a period), use of the records of educational institutions, obituaries, year books, army records, naturalization certificates, questions submitted to Wikipedia Reference Desk, to quote just some of the methods used. With married women teachers, there was a further problem since I did not know their surnames before marriage.

In some cases, one small fact led to a mass of material. Examples included finding the name of a teacher on a receipt of an item purchased by the teacher; an alumnus recalling that a teacher's only son had been killed in the Yom Kippur War; and another alumnus' recollection that a teacher had been involved with the "Little Missenden Festival."

Most of the schools and universities the teachers had attended, were cooperative (or even over-cooperative) in supplying me with information, which included sending me the pupils' or students' marks, form positions and testimonials. However, some wanted me to send proof that the teacher had since died, quoting the Data Protection Act. In all but one case, I was able to send such proof. In the case of the one exception, I pointed out that the teacher would have been by then 118 years old. They still insisted on proof of death and I pointed out that such a teacher would be world news. They then relented and sent me the requested information with "apologies for the confusion"!

Rabbi Dr. Chaim Simons

⚜ ⚜ ⚜ ⚜ ⚜ ⚜ ⚜ ⚜ ⚜ ⚜

Published in "Mishpacha Family First" dated 10 May 2017

In "Family First" issue 540, 'build your best... Quinoa" you write that one may eat Quinoa on Pesach. However, this is not completely correct. Although there are some Rabbonim in America who hold that it is not kitniyos, there are many others in America who hold that it *is* kitniyos. In Israel, it seems that all the Rabbonim hold that it is kitniyos and therefore Ashkenazim, at least in Israel, do not eat Quinoa on Pesach.

Rabbi Dr. Chaim Simons

⚜ ⚜ ⚜ ⚜ ⚜ ⚜ ⚜ ⚜ ⚜ ⚜

Sent to "Mishpacha" 2 July 2017

Zvi Weiss wrote an excellent letter headed "Don't Lionize Trump" (Inbox Mishpacha issue 666) showing how President Trump went back on his election promises regarding Israel. It is essential to inform not only Trump, but the entire world (including, sad to add, members of the Knesset and the Israeli government) of the following facts:

1. The area of Judea and Samaria ("West Bank") belonged to no country, and thus Israel is not occupying territory which belongs to another country. Indeed, many renowned international lawyers state that the State of Israel has a better title to this area than any other country in the world. Furthermore, the Court of Appeal of Versailles France, in 2013 ruled that "Israel is the legal occupant of the West Bank".
2. UN Security Council resolution 242 of 1967 only requires that Israel withdraw to "secure and recognized boundaries." Leading military authorities have ruled that the 1949 Armistice lines are by no means secure boundaries, and the various Armistice agreements signed with the Arab neighboring countries clearly state that these Armistice lines are not recognized boundaries.
3. In accordance with Article 80 of the United Nations Charter, Jews have every right to settle, even if organized by the Israeli Government, anywhere in Judea, Samaria and the Gaza strip.
4. The existence of a "Palestinian" Arab nation is one of the greatest hoaxes of the 20th and 21st centuries and even Arab historians admit that it is a myth. The recently published 120-page book, "A History of the Palestinian People" by Assaf Voll, of which all the pages are blank, amply illustrates this point.

Although Pirkei Avos advises "syog lachochmoh shsikoh" (a preventive fence to wisdom is silence), the facts given in this letter of mine are obviously an exception to this dictum.

Rabbi Dr. Chaim Simons

Sent to "Mishpacha 15 August 2017

I read with interest your article "Field of Silence" (Mishpacha issue 669) on the Lodz ghetto and those buried in the Lodz Ghetto Field.

Several years ago, I was researching my family genealogy and came across two lists (from 1940 and around 1942) of the Lodz ghetto residents. On these lists I found the names of the wife and two young children of my mother's cousin Reuven Zielinski. However, the name of Reuven was missing from both these lists. It was suggested that he may have died at an earlier date. I accordingly examined the list of those buried in the Lodz Jewish cemetery, (which was only a partial list) but could not find his name on it.

At a later date one of my daughters was on a Holocaust Study Trip which included a visit to this cemetery. Whilst there, she went to the office and they found his burial registration. (He had died in 1937 at the age of 28.) With this information she was able to find his grave and saw that his tombstone was still in excellent condition.

From the second Lodz ghetto residents list, one can see that sadly his widow and two children did not survive and were deported to Chelmno on 25 March 1942.

Rabbi Dr. Chaim Simons

🕴️🕴️🕴️🕴️🕴️🕴️🕴️🕴️🕴️🕴️

Published in "Mishpacha" issue 673 dated 16 August 2017

Your excellent and informative article entitled "Dust to Ashes" (Mishpacha issue 670) reminded me of what could have happened, but fortunately did not, with my uncle's body.

Nearly fifty years ago my uncle died in a London hospital. After his death, the hospital authorities handed over a body to the Chevra Kadisha who then did a taharah on it and put it in a coffin. The levaya started from the area of my parent's house and proceeded to the Jewish burial ground. The tefillos prior to the levayah were recited in the ohel of the cemetery.

Whilst the coffin was then being taken to the prepared grave for burial, one of the Chevra Kadisha happened to ask my father what they should do with my uncle's clothes. My father replied "but he was wearing pajamas." "No," they replied, "he was fully clothed." My father immediately realized that something was wrong and demanded that they open the coffin. They did this and discovered that they had the wrong body, almost certainly that of a non-Jew.

Immediately, together with my father, the Chevra Kadisha drove back at top speed to the hospital with the body of the stranger, identified the body of my uncle, and performed a taharah on it in the presence of my father, who insisted on being present this time in order to make sure that there were no further mistakes. They then returned to the cemetery and my uncle was given a proper Jewish burial.

Fortunately, in this case, there was a positive ending, but one shudders to think what would have happened had the member of the Chevra Kadisha not made this chance remark to my father. It was surely Siyata Dishmaya and not just "chance." The non-Jew would have had a Jewish burial and in his place my uncle might well have been cremated.

Rabbi Dr. Chaim Simons

♔♔♔♔♔♔♔♔♔♔♔

Sent to "Mishpacha" 14 March 2019

In your very interesting article on "Pi" (the ratio between a circle's circumference and its diameter), which appeared in the English Mishpacha Junior section (issue 751), you make no mention of the value of Pi in halachah. There is already a source for the value of Pi in sefer Melachim (aleph 7:23) in the Tanach. There it states that the circumference of the "Yam shel Shlomo" was 30 amos and its diameter 10 amos, thus giving a value of 3 for Pi. From this, the Mishnah in Eruvin (1:5) states that the circumference of a circle is three times its diameter.

A more recent suggestion states that there is a hint of a far more accurate value for Pi in this verse in sefer Melachim. In it there is a kri-kesiv on the word "kaveh" namely the kesiv has the letter "hey" at the end whilst according to the kri one reads it without the "hey" at the end. The gematria of the kri is 106, whilst that of the kesiv is 111. The ratio of these two numbers multiplied by 3 gives the value of pi accurate to four decimal places.

A much more detailed article on this subject can be found in an excellent article by Moshe Taub entitled "Pi or 'What Did Chazal Know and When Did They Know It?'"

Rabbi Dr. Chaim Simons

🌿 🌿 🌿 🌿 🌿 🌿 🌿 🌿 🌿 🌿

Sent to "Mishpacha" 16 March 2019

In his letter "Three More Indicators" (Mishpacha issue 752) on the reliability of the kashrus at a hotel, Rabbi Avrohom Juravel gives three indicators to check. The second one is whether towards the termination of the first day Yom Tov of Pesach the staff are already preparing for the second Seder and whether the tables in the dining hall are already set up.

In practice, one does not need to wait for Seder night to check this, since it can be verified on a Shabbos, in particular during the summer months when Shabbos finishes very late in the evening. Just before the termination of Shabbos, one can take a look in the dining hall and see if the tables are already set up for Sunday morning's breakfast.

Rabbi Dr. Chaim Simons

🌿 🌿 🌿 🌿 🌿 🌿 🌿 🌿 🌿 🌿

Sent to "Mishpacha" 8 November 2020

I was very happy to read that after an 18-year-old battle, Ari Zivotofsky's son's passport gives his place of birth as Jerusalem Israel, instead of Jerusalem with no country.

This reminded me of a similar fight I had in 1970 regarding the registration of my eldest daughter's British birth certificate. At the time my family was among the Mitnachalei Hevron living in the Military Compound in Hebron. Having British citizenship, my daughter was automatically British. I went to the British Consulate in West Jerusalem (on Mount Zion) with the various documents and was given a form to complete. I wrote my place of residence as Hebron Israel. The clerk there immediately crossed out the word Israel and said one must write Hebron Jordan. Britain had recognised the area of Yehudah and Shomron as a part of Jordan. I strongly objected to this. He then telephoned to someone - I don't know who - and said that he had a person who strongly objected to having Hebron Jordan on his daughter's birth certificate. They then agreed to write just Hebron. Needless to add, that the hospital of her birth, Shaarei Tzedek, was just written on her British birth certificate as Jerusalem without the addition of Israel.

Rabbi Dr. Chaim Simons

🌳 🌳 🌳 🌳 🌳 🌳 🌳 🌳 🌳 🌳

Sent to "Mishpacha" 1 January 2021

"The Milchig Clock"

The item in issue 842 "Ben Yomo Clock" on the Kichel page "The Hopefully Still Kosher Kitchen," reminded me of the comments I wrote about ten years ago on one of Rav Aryeh Lebowitz' of Yeshiva University "Ten Minute Halacha" shiurim. I wrote that it often happens that one has eaten a fleishig meal but does not note the time that one has finished eating the meat. How does one then know that 6 hours have passed so that one can now have milchig? A clock needs to be designed that could be set after eating fleishig and which after 6 hours (or however long one's minhag was to wait) would ring and/or show some sign that 6 hours was up!

Rabbi Dr. Chaim Simons

Section Nine

Seven stairs – but no more!

THE GERRER REBBE ASCENDED
AN ADDITIONAL STAIR!

Rabbi Dr. Chaim Simons

Paper written in Hebrew in 1987 and translated into English in July 2021.

(For 700 years the Moslems would not allow Jews to go higher than 7 steps leading to the entrance to the Cave of Machpelah. However, in 1935, the Gerrer Rebbe tried to go beyond the seventh stair and this led to an unpleasant situation.

In 1987 I decided to research this subject and my main source of information came from newspaper articles on this event. I then wrote up a paper in Hebrew on it. This paper of mine was published in July 1987 in the Kiryat Arba Local Council magazine "Chavruta.")

ENGLISH TRANSLATION OF PAPER

When the Zionist leaders (including David Ben-Gurion) appeared before the Woodhead Commission in 1938, they spoke about the "shameful conduct" towards the Gerrer Rebbe which occurred near the Cave of Machpelah several years earlier.

What and when was this "shameful conduct"?

It occurred in the month of Elul 5695 (1935) and details about it appeared in the newspapers of that period ("Ha'aretz," "Doar Hayom," "Davar," "Palestine Post ") and also in an article in "Sefer Hebron" written by Rabbi Yitzchak Meir (p. 326) (I could not find archival material on this subject in the files of the British Government, nor in the Central Zionist Archives. In addition, there is no material on this incident in the archives of the Gerrer Rebbe.)

At that period, the Gerrer Rebbe lived in Poland, and in the month of Elul 1935 he came to visit Israel. On 27 Elul, he visited the Cave of Machpelah accompanied by his sons, Rabbis and Hassidim – several of them students of the "Sfat Emet" Yeshivah in Jerusalem. All together there were about thirty-five people who came, travelling in small cars, including one car filled with women.

There are several versions as to what actually happened when they reached the stairs by the Cave of Machpelah:

a) The guard, who was standing by the Cave of Machpelah, gently explained to the Rebbe who wanted to ascend above the seventh step, that it was forbidden to do so (Doar Hayom 27.9.35); this is also the version of Rabbi Yitzchak Meir in his book.

b) The Rebbe was unaware of the existing restrictions on Jews (Doar Hayom 26.9.35, Palestine Post 26.9.35).

c) One of those accompanying the Rebbe said that it was explained to the guard that the Rebbe was a "great sage," and therefore the guard allowed the Rebbe and those accompanying him to go above the seventh step, and then in return asked them for a "tip." (Ha'aretz 3.10.35)

According to all opinions, the Rebbe went beyond the seventh step (some say that he reached the eleventh step). According to Rabbi Yitzchak Meir, at that moment Arab louts, who had been called by the guard, jumped onto the stairs. The Rebbe said, "They the 'shkatzim' [loathsome creatures] are allowed to ascend, only we are forbidden."

The policeman who was guarding the place rudely pushed against the chest of the Rebbe. The Rebbe's followers immediately started shouting that he was "a wise man" and it was forbidden to touch him, and according to the police they beat the policeman. The Rebbe finished his prayers and returned to his car. When the British police arrived, they arrested ten young Hasidim students of the "Sfat Emet" yeshiva who had not yet had the time to leave the place. They were accused of beating a policeman.

The next day, the ten defendants appeared before a police officer in Hebron. Among the witnesses was the Mufti of Hebron, who testified that "Jews are not allowed to ascend more than seven steps, and no Jew has ever ascended above that." The attorney for the defendants asked the Mufti "how can you say this when I myself went up all the stairs and also went down into the Cave itself." The Mufti replied "However, it is possible for a Jew to go to the Cave if he has special permission." (Doar Hayom 27.9.35)

The trial continued in Jerusalem on the Fast of Gedaliah, but there was contradictory evidence regarding the guilt of the defendants. The Gerrer Hassidim claimed that the defendants did not beat the police officer. In contrast, the police, the caretaker of the Cave of Machpelah. and an old Arab (who was almost blind)!) testified the opposite.

In the verdict, five of the defendants were found guilty and each received a fine of two lirot, or eight days in jail. They paid the fine and were released.

A year after the liberation of Hebron, the "famous" stairs were demolished on the orders of Defense Minister Moshe Dayan, but the "shameful conduct" towards the Jews still continues ....

(The reason these stairs were demolished was that on the previous day which was during Chol Hamoed Succot 1968, a grenade was thrown in the Cave of Machpelah injuring many people. On the following day Moshe Dayan came to Hebron, and even went up to the top of the tower of the Muezzin. He gave an order to destroy the "famous stairs." In retrospect, this was a pity since these stairs were part of the history of the Cave of Machpelah.)

Lightning Source UK Ltd.
Milton Keynes UK
UKHW010742180322
400272UK00001B/11